PREFACE

I embarked on this project to address the questions that have always haunted me as a Muslim growing up in the west. Why does a piece of cloth over a woman's head generate such political and emotional disturbance in the west? And just as peculiarly, how is it that the Muslim woman is discussed and debated with such assurance and conviction?

These questions have always appeared in some shape or form throughout my life despite me not having worn any type of veil. Whether it was always having to explain the reason I did not wear the "proper" uniform in high school (long skirts instead of the usual short ones in junior years or swimming wear or "togs" during swimming) or in the climate of post-9/11, the all-too-frequent conversation that paradoxically identified me both as a question and an affirmation of an accepted and unquestioned truth: where was I from? And the emphatic comments: "You must be glad that you are living in New Zealand!" or "How fortunate that you no longer have to wear those ghastly veils!" I never knew how to respond to strangers, acquaintances and friends, declaring their moral positions on countries far removed from their lives. Their extraordinary certainty about what I "should" be feeling left me perplexed. Later in life, I realised it was not the *othering* of who I was which left me unsettled. Rather, it was the certainty about *what* I came from, the knowledge of my culture and its people that disturbed me. A certainty I never entertained myself. Moreover, I was most deeply unsettled by the expectation that I contained a desire to *escape* this culture; an expectation that came to me through images of veiled women with stern and intimidating bearded faces of Muslim men. The veil's menacing presence in these conversations, and the recurring sense of "being the known", have motivated my inquiry. These familiar scenes and the feelings, evoked and remembered, have remained within and alongside me in the writing of this book. I have aimed here to trace these assumptions and certainties of my desire to escape to the expected destination of my liberation.

The subject of the veil has by now been analysed by numerous scholars. Given the burgeoning corpus on the veil, there remains this pressing question: is there a need for another? Has the veil been successfully situated, dissected, put back together, *made known*? Much of this literature on the veil admirably and cogently unpacks the political and historical dimensions of my persistent questions: colonialism's mission to civilise the Muslim through unveiling and through its contemporary campaign of racialisation of Muslims; the policing of bodies and national identities in the pursuit of a specific modernity and notion of self; the underpinnings of discourses that produce the veiled woman and the racialised modes in which Islam is always presented as an irreconcilable other. These scholarly approaches have taken to task the essentialist representations of Muslim women as abject, voiceless, victims of their culture. The counter discourse of veiling has also emphasised choice and agency to push for a more liberating meaning.

The volume of writing on this topic has overwhelmed me, as it has the scholars who have laboured over these questions in their rich corpus. My aim in this book is not to reinforce the oppressed versus liberated paradigm that dominates the discourse on the veil. Nor am I interested in using the Muslim woman qua the veiled woman as an oppositional strategy. Considering the voluminous extant scholarship that endeavours to understand or demystify the veil, this book attempts to shed a new light on an exhausted corpus. Not to join the choir of voices "explaining away" the veil, but I interrogate the never-ending curiosity about what lies "beneath the veil". I do not aim to answer the endless questions and demands for confession that the conversation provokes: why do Muslim women veil? What does it *really* mean? Do they *really* have a choice? It is not the purpose of my book to make sense, even in the broadest terms, of these questions that have accompanied me for many years—demanding in their persistence, and unique in their appetite for more "detail". My aim, therefore, is not to engage this literature directly but to identify the gaps that remain. I refuse to answer the why question. The question

itself is the object of my interrogation. It is precisely because so much
has been written on the subject that I am motivated to write this book.
The "excess" never satisfies.

Much writing on the subject has obscured rather than illuminated
the discursive puzzle (the focus on multiple meanings of the veil) or
left insufficiently apprehended (the racist violence behind its representations). This book is a departure from a discourse of "too much-ness" and
a paring back to the persistent tension that these repetitive questions are
symptomatic of. Even after historical, political and anthropological inves-
tigations unearth power's hold on representations of Muslim women,
why does the veiled woman make her return *after* the fact and why is the
Muslim woman *always* announced through the veil? This is a represented
"fact", situated in a history, a politics, and a counterfactual dismantling
of how she has been understood. It is a "fact" that I consider contains
the possibility of its own demystification.

My apprehension about my project of examining the west's unease,
and the violence that this can produce, made itself known to me through
my compulsion to repeat. I was overcome by the need to pile explanation on explanation to name the violence. Explaining it one-way, and
then another, and yet I knew my apprehension remained—stretched
out in a fraught tone. It was as if no critique, explanation, demonstra-
tion, counterpoint or image, could adequately name it. Reflecting on
the unconscious impulse to repeat, I had to ask myself why was I not
comfortable with my assembling of words and their meaning or the language as it was? The French psychoanalyst Jacques Lacan explains the
Freudian compulsion to repeat through an illustration of a child's use
of a cotton reel in a game of "presence" (*Fort*) and "absence" (*Da*) to
cope with the anxiety felt with the coming (appearance) and going (disappearance) of the mother. The gap between the child and the reel is
attached through the string, which for Lacan illustrates that something
has been detached but something can possibly be retrieved. Repetition,
Lacan reveals, is never accidental but a symptom of a deeper disturbance,
the return of the Real in the form of the subject's efforts to recover a
loss and the failure to do so. My repeated references to the post-9/11
era, the war on terror, and the racial violence of reductionist representation of the veiled/Muslim woman, disclosed an anxiety associated with
relying on a shared recognition with the Other in language. Faced with
the psychotic certainty of an unveiling imaginary—the hypnotic belief in
the revealed flesh as a signature of freedom—my writing reflected a kind

of strain at the weight of this imaginary fixing. I chipped away at its certainty, attempting to disrupt its trance-like repetition, perhaps to force the west to confront its own castration, its own limit. It is also possibly an unconscious admission on my part that the language is not only my own, but also that of the audience I imagine to be western and secular. The postcolonial theorist Edward Said sullenly suggests this as the *only audience* and one that will never be sufficiently convinced of the actual violence enacted. Although I have attempted to rectify this problem of repetition throughout the rewriting and editing processes, I know there will be times when I have been unsuccessful in this effort, seduced by a desire to hold on to the promise of the new, of an attainable meaning.

In the early stages of writing, I was frequently asked how I could reconcile writing on the veil and Muslim women without speaking to Muslim women? I speak with Muslim women every day, but the question assumed (rather forcefully) was that it was impossible to conduct research on the issues I was concerned with in the absence of women and their voices. These questions made me wonder about the research strategy of shedding light—or to put it in western media lexicon, "lifting the veil"—on the diverse lived experiences of Muslim women achieved? I asked who is the audience that the "veil" is being lifted for and to what end? The Muslim woman continues to appear as a one-dimensional figure of difference, as victimhood and threat, and as I contend, with new anxieties, a subject/object arranged for the consumption of an ever-curious western audience.

The desire for accounts that reflect Muslim women's lived experiences—that is, the need to hear from the victims of orientalism and Islamophobia—demonstrates the limits of epistemological readings. This discourse on representation is pursued in the hope of problematising and diminishing the racist gaze that insists on her oppressive status. The book confronts the gaze that constructs the space between the figure of the veiled woman and the intelligibility of that presence. Through a psychoanalytic lens, one can realise that these unrelenting questions on the veil are not in fact seeking specific answers but are bouts of uneasiness played out on the body. The body here becomes the conduit of masquerading truths.

Melbourne, Australia   Sahar Ghumkhor

ACKNOWLEDGEMENTS

I'm indebted to the kindness and inspiring work of Juliet Rogers whose mentoring has been exceptional. Also, thank you to Maree Pardy for always offering her brilliant input when I need it. Thank you to Lila Abu Lughod whose scholarship is as generous and inspiring as she is. Thank you to my friends for all the thought-provoking conversations and debates. I've learnt so much from them even when we have passionately disagreed. I'm also grateful for the hard work put in by my copyeditor Joel Rodriguez.

Thank you to Hussein Mohamud whose depth of thinking, conversation, inspiration, generosity and love continues to astonish me and has, in so many ways, made this book possible. Special thanks to my family for the wonderful support when I've needed it. My nephews and niece in particular who now and then allow me to escape into their enchanting world.

CONTENTS

LIST OF FIGURES

CHAPTER 1

Introduction: Bodies Without Shadows

So extreme is the concern with Muslim women today that veiled, and even unveiled, women are no longer thought of as individuals: collectively they have become the Muslimwoman. —Miriam Cooke[1]

The image on a 2010 *Time* magazine cover shows a young Afghan girl named Aisha Mohammadzai wearing a loose headscarf, her face visibly disfigured by her missing nose. The gaping wound where her nose was offers a grisly sight. The arresting image has immediacy in its message, underscoring Roland Barthes' claim that the image communicates, "this is what happened there; having been there",[2] as it sears itself into the viewer's mind announcing the violence and horror Aisha has witnessed and experienced.

Aisha is an 18-year-old Afghan girl from the province of Oruzgan. *Time* recounts that after being married at the age of 12, Aisha experienced six years of abuse at the hands of her in-laws. She eventually escaped. However, to make an example of her and prevent other girls from doing the same, the Taliban cut off her ears and nose. Recognising the distressing nature of the image, *Time's* managing editor justified the decision to position Aisha as a window into what is happening in the country and to inform debate:

> But bad things do happen to people, and it is part of our job to confront and explain them. In the end, I felt that the image is a window into the

© The Author(s) 2020
S. Ghumkhor, *The Political Psychology of the Veil*,
Palgrave Studies in Political Psychology,
https://doi.org/10.1007/978-3-030-32061-4_1

reality of what is happening — and what can happen — in a war that affects and involves all of us. I would rather confront readers with the Taliban's treatment of women than ignore it. I would rather people know that reality as they make up their minds about what the U.S. and its allies should do in Afghanistan... We do not run this story or show this image either in support of the U.S. war effort or in opposition to it. We do it to illuminate what is actually happening on the ground.[3]

Time situates Aisha not only as an emblem of a country that disfigures women but also as a symbol of a nation that has been disfigured by war, fundamentalism and the burqa. "Reality" is conveyed through Aisha's violated face. This is a violation that coalesces with the burqa's violations against bodies of women under the excesses of culture. The burqa, as Belgian moral philosopher Etienne Vermeersch described it in 2011 while supporting its ban, "is a symbol of women's oppression... It is worse than the swastika".[4] French philosopher André Glucksmann declared the veil was "stained with blood"[5] and a "terrorist operation".[6] Over the last few years, the burqa has come to represent a formidable image of violence, civilisational difference, subordination, a "veil of terror"[7] on the body, refusing to release an inch of it. Resembling the burqa's erasing presence, Aisha's missing nose functions as bodily erasure.

Previously, in 2002, the image of an un-covered face of an Afghan girl staring back at the reader, surrounded by women in blue burqas, was shown in *The Age*. Titled "Liberated Kabul", the same themes of presence and absence, exposure and closure, veiled and unveiled appear. The girl's face, the only visible face among the crowd, announces the Afghan woman through her unveiling. The veiled women surrounding her, it is inferred, have not yet been identified. Their desires remain unknown, unexplored and unhuman. The representation of the face, as Judith Butler detects in this image, conditions the process of humanisation.[8] While humanisation occurs through a process of revelation, it also requires recognition by another. Like the women who remain unannounced beneath the veil, Aisha's disfigured face is still to be recognised. She is not yet human. Aisha remains under a *veil of violence*. This is a violence that cuts and mutilates women's bodies, a visible "SOS" violence fixing the viewer to the spectacle of her disfigured face, and a symbolic erasure which imposes a "universe of meaning"[9] of what needs to be done: the mission yet to be completed.

Aisha's face symbolises the continued threat of the Taliban, authorising the mission of Operation Enduring Freedom,[10] and as Gayatri Spivak describes the underpinning principle of the project of gender and development: "white men saving brown women from brown men".[11] Aisha's image is captioned with an urgent statement of this mission: "What happens if we leave Afghanistan". This is not a question but an authorised statement—a universal moral code suggesting the wounds inflicted on the women of Afghanistan are raw and have yet to be healed. The face of the liberated girl from 2002 may also fall victim to the violence that surrounds her. Like the burqa, Freedom is precarious. Yet, it is potentially triumphant. Freedom, as Wendy Brown reminds, has become a compelling symbol of difference, that of conditions of coercion and that of action, representation and absence, domination and participation.[12]

The image of Aisha is framed neither as a case of domestic violence nor of gender-based violence and religious fundamentalism. It is framed through a much deeper imaginary—as the necessity to mobilise "protection". The colonial violence of this imaginary and its exhortations, does not only infer in the compulsion to save Aisha from something, it is implied, as Abu-Lughod observes about the underlying pursuit to go to war for Muslim women, as saving her *to something*.[13] What is the "something" to which Aisha is being saved? Rather than examining what she is being saved from, this book examines the drive, impulses and imaginary investment in this saviour fantasy. It contends that the political nature of the impulse to unveil is driven by deep psychic investment in the west.

My assumed gratitude for the safety in New Zealand and the unrelenting search by my peers and strangers for the meaning of the veil portends something much deeper, which threatens to destabilise psychic investments. To cover is to hide, to refuse something and to suggest one has secrets. What cannot be seen or known carries the allure of transgression. Its profound anxiety appears in the repetitive proclamations about my safety. Repetition is critical to this book in that it is a symptom that promises disclosure, of recovering something lost. Within the framework of the book, anxiety animates the west's impulse to unveil the Muslim woman. Therefore, repetition is critical to this book in that it is a symptom that promises—a body "that does not blush" in its defiance with the world—recovering something lost through disclosure. I examine the veiled woman as a reoccurring symptom of the western imaginary. In so doing, I aim to provide an understanding of the complicated hold she has on the troubled psyche of the west. The intention of this book is therefore, not to understand the veil and its purpose for Muslim women. It is to *think through* the veil to understand *what it means for the west*.

The saviour fantasy is powered by an evolutionary continuum of progress that situates the west in what Butler describes as the "avatar of freedom".[14] This trajectory, where freedom is assumed to unfold through time, produces, among other things, the veil as a spectacle of anachronism and unfreedom (veiled) and regression (veiling). If the perceived growing presence of the veil connotes the erosion of freedom, unveiling is viewed as progressing towards a state of freedom (unveiled). The veiled and unveiled operate in what Laura Soler describes as the "imperial formations", which persist in "processes of becoming". Unveiling, as an act of progressive doing, becomes one of its crucial "promissory notes".[15] In Soler's parlance, the veiled and unveiled imagery are the "imperial debris" chronicling loss and redemption in Aisha's face. Her single portrait, held together by this imagery of lack and deliverance, comprises all that needs to be known. Its elision of other knowledge constitutes an epistemic violence. Not only does it efface other knowledges, it also betrays a tragic lack of self-knowledge.

The veiled and unveiled activates an imagining—the possibility and impossibility of a stable "west" and the epistemic conditions (freedom, truth, knowledge) which sustain it. This book acknowledges that like modernity, the west is a contested concept that lacks an "integrated totality".[16] Nevertheless, it deploys this term because it exists through, what anthropologist Talal Asad contends is, the "political goal" to be "modern" and "western".[17]

An aggressive re-centring of discourses of the west occurred after the events of 11 September 2001. A renewed commitment to the values of democracy and freedom, terms believed to be exclusively affiliated with the western liberal tradition,[18] to prevent an assault not only on the United States but on western civilisation as a whole.[19] In this civilisational discourse of "us and them", the moral imperative of a "crusade" to "defend freedom at any cost" invokes a western fighting spirit against an Islamic enemy.[20] This encounter with others reflects a west that Asad argues has "many faces at home " but "presents a single face abroad".[21] This book traces the making of this unified west through an identity in crisis. This is a west that cannot otherwise be known without its political, economic and legal consolidation of the ideals of freedom, democracy, human rights and women's emancipation around the veil, or more precisely on the body.

The west appears in the singular that has reconciled its inherent contradictions and addressed its ambiguities[22] in the seductive logic of the image's certainty and captured imaginaries. This is a west that sees itself by means of ideological affiliation and projecting what it is not, into its representations of the unfreedom of others. These are others who are both abroad—and in the intimate cultural encounters of the postcolonial world today, *within* its geographical borders but who are always apprehended as antithetical to western values. This imaginary underpins the veiled and unveiled—images that drape the fantasy of western totality over the Muslim woman as it aspires to unveil its freedom, all the while stifling the question of what freedom actually is.

Along the continuum of progress, unveiling comes to stand in for what Spivak's formulation contends is a freedom that *one cannot not want*[23]: Freedom must not only be desired, but can only be imagined as a freedom that cumulates in the act of unveiling performed by the west.[24] In other words, certain images come to stand in for what freedom can and must be. This is the "only" freedom that can be tolerated. To borrow from German phenomenological philosopher Martin Heidegger, this is a "readiness-to-hand" freedom whose neutrality goes unquestioned.[25] What Fredrich Nietzsche termed "the instincts for freedom" find expression in this unveiling fantasy. It is a freedom instinctively prescribed to what it means to be human and only realised as something not quite, when its meaning fails. The readiness of freedom, I contend, appears *through the universalism of flesh*: sexuality, choice and desire made possible through the body as its witness—a freedom that must be seen. A freedom that, like the body, is "natural". A Derridean "naked truth" that lays bare the natural human condition. As such, certain images come to stand in for what freedom can and must be.[26]

The corporeal terrain in which freedom is discovered also provides the coordinates for the secular body, whose boundaries Asad[27] and Hirschkind[28] have attempted to trace but are like quicksand, difficult to grasp. The "secular" and "religious" are words and concepts we use as if we know exactly what they are, how they are neatly classifiable from the other. In addition, the religious and the secular which may at times demarcate metaphysical, spiritual, cultural and political distinctions, can run through the body *unidentified* and apprehend multiple modes of living. The secular body for Asad has fleeting detections in the lived experience, as he attempts to claim the secular in the grammar of oppositions between religion/secular and denotes it as "best pursued in its shadows".[29] This book contributes to detecting the elusive secular body by pursuing the shadows it cast on other bodies. It does this by examining the psychoanalytic makeup of the secular imaginary—what it desires, what sustains it—to build the bridge between the secular and religious.

This book contends that this somatic idiom is underpinned by an imagination of unveiling (symbolically and physically) which restores the west's sense of its own power. Unveiling enables the west to intrude where it is the "other" making itself the centre and the agent (again) by promising universal freedom, assuring its prophetic subjectivity. It is this in potential of unveiling—the possibility of piercing the veil of tradition, constraint and unseen knowledge—that the west has assigned itself as the agent and the author of its ontological origins. The promise of unveiling has the same political effects of imagining oneself returning from the heart of darkness, and narrating the tale of survival, adventurism and heroism—inflating what Hannah Arendt observed as the "boyhood ideals" of the imperialist character.[30] However, if freedom is where the west locates its origins and ideals, it must name its other, unfreedom, as Brown notes "the first imaginings of freedom are always constrained and potentially require the structure of oppression that freedom opposes".[31] The veiled and unveiled is a visual psychic economy in which the question of freedom is imagined resolved as imperial pursuits of knowledge, truth and subjectivity is exposed, sanctioned and secured through bodies.

The book understands subjectivity as one that is decentred, located within the Lacanian psychic registers of the Imaginary where the subject (or child in Lacanian parlance) fixes itself in an ideal image. This is an image that represents its unity with the mother as Other who is called on to affirm its imagined sense of self. The failure to secure this recognition in the Other marks the world of the Symbolic, the order of language, which provides the subject with a means to pursue its desire for its ideal image.[32] Exploring this psychic terrain of subjectivity allows for an analysis of the role of anxiety, desire, fantasy, trauma and *jouissance*. The latter is a form of unconscious enjoyment at the moment when enjoyment ends, and pain begins.[33] I examine how these psychic registers present themselves (or otherwise) in the gaze that looks upon the image of Aisha as exemplar of "the" Muslim woman.

This book traces these psychic coordinates in the terrain of the veiled, unveiled, veiling and unveiling, in terms of the political powers they mobilise or disable.[34] The veiled and unveiled are part of an imaginary investment in the possibility and the impossibility of the western subject— or the making or unmaking of the human. The veiled and unveiled is a haunting return in contemporary analyses of the west and its Other in a theatrical delineation of what is now called "The Muslim Question". It is the scene in which historical enemies are revived only to tell cautionary tales of peril and preordained victory. It is prophylactic for a world which Jason Josephson-Storm describes as "disenchantment" brought on from a "de-spiritualised modernity" as the acceptable mode of modern life.[35] The questions this book asks are most concerned with the governmentality and disciplinary processes of the cultural-political context that the veiled and unveiled fabricate, and the fantasies and *jouissance* that sustain them. This *jouissance* is discernible in Aisha's "wholeness" made possible through replacing her nose. This nose replacement, this book theorises, is a mode of unveiling.

This book reads images, socio-political discourses, historical and political events, scenes, through psychoanalytic themes of trauma, fantasy, anxiety and *jouissance*. The aim here is not to deal with empiricism—that is, searching for the Real of the other, but to identify the imagery of the veiled-veil*ing*-unveil*ing*-unveiled as powerful metaphorical expressions and coordinates of agency, autonomy and freedom in the post-9/11 and postcolonial world of national security, multiculturalism, human rights and women's rights. The images' hold on the historical imaginary is reproduced as part of a "we", the west, by anti-immigration campaigns, activists, politicians, journalists and academics. In this vein, the veiled and unveiled continue to inform "The Muslim Question".[36] The fantasy of unveiling is able to bridge these epistemic conditions, resolve inherent contradictions in western knowledge-making possible the occupation of imagined parameters of modernity/ tradition, freedom and truth—by way of symbolically measuring one's "civilisational proximity".[37]

IMAGING AND IMAGINING AISHA

Judging one's proximity to civilisation purports certainty about causes and urgency for solutions. Something must be done, and it must be done soon. The intimacy of a story invokes a responsibility on the reader.[38] Aisha's image is specular support for violence afflicted by her culture: an appeal to absolute conclusions about what is happening to Afghan women, what will happen to them and what they need. Aisha's disfigured face operates within a regime of, what Wendy S. Hesford describes as, "ocular epistemology", a "seeing-is-believing" paradigm that heightens the truth of the injustice.[39] Aisha's piercing brown eyes looking back to the viewer solicit a response from them to her injustice. Solicitation, however, evokes the absence of her voice as it privileges response over request. The image acts upon those who are imagined or imagine themselves as having moral weight, and who feel compelled to respond. Unlike Aisha, they are imagined or imagine themselves as having the capacity to deliver the rights and freedoms that she is assumed to be seeking but are denied. The "we" in *Time*'s slogan: "What happens if we leave Afghanistan", activates sympathy, outrage and judgement about what has happened to her; a "we" that is imagined in the questions that she provokes: How can "we" not feel disgust, shock and concern at her pain? How can this brutalised sombre face not provoke these sentiments? How can "we" not judge? And how can "we" not act? The answer denotes the promise of the image and the knowledge that it brings. Images serve as an important conduit for political truths in a society that increasingly reads and understands events by consuming their images.[40]

Imagery has a social and psychoanalytic valence here as it ensnares and captivates corporeality in the politics of empire, nationalism, decolonisation, modernity, progress and civilisation. These are sites of imaginaries where deep and intense emotions have been both pronounced and repressed. As Griselda Pollock writes,

> the image is a holding place of meaning, already structured by psychological processes, servicing them as the carrier of affects, phantasies, and displaced meanings. The image can be imaginary. It can inhabit an object, a thing, a picture created visually or in literature. It is never pure, purely visual, or even perceptual.[41]

Though the image holds fixed meaning, the content of possible meanings swells. The image is material in its visibility—a "this happened"—but also metaphorical of the imaginary that produces its meaning. Within a libidinal economy, the imagery of the veiled and unveiled is that carrier of affects, phantasies and displaced meanings, where seductive scenes of imagined loss, ruins and violent possession are fantasised. Aisha, through this lens, exists in what Edward Said observes as the phantasmatic Other, who is constituted through western positional superiority. The imagery that makes Aisha known is a testimonial of a history of civilisational proclamations, both imaged and imagined, that offers visual totality and secured truths. This certain knowing is the object of psychic investment.

This book refers throughout to images encountered through a range of media, including social media, where human rights groups, feminist activists and anti-immigration movements mobilise awareness of their political concerns and generate responses. The image today is increasingly replacing the written text as a means through which knowledge is circulated and consumed. Jean Baudrillard argued that in the era of technology the proliferation of images has initiated the death of the "Real" by over-representation. The hypervisibility of the image contains its opposite effect—that something in it has disappeared. The trafficking and marketing of images, the need to constantly document, is for Baudrillard, an overdose on meaning and is a seduction by illusion that enable us to distance ourselves from the "Real" world.[42] Documenting the historical knowledge production of the East in *Orientalism*, Edward Said understood the salience of images as sites of containment and meaning production about the other. Claiming to be a "neutral" knowledge of the East, orientalist knowledge relied on images as a conduit, a visible citation, announcing an exalted civilised Europe through a dangerous anachronistic Orient. The simplicity of the image for Said allowed Europe to "come to terms with the Orient" and elude its own otherness.[43] But even Said did not foresee the extent to which the image (of others) would become a foremost mode of knowledge transition. Our understanding of events in the world, war, politics, and so on, are increasingly retold and accessed through entertainment and media. Take for example, films such as *Jarhead* (2005), *The Hurt Locker* (2008), *Zero Dark Thirty* (2013) and *American Sniper* (2014); and TV shows like *Homeland*, *24* and *The Honourable Woman*. In addition to war footage, YouTube, photographs and Internet memes make the image/knowledge nexus pervasive. Such images flatten the world into Good and Evil, western virtue and Eastern barbarism. The monotony of the written word, and the labour entailed in its consumption, has been relieved by the entertaining, gripping and easily consumable image.

The image not only reduces complexities by providing certainty in an increasingly interconnected world, it also serves as a single global language. In the postcolonial era, where the East appears more than ever as an image, the other has become more digestible. Images of others who are strange to us are not simply momentary references or visual props, in a fleeting news announcement. Just as orientalism relied on fixed images of the Orient, images like Aisha are *recurring and circulating* fixing the image of otherness within geographical and cultural boundaries of the latest encounter with the strange. The power of the image is secured through its *familiarity* ("we" already believe Aisha is another Muslim woman in crisis), the *intensity* of its viral capacity, and the *accessibility* of its circulation.

The "visual capital" of the image does not exist in a vacuum; it needs to be mediated through particular discourses with interpretive power.[44] As

Said contends, the image of the other is always a highly situated knowledge, one that is organised and produced by discursive power.[45] In Saidian parlance, the image has the power to create meaning and the potential to satisfy the thirst for meaning. More salient, the image is informed by history, a historical imaginary and the production of identity. The image is an imperial site of re-visioning desires, the objects of desire's projection, as it is generated as "symbolic revenge".[46] Identifying this power in the image, Alison Young observes that its force is both "affective and effective", commanding the spectator's response.[47]

The danger of the image is that it assumes its truth by presenting things singularly. The image's applied politics and its illusion of fixing meaning in the comforting certainty of its visibility, erases complexities and grounds the gaze in a reliable and perceptible "fact". However, what has been excluded from the image—that which is beyond the frame—is what Butler has described as the "field of representability", which interprets the image and us.[48] Saba Mahmood similarly argues that "representations of facts, objects and events are profoundly mediated by the fields of power in which they circulate in".[49] Without its field of meaning, what is occluded from the image, it suggests that the image too can slip in meaning. Take for example, the image shown of the girl in "Liberated Kabul" where her uncovered face might have been a temporary gesture of a girl removing her veil to look more closely for American drones as her country enters the next phase of conflict, rather than the reception of freedom in Afghanistan. The image too can be indeterminate, leaving traces of ambivalence. I want to stress here that it is not the discursive field of meaning alone but the mobility and intense circulation of particular images and their reception that secures the image's meaning. Demanding "truth" by arresting the visible and circulating it above all, the image, in Žižekian parlance, is a spectre of subjective violence, which "prevents us from thinking".[50]

It is not just any image that is selected for circulation, but one that enables the western viewer a way of mobilising a knowing of what it conveys. The body's claim to universality, its corporeal familiarity bolsters the power of the image's ocular epistemology. Aisha's disfigured body invites signification. Her body is presented as a body that is prepared for inscription—confessing what has happened. The body here is a consoling familiar (we are all made of flesh and have bodies), which accentuates the affective and effective qualities of the image as meaning: a flesh experience, experience that authenticates a truth, and the body materialises it. It is in "digging into flesh" that Frantz Fanon observed that we find meaning.[51] The body gives credence to Barthes' observation: this is what has happened because it has been felt, experienced and could be re-lived.

Images of liberated, celebrated, detained, injured, tortured, enslaved, mutilated and humiliated bodies saturate today's media landscape.[52] The image of the body fixes "truth", the "reality" of war. It mobilises a response. It is deployed to measure—the victory of political visions; embodying a nation's becoming and a nation's decline; and to mark cultural difference. It is in this new digital age, and in this flesh, Islam and Muslims are brought to the west's attention to inform a western imaginary of the other. This is the "outside" the frame that frames Aisha as a body in crisis, disseminated to the world.

The relationship between the body and the image is in the authority of its visibility. This relationship is addressed in Lacan's conception of the birth of the subject. For Lacan, the subject who looks at a mirror, sees itself through an external image of its body as unified, as "closed". The body for Lacan has material properties, but it is also an object of imaginary construction—an *imago*—an imaginary produced in language. Lacan calls this unified body—the "body of the symbolic". Psychoanalyst Colette Soler explains it as an "incorporeal body, which by embodying itself gives you a body". The body, in other words, is spoken and given to us through signifiers.[53] The body is language, in the order of signifiers, culture, discourse, representation and *images*. Lacan's Symbolic Register suggests that language is never entirely ours because others always determine it. The body is never fully determined in language because, as an image, its meaning is unstable, always exceeding its signifier. It is through the Other as the Symbolic, the order of language, that the body can certify knowledge and secure corporeal meaning—retrieving "The Body" as one.

Lacan calls this other "an Other" to refer to it as a location in which others—like Aisha—can be projected, rather than being a definite presence. The failure to secure meaning in an unidentified Other both stabilises and destabilises the subject's effort to secure its imaginary sense of self, to address the question *Che vuoi?* (what do you want?)[54] For Lacan, the Other's question speaks to the heart of the subject's ontology, its desire to secure its image and meaning, to put together a body imagined whole, and to have the Other sanction it—a question that always follows with dissatisfied answers. *Che vuoi?* is both paranoid ("what"), desiring ("want"), and accusatory ("you") in its demanding tone, reaffirming that the Lacanian subject is not a subject of its own making. It is a subject whose demands and desires stem from, and are invested in otherness, tormented by the possibility of not knowing. In the context of this book, the perennial question—that drives the history of Orientalism and the current mode of Islamophobia—from the west to the Muslim is: *what do you want from me?*

The Other's question appears as fantasy and anxiety in the disfigured face of Aisha. Her missing flesh, as a piece of revealed truth, authorises an imagined certainty that something has gone wrong in Afghanistan. The staging of her wronged (or mutilated) body simultaneously stages the imagined capacity of the west to intervene in a scene of *fantasy*. In psychoanalytic theory, this fantasy screens the trauma of not knowing the Other's desire, the answer to *Che vuoi?* It is an unconscious defence against the impossibility of one's imagined sense of wholeness: the scene of castration.[55] This Fantasy attempts at the totalisation of a revealed truth, unwilling to consider anything else. The image of Aisha's body, or more precisely, how her body is imagined as an emergency, by a western liberal subject, who imagines itself as the one who must respond, gives corporeal and incorporeal consistency to western notions of self. This occurs through the language of freedom, democracy and universalism, and most importantly, in the act of restoring the missing flesh to ward off any future disambiguation and disintegration of the subject.

The Fantasy of Unveiling Freedom

It is the impossibility of bodily and psychic consistency, this lack and the pursuit to fulfil it, which provocatively places a young girl from a small village of Afghanistan on the front cover of an internationally known western magazine. Her unfamiliar journey from this unfamiliar world invites western viewers to imagine themselves as the one who can shield her from violence. This is a dynamic that involves mobilising the fantasies of orientalism, gender, development and subjective violence. Fantasy provides an answer to the impossibility of satisfying the question at the heart of subjectivity by teaching the subject how to desire its possibilities. Fantasy stages the Other's desire with the question to the viewers—what do others want from me? Who am I to others?[56] The "we"—as part of a "Coalition of the Willing", at war with Aisha's adversary on the cover of *Time* – is crucial for an imagined self, for the possibility of satisfying this question. To identify with a "we" is to also agree that something can or has been lost as Butler writes, "Loss has made a tenuous "we" of us all".[57] To invoke the "we" is to perform imagined boundaries.

The urgency of responding to Aisha is a desire for wholeness, of always knowing the truth—that "we" have the freedom to protect her. This is a strategy that prevents the gazing western subject from the destructive confrontation with the impossibility of the image's promise of securing this truth. The Other's desire returns in the west's image of itself because an unveil*ed* freedom is never guaranteed in the Other. Aisha embodies the threatening neighbour who provokes an ontological question by pointing to the possibility of enjoying differently, what Lacan calls the neighbour's *jouissance*.

Jouissance is an important concept for this book as it enables us to understand the continued investment in others because it undergirds the structure of subjectivity and the workings of knowledge production. Though a difficult concept to define, Lacan provides some guidance about how to understand it. *Jouissance* is like an unconscious enjoyment, an intolerable pleasure that "strangely" repeats—strange because what it repeats cannot be described as pleasure either.[58] *Jouissance* can be experienced in pain, anxiety, transgression and even disgust. Therefore, *jouissance* is not desire which "comes from the Other" but "located from the side of the Thing"—a point of limit.[59] *Jouissance* is inscribed on the body, as the Other's symbolic inscription, locating the *making and the unmaking* of the subject,[60] and the limit of knowing and not knowing the body. Aisha's unveiled injured face marks the failure of this inscription as the impossibility to guaranteeing the freedom that unveiling promises—the death of its *jouissance*. Her injured face reveals that what lies beneath the veil is further mutilation, a fragmented body that has yet to be made whole. This can only occur through her unveiling.

The encounter with Aisha's unveiled injured face is akin to the encounter with the hidden/veiled face, both traumatic because it destabilises one's certainty about one's self and its relation to *jouissance*—the universal formula of enjoying freedom as unveiled is brought into question. The uncovered face as mutilated, raises the question as to whether unveiling Afghan women can guarantee their freedom? Aisha's unveiled face makes known the question: what does the Other want from me if unveiling is not enough? If freedom is not enough? This question is answered by an agent of her unveiling whose freedom is postponed (but always promised) by another corporeal affliction, another *veil of violence*. This veil is a permanent *racial shadow* on her body, exhibiting symptoms of difference. The violence is imagined as afflictions of "cultural practices" (veiling, honour crimes, female genital mutilation, etc.)—symptoms of constraints of difference that produce "The Muslim Woman". The veil of violence is what Taussig describes as "epistemic murk",[61] the terrifying fictional explorations of the Muslim other—feminine and unknown—while it aestheticises horror. Veiled or unveiled, Aisha *is* the veiled woman, whose veil of (subjective and symbolic) violence can only be lifted by another. The veil of violence, both material and metaphorical, sustains the fantasy of an unveil*ing* freedom.

Knowing the Other

Shortly after Aisha's debut in *Time*, new photos of her began to circulate. These images depicted her face after she underwent surgical reconstruction in California. She appears smiling, happy with her "new" nose, which was later revealed to be a cosmetic replacement until she was mentally well for reconstructive surgery. With her prosthetic nose, she appeared at press galleries, meeting Laura Bush and former First Lady of California Maria Shriver.[62] This new offer of freedom via the reconstruction of Aisha's nose by American doctors propels the fantasy of her unveiling. She can be made whole through reconstructive surgery. Her missing nose aroused a desire for the west to recoup the "missing pieces". However, this desire points in an opposite direction. Not so much to the absent nose and the mutilated face, but to the west's own ontological fragmentation, its own mutilation, and its imagining of itself as the one in possession of the wholeness that Aisha lacks.[63] Aisha's popular reception in the west (before and after her surgery) is driven by an imaginary of *knowing* the desire of the Other which stabilises the west's image of itself as an unveiled whole. With or without her nose, Aisha symbolises the violence that is done to other women and signifies the capacity to do "good". The removal of the violence of the first image is made possible only by the intervention of the benevolent west, who imagines itself as the permissible agent of her salvation. However, the narrative of responsibility lingers as a joy and a burden because this missing piece of flesh suggests that "progress" has yet to arrive in a country where bodies remain disfigured.

Aisha's name mobilises other imaginaries too. Aisha, the "child bride" of Islam's Prophet Mohamed—the Muslim woman already present in this image. That is, the Muslim woman as always inflicted by violence. Islam is constructed here as descending violence on Aisha of the seventh century to the Aisha of the twenty-first century. The name Aisha echoes another historical naming: European artists often named their paintings and photographs of unveiled woman of the Orient as Aisha. Examples of this include *Aisha Refena* by George Owen Wynne Apperley (1884–1960) and Jean-François Portaels' *Aisha* painted in Tangier around the second half of the nineteenth century, *Aicha, A Woman of Morocco* by Frederick Arthur Bridgman 1883.[64] The significance of naming these unveiled women "Aisha" alongside the contemporary Aisha on *Time*, should not be overlooked. Having a religious and cultural potency, symbolic of a powerful female figure in Islamic tradition—scholar, military leader and poet—Aisha has a special status in Islam and is considered an ideal female model for Muslim women to aspire to. As such, the unveiling of "Aisha" within the realm of the Orientalist imaginary not only presupposes an unveiled figure of emulation, but also denotes satisfaction by revealing the secrets of the Orient. The repeated unveiling of Aisha fulfils the fantasy of entering the heart of Islam through rescuing the Muslim woman.

The relationship between the west and the veiled woman is one of a subject–object relationship integral to orientalism's positional superiority where she is always placed as other, churning racial narratives.[65] The perpetual defacing of the other within imperial fantasy is a never-ending endeavour of *projecting one's desire into the desire of the Other*.[66] Here, it is recast through imagining the native, who is always in need of improvement, in a state of cultural immaturity.[67] Once the Muslim woman is unveiled, there are other layers of violence, other "evidence" of regression, other veils beneath the flesh. The anxiety of an ontological limit of the west in Aisha's image is recast as the horror of the brute, the Islamic neighbour. In the frequent conflations of Taliban fundamentalism and Islam, terrorism and Islam, Aisha's experience is also a cautionary tale for all women, who take the path of Islam, whose *jouissance* is elsewhere, and whose missing pieces are yet to be revealed.

RETURNING TO THE VEIL

The production of Aisha's image, or rather, the imagining of Aisha as an image, captures the theoretical intervention this book aims to make. It examines the west's historical fixation on the veiled woman as a figure whose image has organised and absorbed historical, cultural and political complexities of the East in relation to the west. It does so not to disprove but to improve the understandings of her reoccurrence today. The question of why there is always a return to the veiled woman has more traction today when we consider the host of pressing economic and social issues that can be put aside, to make way for an exaggerated fear and anxiety of Muslims. Islamophobia takes the most visible representation of Islamic difference, the veiled woman, as its object of worry.[68] For instance, writing about the veil debate in France, Joan Wallach Scott observes how the "veil served to cover a body of intractable domestic issues even as it revealed the anxieties associated with them".[69] In the west, the veiled woman is frequently referred to as a sign of danger and national loss. We encounter frequent reports of incidents where veiled women, as visible Muslims, are attacked by members of the public.[70] Even in a headscarf form, she is seen as a carrier of dangerous ideas and identified as a marker of "passive terrorism".[71] The growing hysteria surrounding the political loyalties of Muslim women is directly proportion to the weight of their veil: from the hijab (headscarf), niqab (face veil, revealing just her eyes), to the burqa (full face cover). Much of this book refers to the veil to capture the practice of veiling the body of which the veiled face is its most powerful imagery; but it will specify when the distinctions are necessary. Controversies around the veiled woman are, often and increasingly, couched within the language of security, cultural oppression and the need to guarantee cultural integrity and civic peace.[72] It is the obsessive resort to banning the veil in a time of other bans—travel bans and immigration bans—that deserves closer examination of what is behind this investment.[73]

The veil—usually representative of the burqa and niqab, but sometimes the hijab too—as a cultural menace and a national security threat predominates in the west despite the empirical evidence to the contrary. Countries like France, Belgium, the United Kingdom, the Netherlands and Australia, each have a low number of Muslim populations and a lower number of women who veil.[74] A 2018 Pew Study of 15 countries showed most western Europeans want some forms of restriction on Muslim women's dress.[75] This is not to say, however, that there would be a justification for banning and legitimate security issues if these countries had higher number of Muslims. In either case, the intense attention and overreaction to the visibility of Islam vis-à-vis the veiled woman require closer consideration. What is it about the veiled woman that draws the west's attention to matters of multiculturalism, anti-immigration, citizenship, terrorism, women's rights and human rights?

In the political atmosphere of security and terrorism, the veiled woman is imagined as someone who represents no faith (in us) or too much faith (in an Other). The west's grappling with this tension appears as a bodily terror, a symptom of culture's menacing effects on the universal reception of rights and the prospect of arresting the universal body. The reappearance of the veiled woman in the west, in the wake of the supposed liberation of Afghanistan and the defeat of tyrants in Iraq, Syria and Somalia, as part of the war on terror, is occurring at a time of great political change in parts of "the Muslim world". "The Arab Spring" and the upheavals since these uprisings have brought about a new threat to some totalitarian governments. Images of these events over the past few years depict Arab women participating, if not mobilising, in a culture of dissent. These noteworthy images of protesting women have shaken long-held western perceptions of women in this region as docile and lacking agency. I consider the significance of these changes within the post-revolution Arabo-Muslim discourse, in particular these changes that mark a departure from the western-inspired perceptions of the Muslim woman. I raise the possible correlation between the rise of Muslim female agency and the imperilled Muslim (veiled) woman and suggest the need to reflect on how the confounding pattern of orientalist images are forcefully circulated at a time when incompatible representations of Muslim women have increased.

My objective is to sidestep the discourse of multiplicity and resistance[76]—as a form of the celebration of the empowered Muslim woman—to add to the differently oriented interventions of Sherene H. Razack, Joan Wallach Scott, Saba Mahmood and Lila Abu-Lughod who locate power at the intimate scale of representations of the *other* woman and the politics of a rescue narrative. Abu-Lughod's well-known question *Do Muslim Women Need Saving?* which relies on decades of anthropological work to illustrate the disconnect between The Muslim Woman, told us through political campaigns to save her from "honour killings" and the veil, the reality of Muslim women's lives. Abu-Lughod explains how these campaigns mark a "new common sense", which deploys gendered orientalism—the helpless woman of "Islamland"—to convince us of the justice Muslim women seek. The Muslim woman's story is expressed through the indictment of her religion and culture to the exclusion of political, economic and historical contributions.[77] Interrogating this racist logic of Muslim representation, Razack argues that responses both in law and popular culture to issues like "forced marriages", the veil, and so on, assert the figures of the "civilised European", the "imperilled Muslim woman" and the "dangerous Muslim man". These figures culturalise violence and animate the war on terror as they are also used to justify stigmatising Muslim communities, and to authorise the invasions of Muslim countries.[78]

Mahmood's *The Politics of Piety* is a ground-breaking critique that problematises poststructuralist feminist subjectivity, womanness and women's relationship to agency, freedom, autonomy and personhood. Mahmood attempts to convey a different mode of female subject constitution, one that refuses to subscribe to hegemonic notions of a liberal self with agency. Her observations of the practices of piety in Egypt show that human activities do not always subscribe to liberatory projects and can indeed demonstrate the opposite: an empowering submission to the transcendental through bodily practices, such as veiling, prayer and fasting as acts of agency. In doing so, Mahmood posits the parochialism of western liberatory conceptions of subjectivity, which define agency only through oppositional practices.[79]

My own intervention can be considered a contribution to responses that reject orientalist depictions of Muslims. My focus, however, is neither one that contests or explores the discursive representation nor outlines how these representations work to sustain racist narratives. This is not a book about veiling practices or to humanise women who wear it. It returns to the deeper questions that Joan Wallach Scott raises in *The Politics of the Veil* about the historical and political investment in the veil. My book attempts to trace the political *and* psychic dimensions of hegemonic discursive power and bring to light the fantasies and anxieties, that underpin it. It aims to explore the psychic mechanics of the discourse of the Muslim Question via the veil.

Discursive representations have effectively unearthed the imperial underpinnings of figures like Aisha to release her from reductionist representations. The focus on representations contends that she is not reflective of all Muslim women and that the violence she has experienced is not contextualised in material or historical terms. There remains a sense there is more to unearth and why the veil haunts conversations on Muslim women. These extant interventions do not sufficiently address what Frantz Fanon describes as the phobogenic condition of the Muslim Woman in the west. Why does the (veiled) Muslim woman persist in the western imaginary *after* the fact of who she really is? I contend that the fascination, anxieties and even revulsion she engenders, cannot simply be explained as misunderstanding, misrepresentation, imperial appropriation of meaning, an interpellation of discursive practice through gender and race, or an anthropological study of Muslim women's "every day" life. Narratives of the veiled woman are not sustained on material and ideological motives alone but exist together with psychic drives that supersede any rational and factual accounts. The imagining of the Muslim other beneath the veil is emblematic of a tension, a trauma in the psychoanalytic sense that is constantly concealed in the call to police or "unveil" Islam. I delve further into why and how the veiled woman produces such a violent demand to unveil for the west. What is the psychic investment in the imagery of the veiled and unveiled that bloats bodies with civilisational value? Why is it that freedom in the liberal secular imaginary must be found through the unveil*ing* body?

The veil is a metaphor of violence that can be both material and immanent to the imagined ontology of the Muslim woman. Miriam Cooke's neologism of "the Muslimwoman" similarly invokes the veil and locates identity boundaries between "us and them". Cooke states "'the veil, real or imagined'", functions like race, a marker of essential difference that Muslim women today cannot escape".[80] Cooke argues that the new visibility of Muslim women has meant the Muslim woman is already a site on which both Muslim women's activism and the racialising discourses of the war on terror and Islamophobia are taking place. However, Cooke's use of the "Muslimwoman" is strategic in that it can anchor, empower and raise a collective political consciousness for Muslim women to break out of the "cage"—signified by the veil—and aspire to a cosmopolitan identity. My intention is not to pave the way for her "escape"; it is to ask why is there the need to escape? Why is she always announced through the veil? And why is she always asked why? Why the why? I examine how she is a symptom of the limit, of relating to the big Other and why she provokes such contradictory responses: fascination and anxiety; disgust and desire. I explore this encounter between western dominant culture with the Muslim woman—vis-à-vis the veiled woman—not so much to point to how *the* Muslim woman is erased entirely by the violence of the western gaze. Rather, I explore what lays beneath "the epistemic violence of this vision".[81]

A psychoanalytic lens reveals the excess that sustains these representations. In Lacanian parlance, the veiled woman is both the *master signifier*— she stands in for the fullness of the meaning of the Muslim woman—and the *objet petit a*—the cause of desire that never entirely captures the Muslim woman. Those who aim to collapse Cooke's neologism—to "complicate" the "Muslimwoman", ignore the imaginary of the west in which the veiled woman cannot be divorced from the discourses that produce her. She always returns as a symbol to be appropriated, examined, disputed and scrutinised—or more precisely, she is always a problem from the start. She is both the discursive space, the hidden ground that allows and disallows one to talk about the Muslim woman/Islam *and* the figure that represents her but never entirely arrives at an explanation of her. What these psychic components of discursive representations reveal is beyond the image are other interpellative forces—what psychoanalyst Mark Bracher argues are "the important elements of subjectivity (ideals, values, fantasy, desire, drives and jouissance)".[82] For Lacan, knowledge is motivated by some failure of pleasure, a dissatisfaction or lack,[83] and it is in this sense that psychoanalysis enables examining why meta-narratives and discourses are produced *and* received.[84] In Suzanne Barnard's terms, it confronts "their founding fantasies and modes of jouissance".[85]

The economy of the veiled and unveiled produces a western desire for the invisible—what is beneath the veil? In turn imagining her being unveiled fulfils the fantasy of what Lacan calls the knowing subject: securing its epistemological claims through reaffirming its scopic field by discovering corporeal freedom and establishing its universalist truths. The "western subject" then comes to secure itself in this relationship, as something, which speaks to the heart of what it means to be free; the Muslim woman is at once an object of anxiety, a mode of enjoying, and a marker of unbearable difference. This difference causes all categories of "Woman" to fail. The return to the veil then is a return to a scene of seduction that locates the veiled *and* unveiled (veiling and unveiling) where the west discovers itself, where the west enjoys itself as western.

CHAPTER OUTLINE

The book is structured around psychoanalytic themes of fantasy, trauma, *jouissance* and anxiety, and how they are situated in subjectivity, the image and the body. These sites come to terms with the fundamental lack in the question of *Che vuoi?* by fixing a universal atemporal answer to this question. Each chapter approaches this ontological tension from within history, the nation, international human rights, and racial and gender spaces. The imagery of the veiled and unveiled, veiling and unveiling, serve as epistemic, ontological and psychic vocabularies in which these psychoanalytical themes and their strains are made politically meaningful.

In Chapter 2 I contend, in line with Kalpana Seshadri-Crooks, that the body ultimately founds the trauma of one's being, or lack of being, and the subject's image of itself. It is through the body that the lack can be identified, and the fantasy of fulfilment can be imagined. I further unpack the Lacanian fantasy of freedom by an unveiled subject by probing the relationship between wholeness and the unveiled. What is it about the unveiled body that embodies ideas of universality and freedom? This chapter makes use of theoretical insights such as Seshadri-Crooks' framing of whiteness as a pre-discursive whole, an unsaid, which frames the modern "natural" body.[86] The body that is neutral, beyond politics, is a "secular body" as examined by Hirschkind and Asad and materially, psychically and discursively distinguishes itself from not only the religious body, but the racial stains of culture left on the body. Tracing this secular body to the "human", I explore how unveiling—both material and imaginary—is linked to a body that is assembled within a progressive history of humanity from natural law to modern human rights. The chapter traces Giorgio Agamben's notion of the political[87] as it shapes the secular body by establishing its civilisational markings of the veiled and unveiled. Within a trajectory that evokes an end of history, I contend that the fantasy of a completed subject, who freely constitutes and perpetuates its own freedom, can only exist by the presupposition of a pre-discursive "neutral"—secular—*unified* body.

Chapter 3 traces the migration of secular freedom qua the impulse to unveil to the international scene of rights campaigns. This chapter explores how human rights are already underpinned by a presupposition of a global human wholeness. I examine images used in human rights campaigns which construct the Muslim woman as always in an emergency appearing in a veil of violence. These images of corporeal afflictions elicit a response by the free and morally certain west. The repeated appearance of the veiled woman as *object a*, always imagined beneath a threatening veil, is recast here as a practice of deferring the "freedom" of unveiling because it can never completely arrive. Using Renata Salecl's Lacanian framework of rights as a language that can fulfil the subject's ontological lack with more rights,[88] the image of the veiled woman in crisis is rendered as an insurance of the promise of human rights. Images of the Muslim woman under the shadow of the veil of violence, therefore, link desiring rights with the wholeness of freedom's arrival on the body. The veiling of the Muslim woman in the human rights imaginary maintains the economy of rights and desire as a constant deferral of the arrival of rights. There are always more rights and more desires to be fulfilled, thus securing the western subject's fantasy of the possibility of corporal and psychic wholeness. This chapter argues that all these images of the Muslim woman, veiled or unveiled, are iterations of the veiled woman.

Chapter 4 considers the possibilities of attaining, in Lacanian parlance, the signifier of Woman in the fantasy of the phallic west that has already claimed universalism and freedom. I examine what it is about unveiling in and of itself that carries notions of freedom and women's agency? Building on the discussion of the fantasy of unveiling freedom, I consider the role of women in the fantasy of freedom. Revising the Oedipal paradigm of castration, beyond biology, in Lacan's account, the masculine and feminine is viewed through having or not having language. In this vein, wholeness for Lacan is phallic or masculine because the Symbolic/language can be mobilised to secure its fantasy. It is the regulation of *jouissance*, through masculine and feminine structures of being, that reveals the Lacanian formula of Woman's non-existence. I contend that the concern for the *other* woman, the Muslim woman, by secular female critics in the west is an attempt to overcome the inexistence of Woman by unveiling the veiled masquerade which conceals women's lack. Within the Symbolic structure of modernity, the fantasy of unveiling freedom identifies a *hyper-unveiling* which makes possible the arrival of the universal Woman by projecting lack on to the veiled other thereby attuning herself with an unveiled west and its master signifiers of universality and freedom.

Chapter 5 broadens the discussions of the previous chapters and situates their relevance in the climate of Islamophobia by examining the politics and emotional investment in "The Muslim Question". With the relationship between subjectivity, the body, and the image in mind, this chapter asks what does this question reveal about the postcolonial condition? While Orientalism for Edward Said was about the other in exotic places made intelligible through orientalist fantasies, what does Islamophobia reveal about the west's relationship to the other who enjoys differently within its borders? The chapter contends that the prominence of the veil in Islamophobia is a hysterical preoccupation with "The Body" and its potential contamination in contact with others: the Muslim as terrorist, the Muslim as terrorising. Both these discourses are symptoms of paranoid knowledge as they strive to manage knowledge of the other, but this paranoia spills out as Islamophobia when it imagines being overwhelmed by the other. This fixation on the body reveals itself as a hypochondria that demands to know the "universal" body. In Islamophobia, the perpetual questioning of the Muslim—Why is she veiled? What is she hiding? What is Islam? Why are Muslims not condemning terrorism?—are the hysteric's questions to the Other to secure truth through the unveiling (knowing of) the body—a body whose boundaries and knowledge cannot be guaranteed. In the fantasy of freedom, it is only the repetition of the image of the veiled woman, who circulates as the foreign identified and contained as an image that is a substitute for absolute knowledge over the body, offering momentary relief to these questions. A form of "hyperveiling"—"complete forms of covering"[89] —occurs as a new mode of knowing the Muslim and therefore, securing the universal body.

Chapter 6 shifts the focus to examine what women's pursuit for wholeness portends to "unveiled" women from Muslim communities. This chapter examines confessional narratives of Muslim women or former Muslim women, such as "unveiling" stories of Iranian women facing the forces of Islamic fundamentalism on social media pages, the curious alliance between "secular Muslims" and far-right anti-Islam activists, and journalist Mona Eltahawy. Using Michel Foucault's politics of confession—the demand to uncover truth,[90]—the other's confession satisfies the question which haunts the subject's desire to know. In this vein, these "native" discourses are symptoms of an internalised Islamophobia that treats their bodies as diseased and needing to be cured through confessing its bodily symptoms. The other, confessing their desires, in Foucauldian parlance, is an obedience to power in that it relies on a belief in the "natural" body as not yet discovered. The chapter explores the relationship between native informant figures and the desire to confess in the post-9/11 epoch as the new postcolonial condition for those who hail from "former colonies". They situate themselves in heroic narratives of surviving the violence of the veil and declaring the "truth" of Islam, narrating the ordeal of experiencing bodily (sexual) constraints of cultural and religious imposition. Their subversive commentary adopts a language of agency, thereby, evoking a perpetual reinstalment of the fantasy of unveiling through confession. In other words, there is always a veil (of violence) that identifies the potential of (self) discovery. The unveiled Arab (read as Muslim) body realises what Joseph Massad observes as empire's crusading sexual identitarian impulses, assimilating identities[91]—and this book argues, bodies—and practices under what is normalised as "sexuality"

This book aims to shed new light on the west's fixation on the veiled woman through the question of what is in the veil more than a Woman? Though an awkward question, the book hopes to demonstrate its metaphysical makeup by locating it in the repetition of how Muslim women like Aisha are imagined. The book identifies how this repetition is about failure and the seductive possibility of recovering next time something lost. Looking at both the veil and the body that possess it, or is possessed by it, this book traces the symptoms of loss for a west absorbed by the question of the Other, raised in the body that refuses to confess. I argue in this book that the preoccupation with the veiled woman is part of an imperial fantasy of constant discovery of a western all-knowing subject in pursuit of unveiling freedom to secure bodies without shadows. These are shadows that detect possibilities of new epistemological discoveries, new means of enjoying, but also new torments, laid bare for a panoptic gaze that declares *unlimited* knowledge, the removal of any veil on corporeal terrains. The fantasy of freedom is only secured by imagining there is another veil, another violence on Muslim women's bodies whose shadows always linger and in need of being unveiled. The return to the veiled woman is a veiling of the Muslim as part of a strategy to discipline and contain knowledge of the Other—of any*body* that alerts one to the unsettling possibility that liberal freedom lacks universal prescription.

NOTES

1. Miriam Cooke, "Deploying the 'Muslimwoman', Roundtable Discussion: Religion, Gender and the Muslimwoman," *Journal of Feminist Studies in Religion* 24, no. 1 (2008): 91.
2. Roland Barthes and Stephen Heath, *Image, Music, Text* (New York: Hill and Wang, 1977), 44.
3. Richard Stengel, "The Plight of Afghan Woman: A Disturbing Picture," *Time*, July 29, 2010.
4. Cited in Jogchum Vrielink, "Symptomatic Symbolism: Banning the Face Veil 'As a Symbol'," in *The Experience of the Face Veil Wearers in Europe and the Law*, ed. Eva Brems (Cambridge: Cambridge University Press, 2014), 184.
5. Joan Wallach Scott, *The Politics of the Veil* (Princeton: Princeton University Press, 2007), 158.
6. Joan Wallach Scott, *Sex and Secularism* (Princeton and Oxford: Princeton University Press, 2018), 169.
7. Ellen McLarney, "The Burqa in Vogue: Fashioning Afghanistan," *Journal of Middle East Women's Studies* 5, no. 1 (2009): 2.
8. Judith Butler, *Precarious Life: The Powers of Mourning and Violence* (New York: Verso, 2004), 141–142.
9. Slavoj Žižek, *Violence: Six Sideways Reflections* (London: Profile Books, 2008), 1–3.

10. In the wake of the events of 11 September 2001, the United States and its allies invaded Afghanistan on 7 October 2001 because it was believed that the Taliban were harbouring al-Qaeda, and to stop al-Qaeda from using it as a base for future attacks. This militarised action was called Operation Enduring Freedom.

11. Gayatri Chakravorty Spivak, "Can the Subaltern Speak?" in *Colonial Discourse and Post-Colonial Theory: A Reader*, ed. Patrick Williams and Laura Chrisman (New York: Columbia University Press, 1994).

12. Wendy Brown, *State of Injury: Power and Freedom in Late Modernity* (Princeton: Princeton University Press, 1995), 5.

13. Lila Abu-Lughod, *Do Muslim Women Need Saving?* (Cambridge, MA: Harvard University Press, 2013), 47.

14. Judith Butler, "Sexual Politics, Torture, and Secular Time," *The British Journal of Sociology* 59, no. 1 (2008): 4.

15. Anne Laura Stoler, "Imperial Formations: Reflections on Ruins and Ruinations," *Cultural Anthropology* 23, no. 2 (2008): 192.

16. Asad, *Formations of the Secular: Christianity, Islam, Modernity*, 13.

17. Asad, *Formations of the Secular: Christianity, Islam, Modernity*, 13.

18. Democracy and freedom are principles that emerge from European liberal traditions of tolerance, individual freedoms and enhancing the capacity to choose, private-public divisions, and secularism as a doctrine that maintains the political as "empty"—not prejudiced by culture and religion. Seth's unpacks the problematics of both the "pre-social" liberalism of John Stuart Mill and the procedural liberalism of Immanuel Kant. Despite its principles of universal equality and rights, they fail to recognise difference unless it is brought under the "sign of the same". See Sanjay Seth, "Liberalism and the Politics of (Multi) Culture: Or, Plurality Is Not Difference," *Postcolonial Studies* 4, no. 1 (2001).

19. Goldie Osuri and Bobby S. Banerjee, "White Diasporas: Media Representations of September 11 and the Unbearable Whiteness of Being in Australia," *Social Semiotics* 14, no. 2 (2004): 158.

20. Sunera Thobani, "War and the Politics of Truth-Making in Canada," *Qualitative Studies in Education* 16, no. 3 (2003): 402.

21. Asad, *Formations of the Secular: Christianity, Islam, Modernity*, 13.

22. Contradictions and tensions include the assumed separation between religion and state in the doctrine of secularism which are not separate practices but flow into each other. Though liberalism is a complex tradition with varying currents, its tensions such as the division between public and private and individual and collective freedoms, have been an unresolved theme. Both secularism and liberalism assume themselves to be impervious to religious and cultural bias which the debate on multiculturalism, and the issues of race, gender and sexuality, have put into question. See Seth, "Liberalism and the Politics of (Multi) Culture: Or, Plurality Is Not Difference". Asad,

Formations of the Secular: Christianity, Islam, Modernity. For how these tensions can manifest more specifically, see fieldwork on Muslims in France in Mayanthi L. Fernando, *The Republic Unsettled: Muslim French and the Contradictions of Secularism* (Durham: Duke University Press, 2014).

23. Gayatri Chakravorty Spivak, *A Critique of Postcolonial Reason: Toward a History of the Vanishing Present* (Cambridge, MA: Harvard University Press, 1999), 9.

24. This is a freedom that Butler argues is tied to temporal secular time: always moving forward. Butler, "Sexual Politics, Torture, and Secular Time," 3.

25. Marylou Sena, "A Purview of Being: The Ontological Structure of Reference (*Verweisung*) and Indication (*Indikation*)," in *Heidegger, Translation, and the Task of Thinking: Essays in Honour of Parvis Emad*, ed. Frank Schalow (New Orleans: University of New Orleans, 2011), 85.

26. Butler, "Sexual Politics, Torture, and Secular Time," 4.

27. Talal Asad, "Thinking About the Secular Body, Pain and Liberal Politics," *Cultural Anthropology* 26, no. 4 (2011): 657–675.

28. Charles Hirschkind, "Is There a Secular Body?" *Cultural Anthropology* 26, no. 4 (2011): 633–647.

29. Asad, "Thinking About the Secular Body, Pain and Liberal Politics," 657–675.

30. Arendt here is referring to those who did not "outgrow their boyhood ideals" and who became ideal candidates for colonial services. "Imperialism to them was nothing but an accidental opportunity to escape a society in which one had to forget his youth if he wanted to grow up". See Hannah Arendt, "The Imperialist Character," *The Review of Politics* 12, no. 2 (1950): 303–320.

31. Wendy Brown, *State of Injury: Power and Freedom in Late Modernity* (Princeton: Princeton University Press, 1995), 7.

32. These three registers can be approached from multiple angles such as the specular image and the role of the signification; but most refer to the oedipal scene which builds on Freud's notion of the child's castration from the mother by the father's intervention. This Lacan reads as not simply about the oedipal family, but the subject's relation to desire. The phallus a marker of wholeness also represents the subject's division; forbidding the child from desiring fully by reconnecting with the mother. See Bruce Fink, *The Lacanian Subject: Between Language and Jouissance* (Princeton: Princeton University Press, 1995), 44–60.

33. Paul Verhaeghe, "Enjoyment and Impossibility: Lacan's Revision of the Oedipal Complex—Reflections on Seminar XVII," in *Jacques Lacan and the Other Side of Psychoanalysis*, ed. Justin Clemens and Russell Grigg (Durham: Duke University Press, 2006), 30–31.

34. Asad, *Formations of the Secular: Christianity, Islam, Modernity*, 17.

35. Jason Josephson-Storm, *The Myth of Disenchantment: Magic, Modernity and the Birth of the Human Sciences* (Chicago and London: University of Chicago, 2017).
36. This is a question that marks the Muslim and Islam as a limit, a "preeminent danger" to Enlightenment principles, to governance, to Christians, Jews, secular humanists, women, sex and sexuality, and all things that constitute as civilisational practices of "the west". See Anne Norton, *On the Muslim Question* (Princeton: Princeton University Press, 2013), 2–3.
37. Chetan Bhatt, "The Times of Movements: A Response," *The British Journal of Sociology* 59, no. 1 (2008).
38. Arthur Kleinman and Joan Kleinman, "The Appeal of Experience; The Dismay of Images: Cultural Appropriations of Suffering in Our Times," *Daedalus* 125, no. 1 (1996): 7.
39. Wendy S. Hesford, *Spectacular Rhetorics: Human Rights Visions, Recognitions, Feminisms* (Durham: Duke University Press, 2011), 29.
40. Jean Baudrillard, *The Spirit of Terrorism* (London: Verso, 2003), 26–27.
41. Griselda Pollock, *Psychoanalysis and the Image: Transdisciplinary Perspectives* (Malden, MA: Blackwell Publishing, 2006), 4.
42. For an analysis of the conflation between the "real" and the image, see Jean Baudrillard, *The Spirit of Terrorism* (London: Verso, 2003), 26–27.
43. Edward Said, *Orientalism*, 1st ed. (New York: Pantheon Books, 1978), 1.
44. Hesford, *Spectacular Rhetorics*, 8.
45. See Said, *Orientalism*.
46. Bullock, *Rethinking Muslim Women and the Veil*, 17.
47. Alison Young, *Judging the Image: Art, Value, Law* (New York: Routledge, 2005), 13.
48. Judith Butler, "Torture and the Ethics of Photography," *Environment and Planning D: Society and Space* 25, no. 6 (2007): 953.
49. Saba Mahmood, "Feminism, Democracy and Empire: Islam and the War on Terror," in *Women's Studies on the Edge*, ed. Joan Wallach Scott (Durham: Duke University Press, 2008), 97.
50. Žižek, *Violence: Six Sideways Reflections*, 3.
51. Frantz Fanon, *Black Skin, White Masks* (London: Grove Press, 2008), 3.
52. For instance, the "liberated" body of unveiled Afghan women; the "celebrated" body of FEMEN's sexual revolution; the tortured and humiliated bodies of Abu Ghraib in Iraq.
53. Colette Soler, "The Body in the Teaching of Jacques Lacan," trans. Lindsay Watson, http://jcfar.org.uk/wp-content/uploads/2016/03/The-Body-in-the-Teaching-of-Jacques-Lacan-Colette-Soler.pdf
54. Jacques Lacan, *Ecrits: The First Complete Edition in English* (New York: W.W. Norton, 2006), 690.
55. Juliet Rogers, *Law's Cut on the Body of Human Rights* (New York: Routledge, 2013), 10.

56. Slavoj Žižek, *How to Read Lacan* (New York: W.W. Norton, 2007), 49.
57. Butler, *Precarious Life: The Powers of Mourning and Violence*, 20.
58. Verhaeghe, "Enjoyment and Impossibility," 30–31.
59. Lacan, *Ecrits: The First Complete Edition in English*, 853.
60. Verhaeghe, "Enjoyment and Impossibility," 31–32.
61. Michael Taussig, "Culture of Terror--Space of Death. Roger Casement's Putumayo Report and the Explanation of Torture," *Comparative Studies in Society and History* 26, no. 4 (1984): 471.
62. Jessica Ravitz, "Saving Aesha," *CNN*, May 2012, http://edition.cnn.com/interactive/2012/05/world/saving.aesha/index.html
63. Rogers, *Law's Cut on the Body of Human Rights*, 26.
64. Pino Blasone, "Orientalism, Veiled and Unveiled," (2011), https://www.scribd.com/document/51101694/Orientalism-Veiled-and-Unveiled(PDF).
65. Said, *Orientalism*, 7.
66. Fink, *The Lacanian Subject: Between Language and Jouissance*, 59–61.
67. Butler, "Sexual Politics, Torture, and Secular Time," 15.
68. Dekker and Van Der Noll (2009) quoted in Vladiana-Ioana Apetroaie, "The Trembling Veil: Issues of Gendered Islamophobia and Intolerance Towards Veiled Muslim Women, Current Issues of Islam" (Faculty of Social Sciences, 2012), 4. For example, the correlation between the rise of veil debates in the past six years and rise in unemployment and austerity measures throughout Europe.
69. Joan Wallach Scott, *The Politics of the Veil* (Princeton: Princeton University Press, 2007), 18.
70. Across western countries, studies show that women are disproportionately the target of anti-Muslim attacks. For example, in the UK: https://www.theguardian.com/uk-news/2018/jul/20/record-number-anti-muslim-attacks-reported-uk-2017
    Australia: https://theconversation.com/islamophobia-is-still-raising-its-ugly-head-in-australia-80682
    United States: https://www.washingtonpost.com/posteverything/wp/2016/09/16/how-muslim-women-bear-the-brunt-of-islamophobia/?utm_term=.cab2d756243e.
71. Laurie Fenstermacher, "Countering Violent Extremism; Scientific Method and Strategies" Revised White Paper, Air Force Research Laboratory, July 2015, https://info.publicintelligence.net/ARL-CounteringViolentExtremism.pdf
72. It is worth noting that the question of the veil has also been raised in Muslim majority questions such as Iran, Tunisia and Turkey that have either enforced it or restricted it. In the past year, restricted or total bans on the veil have occurred in Syria, Cameroon, Egypt and Chad and Congo-Brazzaville, citing

security. The nature of these debates must be considered within the dynamics of local histories, colonialism, statecraft and contemporary geopolitical alliances amidst the war on terror. Whether imposing the veil or banning it, the veil's over-determination in such localities works within the already established discursive parameters of western socio-political interests which aims to frame Islam as a threat to secular freedoms and a domestic and international security issue.

73. Sherene H. Razack, "A Site/Sight We Cannot Bear: The Racial and Spatial Politics of Western of Banning of the Muslim Woman's Niqab", *Canadian Journal of Women and the Law* 30, no. 1 (2018).

74. In France, it was predicted around 1900 women are reported to wear a veil. Salman Sayyid, "Veiled Threats?" *International Centre for Muslim and Non-Muslim Understanding* (2011), http://www.unisa.edu.au/Documents/EASS/MnM/commentaries/sayyid-veiled-threats.pdf In the Netherlands, around 100 women are reported to have worn it. In Belgium between 200 and 400. See Yaiza Janssens Eva Brems, Kim Lecoyer, Saila Ouald Chaib, Victoria Vandersteen and Jogchum Vrielink, "The Belgian 'Burqa Ban' Confronted With Insider Realities," in *The Experiences of Face Veils Wearers in Europe and the Law*, ed. Eva Brems (Cambridge: Cambridge University Press, 2014), 71–78. In Australia, with a Muslim population of only 1.7%, it has been estimated between 500 and 1000 in Shaista Gohir, "Is the Face Veil Really a Threat to Western Culture?" *The Huffington Post*, September 20, 2011.

75. https://www.pewresearch.org/fact-tank/2018/09/17/most-western-europeans-favor-at-least-some-restrictions-on-muslim-womens-religious-clothing/?fbclid=IwAR1GMneQycfHWlVNKJBpRfsga2UD8Iw6y9ddUAu50nHe6YXZzMwUoJNnNVA.

76. See the emphasis on the veil's shifting meaning in varying social, historical and political context in Faegheh Shirazi, *Women in War and Crisis: Representation and Reality* (Austin: University of Texas Press, 2010); Jennifer Heath, ed. *The Veil: Women Writers on Its History, Lore and Politics* (Berkeley: University of California Press, 2008). See also initiatives that aim to "shatter stereotypes" by giving "voice" to Muslim women and their lived experiences. Nazma Khan, "World Hijab Day," http://worldhijabday.com; "Faith, Fashion and Fusion: Muslim Women's Style," http://www.powerhousemuseum.com/faithfashion/; "Muslima—International Museum of Women," http://muslima.imow.org/content/aboutmuslima.

77. Abu-Lughod, *Do Muslim Women Need Saving?* 54–80.

78. Sherene Razack, "Imperilled Muslim Woman, Dangerous Muslim Men and Civilised Europeans: Legal and Social Responses to Forced Marriages," *Feminist Legal Studies* 12, no. 2 (2004): 131.

79. See Saba Mahmood, *Politics of Piety: The Islamic Revival and the Feminist Subject* (Princeton: Princeton University Press, 2005).
80. Cooke, "Deploying the 'Muslimwoman', Roundtable Discussion: Religion, Gender and the Muslimwoman," 91.
81. Razack, *Looking White People in the Eye*, 16.
82. Mark Bracher, *Lacan, Discourse, and Social Change: A Psychoanalytical Cultural Criticism* (Ithaca: Cornell University Press, 1994), 10.
83. Suzanne Barnard and Bruce Fink, *Reading Seminar XX, Lacan's Major Work on Love, Knowledge, and Feminine Sexuality* (New York: SUNY Press, 2002), 34.
84. Bracher, *Lacan, Discourse, and Social Change: A Psychoanalytical Cultural Criticism*, 10.
85. Barnard and Fink, *Reading Seminar XX*, 13.
86. Kalpana Seshadri-Crooks, *Desiring Whiteness: A Lacanian Analysis of Race* (New York: Routledge, 2000), 21.
87. Giorgio Agamben, *Homosacer: Sovereign Life and Bare Life* (Stanford, CA: Stanford University Press, 1998).
88. Renata Salecl, *The Spoils of Freedom: Psychoanalysis, Feminism and Ideology After the Fall of Socialism* (London: Routledge, 1994), 127.
89. Neil Macmaster and Toni Lewis, "Orientalism: From Unveiling to Hyperveiling," *Journal of European Studies* 28, no. 1 (1998): 122–130.
90. Foucault, *The Will to Knowledge: The History of Sexuality I*, 19.
91. Joseph A. Massad, *Islam in Liberalism* (Chicago and London: University of Chicago Press, 2015).

REFERENCES

Abu-Lughod, Lila. *Do Muslim Women Need Saving?* Cambridge, MA: Harvard University Press, 2013.

Agamben, Giorgio. *Homosacer: Sovereign Life and Bare Life*. California: Stanford University Press, 1998.

Asad, Talal. "Thinking About the Secular Body, Pain and Liberal Politics." *Cultural Anthropology* 26, no. 4 (2011): 657–675.

Asad, Talal. *Formations of the Secular: Christianity, Islam, Modernity*. Stanford, CA: Stanford University Press, 2003.

Barnard, Suzanne and Bruce Fink. *Reading Seminar XX, Lacan's Major Work on Love, Knowledge, and Feminine Sexuality*. New York: SUNY Press, 2002.

Barthes, Roland and Stephen Heath. *Image, Music, Text*. New York: Hill and Wang, 1977.

Baudrillard, Jean. *The Spirit of Terrorism*. London: Verso, 2003.

Bhatt, Chetan. "The Times of Movements: A Response." *The British Journal of Sociology* 59, no. 1 (2008): 25–33.

Blasone, Pino. "Orientalism, Veiled and Unveiled." (2011). https://www.scribd.com/document/51101694/Orientalism-Veiled-and-Unveiled(PDF).

Bracher, Mark. *Lacan, Discourse, and Social Change: A Psychoanalytical Cultural Criticism*. Ithaca: Cornell University Press, 1994.

Brown, Wendy. *State of Injury: Power and Freedom in Late Modernity*. Princeton: Princeton University Press, 1995.

Butler, Judith. "Sexual Politics, Torture, and Secular Time." *The British Journal of Sociology* 59, no. 1 (2008): 1–23.

Butler, Judith. "Torture and the Ethics of Photography." *Environment and Planning D: Society and Space* 25, no. 6 (2007): 951–966.

Butler, Judith. *Precarious Life: The Powers of Mourning and Violence*. New York: Verso, 2004.

Cooke, Miriam. "Deploying the 'Muslimwoman', Roundtable Discussion: Religion, Gender and the Muslimwoman." *Journal of Feminist Studies in Religion* 24, no. 1 (2008): 91–199.

Fanon, Frantz. *Black Skin, White Masks*. London: Grove Press, 2008.

Fenstermacher, Laurie. 'Countering Violent Extremism; Scientific Method and Strategies' Revised White Paper. Air Force Research Laboratory, July 2015. https://info.publicintelligence.net/ARL-CounteringViolentExtremism.pdf.

Fernando, Mayanthi L. *The Republic Unsettled: Muslim French and the Contradictions of Secularism*. Durham: Duke University Press, 2014.

Fink, Bruce. *The Lacanian Subject: Between Language and Jouissance*. Princeton: Princeton University Press, 1995.

Heath, Jennifer, ed. *The Veil: Women Writers on Its History, Lore and Politics*. Berkeley: University of California Press, 2008.

Hesford, Wendy S. *Spectacular Rhetorics: Human Rights Visions, Recognitions, Feminisms*. Durham: Duke University Press, 2011.

Hirschkind, Charles. "Is There a Secular Body?" *Cultural Anthropology* 26, no. 4 (2011): 633–647.

Josephson-Storm, Jason. *The Myth of Disenchantment: Magic, Modernity and the Birth of the Human Sciences*. Chicago and London: University of Chicago, 2017.

Kleinman, Arthur and Joan Kleinman. "The Appeal of Experience; The Dismay of Images: Cultural Appropriations of Suffering in Our Times." *Daedalus* 125, no. 1 (1996): 1–23.

Lacan, Jacques. *Ecrits: The First Complete Edition in English*. New York: W.W. Norton, 2006.

Macmaster, Neil and Toni Lewis. "Orientalism: From Unveiling to Hyperveiling." *Journal of European Studies* 28, no.1 (1998): 122–30.

Mahmood, Saba. "Feminism, Democracy and Empire: Islam and the War on Terror." In *Women's Studies on the Edge*, edited by Joan Wallach Scott, 193–215. Durham: Duke University Press, 2008.

Mahmood, Saba. *Politics of Piety: The Islamic Revival and the Feminist Subject.* Princeton: Princeton University Press, 2005.

Massad, A. Joseph, *Islam in Liberalism*, Chicago and London: University of Chicago Press, 2015.

McLarney, Ellen. "The Burqa in Vogue: Fashioning Afghanistan." *Journal of Middle East Women's Studies* 5, no. 1 (2009): 1–20.

Norton, Anne. *On the Muslim Question.* Princeton: Princeton University Press, 2013.

Osuri, Goldie and Bobby S. Banerjee. "White Diasporas: Media Representations of September 11 and the Unbearable Whiteness of Being in Australia." *Social Semiotics* 14, no. 2 (2004): 151–171.

Ravitz, Jessica. "Saving Aesha." *CNN*, May 2012. http://edition.cnn.com/interactive/2012/05/world/saving.aesha/index.html.

Razack, H. Sherene. "Imperilled Muslim Woman, Dangerous Muslim Men and Civilised Europeans: Legal and Social Responses to Forced Marriages." *Feminist Legal Studies* 12, no. 2 (2004): 129–174.

Razack, H. Sherene. "A Site/Sight We Cannot Bear: The Racial and Spatial Politics of Western of Banning of the Muslim Woman's Niqab." *Canadian Journal of Women and the Law* 30, no. 1(2018): 169–189.

Rogers, Juliet. *Law's Cut on the Body of Human Rights.* New York: Routledge, 2013.

Said, Edward. *Orientalism.* New York: Pantheon Books, 1978.

Salecl, Renata. *The Spoils of Freedom: Psychoanalysis, Feminism and Ideology After the Fall of Socialism.* London: Routledge, 1994.

Scott, Joan Wallach. *The Politics of the Veil.* Princeton: Princeton University Press, 2007.

Scott, Joan Wallach. *Sex and Secularism.* Princeton and Oxford: Princeton University Press, 2018.

Sena, Marylou. "A Purview of Being: the Ontological Structure of Reference (*Verweisung*) and Indication (*Indikation*)." In *Heidegger, Translation, and the Task of Thinking: Essays in Honour of Parvis Emad*, edited by Frank Schalow, 71–94. New Orleans: University of New Orleans, 2011.

Seshadri-Crooks, Kalpana. *Desiring Whiteness: A Lacanian Analysis of Race.* New York: Routledge, 2000.

Shirazi, Faegheh. *Women in War and Crisis: Representation and Reality.* Austin: University of Texas Press, 2010.

Soler, Colette. "The Body in the Teaching of Jacques Lacan." Translated by Lindsay Watson. http://jcfar.org.uk/wp-content/uploads/2016/03/The-Body-in-the-Teaching-of-Jacques-Lacan-Colette-Soler.pdf.

Spivak, Gayatri Chakravorty. "Can the Subaltern Speak?" In *Colonial Discourse and Post-Colonial Theory: A Reader*, edited by Patrick Williams and Laura Chrisman, 66–111. New York: Columbia University Press, 1994.

Spivak, Gayatri Chakravorty. *A Critique of Postcolonial Reason: Toward a History of the Vanishing Present*. Cambridge, MA: Harvard University Press, 1999.

Stengel, Richard. "The Plight of Afghan Woman: A Disturbing Picture." *Time*, July 29, 2010. http://content.time.com/time/magazine/article/0,9171,2007415,00.html.

Stoler, Anne Laura. "Imperial Formations: Reflections on Ruins and Ruinations." *Cultural Anthropology* 23, no. 2 (2008): 191–219.

Taussig, Michael. "Culture of Terror—Space of Death. Roger Casement's Putumayo Report and the Explanation of Torture." *Comparative Studies in Society and History* 26, no. 4 (1984): 467–497.

Thobani, Sunera. "War and the Politics of Truth-Making in Canada." *Qualitative Studies in Education* 16, no. 3 (2003): 399–414.

Verhaeghe, Paul. "Enjoyment and Impossibility: Lacan's Revision of the Oedipal Complex—Reflections on Seminar XVII." In *Jacques Lacan and the Other Side of Psychoanalysis*, edited by Justin Clemens and Russell Grigg. Durham: Duke University Press, 2006. 30–31.

Vladiana-Ioana Apetroaie. "The Trembling Veil: Issues of Gendered Islamophobia and Intolerance Towards Veiled Muslim Women, Current Issues of Islam." Thesis (Faculty of Social Sciences, 2012).

Vrielink, Jogchum. "Symptomatic Symbolism: Banning the Face Veil 'As a Symbol'." In *The Experience of the Face Veil Wearers in Europe and the Law*, edited by Eva Brems, 184–193. Cambridge: Cambridge University Press, 2014.

Young, Alison. *Judging the Image: Art, Value, Law*. New York: Routledge, 2005.

Žižek, Slavoj. *How to Read Lacan*. New York: W.W. Norton, 2007.

Žižek, Slavoj. *Violence: Six Sideways Reflections*. London: Profile Books, 2008.

CHAPTER 2

The Unveil*ing* Body

anatomy is destiny. —Sigmund Freud.[1]

The following series of images by internationally recognised Yemeni artist Boushra Almutawakel represents the complex lives of Yemeni women. The images were produced to counter fundamentalist representations while also challenging western interpretations. The first image of the artist wearing hijab with her unveiled child on her lap holding a doll, gradually morphs into images of the two of them wearing different forms of veils. Almutawakel explains she used the image of the veil to illustrate how it reflects "convenience, freedom, strength, power, liberation, limitations, danger, humour, irony, variety, cultural, social and religious aspects, as well as the beauty, mystery and protection".[2] The image's meaning shifts beyond the purpose of identifying the diversity of experience among women in the Arab and Muslim world. Almutawakel's western audience have been heavily exposed to oriental and Islamophobic tropes in a post-9/11 climate overshadowed by The Muslim Question.[3] The circulation of her images cannot be contained by the spaces in which her art has been presented. I encountered these particular images, for instance, on a Facebook page of a western women's rights organisation where it was negatively depicting the practices of veiling and the threat of fundamentalism to Muslim women. These images, like many of the images examined in this book,

S. Ghumkhor, *The Political Psychology of the Veil*,
Palgrave Studies in Political Psychology,
https://doi.org/10.1007/978-3-030-32061-4_2

have been repeatedly used for other purposes. Encountering Almutawakel's images in a different context, not of her own, generates loss of translation, as the content of the image flattens meaning and seduces the viewers into their own process of unfolding. Through what Wendy S. Hesford calls an ocular epistemology, a seeing-is-believing paradigm that heightens a truth,[4] the content of these images produces a sense of inevitability of fundamentalist oppression of not just Yemeni women but all Muslim women. What purpose does the veil have in such an image? Why is it such a powerful signifier of the human experience? I argue in this chapter that images of women in veil are seen through a fantasy of unveiling, which casts a menacing shadow in each depiction of bodies falling under the veil's imprisoning grasp as they attach lack to difference. This fantasy appears as a totalising truth of the promise of an unveiled liberation made certain only by the veil's visible smear on the body.

The images by Almutawakel, however, reveal more than simply the veil's ominous presence. They presuppose knowledge of the veil and the accessible body that simply succumbs or flees it. In this chapter, I explore how the body is presented as a "fact" that is reachable, containable and a naturalised beginning in the socio-political theatrics of masking and unmasking, veiling and unveiling. This axiological ground discovers the liberal subject of human rights and its claims to truths like universalism, freedom, democracy and knowledge. In the mode of the body's material presence, its visibility, Almutawakel's images become a projection of a western imaginary that extols the virtues of unveiling.[5] An unveiling that carries a linear trajectory and the arrival of universal truths in the material body. Strangely, this body is a futurity that has already arrived, announced by the marks it has left on the bodies of others, like the veiled women. The images narrate the historical and material becoming of bodies on a linear plane, with each frame marking progress from modernity to tradition. As the veil becomes visibly heavier, the bodies in the image blend with the black backdrop, suggesting not simply the different experiences of veiling, but the all-consuming nature of the veil. Each image dreads the future veil*ing* until there is nothing but darkness. Like a shattered mirror, the images of veiled bodies are a specular failure, "sprawled out" in Fanon's despair, expressions of ontological departures from an imagined totality. Nevertheless, bodily integrity as whole is not always realised in such palpable sequence. It is imagined in the very positioning of the body *in* bodies.

The body, scattered, across a dark contextless plain, appears again, this time in a photo essay in *The New York Times*. Titled "Portraits of Dignity:

How We Photographed Ex-Captives of Boko Haram", the images are of Nigerian women, each in a solemn pose, looking away from the camera. We know little about these women beyond their kidnapping ordeal by the Nigerian Islamist movement Boko Haram. These are the girls that inspired the worldwide trending hashtag #BringBackOurGirls in 2014. The author explains that all "we" know of "them" since are dreary images of "dark robes and sad faces". Thus, the aim was to portray the young women in a more dignified way. The images show an uncanny resemblance to its bleak counterpart. This unveiling of Nigerian women reveals the same sad faces, only this time looking away in shame into a looming veil of darkness that surrounds them and intimidates to swallow them at any moment. Turning away from the viewer, the camera is an intruding presence, photographing them in a memory of their ordeal. The experience of looking at this series of images is one that objectifies them by presenting them as violated bodies or bodies in the throes of injury. We do not know them individually or their aspirations and their personal stories beyond this memory.[6] It does not matter if some of them are Christian; in their ordeal with Islamist violence, *they are imagined as Muslim women* qua the injured women of Islam's fundamentalism. Both images are bodies scattered across "the dark continent"; snapshots of corporeal fragments—afflicted, violated, traumatised and repressed. These are bodies marked with impossibility—broken bodily pieces, frames of un-selfing, needing to be assembled and seeking meaning beyond the descending veil. Both are images coping with disappearance before the call to "bring back"—make visible again—what is ours (Figs. 2.1 and 2.2).

This chapter interrogates the political imagination that imbues unveiling with the promise of bodily integrity, empowerment and dissent, and what sustains the lifeblood of liberal progressive politics. It asks, why is the removal of the veil and the revelation of flesh, an investment in freedom? Why is freedom imagined unveiled? What is it about the body—as veiled and unveiled flesh—that burdens it with a Manichean divide of the boundaries between constraint and freedom? The body that *is*, or can be exposed, is a body that is modern, free, secure, conscious and human in its visibility and presence. This body sits in contrast to the invisible body, veiled in insecurities, vulnerability and most saliently, subhuman in its *absence*. As part of modernism's claim to truth, what Jacques Derrida described as "the naked truth"—knowledge as exposed, the veiled body conceals the knowable. Modernism's fantasy of unveiling freedom fixates on the *potential* of the body to secure, akin to what Michel Foucault observes as the secrets

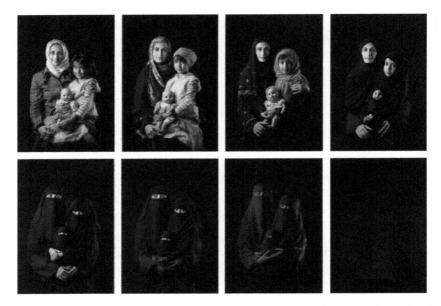

Fig. 2.1 "Mother, Daughter, Doll", Boushra Almutawakel (Re-used with kind permission from Almutawakel)

of life and death.[7] This potential resides beyond the veil, in the promise of its removal.

To understand the politics that sustains such a reading of Muslim women's bodies, one must examine the historical processes that have been central to the materialisation and intelligibility of bodies, which seeks to identify the relationship between politics, power and the corporeal. One could go further, by attempting to understand this relationship's relevance in the imagining of self and other; of locating western master signifiers of freedom, knowledge, subjectivity and universalism. In doing so, we come to understand how Muslim women's bodies are entangled in a political imaginary, which Anne Anlin Cheng observes to be modernity's "fascination with transparency" and "a pleasure about seeing *into* and *through* things"[8] that this chapter explores through the making of the "natural" body in the pursuit of the universal human. In the first half, I trace this fascination with transparency, an insatiable desire to know through the lens of the veiled and unveiled. I begin with the body as a pre-symbolic (or pre-discursive) unsaid,

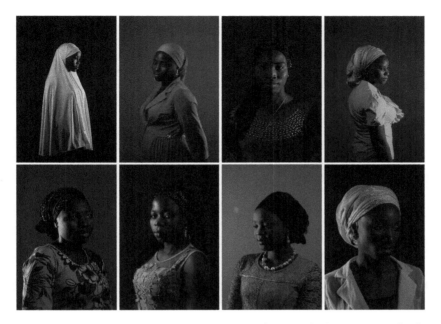

Fig. 2.2 NYT/ "Portraits of dignity: How we photographed ex-captives of Boko Haram". April 11, 2018 (Re-used with kind permission from Headpress Pty Limited)

and the role this factuality of the body, its "brute givenness"[9] plays in the imagining of a universal free subject. I trace this pre-symbolic as something "natural" by beginning with the example of race's stubborn presence in the way we think about and imagine bodies. I engage with the work of Kalpana Seshadri-Crooks whose psychoanalytic lens sheds a curious light on the continued belief in race due to its emphasis on corporeal visibility as a natural citation to identifying racial difference. This is a difference, she argues, that compensates for the inherent lack in Jacques Lacan's reassessment of Freudian biologism in his theory of sexuation. The question of sexuation for Lacan is the question of the subject and its relationship to the body, a relationship that is never entirely reconciled with the haunting ontological question: *Che vuoi?* Where do I come from? What do these bodies mean?[10] Seshadri-Crooks argues that whiteness comes to reconcile the difference in bodies by measuring, and thus making intelligible, other bodies in a racial hierarchy that presupposes a natural wholeness beyond race. I argue that in the fantasy of unveiling, the fascination for transparency (to know), is fulfilled in imagining the body as "natural". Like whiteness, this "natural" body appears as *more than* symbolic, beyond the veil of difference, which imprints the body like race. Like race, the unveiled comes to satisfy the question of sexual difference by claiming the "natural" and thus, the *unified* body.

In the second half of the chapter, I examine how this "tenacious pull of biologism and fact"[11] vis-à-vis the natural body become a locus for the realisation of the universal human and gives political impetus to the pursuit of human rights. While the notion of universalism has increasingly fallen into question in recent years, human rights have become its most articulate expression[12] with the self-evident declaration of "all human beings are born free and equal in dignity and rights".[13] In a "post-racial world", where society in this vision has triumphed over the past and an end of history is declared possible, this is a mastery that is most powerfully expressed in the adulation and protection of secular gains: rights, freedom, security and knowledge. With these gains come certain bodily practices, beliefs and sensibilities, which Charles Hirschkind and Talal Asad recognise as clues to modernism's most salient yet elusive concept: the secular.[14] This chapter argues that the act of unveiling the body arranges the borders of where the religious and the secular can be most powerfully pronounced, making the "secularbody" conceivable. The all-encompassing pull of human rights is its global moral proclamation that seduces one into presuppositions of a "natural" pre-discursive human and a body that exists before or beyond culture, politics and religion. How this human body is imagined is sustained by the secular as modernism's political, ethical and affective attachment and investment in "bare surface"[15] which connotes the *absence of shadows of cultural partiality*. In contrast, the "discursive" (symbolic) body, like the raced and veiled body, is one that is fragmented like the snapshot of bodies in the two images above. Aided by the theories of Costas Douzinas and Giorgio Agamben, particularly their historical tracing of rights in natural law, this chapter further builds on the salience of the natural body through the discourse of human rights. Unpacking beyond the political nature of human rights, Douzinas assists with tracing the body in a progressive teleology from natural law to human rights. From these discussions, he extrapolates that the body which presupposes all bodies, is a discontinuity, spaced out across historical time, animated into a specific type of assemblage through a desire for a not-yet-arrived human. The body here is mythically inscribed as a judgement in history: carrying its lessons, maturing, accumulating freedom and emerging whole as it advances in history. As these two images of fragmentation suggest, the body can catalogue history in what Anne McClintock describes as "global progress consumed visually as a single image" from "anachronistic space" (veiled) to "panoptical time" (unveiling),[16] and the possibility of this regression (veiling). In the Derridean sense, the body anchors the dizzying anxiety of the animal-human binary, naturalising the multiplied—and I argue, racial—differences, that mark the edges of "the abyssal limit".[17] However, the path to humanisation is an advancement that is aided by the law, which Agamben contends, signals the appropriation of natural law by sovereign power to serve the governing agenda of biopower and allowing politics to reduce natural life to political existence.[18] In this vein, the body is one that is constituted and *disciplined* into freedom through law.

Freedom as a practice of the body is identified in the western imaginary as the performativity of unveiling—the always unveil*ing* body—that signals the accretion of modernism's desire for transparency, its fixation on the revelation of flesh, in its pursuit for knowledge. Knowledge in this idiom can only be found in the discarding of irrational beliefs, attachments to tradition, and a commitment to the foundations of Europe's Enlightenment and the birth of science as the universal truth. The secular prescription that drives the fantasy of unveiling is not simply the unveiling of Muslim women's bodies, but I argue here and throughout the book, it is an unveiling of *all bodies*.

THE "NATURAL" BODY

The body, like the image, is often spoken about as a fact.[19] Not only can we see and observe it, we can measure, touch, taste and smell it. Our capacity to experience the body through our senses has meant that it can materialise and secure meaning—we can attach knowledge (of sexual and racial difference, for instance) in and on the body. The body is a visible locus where desire comes to be ascribed, manifested and aligned with universal knowledge. The notion of this material body as a locus of the universal human and a source of its fundamental truths (because it can be scientifically studied and known) has become normative in western modernity.[20] Meaning is sought in what is manifested on its corporeal terrain, and the corporeal secures assumptions of its self-evidence. In an era where grand narratives and universal abstractions—democracy, freedom, human rights—seem increasingly difficult to ground, the body has become the site on which these political truths are settled; where the veiled and unveiled imagery and the imaginary that underpins them, materialise. Alain Badiou also posits that the body is the only concrete instance for desolate individuals aspiring to enjoyment. Human being, in the regime of the "power of life", is a slightly sad animal, who must be convinced that the law of the body fixes the secret of his hope".[21] Belief is, therefore, grounded in the body because the body presents itself as a concrete truth, a material reality. What occurs and what is experienced happens to bodies[22] and its fleshly certainty is the origin of all meaning.

While the body is perhaps a biological fact, or set of facts, it is produced contextually, culturally and discursively, and therefore, shaped and disciplined into meaning. It is in this mode that Michel Foucault's investigation into the relationship of knowledge/power pinpoints the body as crucial to producing, governing and securing knowledge.[23] The body for Foucault performs knowledge and is "directly involved in a political field; power-relations have an immediate hold on it; they invest it, mark it, train it, torture it, force it to carry out tasks, to perform ceremonies, to emit signs".[24] This biopolitical body whose aim is to survive and flourish, is a place of information stored and that needs to be released. This is the body that is made known through its visibility.[25] However, as feminist and psychoanalytic philosophers such as Elizabeth Grosz and Judith Butler have argued, if the body is a discursive site, it presupposes a blank screen "awaiting the imprint".[26] The body, through such lens, is not a thing in itself, but something that is narrated into a particular meaning. As Butler states, the body itself is the "materialisation" of its "intelligibility".[27] For them the body comes into existence through language (sex, gender, race, ideology)—not simply inscribed with language. The naturalness of the body, Butler argues emerges through the performance of social practice and its repetition so that bodies are no longer read but just are. Repetition may produce a "naturalised effect", it also suggests a state of bodily insecurity.[28]

As language fails to produce total meaning, Lacan reminds us, the body's intelligibility occupies the space of both the *symbolic* and the *pre-symbolic*. The *objet petit a* as the object cause of desire is that which reminds us of the body both as Symbolic and that which alludes capture (in the Real). This failure for Lacan is what makes the body an "enjoying substance" which, as we recall from the introduction, locates the link between knowledge and *jouissance*. *Jouissance* "invades" the body and acquires markings on the body through the intervention of the Other (as symbolic inscription—knowledge).[29] The subject's ambivalence lies in how the body is both "ours" and Other triggering the anxious question of one's identity. Unlike Foucault's knowing body, the psychoanalytic body is the body that does not aim at its own good. It is one that is difficult to control and trace its boundaries because of its intimate relation with the psyche, and its relationship to the mind and body.[30] This is the body that is in question. Whereas the biopolitical body is knowable, the psychoanalytic body reminds us that subjectivity—or who we are, or think we are—is located at the intersections of body and mind and therefore cannot be reduced to either. The psychoanalytic body challenges the Dualistic and Cartesian readings of mind/body oppositions[31] and one that escapes signification.

From an anthropological perspective, Hirchkind (2011) and Asad (2011) in their probing discussion of the possibility of a secular body, similarly recognise the body's ambivalence. That is, its unpredictability in securing knowledge of what we interpret to be "secular" and "religious". While these concepts allude us, at the same time we insist on their distinctive knowability. The "disinterested" knowledge of the secular is most successfully mapped on to the body as the coordinates of western universal desire for freedom and the natural condition of the secular. However, this naturally "wild body",[32] unconstrained and no longer mired in cultural protocols, is inaccessible; its "behaviour depends on unconscious routine and habit, because emotions render the ownership of actions a matter of conflicting descriptions, because body and mind decay with age and chronic illness".[33] Recognising the failure to contain a fixed intelligible body, Asad challenges the liberal secular notion of a free active subject with clear intention in control of history and the social world.[34] The body's ocular and phenomenological persuasions, however, continue to promise an objective knowledge that can be obtained from the material body beyond the symbolic. Western demands to see Muslim women's face are so forceful, for instance, because the body has a particular hold on the modern imagination linking knowability to fleshly recognition and visibility. Australian political commentator and former Member of Parliament Jacqui Lambie who opposes the veil does so because it obstructs this knowingness and familiarity: "Because what I believe is we must be able to tell the body language and we can do that by the face".[35] The body, like science, is what Lacan has described as the pursuit for the real, securing what we believe; but both are already grounded in signification, seeking to fasten a *gestalt*: the image of wholeness in the presupposition of a knowing subject.[36]

Pushing back against the devaluation of a material body by arguing for its potential in securing universal truths, Annabelle Mooney describes the body as a "zero institution"—the "base" that structures our world.[37] Without it there is no meaning, and if only "we are willing to look" we see what it exposes. The body for her is an index of its own meaning and does not require representation. Bodies show us that they can perish, need food, drink, rest, sleep, air to breathe; embodying truths that denounce "other discourses or images as fictions".[38] Mooney, therefore, sees the body not as a signifier, as Butler and others have argued,[39] because she casts the body as more than signification. When we experience pain, we can only communicate or index that experience. The index is, therefore, always cataloguing something real, something embodied. However, Mooney's phenomenological attempts to find the Real through the body does not sufficiently account for a number of things. The body's capacity for exposure is compromised as encounters with bodies also occur through *images of bodies*. When we look, we are not simply looking at another body, but images of *other bodies*, bodies in representation, symbolically inscribed which then inform our own bodily imaginary. To simply look at the body in order to access a truth fails to account for the gaze that facilitates looking and nominates the one who is doing the looking. This is crucial to how bodies produce meaning as the body is brought into being, categorised and experienced through looking. We are taught how to see the body. Moreover, our experiences with the body and of other bodies are not simply our own but determined by libidinal structures—the psychological and morphological forces more so than the biological.

The body, as psychoanalytic theorist Derek Hook argues is a dormant register, a vessel of the (corporal, libidinal, extra-discursive) experience that is never completely domesticated by discourse.[40] However, even this extra-discursive body is a body imagined within symbolic restraints because as Butler has observed, whatever is "posited as prior to construction will, by virtue of being posited, becomes the effect of that very positing".[41] Those indexes of bodily experiences: sleep, hunger, exhaustion, pain and so on, are on the one hand experienced in bodies but not necessarily the bodies we imagine and see experiencing. Racist fantasies reveal that looking is also about *phantasmatic imaging of the body*, imaginary projections grounded in a belief in the seen. Using an ocular epistemological lens, Seshadri-Crooks contends, as I discuss below, that race's reliance on corporeal visibility, *naturalises the body*[42] or to put it another way, how the Symbolic masquerades as the "brute giveness"[43] of the Real.

A contemporary illustration of the limits of thinking about the universal material body is seen in the United States in response to a video of a police officer with his arms around the neck of a black man, Eric Garner. Garner struggles to breathe, repeatedly stating, "I can't breathe". Garner's pleas for help were ignored and he died from choking. Epitomising Fanon's "postcolonial breathlessness", where he too declared that anti-colonial struggles were the result of an inability for colonised peoples to breath,[44] this encounter between white uniformed bodies and the black body sheds a critical light on shared bodily experience.[45] What does it mean for the body to share in universal experiences when Garner's racialised body raises the question: when is breathing not breathing? In white America's racist fantasy, the body becomes a barrier to the universality of breathing. The incident raises the broader tension Fanon's reflections grappled with: where is the self when the body has been taken up by another for signification? Or how do we locate the pre-symbolic body from the symbolic body when we can only imagine, identify and understand bodies within a symbolic logic of race, sex, gender? How do we access this "natural" body? Further, some bodies give birth and frequently bleed. Some bodies are unwanted, some are phantom bodies, others are digitised and siliconised—the "stuff" of bodies is increasingly brought into question.[46] Then there those that one can imagine simply do not exist as bodies. The veiled body, for one, does not fit the "normative notion of what the body of the human must be".[47] Mooney's index, in other words, is already determined by the symbolic. The purpose here is not to deny that there is no such thing as the body but the *thingness* of the body in the making of the corporeal human is malleable and interactive with the world. The body, as Pierre Bourdieu reminds is a "hexis" and is "political mythology realised, *em-bodied*, turned into a permanent disposition, a durable way of standing, speaking, walking and thereby of feeling and thinking". The body in this schema is a "site of incorporated history".[48] The purpose in situating the body is not to, as Derrida contends, "isolate ourselves in language",[49] but to understand how its naming rehabilitates the psychic and sexual ambivalence in the body, by safeguarding an organic surface for meaning-making which explains race's sticking hold on us today. The belief in the "natural" condition of the body, what it is destined for, will be imperative to understanding modernism's investment in the unveiling of Muslim women's bodies.

Race and the Body

Identifying the disjuncture between the discursive (of the Symbolic) and the pre-discursive (the body as pre-symbolic, the Real) in *Desiring Whiteness,* Seshadri-Crooks turns to the persistence of race, contending that race as a difference resolves the tension between the naturalness of the body (pre-discursive) and its Symbolic inscriptions. Why is there so much investment in visible difference, such as the veiled Muslim woman? Or, as Hook asks, "why is it… that the body never 'falls out' of racism?'"[50] Hook argues that it is about boundary-anxieties and "bodily mimicking" in an attempt to measure against[51] to secure a "whole" and known body—a theme I return to in Chapter 6. Seshadri-Crooks focuses on the body's capacity to fasten its hold on truths, that is, race persists because we believe it to be a natural reference that makes sense of "difference". What Seshadri-Crooks has in mind is the Lacanian subject that lacks full representation, the capacity for satisfied meaning of the body. It is to this unfulfilled subject that race offers coherence and meaning.

Addressing the current political and social landscape, Seshadri-Crooks contends that the contemporary west has been refused the enjoyment of openly racist rhetoric. Racism, it is believed, is no longer an accepted way of thinking but race is deployed as a "neutral description of human difference", grounded in the phenotype. Racism is, thus, conjectured as misappropriation of difference.[52] The calls for multiculturalism in liberal democracies are underpinned by a belief that we must purge racism from society but value the "fact" of race and "celebrate difference".[53] Despite these celebrations, Seshadri-Crooks insists that belief in race as a "neutral difference" continues both for its capacity to establish specific relations and to justify power and domination. Foucault has earlier reminded us of race's key role in the emergence of colonial-style regulatory technologies which enabled the modern state "to create caesuras within the biological continuum addressed by biopower" in order to measure life against others who are eliminated (physically or symbolically) in its name.[54] Similarly, Anne McClintock observes that in the nineteenth century, race functioned as a category of class to *invent* difference in order to manage European communities like the British and the Irish, by establishing markers of degeneration, signs of otherness. The signs of otherness, or "domestic barbarism", was identified in accents, in exaggerated lips and receding foreheads, which continued to be postulated as natural differences.[55]

The signs of otherness on the body are visible but also rely on the unseen within the body through which difference is made. As Cheng reminds us, racial difference is not only symptomatic of how we see but teaches us also *to see*.[56] That is, to see race is to see beyond the discursive. The western mode of seeing is important for considering both how Muslim women are seen through the lens of histories of naming Islam marked on their bodies, and seeing as a mode of knowing.

In the scene of castration, Freud demonstrates this difference as teaching to see how the absence of the penis, rather than the presence of the penis, identifies the lack. Lacan recognises this appellation as demonstrating the importance of how language assists in the seeing and naming of bodies. In Lacanian parlance, the visibility of difference (sexual or racial) as lack, instils a desire for phantasmatic and morphological wholeness—that is, overcoming one's difference or fragmentation. The capacity of race to resolve the indeterminacy of subjectivity and the anxiety and antagonisms of difference generates a fantasy of something beyond difference—an attainable wholeness.[57] Seshadri-Crooks' inquiry into the investment in race is pertinent to a link between the imaginary self, the fantasy of ontological wholeness and the body through which it is secured. Just as images rely on an ocular knowledge Seshadri-Crooks maintains "we believe in the factuality of difference in order to *see* it". It is always a belief in what exists prior to and outside of the image, outside of "race", that enables the "fact" of the image and race to be read in particular ways.

> Race organizes difference and elicits investment in its subjects because it promises access to being itself. It offers the prestige of being better and superior; it is the promise of being more human, more full, less lacking. The possibility of this enjoyment is at the core of "race".[58]

The racialised other is constituted through a stain of lack in a racial hierarchy that infers completion as something beyond difference. Overcoming difference, therefore, becomes not only possible but desired. The body that attains wholeness is one imagined to be without symbolic shadows—that is, without its shades of difference—the racial symptoms of fragmentation. Seshadri-Crooks' emphasis on the body as a site of making and unmaking proposes a logic of bodily exposure, revealing the body in its "natural" form. But why does the body need exposure to announce its presence? Here, Seshadri-Crooks alludes to Lacan's notion of sexuation in order to addresses the inherent lack in the Lacanian subject. She reads sexuation through race. For Seshadri-Crooks, race compensates for sex's failure to address these questions, its inability to make sense of bodily differences. As Lacan famously, and radically, states, "there is no such thing as a sexual relationship"[59]—in the process of becoming gendered there is no signifier for "Man" and "Woman" that would symbolically recognise and guarantee their sexual positions in language. In other words, there is no direct relationship between men and women. There is only a "non-relationship" in place of it; insofar as there are men *and* women *this very* difference itself[60] is the name for the deadlock. In regard to sexual difference, there is something that resists every attempt at symbolisation—every translation of this difference fails.[61] "Masculine" and "feminine" signifiers are ways of marking this failure, by gendering or sexualising bodily difference.

The ambivalence or failure to reconcile the body and sexual difference is understood through castration. This is at the heart of Lacanian theories of the subject who emerges after experiencing a split—a lack and absence. Castration marks the limit of *jouissance*, the law of prohibition that forbids the child's desire for the mother—the desire for oneness. The "No!" of the Father (the law) identifies man and woman by their mode of desire as a way to deal with the lack of being in language that regulates one's relationship with the body. As Lacan explains, "It is in the *name of the father* that we must recognise the basis of the symbolic function which, since the dawn of historical time, has identified his person with the figure of the law".[62] The limit of this law causes the disjunction between sex (the radically Other body)—the body's meaning beyond language—and sexuality (the symbolic body). However, *jouissance*—the (dis)satisfaction that replaces the mother-child wholeness, the enjoyment that one gets in the proximity of achieving this unity or the impossibility of it—is made possible by the law's failure to guarantee meaning for the subject. This disjuncture fills and is soothed through fantasy.[63] Fantasy offers a totalised truth—the body as one.

In addition, racial exclusion contains the fear of losing one's symbolic status: whiteness signifying the phallus, the law. Race functions like kinship relations' law, punishing transgressions and positioning subjects within a racial order. Unlike sexual difference, which is founded on the Real-Symbolic law of the prohibition of incest, the law of racial difference is symbolically determined, culturally based and historicised.[64] Race is not missing a signifier, a signifier which locates the Real (the limit of language, the law) but imagined as universal, a fact, a legal sanction and that which can offer the sexed body its total meaning. Race attempts through a purely symbolic means to signify the very thing that is lacking in the moral law (the traditional family), yet at the same time, superficially resembles the moral law insofar as maintaining a racial family.[65]

Put more specifically, Seshadri-Crooks argues that the category of race undoes the law of the No! The taboo against incest—which Freud posits is the origin of the law—plays no role in race, as those racially othered can never be admitted or acknowledged within the traditional family structure. The prohibition constitutes the subject before the law, but by prohibiting *jouissance* it discloses the subject's potential for it. The law legitimates certain alliances and refuses others as transgressive. Thus, without the law the subject's place in the symbolic order is out of place. Seshadri-Crooks uses the example of slavery in the United States to illustrate that the law's limit makes *jouissance* possible by making slave women entirely sexually accessible to their male owners. The "master" could cohabit with his slaves, and the children he had with his slaves, with impunity. The slave owner was free to play out his fantasy of the primal father of the original horde, whose murder Freud posits as the origin of the moral law. For Seshadri-Crooks, the racial symbolic makes possible this time of unrestrained *jouissance,* before the enforcement of moral law. One could live with slave mistresses and even acknowledge her children, but she was still a "whore and her children nothing but bastards".[66]

Race's promise of fullness is founded on a belief in an *absolute human-ness* (aspiring to be part of the human family) beyond the law. Different racialised groups hold the fantasy separately—each aiming to monopolise the commonly understood category of "human" qua—with whiteness as a master signifier. By not missing a signifier, whiteness generates a desire for recognition and completion by providing the "illegal enjoyment of absolute wholeness". Like the prohibition against miscegenation, multiculturalism, as a respect for difference, ultimately serves to protect the paradox of whiteness, its ability to signify the unsignifiable: humanness/oneness merged with a "whole" body.[67] The desire for whiteness, the desire to be more human, is the fantasy of going beyond the symbolic, where one can recover *or unveil* the missing substance of one's being that annihilates difference.

How is race able to do this? Race becomes an indeterminacy of sexual difference by addressing the subject's desire for bodily meaning. Race posits something *natural, pre-discursive*, and I contend, *unveiled* about the racialised subject. It also considers the visibility of flesh as neutral and therefore natural. Seshadri-Crooks argues race has captured the social imaginary due to its reliance on visibility. Race disavows its historical/symbolic origins and presents itself as universal with "more than symbolic"[68] effects on the body. In this sense, it has a "naturalising" effect on the body by attaching itself to visible differences, phenotype, bodily marks, which are considered to be appear inherited, like sex, and exceed language like a "fact of nature".[69] In these ways, race supports and defends against the fantasy of a totalised subject. The body then comes to play an essential role in carrying traces of something else—the pre-discursive marks (hair, skin) which sustain the fantasy of neutral categories of difference that are not yet whole. These marks on the body are an "imaginary fixing"[70] stains on the body that sustains the fantasy that difference can be overcome by their removal. The removing of these bodily stains refers to aspirations to whiteness which functions as a pre-discursive sameness, a universal body, that both the anxiety of lack (difference) and the anxiety of race's own cultural origins are foreclosed. This sameness operates as lacking the stain of difference, which attracts the subject and promises being itself. The phenotype secures the belief in racial difference perpetuating the desire for whiteness, or rather, wholeness.

Seshadri-Crook's observations of race and the body as securing wholeness or truth resonates with Eric Santner's psychoanalytic reading of the remnants in modernity. Santner traces the development of sovereignty from European kingship to democracy. Putting to use Ernst Kantorowicz' *The King's Two Bodies* which outlined the monarch as having a fleshly body that experienced death and a transcendental eternal body, Santner posits that today's modern society is trying to secure the latter. "In order to become a human subject, the "flesh-and-blood" of our existence as animals – even social animals – must be supplemented by a surplus of "flesh": that is the very stuff of a missing link or gap".[71] Identifying the Lacanian concept of the *object a* in the king's sacral substance of the flesh, the sublime body results from the missing gap that has been democratised by migrating to the new bearer of sovereignty, the people who now struggle to secure the flesh of sovereignty. The new bearers are "in some sense stuck with an excess of flesh"—what he calls a surplus of immanence; that their own bodies cannot fully embody and thus, must be handled in other ways.[72] The flesh is the "organ not cut to the measurement of the human body"[73]—marking the failure of sexual difference. It is through tracing the flesh—the "too muchness" of kingly power—that conceives corporeality as a way to secure this new symbolic authority: the sovereign in the democratic subject, the body that best secures the flesh of which other bodies are measured against. For Santner, the body masquerades as flesh—"veiled by this sub-lime (im)posture" of the "neutered royal".[74] I add here that the quest to unveil the natural condition of the universal human subject is circumscribed by the desire to locate the body that identifies the flesh—the impossibility of embodying sovereign power (wholeness), which is then concealed by the fantasy of unveiling.

The Unveiled

Access to being, through whiteness as a fantasy of the whole, resonates with the fantasy of an (unveiled) west as the agent of unveiling freedom. While Seshadri-Crooks' focus is on the master signifier of whiteness, which sustains desire for a pre-discursive wholeness, I maintain that the fantasy of unveiling similarly produces a desire for a pre-discursive whole vis-à-vis the unveiled. Seshadri-Crooks' reminds us that that which fails *is written on the body*, and its failure marked by what is imagined to give the body meaning. Wherein whiteness produces racial bodies measured against a whole, the unveiled makes visible the veil as an imagined marker of bodily difference. Here we encounter a problem with such a comparison. Seshadri-Crooks argues that race relies on "pre-discursive" differences on the body, the "real" of phenotype. The veil, however, is a cultural marker of difference that attaches to the body in another way. Curiously, this distinction is often expressed in the insistence by critics of Islam that Islamophobia is not racism because Muslims are a diverse racial group.[75] Not only does this clarification reveal the persisting belief in the notion of race, it demonstrates how modern racism is rationalised more effectively by seeking cultural inscriptions. The veil is both master signifier and *object a* which induces, to paraphrase Seshadri-Crooks, the belief in difference in order to *see* it. What the west sees here is a racial marker of permanent culturally sanctioned violence inflicted on the body. The impulse to reveal the body beneath the veil, to tear off the veil of tradition, similarly presupposes the pre-discursive universal body, untainted by the markers of (cultural) difference. Returning to Almutawakel's image, we assume that the image before the first shot of the woman and child in hijab would be of them with their heads uncovered. This is not an image of them unveiled. They remain under a veil in some form (an unveiled-veiled), because the west desires *to see the veil* in the mode of a difference that produces Muslim women's bodies.

The impulse to unveil is rooted in western modernity's yearning to expose the hidden truth,[76] laying claim to corporeal knowledge.

Thus, overcoming the ontological tension at the heart of the subject through a belief in universal pre-symbolic sameness. Unveiling invests in signifying the unveiled body *as natural*, a pre-discursive sameness that signals the universal. This investment in the experiences of the flesh as a measurement of modernity is imbued with historical European encounters with others in the Orient,[77] and like race, has also been contested. Like whiteness and thus race, the unveiled has a similar attachment to nature, it is *imagined* through a "so-called pre-discursive body" that is *more than* symbolic. This impulse to see the body without cover is a modern preoccupation with skin, according to Cheng. The aesthetics of surface she contends cannot be separated from the history of race which is founded on a similar notion of a "desire for pure surface"[78]—what she calls "the second skin" as an attachment to the visible. The metonymic meaning this surface produces are "purity, cleanliness, simplicity, anonymity, masculinity, civilisation, technology, intellectual abstracism",[79] in contrast to skin that carries the stain of excess: race and femininity.

If nakedness has historically imagined as primitive, raw animality, mere flesh and devoid of the human, how it is that modernism's investment in "pure surface" (the unveiled) does not get attached to nakedness? How do we account for this seeming contradiction? There are two forms of nakedness at work here. Modern nakedness is one about *clearing away* and disciplining the body to reveal bare skin whereas primitive nakedness has no trace of the veil's removal which exists as an unenlightened state with the absence of desire for universal knowledge. Reflecting on colonial nakedness, Levine observes how undressed natives were described as "not of their right mind... lacking history, lacking shame, lacking clothes... the absence of civilisation".[80] It is in the *act* of unveiling rather than being in a timeless state of nakedness is where the distinction between nakedness and the unveiled finds civilisational pronouncement.

In contrast to this "will to unwrap"[81] Joan Copjec's analysis of the "erotic and despotic colonial cloth" in the Moroccan photographs by French psychiatrist G. G de Clérambault—a man of the cloth—who draped the body in cloth, reads his attachment to these draped bodies as identifying functionalist types—the different ways drapery falls on the body. Using these images to critique utilitarian's repressed desire—what it deemed "useless enjoyment and all but functional clothes", Copjec observes how on the "borders of the whole cloth of the greatest happiness, there emerged a phantasmatic figure veiled, draped in cloth—whose existence, posed as threat". This abandoned neighbour, whose useless enjoyment colonial powers attempted to strip away, showed the refusal to "release itself into the universal pool".[82] The lack of functionality, greater purpose, even "extremism" of a body draped in veils one could argue, Copjec's reading is identifying the *unnatural* state, its obscenity, that is being projected in these photographs. Clérambault's fetishistic gesture of veiling for the Other, is an anxious repetition of containing bodies that enjoy differently to be marked off as uncivilised, wasteful bodies.

With the act of unveiling came a universal enjoyment, a raising of consciousness and the embracing of knowledge of the body and its place in the world. Through Butler's lens, unveiling is a perpetual "performance" that "compel belief" in the truth of the body—the unveiled "natural" body as the conduit for accumulating freedom and the measure for all bodies.[83] However, these boundaries require vigorous policing while being in the throes of unveiling succour. The clearing away serves as a prophylactic against the anxiety of the security of one's symbolic structure in the possibility of nakedness as just being another form of veiling or other *jouissance* and other (animalistic) ways of enjoying beyond the race-based master signifiers of the (unveiled) law.

The visibility of difference, as embodied by the veiled woman, has a contradictory function: it protects against lethal sameness but it also facilitates the possibility of sameness through the fantasy of phallic wholeness/unveiling.[84] The body enters here as a marker of civilisational boundaries, demarcating "us" from "them". This "denaturing" (that which is raced, as oppose to unraced) occurs in how the veiled body is imagined as what makes the other *other*—a constrained body, embedded in the particularities of culture and not yet sufficiently evolved to desire more. It is the positing of a particular body that occupies the unveiled or in the process of unveiling, not subject to symbolic determinism, as a neutral point of reference of what it means to be "human", against which other bodies are measured. In Almutawakel's image, the unveiled "whole" body exists beyond the frame, beyond the symbolic imagery of the layers of veils yet it is also the overall frame, which locates its consistency, its allure of completeness, on the partial veiled bodies in each image.

The body in the fantasy of unveiling freedom, like whiteness, is the Lacanian whole body assuming a position of neutrality, invisibility and universalism as the complete boundaries of what Charles Taylor describes as the "buffered self".[85] When unveiled in its natural or "real" state, this universal body is the biopolitical body that indexes knowledge of human experience, and which "other bodies" suggest has been veiled by symbolic layers.

This is a body that is both material and metaphorical, imaged and imagined and against which other bodies are judged. When one looks, this is the body one seeks to find, believing it to be there, because it promises the subject security, fulfilment and *power over the body*. In this fantasy, "difference" is fulfilled and *materialised* in the image of an unveiling freedom to uncover an autonomous subject who can overcome cultural constraints and embrace the prestige of being dignified, progressive and modern.[86] If freedom is something one cannot want and freedom is imagined cumulative, inherited in unveiling is modernism's arc of enjoyment where fleshly knowledge discovers supressed desire. Here, we see the merging of the biopolitical (knowable; pure surface) and the psychoanalytic (unknowable; fragmented) body, in modernism's fantasy of human development. This progressive thrust has recently been described by Jason Josephson-Storm as modernity's myth of the "disenchantment" of the world[87]—a process of logocentrism, secularisation, de-magnification and scientification that dominates nature, and I contend, repurposes *our* nature to fulfil an imagined human totality.

THE BODY AS LAW

The imaginary that underpins the fantasy of unveiling the Muslim woman presupposes a body that has an innate or natural desire that is imagined as dormant. The invocation of natural desire emerges from political progressions with origins in the history of natural law—a desire to perfect human nature by a spirit of progress that privileges rationality, reason, liberty and autonomy. The *telos* of the human and the project of history is freedom.[88] This desire for freedom—that which we cannot *not* want—attaches itself to the body and secures itself to corporeal truths. The body itself offers what Lacan calls a universal satisfaction[89]—satisfying the authenticity of meaning, because of its framing in natural law. Italian philosopher Giorgio Agamben identifies the role of the body and the modes of its exclusion within the law through the history of natural law. Traced back to Greek teleology, natural law posits a subject with certain natural (and therefore universal) moral capacities, a natural life (*zoe*) whose purpose was to fulfil it. The *bios* (political life) was to build on *zoe* by inscribing rights and duties on the body to reach its potential.[90] Natural law revealed the potential in everyone as part of a historical quest for the universal and what Ernst Bloch has described as a forward-pressing, not-yet-determined nature of human being.[91]

Sophocles' much-cited play *Antigone* provides a crucial case in point as an early application of natural law. Antigone, the heroine, disobeys the law of her Uncle Creon who forbids the burial of Polyneices, her brother. Polyneices is killed after he leads an army against his brother Eteocles in order to gain what he believed to be his rightful position as the inheritor of the kingdom of Thebes. Antigone's refusal to deny her brother the sacred burial right draws on unwritten laws of nature that supersede the law. In this case, one's familial and spiritual obligation. As Butler argues, Antigone's defiance of Creon's claim to sovereignty questions the very basis of the "social deformation of both idealised kinship and political sovereignty that emerges as a consequence of her act".[92] In Lacan's own reading of Antigone's act, represents an unrelenting desire to recuperate her symbolically and physically dead brother, is a desire so pure, it falls into the realm of the death drive, marking the limits of the symbolic order that cannot locate her desire though it speaks in desire's name. Antigone's act, for Lacan is beautiful because she identifies the subliminal limit, the place of feminine *jouissance* which has never been, or can be, determined.[93] It also raises the possibility of what Collette Soler has observed about language exceeding the subject as a body because it assures one of the non-symbolic beyond.[94] The body here is nothing more than dead flesh, decomposing, losing its symbolic significance.[95]

Speaking to an Other law beyond kinship and political sovereignty, Antigone's story offers an illustration of the tension between the Law (*bios*) and natural law (*zoe*) exposing how the latter exists regardless of the absence or presence of the Law. Natural law developed the naturally free and authorising individual, and that which guided this individual on its natural progression: a "forward march" of "all-conquering reason" which erases mistakes and aspires to a human end, an ideal.[96] Like McClintock's "panoptical time" as a scopic drive of modernity, compartmentalising the world into progress and "anachronistic space",[97] this trajectory has historically presaged and announced a desire for all knowledge, for modernity's Enlightenment. Embedded in modernity's trajectory is an imaginary of continued disclosure, a seeking out of an unveiled authenticity: the naked truth.

The Secular Body: Corporealising the Human

Despite critical assaults on this always-improving human body, Friedrich Nietzsche's announcement of the death of man, and the anti-humanist discourses of Michel Foucault, Martin Heidegger and the Freudian tradition, human rights discourse, which relies on the notion of the universal human, has managed to endure through its own constant renewal. The mainstreaming of human rights propels the desire to return to the human's pristine condition of selfhood to reinstate its freedom.[98] Examining the development of natural law and its contribution to the universalist claims of human rights, Douzinas refers to Thomas Hobbes' "natural man" who was a "naked human being" endowed only with logic, strength, survival instincts and a sense of natural morality; however, this being was not entirely naked but one whose "natural" instincts[99] became bound to the "human" as part of improving its nature through human emancipation. For Douzinas, unlike myths, which rely on beginnings, reason as a historical process of which human rights is its legacy, looks to *telos* or ends.[100] Like race, natural law has an anti-historicist claim that presents it as *beyond* the law and culture, a universalist Hegelian *geist* assisting individuals to perfect their nature and reach their full potential.[101] The law functions here to release the human to realise free will as a principle that society is ultimately founded on and which is itself integral to the quest of perfecting the natural self.[102]

With the end of the Cold War and the perceived victory of western civilisation over ideology, an end of history was declared.[103] History and civilisation had reached the apotheosis of human development, signalling the need for the rest of humanity to perfect itself with the tools of western civilisation: secularism, liberalism, democracy and human rights. Identifying the desire to couple a specific selfhood with freedom, in the extolling of human rights today, Badiou frames this as a desire to return to the abstract Kantian subject—indicative of a hegemonic constitution of a western-inspired universal subject.[104] It is within the teleology of the desire for reaching this never actualised potential—a universal "human"—that the unveiled and unveiling has held so much traction in recent years.

This progressive notion of history-making and self-empowerment of the human is embedded in what Asad contends is the notion of the secular and its drive to replace not simply "religious passion" with dispassionate reason, but pain with pleasure. He expands, if the body is afflicted, this puts a limit to the body's ability to act effectively in the real world.[105] The political impulse to empower the human, and aid the body that occupies it, is encapsulated in global human rights campaign as imagining the effective realisation of universal humanity transcending geographical and national boundaries, and here I argue, *bodily difference*. Difference here appears as human rights violations to the body.

Linking the corporeal with the body, Asad observes how the body must experience in a particular way in order to attain (and thus, identify) the human.[106] This human occupies the position of the universal, the natural, that exceeds difference and is in the realm of the secular. The secular, for Asad, is a critical act of unmasking that if we were to think of it as a body, would detect bodily harm or sickness. In other words, the secular body is possible if we think of it as how it comes into a practice.[107] As a knowledge of truth-making, the secular serves as a prophylactic to the body in crisis, shattered by the demands of tradition and history. If the secular body isn't definitive, what we can derive from this investment in knowing the body is an attempt to claim the body for the secular.

Examining possible answers to the directness of the question—what is the secular body? Jelle Wiering proposes that thinking about the secular in relation to how the body is presented—how one dresses, eats or practices sex—is helpful to establishing its boundaries. Following Joan Wallach Scott's observation of the intimacies between secularity and sexuality, what she coins "sexularism", Wiering offers a way of thinking about the secular body as the "the sexular body"—a "wild body"—which mobilises secular principles of unconstrained desires through the openness of sex, the enjoyment of sex—it is a body "that does not blush".[108] This secular entitlement of the body is not possible without efforts to expunge the compromised or contaminated body, identified as the religious body (a theme I turn to in Chapter 6). As we so far have deduced, unveiling is imperative to modernism's practicing of truth-telling where sensorium and corporeal boundaries are registered. Unveiling's investment in discovering the universal body, the natural body, undeterred by sickness or injury, I propose, is a practice of embodying the secular, *the unveiled as the secular body*. The secular as an ethical and social ritual of the body, detects the coordinates for the body's universal satisfaction beyond the constraining demands of cultural and religious traditions. Unveiling is a disciplinary process of secular self-management that educates oneself about the body: what to feed it, how to dress it, and how it desires.[109] It is a process that Foucault discerns as a way to be disciplined by freedom.

Difference is that which thwarts or denies secularism's promise of freedom and misrecognises the natural constitution of the human whose body is meant to enjoy freedom as it exposes itself to more rights, discovers more ways of protecting oneself from violations and from racial injury. In the trajectory of the human, the "natural" body is *almost always already unveiled*, but not yet arrived.

In the following chapter, I argue that human rights campaigns provide ways of fulfilling the fantasy of unveiling with the acquisition of more rights in a teleology of bodily wholeness, made possible by imaging the body. But before we can explore the role of these images in the fantasy of freedom, we need to understand its underlying imaginary by unpacking it further. In the political imaginary of universalising the human, natural rights are a force for good, moving history towards a destination: an unveiled subjectivity that can unfailingly *enjoy freedom*. People now attain their concrete nature, their humanity, by *unveiling* their intrinsic rights in nature *through* the acquisition of universal human rights.[110] This is the broken body that is then put back together through rights, the law. The legalisation of desire and the authority that human rights has assumed in guiding the development of humanity has also meant the naked human is based on violent exclusions, revealing the reduction of the human to a universal category subject to biopolitical policing of state power[111] or as Asad describes it, "the essence of the human comes to be circumscribed by legal discourse".[112]

Building on Foucault's notion of biopower—the surveillance and disciplinary technologies of the state to govern bodies,[113] Agamben contends, that human rights relies on docile bodies: the politicising theological body that is posited as lacking its nature and thus, put to use by powerful disciplinary strategies to relocate it.[114] Unlike Foucault, who links biopower to modern forms of micro-governing that require a "destruction of the body",[115] Agamben argues biopower can be traced to the Ancient Greeks. The unwritten laws of nature in Ancient Greece came under the fold of politics which saw the *bios* (political life) appropriate *zoe* (natural life) and put it to use for the *bios*.[116] It is because bodies are politicised but never entirely determined by discourses that human rights can render bodies as "bare life"—a "life exposed to death[117]" or what Badiou, in his own concerns about human rights, has called "human animals".[118] We are reminded of the quicksand boundaries of human/animal, naked/unveiled, self/other, that modernism's progressive impetus has attempted to preserve but never mastered. Humanity is reducible because human lives become, in the words of Agamben, the "principal objects of projections and calculations" of the sovereign state. The bare life of the citizen is the new biopolitical body of humanity and the source of sovereign power.[119] Refugees, terrorists and even Muslims in the age of surveillance and security are symptoms of how we are subject to sovereign power, capable of being stripped of rights, *all* potentially reduced to bare life, exposing the state of primitive nakedness.

What we see through Agamben's lens is the colonising effect of *bios* over the *zoe*. That is, we see the appropriation of natural law by sovereign power to serve the governing agenda of biopower, thus allowing politics to reduce natural life to political existence.[120] The disciplining of bodies is to be constituted as natural (governed) and those that are unnatural, excluded from political and symbolic life, show the reduction of bodies to *bios* and the illusion of a universal nature that underpins them. Just as race attaches itself to the material "natural" body, we see politics harness nature as the colonisation of *zoe* by *bios* to produce a desire for unveiling as a practice of secular agency, of *feeling free*.

In this mode of universalising freedom, universalist claims of human rights has reduced bodies to the calculations of political rights—to modernism's aestheticisation of the inorganic in the name of the organic[121]: having them, accumulating more of them, lacking them, or *unworthy* of them. Freedom and suffering are a *visible* spectacle, evidence of one as either lacking human rights—manifested in the mutilated and veiled body—or receiving them through gestures of unveiling. These examples indicate how "human rights" make itself known through the body, composing some as suffering—injured bodies in need of "fixing", being put back together, by rights. The body actualises human potential and is a concrete means of experiencing human rights because it is through its "material factualness" that one can be convinced of their political truths. Cultural constructs always maintain "the aura of realness" as we saw earlier.[122] The body becomes the alibi of the individual as human, desiring and living, and invested in the Real performed on its corporeal terrain.

In the fantasy of the west of unveiling, the unveiled appears as the "naked" body represented as an isomorphic alignment with the flesh, securing the "thing", by reifying a matured secular body. Maturing through the realisation of desire, practice of self-governing, autonomy, the body is retrieved as it actualises human potential. It is the body that represents what Collette Soler calls the "unisex effect"—sexual difference is now being *covered over* rather than being made visible under discourses of equality (such as human rights), which do not know of sexual difference.[123] The "naked liberated" body exists as a universal epidermal surface, mollifying the ontological uncertainty of sexed bodies by positing a self-fashioning individual that consumes freedom, has tamed nature, and shapes it through the procurement of human rights. The unveiled in this sense is an "immanent absence"[124] and the "lure" that necessitates the unveiling of the "unfinished person" of the future[125] of which human rights is fundamentally its tool. The unveiled as a secular aspiration, promises fulfilment of the human and the possibility of its perfect truth: the natural body unburdened by cultural bias, irrational demands of tradition, racial stain—each which human rights has neutralised and deposed.

The unveiling of history's suppressed freedoms, desires and truths in the pursuit of perfecting the human, appeals to a freedom that "must always be increasing.[126] If freedom is always on the rise in the acquisition of more rights, and is attached to the body in specific ways, the body must also always be unveiling to receive it because unveiling attaches itself to the political impulse of releasing oneself from constraints. The very idea of unveiling portends something that has been hidden and is being laid bare for both visible and psychic relief. The idea of exposing the body is itself invested with imagining releasing oneself from the chains of tradition, the suppression of desires and discovering an authentic secular self-exerting agency. The body being unveiled is the fantasy defence for actualising desire for secular rights and freedom.

Conclusion

It is within the historical fantasy of unveiling the human that a valorised (unveiled) west is harvested, and like whiteness, represents a "complete mastery, self-sufficiency and the *jouissance* of oneness".[127] History's progressive thrust, couched in a natural desire for a perfect truth embodied in the not-yet-*wholly*-human, is linked to the promise of unveiling. Within this historical imaginary, the singular and innocuous truth remains hidden. That is, re-assembling the unveiled secular body—the oneness that sexual difference fails in—is attained through the biopolitics of rights, shaping and disciplining the body into political completeness. This humanising narrative is continually reproduced through stories that link desire with unveiling, and the normal with the unveiled. Often these stories are about the restrictions forced upon women by fundamentalist regimes. For example, Iranian women earn their humanity through the presence of consumerism in their lives and on their bodies—from the desire to paint faces, smoke, or to don fashion-chic.[128] In these "human" or humanising stories, a recognisable natural personhood exists beneath the incomprehensible veil.[129] It is only with the removal of the veil that bodies are made intelligible, familiar and "normal" in seeking visible signs of pleasure—imagining a mastery over the body. The body *must confess* and perform its rights—rights that are often linked to a secular freedom to consume without constraints, and through consumption, come to earn their place in the human family.

This chapter has established the link between the fantasy of the west as an exalted subject through the image of the unveiled, wholeness made manifest through the body. In the captivating politics and psychic terrain of the veiled and unveiled, Almutawakel's image of herself with her child and doll invites a reading of an unsuccessful attempt at the "natural human" who is the very frame that reads these images. The disappearance of their bodies under the veil triggers an impulse to unveil, to release the body from its constraints. It is the body presupposed through other bodies, that frames Almutawakel's image. Read through the discourse of progress in the west, the image promises the liberation of the body which unveiling ensures. Veiling here is represented as a transgression of natural desire, restricting the body from enjoying, from experiencing and interacting with the world. Unveiling the body marks the biopolitical mode of disciplining modern subjects into their universal human status and into a freedom of corporeal consumption.

To conclude, the visible body is constitutive of the self-authorising secular liberal subject. Its claims are grounded in a visible truth, and its subject is its corporeal confirmation. Freedom is imagined and "fixed" through the promise of the unveiled body. The partial representations of the body as incomplete bodies activate a desire for fulfilment that comes with revealing the complete body beneath the veil. The veiled body, a distortion of the natural state of *zoe*, holds out the promise of wholeness, the law of the unveiled. Her veiledness exhibits her unfreedom that is violently emblazoned on and through her body. Her body is always in the process of becoming through the act of unveiling. It is through the body in action, that the fantasy of freedom is grounded and imagined as ultimately satisfied.

NOTES

1. Cited in Helen Block Lewis: 'Anatomy is Destiny: The Problem of Freud's Sexism in *Freud and Modern Psychology: The Emotional Basis of Human Behaviour* (Springer: Boston, 1983).
2. Boushra Almutawakel, "The Hijab/Veil Series," http://muslima.imow.org/content/hijab-veil-series.
3. This particular image has been posted on social network pages that are either less critical to the war such as liberal feminists "*Stop the World War on Girls*", or directly identify with it, such as right-wing nationalists Australian Defence League.

4. Hesford, *Spectacular Rhetorics: Human Rights Visions, Recognitions, Feminisms*, 29.
5. This would not be the first time that this kind of image of a young girl with a doll being threatened by the veil has been shown. In 2002, Harriet Logan's book *Unveiled* about a Western photographer who goes to Afghanistan and interviews a group of women, documenting their lives through photographs before and after the Taliban. The front page is a close-up of a woman's face in a burqa. The back cover contains a young girl holding her doll smilingly. The front and back covers encapsulate this narrative of "before" and "after".
6. The article was also critiqued by Africa is a Country. https://africasacountry.com/2018/05/how-not-to-photograph-nigerian-women-again.
7. Michel Foucault, *Birth of the Clinic* (Routledge, 2003).
8. Anne Anlin Cheng, *Second Skin: Josephine Baker and the Modern Surface* (Oxford and New York: Oxford University Press, 2011).
9. Elizabeth Grosz, *Volatile Bodies: Toward a Corporeal Feminism (Theories of Representation and Difference)* (Bloomington: Indiana University Press, 1994).
10. Scott, *The Politics of the Veil*, 16.
11. Cheng, *Second Skin*, 8.
12. Costas Douzinas, *The End of Human Rights: Critical Legal Thought at the Turn of the Century* (Oxford: Hart Publishing, 2000), 1–2.
13. United Nations, "The Universal Declaration of Human Rights," http://www.un.org/en/universal-declaration-human-rights/.
14. See responses to this concept from Charles Hirschkind, "Is There a Secular Body?" *Cultural Anthropology* 26, no. 4 (2011); Talal Asad, "Thinking About the Secular Body, Pain and Liberal Politics," *Cultural Anthropology* 26, no. 4 (2011).
15. Cheng, *Second Skin*.
16. Anne McClintock, *Imperial Leather: Race, Gender, and Sexuality in the Colonial Contest* (New York: Routledge, 1995), 58.
17. Jacques Derrida, "The Animal That Therefore I Am (More to Follow)," trans. David Wills, *Critical Inquiry* 28, no. 2 (2002): 369–418.
18. Giorgio Agamben, *Homosacer: Sovereign Life and Bare Life* (California: Stanford University Press, 1998), 75.
19. For a discussion on how "sex" is used as a reference for material difference and its limits, see Judith Butler, *Bodies That Matter: On the Discursive Limits of "Sex"* (Oxon: Routledge, 2011).
20. For instance, using a Foucauldian approach in her examination of the role of Muslim women's bodies in orientalist knowledge production in the colonial era, Meyda Yeğenoğlu argues that it stemmed from the Enlightenment notion of visibility as a "precondition for true knowledge". See Meyda

Yeğenoğlu, *Colonial Fantasies: Towards a Feminist Reading of Orientalism* (Cambridge: Cambridge University Press, 1998), 116.

21. Alain Badiou, "Bodies, Languages Truth," 2006, http://www.lacan.com/badbodies.htm.

22. Elaine Scarry, *On Beauty and Being Just* (Princeton: Princeton University Press, 1999), 111.

23. Michel Foucault, *The Will to Knowledge: The History of Sexuality I*, trans. Robert Hurley (London: Random House, 1978), 107.

24. Michel Foucault, *Discipline and Punishment: The Birth of the Prison*, trans. Alan Sheridan (New York: Random House, 1995), 25.

25. Hilary Neroni, *The Subject of Torture: Psychoanalysis, Biopolitics in Television and Film* (New York: Columbia University Press, 2015), 25.

26. Judith Butler, "Foucault and the Paradox of Bodily Inscriptions," *The Journal of Philosophy* 86, no. 11 (1989): 603. "The body posited as prior to the sign, is always *posited* or *signified* as *prior*. This signification produces as an *effect* of its own procedure the very body that it nevertheless and simultaneously claims to discover as that which *precedes* its own action. If the body signified as prior to signification is an effect of signification, then the mimetic or representational status of language, which claims that signs follow bodies as their necessary mirrors, is not mimetic at all. On the contrary, it is productive, constitutive, one might even argue *performative*, inasmuch as this signifying act delimits and contours the body that it then claims to find prior to any and all signification". *Bodies That Matter: On the Discursive Limits of "Sex"*, 30. "…the neutral body can only be filled in by the male body and men's pleasures". Also See Elizabeth Grosz, *Volatile Bodies: Toward a Corporeal Feminism (Theories of Representation and Difference)* (Bloomington: Indiana University Press, 1994), 156.

27. Butler, *Bodies That Matter: On the Discursive Limits of "Sex"*, 32.

28. Butler, *Bodies That Matter: On the Discursive Limits of "Sex"*, 88.

29. It is both a "being of jouissance" (invasion) and "jouissance of the Other" (inscription). Verhaeghe, "Enjoyment and Impossibility: Lacan's Revision of the Oedipal Complex—Reflections on Seminar XVII," 30–33.

30. Neroni, *The Subject of Torture*.

31. Grosnz, *Volatile Bodies: Toward a Corporeal Feminism*, 5–10.

32. Jelle Wiering "There Is a Sexular Body: Introducing a Material Approach to the Secular," *Secularism and Nonreligion* 6, no. 8 (2011): 6.

33. Asad, *Formations of the Secular: Christianity, Islam, Modernity*, 72. For an application of Asad's argument, see Saba Mahmood's work on the piety movement in Egypt. She explores how the body is not simply an index to experience but helps to transform the bodily act into a particular kind of meaning, reflective of the world in which bodies are located. Mahmood, *Politics of Piety: The Islamic Revival and the Feminist Subject*, 26–27.

34. Asad, *Formations of the Secular: Christianity, Islam, Modernity*, 72.

35. Latika Bourke, "Burqa Debate: Jacqui Lambie Goes Head-to-Head With Female Islamic Leader on Sunrise," *The Sydney Morning Herald*, October 2, 2014, https://www.smh.com.au/politics/federal/burqa-debate-jacqui-lambie-goes-headtohead-with-female-islamic-leader-on-sunrise-20141002-10ozui.html. During the national debate on France's decision to ban the face veil in 2010, French MP Jacques Myard's, one of the main advocates of the ban, defended the move in an interview with ABC's *Foreign Correspondent*, with a rather personal note: "When you hide your face... I am the victim. I am—because you refuse [to let me see] who you are, and this is not acceptable." The body here speaks to the condition of not knowing and is policed by securing identity, social relations and imagined national boundaries. Also see, Jacqui Pavey, "The Burqa or the Ban: Which Is Worse?" *Right Now: Human Rights in Australia*, February 14, 2011, http://rightnow.org.au/opinion-3/the-burqa-or-the-ban-which-is-worse/.

36. Bruce Fink, "Knowledge and Jouissance," in *Reading Seminar XX: Lacan's Major Work on Love, Knowledge and Feminine Sexuality*, ed. Susanne Barnard and Bruce Fink (New York: State University New York Press, 2002), 26–30.

37. Annabelle Mooney, *Human Rights and the Body: Hidden in Plain Sight* (Surrey: Ashgate Publishing Company, 2014), 91.

38. Mooney, *Human Rights and the Body*, 98–99.

39. The body is not "an originating point nor yet a terminus; it is a result or an effect". See Denise Riley, *"Am I That Name?" Feminism and the Category of "Women" in History* (Minneapolis: University of Minnesota, 1988), 102.

40. Derek Hook, *A Critical Psychology of the Postcolonial: The Mind of Apartheid* (London: Psychology Press, 2012), 47.

41. Butler, *Bodies That Matter: On the Discursive Limits of "Sex"*, 5.

42. Seshadri-Crooks, *Desiring Whiteness: A Lacanian Analysis of Race*, 19.

43. Grosz, *Volatile Bodies: Toward a Corporeal Feminism*, 6.

44. See Arthur Rose, Stefanie Heine, Naya Tsentourou, Corrine Saunders, and Peter Garratt, *Reading Breath in Literature* (Cham: Palgrave Macmillan, 2019).

45. Josh Sanburn, "Behind the Video of Eric Garner's Deadly Confrontation with New York Police," *Time*, July 23, 2014, https://time.com/3016326/eric-garner-video-police-chokehold-death/.

46. For a discussion of technoculture and its impact on the corporeal, see Vicky Kirby, "Reality Bytes: Virtual Incarnations," in *Telling Flesh: The Substance of the Corporeal* (London: Routledge, 1997).

47. Butler, *Precarious Life: The Powers of Mourning and Violence*, 33.

48. Pierre Bourdieu, *Language and Symbolic Power*, trans. Gino Raymond and Mathew Adamson (Cambridge, MA: Harvard University Press, 1991), 13.

49. Geovanna Borradori, "Autoimmunity: Real and Symbolic Suicides—A Dialogue of Jacques Derrida," in *Philosophy in a Time of Terror: Dialogues with Jürgen Habermas and Jacques Derrida* (Chicago: The University of Press, 2003), 87.
50. Hook, *A Critical Psychology of the Postcolonial: The Mind of Apartheid*, 3.
51. Hook, *A Critical Psychology of the Postcolonial: The Mind of Apartheid*, 4.
52. Seshadri-Crooks, *Desiring Whiteness: A Lacanian Analysis of Race*, 7.
53. Seshadri-Crooks, *Desiring Whiteness: A Lacanian Analysis of Race*, 9.
54. Michel Foucault, *Society Must Be Defended: Lectures at the Collège de France, 1975–76* (London: Penguin, 2004).
55. McClintock, *Imperial Leather: Race, Gender, and Sexuality in the Colonial Contest*, 53.
56. Cheng, *Second Skin*, 6.
57. Seshadri-Crooks, *Desiring Whiteness: A Lacanian Analysis of Race*, 7.
58. Seshadri-Crooks, *Desiring Whiteness: A Lacanian Analysis of Race*, 7–8.
59. Jacques Alain-Miller and Jacques Lacan, eds., *The Seminar of Jacques Lacan on Feminine Sexuality: The Limits of Love and Knowledge, Book XX, Encore 1972–1973* (New York: W.W. Norton, 1998), 71.
60. Fink, *The Lacanian Subject: Between Language and Jouissance*, 104–105.
61. Slavoj Žižek, "The Real of Sexual Difference," in *Reading Seminar XX: Lacan's Major Work on Love, Knowledge, and Feminine Sexuality*, ed. Suzanne Barnard and Bruce Fink (New York: State of University of New York Press, 2002), 61–62. Žižek uses the example of Claude Levi-Strauss' notion of the "zero-institution" as an example of how sexual difference works. The Winnebago tribe, divided into two subgroups and located in different part of the village (above and below) were asked to draw the ground plan of his or her village and obtained two different answers depending on which subgroup he or she belonged to. Both groups configured the village differently but referenced a constant: not some objective "actual" disposition of the houses in the village, but the traumatic kernel, a fundamental antagonism the inhabitants of the village were unable to symbolise or come to terms with—suggesting an imbalance in social relations that prevented the community from stabilising as a whole. The two perceptions were only attempts or coping mechanisms in dealing with this lack of wholeness.
62. Lacan, *Ecrits: The First Complete Edition in English*, 230.
63. Seshadri-Crooks, *Desiring Whiteness: A Lacanian Analysis of Race*, 40.
64. Seshadri-Crooks, *Desiring Whiteness: A Lacanian Analysis of Race*, 40–43. See also Henry Krips' discussion of this slave-master relation, "A Slave to Desire: Defetishising the Colonial Subject," in *Fetish: An Erotics of Culture* (New York: Cornell University, 1999).
65. Seshadri-Crooks, *Desiring Whiteness: A Lacanian Analysis of Race*, 23.
66. Seshadri-Crooks, *Desiring Whiteness: A Lacanian Analysis of Race*, 43.

67. Seshadri-Crooks, *Desiring Whiteness: A Lacanian Analysis of Race*, 45.
68. Seshadri-Crooks, *Desiring Whiteness: A Lacanian Analysis of Race*, 21.
69. Seshadri-Crooks, *Desiring Whiteness: A Lacanian Analysis of Race*, 4.
70. Seshadri-Crooks, *Desiring Whiteness: A Lacanian Analysis of Race*, 21.
71. Eric L. Santner, *The Royal Remains: The People's Two Bodies and the Endgames of Sovereignty* (Chicago: University of Chicago Press, 2011), 74.
72. Santner, *The Royal Remains*, xxi.
73. Santner, *The Royal Remains*, 76.
74. Santner, *The Royal Remains*, 81.
75. For an analysis of these claims, see David Tyrer and Salman Sayyid, "Governing Ghosts: Race, Incorporeality, and Difference in Post-Political Times," *Current Sociology* 30, no. 3 (2012): 353–367. Also see, Yassir Morsi, "Islamophobia Is Racism," *Right Now*, October 31, 2014, http://rightnow.org.au/opinion-3/islamophobia-is-racism/.
76. Michel Foucault traces this desire for disclosing truth in what he describes as modern power's confessional demands. Knowledge became a tool of power that established the boundaries between the natural and unnatural body and policing sex and sexuality. See Foucault, *The Will to Knowledge: The History of Sexuality I*.
77. See Leila Ahmed, *Women and Gender in Islam: Historical Roots of a Modern Debate* (New Haven: Yale University Press, 1992).
78. Cheng, *Second Skin*, 12–13.
79. Cheng, *Second Skin*, 25.
80. Phillipa Levine, "States of Undress: Nakedness and the Colonial Imagination," *Victorian Studies* 50, no. 2 (2008): 195–196.
81. Joan Copjec, *Read My Desire: Lacan Against the Historicists* (Cambridge, MA: MIT Press, 1994), 69.
82. Copjec, *Read My Desire,* 106.
83. Butler, *Bodies That Matter: On the Discursive Limits of "Sex"*, 88.
84. Seshadri-Crooks, *Desiring Whiteness: A Lacanian Analysis of Race*, 8.
85. Charles Taylor, *A Secular Age* (Cambridge, MA: The Belknap Press of Harvard University Press, 2007).
86. Seshadri-Crooks, *Desiring Whiteness: A Lacanian Analysis of Race*, 7.
87. Josephson-Storm, *The Myth of Disenchantment*.
88. Wendy Brown, *States of Injury: Power and Freedom in Late Modernity*, 4.
89. Lacan, *Ecrits: The First Complete Edition in English*, 689.
90. Tom Frost, *Giorgio Agamben: Legal, Political and Philosophical Perspectives* (London: Routledge, 2013), 56.
91. Douzinas, *The End of Human Rights*, 15.
92. Judith Butler, *Antigone's Claim: Kinship Between Life and Death* (New York: Columbia University Press, 2002), 6.

2 THE UNVEILING BODY   67

93. Jacques Lacan, *Seminar VII: The Ethics of Psychoanalysis*, ed. Jacques-Alain Miller, trans. Dennis Porter (New York: W.W. Norton, 1992), 243–256.

94. Soler, "The Body in the Teaching of Jacques Lacan."

95. Silvia Federici's fascinating insights on the role of the body in the service of European capitalism identifies a similar tension between the body that is entirely disciplined by the symbolic, and the body that exceeds it, preserving a sacredness. In the eighteenth century England, there emerges two opposite investments in the body: the body seen as imbued with powers even after death. People believed that the body could "come back again" in revenge against the living. Though Federici does not make this link, the belief in the body that returns echoes Haitian belief around the same period (seventeenth to eighteenth century) where a country, enslaved by Europe, saw dying as the only escape from slavery into an afterlife of freedom. However, slaves who committed suicide to escape would be condemned as an undead slave, still denied their bodies. The zombie, as the enslaved body, emerges in this period as an embodiment of the horrors of slavery. The undead, in other words, could be utilized beyond death, as part of the inescapability of the slave institution. This is Federici's second body that, unlike the first body that continues to live after death, is the body that is seen as dead even when still alive. Like the enslaved body, dead or undead, this is the body that could be mechanised, serviced for capitalist labour and scientific discoveries. See Silvia Federici, *Caliban and the Witch: The Woman, the Body and Primitive Accumulation* (New York: Autonomedia, 2004), 144–145. For the link between zombies and slavery see Mike Miriani, "The Tragic, Forgotten History of Zombies," *The Atlantic*, October 28, 2015, https://www.theatlantic.com/entertainment/archive/2015/10/how-america-erased-the-tragic-history-of-the-zombie/412264/.

96. Douzinas, *The End of Human Rights*, 9.

97. McClintock, *Imperial Leather: Race, Gender, and Sexuality in the Colonial Contest*, 30–37.

98. Douzinas, *The End of Human Rights*, 17.

99. Douzinas, *The End of Human Rights*, 65.

100. Douzinas, *The End of Human Rights*, 6.

101. Douzinas, *The End of Human Rights*, 29.

102. Douzinas, *The End of Human Rights*, 20.

103. Fukuyama argued in 1989 that with the death of fascism and the decline in community with the end of the Cold War, liberalism had triumphed the battle of ideas and emerged as the universal project that would achieve history's end. Liberal institutions would be challenged, however, by ethnic and cultural rivals but ultimately will remain an unparallel force to guide the global community. Francis Fukuyama, *End of History and the Last Man* (New York: Free Press, 2006).

104. Alain Badiou, *Ethics: An Essay on the Understanding of Evil*, trans. Peter Hallward (London: Verso, 2001), 8.
105. Asad, *Formations of the Secular: Christianity, Islam, Modernity*, 68.
106. Asad, *Formations of the Secular: Christianity, Islam, Modernity*, 148–155.
107. Talal Asad, "Thinking About the Secular Body, Pain and Liberal Politics," *Cultural Anthropology* 26, no. 4 (2011): 659.
108. Wiering, "There Is a Sexular Body," 1–11.
109. Cheng, *Second Skin*.
110. Douzinas, *The End of Human Rights*, 11.
111. Douzinas, *The End of Human Rights*, 20.
112. Asad, *Formations of the Secular: Christianity, Islam, Modernity*, 135.
113. The transition from monarchical power to modern power was about regulation of bodies through new regimes of disciplinary technologies such as institutional surveillance and a panoptic gaze of normalisation. Biopower becomes a tool for modern compliance by using health practitioners, social workers, educators, etc. to normalise disciplinary practice that governed bodies. See Foucault, *Discipline and Punishment: The Birth of the Prison*. See also, Michel Foucault, Michel Senellart, and Collège de France, *The Birth of Biopolitics: Lectures at the Collège de France, 1978–79* (Basingstoke: Palgrave Macmillan, 2008).
114. See Agamben, *Homosacer: Sovereign Life and Bare Life*.
115. Butler, "Foucault and the Paradox of Bodily Inscriptions," 604.
116. Frost, *Giorgio Agamben: Legal, Political and Philosophical Perspectives*, 56.
117. Agamben, *Homosacer: Sovereign Life and Bare Life*, 88.
118. Badiou, *Ethics*, 11.
119. Badiou, *Ethics*, 12–13.
120. Badiou, *Ethics*, 75.
121. Cheng, *Second Skin*.
122. Elaine Scarry, *The Body in Pain: The Making and Unmaking of the World* (New York: Oxford University Press, 1985), 13.
123. Soler, *What Lacan Said About Women: A Psychoanalytic Study*, 158.
124. Seshadri-Crooks, *Desiring Whiteness: A Lacanian Analysis of Race*, 58.
125. Douzinas, *The End of Human Rights*, 15.
126. Butler, "Sexual Politics, Torture, and Secular Time," 6.
127. Seshadri-Crooks, *Desiring Whiteness: A Lacanian Analysis of Race*, 7.
128. Marguerite Ward, "Young Iranians Continue to Shock the Internet by Being Normal," *Policy Mic*, February 13, 014, https://www.mic.com/articles/82199/young-iranians-continue-to-shock-the-internet-by-being-normal.
129. See also Sex and the City 2 (2010) where four white American women travel to the United Arab Emirates. After feeling alienated by the cultural conservatism, they identify with the heavily veiled local women through their shared desire for designer clothes.

REFERENCES

Agamben, Giorgio. *Homosacer: Sovereign Life and Bare Life.* California: Stanford University Press, 1998.

Ahmed, Leila. *Women and Gender in Islam: Historical Roots of a Modern Debate.* New Haven: Yale University Press, 1992.

Alain-Miller, Jacques, and Jacques Lacan, eds. *The Seminar of Jacques Lacan on Feminine Sexuality: The Limits of Love and Knowledge, Book XX, Encore 1972–1973.* New York: W.W. Norton, 1998.

Alinejad, Masih. "My Stealthy Freedom," (Facebook page, 2014).

Almutawakel, Boushra. "The Hijab/Veil Series." http://muslima.imow.org/content/hijab-veil-series.

Asad, Talal. *Formations of the Secular: Christianity, Islam, Modernity.* California: Stanford University Press, 2003.

Asad, Talal. "Thinking About the Secular Body, Pain and Liberal Politics." *Cultural Anthropology* 26, no. 4 (2011): 657–675.

Badiou, Alain. *Ethics: An Essay on the Understanding of Evil.* Translated by Peter Hallward. London: Verso, 2001.

Badiou, Alain. "Bodies, Languages Truth," 2006. http://www.lacan.com/badbodies.htm.

Borradori, Geovanna. "Autoimmunity: Real and Symbolic Suicides—A Dialogue of Jacques Derrida." In *Philosophy in a Time of Terror: Dialogues with Jürgen Habermas and Jacques Derrida.* Chicago: The University of Press, 2003.

Bourdieu, Pierre. *Language and Symbolic Power.* Translated by Gino Raymond and Mathew Adamson. Cambridge, MA: Harvard University Press, 1991.

Brown, Wendy. *States of Injury: Power and Freedom in Late Modernity.* Princeton: Princeton University Press, 1995.

Butler, Judith. "Foucault and the Paradox of Bodily Inscriptions." *The Journal of Philosophy* 86, no. 11 (1989): 601–607.

Butler, Judith. *Antigone's Claim: Kinship Between Life and Death.* New York: Columbia University Press, 2002.

Butler, Judith. "Sexual Politics, Torture, and Secular Time." *The British Journal of Sociology* 59, no. 1 (2008): 1–23.

Butler, Judith. *Bodies That Matter: On the Discursive Limits of "Sex".* Oxon: Routledge, 2011.

Cheng, Anne Anlin. *Second Skin: Josephine Baker and the Modern Surface.* Oxford and New York: Oxford University Press, 2011.

Copjec, Joan. *Read My Desire: Lacan Against the Historicists.* Cambridge, MA: MIT Press, 1994.

Derrida, Jacques. "The Animal That Therefore I Am (More to Follow)." Translated by David Wills, *Critical Inquiry* 28, no. 2 (2002): 369–418.

Douzinas, Costas. *The End of Human Rights: Critical Legal Thought at the Turn of the Century.* Oxford: Hart Publishing, 2000.

Elston, Helen. "Behind the Veil: Iranian Women Cast the Hijab— In Pictures." *The Guardian*, January 7, 2018. https://www. theguardian.com/artanddesign/gallery/2018/jan/06/behind-the-veil-iranian-women-cast-off-their-hijabs-in-pictures?fbclid=IwAR2P_duIhbCSdbp0PsXkZNgjaYtyNJ3lj1TuvGqUrHhsVNk59JJlZV9DB2g.

Fanon, Frantz. *Black Skin, White Masks*. London: Pluto Press, 2008.

Federici, Silvia. *Caliban and the Witch: The Woman, the Body and Primitive Accumulation*. New York: Autonomedia, 2004.

Fink, Bruce. *The Lacanian Subject: Between Language and Jouissance*. Princeton, NJ: Princeton University Press, 1995.

Fink, Bruce. "Knowledge and Jouissance." In *Reading Seminar XX: Lacan's Major Work on Love, Knowledge and Feminine Sexuality*, edited by Susanne Barnard and Bruce Fink. New York: State University New York Press, 2002.

Foucault, Michel. *The Will to Knowledge: The History of Sexuality I*. Translated by Robert Hurley. London: Random House, 1978.

Foucault, Michel. *Discipline and Punishment: The Birth of the Prison*. Translated by Alan Sheridan. New York: Random House, 1995.

Foucault, Michel. *Society Must Be Defended: Lectures at the Collège de France, 1975–76*. London: Penguin, 2004.

Foucault, Michel, Michel Senellart, and Collège de France. *The Birth of Biopolitics: Lectures at the Collège de France, 1978–79*. Basingstoke: Palgrave Macmillan, 2008.

Frost, Tom. *Giorgio Agamben: Legal, Political and Philosophical Perspectives*. London: Routledge, 2013.

Fukuyama, Francis. *End of History and the Last Man*. New York: Free Press, 2006.

Grosz, Elizabeth. *Volatile Bodies: Toward a Corporeal Feminism (Theories of Representation and Difference)*. Bloomington: Indiana University Press, 1994.

Hesford, Wendy S. *Spectacular Rhetorics: Human Rights Visions, Recognitions, Feminisms*. Durham: Duke University Press, 2011.

Hirschkind, Charles. "Is There a Secular Body?" *Cultural Anthropology* 26, no. 4 (2011): 633–647.

Hook, Derek. *A Critical Psychology of the Postcolonial: The Mind of Apartheid*. London: Psychology Press, 2012.

Josephson-Storm, Jason. *The Myth of Disenchantment: Magic, Modernity and the Birth of the Human Sciences*. Chicago and London: University of Chicago, 2017.

Kamali Dehghan, Saeed. "Iranian Woman Wins Rights Award for Hijab Campaign." *The Guardian*, February 24, 2015. https://www.theguardian.com/world/2015/feb/24/iranian-woman-wins-rights-award-hijab-campaign.

Kirby, Vicky. "Reality Bytes: Virtual Incarnations." In *Telling Flesh: the Substance of the Corporeal*. London: Routledge, 1997.

Krips, Henry. "A Slave to Desire: Defetishising the Colonial Subject." In *Fetish: An Erotics of Culture*. New York: Cornell University, 1999.

Lacan, Jacques. *Seminar VII: The Ethics of Psychoanalysis*. Edited by Jacques Alain-Miller. Translated by Dennis Porter. New York: W.W. Norton, 1992.

Lacan, Jacques. *Ecrits: The First Complete Edition in English*. New York: W.W. Norton, 2006.

Levine, Phillipa. "States of Undress: Nakedness and the Colonial Imagination." *Victorian Studies* 50, no. 2 (2008): 189–219.

Mahmood, Saba. *Politics of Piety: The Islamic Revival and the Feminist Subject*. Princeton: Princeton University Press, 2005.

McClintock, Anne. *Imperial Leather: Race, Gender, and Sexuality in the Colonial Contest*. New York and London: Routledge, 1995.

Miriani, Mike. "The Tragic, Forgotten History of Zombies." *The Atlantic*, October 28, 2015. https://www.theatlantic.com/entertainment/archive/2015/10/how-america-erased-the-tragic-history-of-the-zombie/412264/.

Mooney, Annabelle. *Human Rights and the Body: Hidden in Plain Sight*. Surrey: Ashgate Publishing Company, 2014.

Morsi, Yassir. "Islamophobia Is Racism." *Right Now*, October 31, 2014. http://rightnow.org.au/opinion-3/islamophobia-is-racism/.

Neroni, Hilary. *The Subject of Torture: Psychoanalysis, Biopolitics in Television and Film*. New York: Columbia University Press, 2015.

Pavey, Jacqui. "The Burqa or the Ban: Which Is Worse?" *Right Now*, February 14, 2011. http://rightnow.org.au/opinion-3/the-burqa-or-the-ban-which-is-worse/.

Riley, Denise. *"Am I That Name?" Feminism and the Category of "Women" in History*. Minneapolis: University of Minnesota, 1988.

Rose, Arthur, Stefanie Heine, Naya Tsentourou, Corrine Saunders, and Peter Garratt. *Reading Breath in Literature*. Cham: Palgrave Macmillan, 2019.

Sanburn, Josh. "Behind the Video of Eric Garner's Deadly Confrontation with New York Police." *Time*, July 23, 2014. https://time.com/3016326/eric-garner-video-police-chokehold-death/.

Santner, Eric L. *The Royal Remains: The People's Two Bodies and the Endgames of Sovereignty*. Chicago: University of Chicago Press, 2011.

Saul, Heather. "Iranian Women Discard Their Hijabs for 'Stealthy Freedom, Facebook Page'." *The Independent*, May 13, 2014. https://www.independent.co.uk/news/world/middle-east/iranian-women-discard-their-hijabs-for-stealthy-freedom-facebook-page-9361388.html.

Scarry, Elaine. *The Body in Pain: The Making and Unmaking of the World*. New York: Oxford University Press, 1985.

Scarry, Elaine. *On Beauty and Being Just*. Princeton: Princeton University Press, 1999.

Scott, Joan Wallach. *The Politics of the Veil*. Princeton: Princeton University Press, 2007.

Seshadri-Crooks, Kalpana. *Desiring Whiteness: A Lacanian Analysis of Race.* New York: Routledge, 2000.

Soler, Colette. "The Body in the Teaching of Jacques Lacan." http://jcfar.org.uk/wp-content/uploads/2016/03/The-Body-in-the-Teaching-of-Jacques-Lacan-Colette-Soler.pdf.

Soler, Colette. *What Lacan Said About Women: A Psychoanalytic Study.* Detroit, MI: Other Press, 2006.

Taylor, Charles. *A Secular Age.* Cambridge, MA and London: The Belknap Press of Harvard University Press, 2007.

Tyrer, David, and Salman Sayyid. "Governing Ghosts: Race, Incorporeality, and Difference in Post-Political Times." *Current Sociology* 30, no. 3 (2012): 353–367.

United Nations. "The Universal Declaration of Human Rights." http://www.un.org/en/universal-declaration-human-rights/.

Verhaeghe, Paul. "Enjoyment and Impossibility: Lacan's Revision of the Oedipal Complex—Reflections on Seminar XVII." In *Jacques Lacan and the Other Side of Psychoanalysis*, edited by Justin Clemens and Russell Grigg. Durham: Duke University Press, 2006.

Ward, Marguerite. "Young Iranians Continue to Shock the Internet by Being Normal." *Policy Mic*, February 13, 2014. https://www.mic.com/articles/82199/young-iranians-continue-to-shock-the-internet-by-being-normal.

Wiering, Jelle. "There Is a Sexular Body: Introducing a Material Approach to the Secular", *Secularism and Nonreligion* 6, no. 8 (2011): 1–11.

Yeğenoğlu, Meyda. *Colonial Fantasies: Towards a Feminist Reading of Orientalism.* Cambridge: Cambridge University Press, 1998.

Žižek, Slavoj. "The Real of Sexual Difference." In *Reading Seminar XX: Lacan's Major Work on Love, Knowledge, and Feminine Sexuality*, edited by Suzanne Barnard and Bruce Fink. New York: State of University of New York Press, 2002.

CHAPTER 3

The 'Pure Defence of the Innocent' and Innocence Lost: Imagining the Veiled Woman in Human Rights

Only the non-human is photogenic. —Jean Baudrillard[1]

INTRODUCTION

Walking into an Afghan restaurant on Brunswick Street in Melbourne, Australia, I see her again. Her stern green eyes staring down at me from across the room as I settle into my *ashak* and *kofta* kebab. She is familiar to many. Three decades before the western public witnessed the harrowing image of Aisha and her story, another image had already appeared on the front cover of National Geographic. In 1985, an Afghan girl's piercing eyes conveyed the plight of the third world refugee child who lived among the struggles of war. The image of this girl invites pity and reflection while reminding that freedom is always vulnerable and never fully secured.[2] The necessity to fight to secure principles of human rights and democracy is reinforced in her majestic innocence and beauty. The Afghan Girl icon has survived decades on the cover of magazines. She is studied, debated, reflected upon, while she also provides aesthetic scenery for those who have a taste for Afghan cuisine. Not only has The Afghan Girl captured the western imagination, but she has also been embraced by the Afghan diaspora. In many Afghan homes, restaurants and the offices of health professionals, I find her

© The Author(s) 2020
S. Ghumkhor, *The Political Psychology of the Veil*,
Palgrave Studies in Political Psychology,
https://doi.org/10.1007/978-3-030-32061-4_3

proudly displayed on a wall for guests, diners and patients to enjoy. Sitting in that Afghan restaurant, I wondered why this particular image has come to define the Afghan experience. Does it convey the Afghan experience? Is it misplaced nostalgia by Afghans for a country lost to war and uncertainty? Perhaps, the magnetism is not towards her, but more towards her reception as the embodiment of the Afghan story as well its beauty. Put another way, the appeal of her image is the western desire to photograph her. It replaces the disgust and anger cited by images of the Muslim woman covered in blue with desire evolved by the innocent child, who is pure, vulnerable, exotic, beautiful. She is a deserving object of compassion and admiration. Afghanistan, seen through her image, is staged for the consumption of the west and Afghans who live within its political and cultural borders who perhaps see themselves captured in the gaze of the other. The production and circulation of this image also suggests, in both accounts, a desire to locate the universal dignified human. This chapter traces this set of interwoven desires in the proliferation of images of Muslim women in recent rights campaigns by examining their purchase for human rights. Its focus is not so much on the non-western other's reception of these images but to illustrate the extent to which these images dominate the modern imaginary and increasingly mediate experiences with liberal ideals: the human, universalism and freedom.

Increasingly seen as an unquestioned good and uniting countries and positions across the ideological and political spectrum, human rights are perceived as a politically neutral solution to global individual and collective political, economic and social injuries.[3] The dominance of human rights today, Costas Douzinas has argued, is paradoxically consistent with its greatest violations.[4] This chapter analyses closely how this paradox is arrested in the circulation of images—akin to those of Aisha, The Afghan Girl, *The New York Times'* portraits of women under Boko Haram—for humanitarian purposes. What does seeing and imagining bodies in a state of stress do to contemporary audience?

Images have a unifying capacity in that they can assemble raw human emotions, empower and seduce one into shared judgement in the very question they raise: how can you not *not* want to help this girl? How can one ignore the *instincts* for freedom? I argue her role in campaigns is symptomatic of both the absence of rights, and rights as her prescription of promise. Put in the framing of the previous chapter, such images present human rights as a promise of a "pre-discursive" universal completion in realising the dignified human. It is what Agamben warns is the reduction of politics to bare life. However, for rights to arrive, there must be bodily debris. As such, human rights and humanitarianism trade in images and an imaginary of bodies in crisis.

Humanitarian and international bodies have over the last two decades adopted frameworks to acknowledge women's role in international relations and the gendered component of security. The UN resolution 1325 *Women, Peace and Security* on 21 October 2000 is a recognition of the violence against women and their salient role in post-conflict resolution and peacebuilding. The following year, the invasion of Afghanistan saw this gendered security framework at work as the rationale for war was dominated by the image of the plight of the Afghan woman in a blue burqa. This representation of women as imperilled and needing to be at the centre of nation-building projects has been challenged by the growing concern over western citizens joining the ranks of the Islamic State in Iraq and Syria and their return. The imperilled Muslim women has also become imperilling. She is not simply a victim of the dangerous Muslim man, but also a participant. In 2015, the Women Peace Security resolution 2242 was passed, which identified women's role to combating counterterrorism and violent extremism, and in so doing, positioning women as subject to being victim and perpetrator of violence. Beyond the legal recognition, this is not necessarily a new social and political reality as her victim status has always been precarious. The donning of the veil as a marker of heightened religiosity also gestured towards not knowing what she desires. Like the Chechen "black widow" and Palestinian female suicide bombers, the "jihadi brides" who flock to militant groups to fight in war are often depicted as victims, *groomed into radicalisation*, rather than its active agent. This new rationale appears to extend the 1990s' discourse on violence against women which has been critiqued for framing violence as "the cause of women's dependency rather than one of its effects, the reason for their sexual, economic and social disempowerment".[5] The "radicalised" Muslim woman therefore is also framed by the same violence which culturally sanctions the injured body by terrorism and sexual slavery, empowering both western conservative and liberal forces to rescue her in the name of sexual freedom.[6] For the purpose of this chapter, I want to reflect on the international dimension and the significance of the insertion of this figure in the human rights imaginary.

This chapter will examine the human rights imaginary and how its puts images of Muslim women to use. Costas Douzinas defines this imaginary as the projection of an ideal-self, a redeemable future projection where man achieves its own *gestalt/*image by no longer being enslaved in the quest for rights.[7] As discussed in the previous chapters, the image for Lacan is integral to the making of the subject. The image anticipates and aspires to the ideal, even when impossible, unity of the subject.[8] In this mode, the image transfixes the subject and lays claim to a reality that does not exist and thus, its promises exist only within the subject's imaginary. Fantasy masks the trauma of this impossibility by producing ways of coping with it. This tension is discernible in the promise of human rights that are never realised. Human rights are "the projection of the not-yet into the "always there", a necessity but impossible promise".[9] Human rights violations aspire to this assurance by sustaining a fantasy of what, Renata Salecl observes, is rights' capacity to fulfil a desire for *more rights*. This promise of more rights, I argue, is assisted and secured through the imagery of the veiled and unveiled and the belief in the secular body that animates them. Desire in the human rights imaginary is generated and sustained through the exchange of *veiling and unveiling*—oscillating between lack and being—within the political economy of the veiled and unveiled that is in contention with the natural and unnatural world. Reflecting on a 2002 exhibition titled *Afghan Women: Behind the Veil* honouring the work of Doctors Without Borders, Lila Abu-Lughod similarly observes the role of fantasy in the fixation on unveiling, what she describes as "fantasies of intimacy". The images were accompanied by text: "When the Taliban came to power in 1996, Afghan women became faceless. To unveil one's face while receiving medical care was to achieve a sort of *intimacy* [my emphasis], find a brief space for *secret freedom* [my emphasis], and recover a little of one's dignity... please join us in helping to lift the veil".[10] The emphasis on intimacy, secrecy, the corporeal and desire are the axioms of the veiled and unveiled and what sustains their active underside: veiling and unveiling.

This chapter builds on the arguments in the previous chapter, positing that the pre-discursive secular body appears in these campaigns through the images of bodies under a veil of violence and therefore, endlessly desiring rights. If the secular is a practice of liberating the body from the constraints of cultural and religious demands, rights become a way of shielding the body from its return. The image of bodily violations secures the fantasy of unveiling freedom as modernity's disciplinary practice of secularising the body. Each bodily violation mourns the denial of bodily integrity and its possibility with the removal of each veil. The invitation to muse over the possible dangers that the body is vulnerable to is morally intoxicating.

Reflecting on the world's fascination with the "political horrors" of vulnerable flesh, Babajide Ishmael Ajisafe argues the "post-political has everything to do with the way exposed flesh, human carrion, and cropped bodies traverse along the horror scenes that comprise the foreground of international relations, the middle ground of international law and the background of international discourse".[11] For Ajisafe, the spectacle of violence are ways of unseeing the histories of violence of slavery and colonialism by the conquest of post-political discourses. Yet this same history, like the history of the Taliban and Islamic State's arrival from the fallout of war, has provoked "ways of killing" that has left its mark on the body as witness.[12] The images or rights abuse that circulate are those that enable looking to others and their past without witnessing accountability.

This chapter explores more broadly the over-representation of violations and the amplified tone of making fleshly wrongs visible through the salient role of the visual in human rights discourses. Images of Muslim women are fashioned by a belief in the transparency of what the visual holds, securing the puritanism of human rights language as a universal good. Like Boushra Almutawakel's snapshots of bodies being veiled (or unveiled), the visual display of bodies in these campaigns functions as Wendy Hesford calls an "ocular epistemology", a "seeing-as-believing paradigm", bolstering its claims as witness to human rights injustices. The "realist mode of representation" in which these images operate presents its content as natural, grounded in the reality of the body as the site of universal experience, and a way of visually measuring the truthfulness of what can and cannot be said.[13] Based on the intention to help those who cannot help themselves,[14] human rights campaigns use the image of bodies in crises to bolster its architecture of universal moral truths.

THE ROLE OF THE IMAGE IN HUMAN RIGHTS

The image in human rights campaigns not only stages lack, but also projects wants and fears. In its recognition of the modern subject's wishes, the image aims at displaying the desire to retrieve and attain the always missing part.[15] Attaining rights is embedded in a belief that "all human beings are born free and equal in dignity and rights",[16] and in the past few decades, human rights have become a "self-evident" language to articulate both human suffering and desire. In a world where universalism is increasingly under question, human rights are often seen as the last sacred and unquestionable space that brings together the left and right, liberals and conservatives, nations and cultures.[17] As a normative imperative, human rights are promoted as beyond politics and the last cry of universal Enlightenment.[18] Their reception, however, has not been smooth. Human rights have been considerably critiqued as an agent of western liberal imperialism[19] and as an epistemic discontinuity, accused of a social Darwinism that generate a desire of the strongest (with rights) to protect the weak (without).[20] Further critiqued within the themes of the universal and the particular, the subject of human rights is charged with excluding the specific experiences of gender, race and culture[21]; their particularising of the human[22] and how human rights has strayed from its emancipatory tradition and is now at the service of liberal capitalism.[23] Responding to Michael Ignatieff, whose defence against such criticism is to argue for a minimalist approach to human rights—limiting human rights to political violence and human misery, Brown argues this "anti-politics" of human rights as a pure defence of the innocent, must also be critically assessed.[24] Even the minimalist defence collaborates with the discursive operations of human rights reproducing the specificity of its history, culture and the politics and the image of justice that it registers. Brown asks of Ignatieff's minimalist position for human rights to reduce suffering: how does it answer the call to minimise suffering?[25] Most relevant to the following discussion is her confronting question: how does it avoid entrenching the injured identity of its victims?[26]

Images used in human rights advocacy campaigns tend to represent injustice as outside the bounds of these political tensions. The image is "self-evident" pain and injury which operates within a visual economy of truth and justice, dressed in the ocular and ontological certainty of good and evil, a moral compass which guides human rights consumers in their judgment.

Tracing human rights in history, Lynn Hunt argues that the popularity of the epistolary novel in the late eighteenth century came to inform a new sense of "imagined empathy" towards those of less fortunate circumstances. Through the inner workings of individual moral struggles, society stirred a *natural* emotional response and judgement, helping to expand the notion of natural rights.[27] This capacity for empathy is integral to the making of the modern subject. Modernisation theorist Daniel Lerner observes that empathy is tied to a "mobile personality", receptive to change, seeing oneself in the other and precipitated by modern lifestyles of urbanisation and new technologies of interaction[28]—both physically and virtually. The image's ability to capture violations against others also makes it a potent channel to produce modern emotions that allow subjects to empathise with others. However, unlike earlier expressions of empathy by those more privileged with those of differences classes, the images I examine below suggest that human rights discourse has evolved to replace empathy with sympathy and pity. The image as witness to horror evokes deep affective responses in the viewer whose humanness is tied to their moral judgment or condemnation. Judgement is secured by "attaching it [the wrong] to a visual image; it is the visual image which accumulates sense; and alongside sense, the image accrues a series of judgement or perceptions, it is made into a new objectivity".[29] Writing about the politics of judgement, Kennon Fergusson observes how judgement is most powerful and most public when it is unthinking.[30]

The structure of emotions is not only a disciplinary exercise of reasoned emotions marking what Talal Asad calls the "modern secular", but also about the learning practices to be fully human by retrieving the secular body. Through this humanising process, one learns to recognise particular sufferings as they are seen as a barrier to realising one's humanity.[31] One also learns to recognise the corporeal contours of the secular through witnessing *other* bodies in crisis. The image's visibility has the power to offer imaginary possession of an otherwise uncertain space,[32] such as the meaning of being "human" and corporeal coordinates for the secular body that occupies it. The visual's capacity to present an uncontested fact produces unthinkingness as a truth that stands outside of politics.

Imaging Rights Violations

Reflecting on the politics of images, Susan Sontag observes that without politics, events and therefore the desire to convey them, do not exist.[33] Images operate and are consumed within processes of knowledge production that establish visibilities and invisibilities, organise ideas, activate and deactivate responses and produce subjects and objects. Akin to colonial exhibitions as "museum without history"[34] of "primitive" cultures that indulged European illusions of progress, or the expressionless and dehumanising photographs of madness in the nineteenth century as a way of capturing absence and alterity,[35] the victim in human rights is similarly stripped of meaningful context and showcased as living alterity. The "victim" is frozen in pain, distracting the gaze from other possibilities of assessment. The over-exposure of pain functions like a "commodity spectacle"[36] for the consumption of human rights voyeurs and amounts to "stealing the pain of others".[37] This is a pain that is imagined as the afflictions of culture and which one can be alleviated but must first be made visible. Like victims of torture, victims in human rights campaigns are "bereft of speech", broken subjects, but whose pain is spoken through a "language of agency", making pain visible only in a mastery of power.[38]

The intensity and intimacy of trafficking identities, cultures, communities and beliefs, across national and international spaces, through Internet technology makes the circulation of images significantly different from technological innovations of the past.[39] The rise of memes and hashtag activism,[40] for example, are indicative of a digital age that prefers concentrated messages based on the need to draw attention and consume visually and efficiently.[41] These cultural trends highlight the salience of iconic images to the universalising practice of human rights. Its moral purity is grounded in the "self-evidence" of the visual. As a technology of truth, a mirage of the real, the visual has a self-evidence persuasive power.

Several of the images I examine here have featured on Facebook, blogs, Twitter and Pinterest, where many NGOs such as Amnesty International promote awareness of their human rights campaigns to mobilise support. However, some of these images are floating signifiers, outside the framework of specific campaigns, reproduced outside of their original context and reappear when concerns about Muslim women are heightened or anti-immigration sentiments and anxiety over terrorism are expressed. Humanitarian politics, therefore, cannot simply be understood within singular campaigns but how the public mobilises it in response to global events.

Visual messages are powerful tools for documenting human suffering, and implicating those who see these images as witnesses to the suffering.[42] Tracing the ethics in international human rights, French philosopher Alain Badiou argues that it is a discourse that was founded around a militant consensus of what is barbarianism and what is Evil.[43] Good is that which visibly intervenes against this Evil and therefore, exists in the locus of an ethical response. Such consensus derives its authority from its claim to self-evidence, as stated in the United Nations Declaration of Human Rights charter: "Whereas recognition of the inherent dignity and of the equal and inalienable rights of all members of the human family is the foundation of freedom, justice and peace in the world". "Whereas" functions in this statement as "it being the fact that"—a legalistic term for self-evidence.[44] The moral imprint on all who carry self-evident rights depoliticises the international terrain by masking the power asymmetries determining "good" and "evil" and mapping the west into spectator zones and all areas outside the west into sufferer zones.[45] The documentation of human suffering vis-à-vis these images, therefore, does not always tell the full story and yet insist a story must be told.

The image of the pain and suffering of others also moves the viewer back, exempting him/her from the experience. The one who looks consumes the image as something that has happened and will forever happen to someone else.[46] This othering is sanctioned by an imagination that is committed to realising itself as truth through a constellation of images. The visual economy of human rights, I will illustrate below, are practices of disavowal, fantasy pursuits, and psychic gratification that materialise in these campaigns in several ways. By replacing empathy with pity, boundaries of freedom and constraint, wholeness and fragmentation are established. Empathy here would have suggested similarity and identification while pity creates the other and distances the viewer. The imagining of this "someone else" is best illustrated in the campaign to rescue Muslim women, under what Abu-Lughod calls a new common sense, marking a "transcendent rightness of going to war for women".[47]

These images project Muslim women in crisis, who have been violated and now exhibit bodily symptoms of rights denial. In this vein, the feminist question of looking for the woman in human rights is reformulated: when will *these* women be human?[48] This process is best illustrated by the image of the Afghan woman in the burqa, an image which has dominated the western imaginary of the war in Afghanistan. As Saba Mahmood writes, "[It] was the visual image of the burqa more than anything else that condensed and organised knowledge about Afghanistan and its women, as if this alone could provide an adequate understanding of their suffering".[49] The circulation of her image as an emergency generates a humanitarian impulse to intervene, resurrecting the Spivakian formula of saving brown women from brown men. This formulation marries the fantasy of Matua's savage culture with the powerless victim metaphor to evoke the missionary zeal of a western (white) liberal saviour[50] with the pseudo-truth of this image. In the discourse of human rights, the image is prominent in arousing emotions and judgement, so that its pseudo-truth becomes objectivity as such, totalising in its expression and actuality that it fronts as its ideological impetus.[51]

Spivak (1991, 1999) and Mohanty (1991) have critically analysed feminist and rights discourses' dependence on tropes of third world women as passive victims, abject and unable to speak. Although the geopolitical interests raised in their critiques have not abated, the war on terror has gravitated towards and embedded itself in international rights and humanitarian pro-grammes.[52] The military interventions of Afghanistan, Iraq, Mali, Somalia and Syria are few. Tied to the Bush agenda, the image of the imperilled Muslim woman gained traction in the early years of the wars in Afghanistan and Iraq (2001–2008). However, there was a brief period in which the arrival of Barack Obama's presidency in 2008 along with the hope of demilitarising US foreign policy spelt possibility that the use of this image would also be dispensed. Aisha appeared on the cover of *Time* in 2010, shortly after Obama's election and the images I examine in are images of the post-2008 era. According to Saadia Toor, the impulse to rescue women did sever itself from the Bush agenda but was given new political life and sophistication through the alliance of western left and liberal feminists *and* feminists of the "Global South" who still see "Islamic fundamentalism" as the main threat to Muslim women.[53] Sara Farris traces this alliance to Europe describing it as "femonationalism"—an overlapping of agendas between far-right nationalists, feminists and neoliberals on The Muslim Question, where women's rights are weaponised against Muslim men.

In recent years, the national debates about the status of the Muslim woman, the banning of the veil, and the increasing visibility of Islam within western borders, have triggered further interest in her. These national debates paradoxically place her as a threat to as well as at the mercy of her community. The narratives that encircle and represent her as evidence of the unassimilability of Islam hinge on the broader discourse of the colonial and "third world" woman. They are blended together as a silent testimony to the violence of Islam and its cultural ills plaguing countries deprived of human rights like Iran, Pakistan, Saudi Arabia and Afghanistan. Human rights concerns have also grown on the dangers of patriarchal violence in the activities of transnational jihadist movements like, Boko Haram in west Africa and Islamic State of Iraq and Levant (ISIS) in the Middle East. These narratives of policing "Islamland" and the over-policing of Muslim men speak to the emotionally and politically charged weight of the endangered Muslim woman.

Stories of honour killings, acid-attacks, forced marriages, forced veiling, stoning and gender segregation are often accompanied by particular geographies: South Asia and the Middle East, and few from Asia and even fewer from Africa with the exception of female genital mutilation (FGM). Nonetheless, even Asian and African contexts are seen through a lens that is Islamophobic or Arab-fixated: Islamic culture vis-à-vis Arab culture is represented as an export of misery to even more abject people. There is an effort to constantly locate Islam in its desert dwellings perhaps due to the history of orientalist imagery that it has inspired. This link is observed in the work of Fareed Zakaria, advisor on foreign policy to the former U.S. President George W. Bush, who links *The Problem With Islam* with the culture and mentality of the Arabs specifically which, he claims, is spreading to non-Arab societies. After September 11, he asked, "why is this region the political basket case of the world?... the straggler in the march of modern society".[54] Similarly, in her call to reform Islam, author of *The Trouble With Islam Today*, Irshad Manji blames the Arab "desert culture" or "desert tribalism" for colonising non-Arab Muslim cultures through what she calls "cultural capitulation".[55] The trouble with Islam for Manji is its literal reading of religious text and refusal to modernise. The desert, dry and barren, is invoked as a metaphor for the blankness of thought, civilisational regression and extinction. In contrast, Muslim women from African countries appear under the trope of what Pamela Scully describes as the "vulnerable African woman" whose victimhood, often related to sexual violence in conflict or post-conflict environment, is in need of humanitarian protection.[56] Orientalist discourses on women from the Middle East and South-East Asia, however, are constructed as vulnerable through harmful cultural practices attributed to Islam.[57] Both are produced and arranged through a politics of pity to discover the depredation of brown and black female bodies. Both position human rights governance as an encounter with "culture".[58] However, with the increasing alarm over the rise of fundamentalism in Somalia (al-Shabab), Nigeria (Boko Haram) and Mali (al-Qaeda), the "vulnerable African woman" has merged with the Imperilled (veiled) Muslim Woman, amid narratives of sexual violence, policing, forced marriage and veiling.[59] These scenes of "flesh in peril",[60] made visible by a history of naming,[61] drive the post-political claims of the modern humanitarianism.

Depoliticising the binary of "good" and "evil", the Muslim woman's visibility authorises the certainty of the dangers women face in imagined deserts, environments of excess violence and destitute, untouched by secular modernity's achievements, and whose veiled bodies have yet to realise and experience the integrity of rights. The image of the veiled Muslim woman, lays bare what Mahmood contends is a terrain of a series of historical assumptions internal to liberal, feminist and secular imaginaries that make benevolent interventions across the globe palatable, if not advisable, to those across the political spectrum.[62] As the ground in which emotions—empathy and moral indignation—convert into the human rights political project, the veiled woman's reoccurring image affirms and secures liberal values, which associate sexuality with liberation, and unveiling with the arrival of unrestrained desires and freedom. The following images of Muslim women feed its progressive narrative, positioning her in different iterations of lack in order to allow her western spectators to re-imagine the possibilities of retrieving the lost object of their pre-discursive self.

THE VEILED WOMAN AS A METAPHOR, THE METAPHOR AS A VEILED WOMAN

Human rights discourse is one of intersubjectivity between others and us, where the west presupposes that others await the experience of their freedom through human rights. Lacan has it that the Other is called upon to reaffirm and provide security for the subject's identity. For instance, when we perceive another individual as someone who lacks rights, it is inferred that "we" have them.[63] The Lacanian mirror stage indicates the importance of the image in the imagining and making of the subject. The image is a mirage[64] because it does not guarantee representation of the subject. It eludes the drives of the subject in their fragmented state. The image suppresses the subject's ontological fragmentation through symbolic stabilisation, by providing it the fantasy of total meaning and ontological security. The other as image, the extension of the subject's imaginary, appears in human rights campaigns to guarantee the possibility of what Lacanian Bruce Fink calls, "unfailing jouissance": if *jouissance* is an enjoyment that always fails, disappoints, terrifies and dissatisfies, unfailing *jouissance* is the possibility of perpetual satisfaction.[65] The documentation of abuse, the political horrors of flesh in crisis, exhibit the *fragmentation of subjectivity* for the human rights advocate in order to make possible the full satisfaction of *jouissance,* vis-à-vis the secular practice of self-cultivation and rights retrieval.

Images of veiled women portray and over-emphasise the lack that human rights promise to fill. As Lacan puts it, the function of the veil is to create an absence, a lack and thus, the desire to fulfil it: "one can even say that with the presence of the curtain [the veil], what is beyond as lack tends to be realised as image" and place where "absence" can be projected.[66] Exploring lack and desire in modernity, Lacanian theorist Renata Salecl argues that rights in modernity's symbolic organisation allow us to articulate our desire to be recognised as whole. Distinguishing between need, demand and desire, Salecl contends that the biological concept of need is already mediated by the symbolic, which transfers it into a demand—a demand to the Other to satisfy. Desire arises from the excess of demand over need, as not everything can be reduced to need and cannot be entirely articulated in language, which as we recall, always fails the subject in articulating its desire.[67] This failure or lack at the heart of the subject is presented in the object that stands in for the demand that remains unsatisfied. In modernity, lack is produced in the modern subject who gives up wholeness—sovereignty—and security, and chooses between joining a community or being excluded.[68] This lack, Eric Santner, describes as being left with the "missing flesh" of sovereignty.[69] Rights, Salecl argues, are the reward for this sacrifice—that is, the prohibition imposed by the symbolic. As a substitute, rights are an *object a*—what is leftover from an imagined social integrity and substitute for lack. It is the *object a* that sustains the fantasy of unveiling's promissory note which makes possible the secular body.

The theme of desiring wholeness through rights or facing exclusion is discerned in a 2012 campaign poster by human rights organisation Amnesty International.[70] The poster title reads "Human Rights for Women and Girls in Afghanistan" with a sub-title, "NATO: Keep the progress going!" Between the veiled women is a little girl, in bright red and pink attire, who is looking directly at the camera that connects the western viewer and the child. This poster, on a Chicago bus-stand, juxtaposes two worlds involved in similar activities, delineated by the presence of the veil—an alien appearance, a barrier preventing emphatic identification by the women walking by. These are the women, the viewer can imagine, who have been excluded from community by the veil. Moreover, daily events are loaded with terrifying possibilities of what "we", supporters of NATO, understand as an everyday "reality" of modern life. This is the cultural stain of the veiled woman; whose hypervisibility distorts the otherwise normal scene.[71]

The poster was aimed for a NATO summit in Chicago in 2012 featuring former United States Secretary of State, Madeline Albright. The summit promoted feminist justifications for the war and claimed that women's conditions have improved over the last 11 years. Such claims, Toor contends, are contrary to evidence of women's status as "seriously *declined*" since the invasion and the consistent critique of Afghan women activists like Malalai Joya.[72] After criticism for its endorsement of NATO, Amnesty issued a statement qualifying that they simply meant life for women has improved since the ousting of the Taliban.[73] By reproducing binaries of humanitarian warriors (NATO) and violent fundamentalism (the Taliban), the poster demarcates civilisational boundaries. Amnesty's poster, however, persuasively situates the viewer to identify with NATO's progress as a positive catalyst for change.

In the Amnesty International image, the girl gestures to the role of the oedipal child, struggling to articulate her demand, her desire for pre-oedipal unity. Her eyes, staring back, will her entry to a "civilised" (modern) community, through the offer of rights. The link is central to introducing the moral agent called upon as witness. The child's presence evokes an ethics of responsibility, reminiscent of the scene from Steven Spielberg's film *Schindler's List*. In the movie, the innocence and vulnerability of the girl in red coat stands out from the dreariness of the Third Reich. Like in *Schindler's List*, the girl in the Amnesty International's poster captures the onlooker's gaze, impressing that lost beneath the sea of dehumanising veils is innocence and purity of self. The Third Reich and the Taliban repress rights. Her red coat connotes endangered morals, evoking the European fairytale of Little Red Riding Hood who is threatened by a wolf posing as her grandmother. The veiled women beside her imitate a similar veiled masquerade in the tale: concealing danger.

The ominous tone is also captured in the little girl who, like little red riding hood, gestures to the anxious beginnings of the liberal subject. Writing about the constitution of liberal subjectivity in the myths and narrative of children's literature, Desmond Manderson suggests that the child prefigures the noble savage who represents the "good" of humanity. The comparison posits the child as vulnerable and innocent, but these traits also mean that the child must be violently disciplined—the "duty to civilise"—to safeguard civilisation from the child's potential contamination.[74] Therefore, the emphasis on the child in these images is not simply about vulnerability but also about the transition from childhood to adulthood, a passage that demands an "educated choice".

The child in red in the Amnesty International poster also humanises the faceless women dehumanised beneath the veil. Like the little girl in red coat from the movie, the girl in the poster infuses the dreary scene with her universal humanity—a "good"—that has not, it is inferred, been entirely obliterated—by the Nazi-like violent fundamentalism of the Taliban. It remains free of the veiled wolf: monstrous and callous in its *consumption* of innocence. The theme of Little Red Riding Hood is reproduced again in a promotional poster, capturing a scene from the fourth season of the TV show *Homeland* in 2014. It conveys the main character, Central Intelligence Agency agent Carrie Mathison (Claire Danes), in a red scarf amid a crowd of black veiled women. White, blonde and blue-eyed, Mathison embodies a similar role of innocence, surrounded by the threat of a veil that may also be imagined through the Little Red Riding Hood metaphor as a pack of black wolves.[75] Lacan reminds us that repetition imagines the subject's connection with the lost object (*object a*) at the same time it misses it.[76] The recurring theme of Red Riding Hood is an anchor that puts together a narrative of good and evil, the rights of the deserving (innocent) and the perpetrators who threaten them.

Hollywood and humanitarianism are curiously interlaced in these three scenes of danger and rescue. As western cultural production, their message congeals under the banner of a freedom that has yet to arrive. Amnesty International's poster postulates that the dehumanising veil is the fate of this young girl, but also indicates the hope—or more precisely, desire—for something else. Desire comes in the form of Progress,[77] conveyed through the magnetic gaze that looks back to its audience. The CIA's intelligence gathering, the NATO and its "coalition of the willing", are summoned to keep the encroaching veil at bay to ensure Afghanistan's (Islamland's) future generations are not denied modernity. The poster is marketed to a western public, identifying the duty of protecting this young girl, and a reminder of why "we"—the coalition are there. The spectator is the individual viewer and international legal institutions[78] of the civilised, both bound to the image and assuming the responsibility to act.[79] The emboldened tone of keeping "progress" going and imagining an Afghanistan with young girls enjoying rights and dignity sets the scene for a western *gestalt*, made possible through the offer of freedom[80] and the only guarantee that the little girl remains unveiled—free.

Desiring Rights

The west here announces itself as the bearer of human rights, or as Salecl posits, *presupposing a subject that has been fulfilled.*[81] The promise of human rights in the image of the NATO is imagined as only possible with the NATO's continued mission in Afghanistan. The offer of rights in the unified discourse of human rights therefore,

> strives to produce the impression that the subject has already been attained. By claiming that we have human rights which the state must guarantee, we presuppose that the object of desire is already ours: all we need to do is to describe and codify it in law. The discourse of human rights thus presents a

fantasy scenario in which society and the individual are perceived as whole, as no-split. In this fantasy, society is understood as something that can be rationally organised, as community that become non-conflictual if only it respects "human rights".[82]

The image in human rights campaigns displays a lack as well as the desire to retrieve and attain what is missing.[83] Desire, which gives purpose to the subject, is maintained by inventing new rights in an endless attempt to fill in the fundamental lack, a completion that is always deferred.[84] Unveiling rights, through Lacan's lens, identifies a "crucial dimension of desire—it is always desire in the second degree, desire of desire".[85] Unveiling guides a possible response to the Other's question, a way of imagining the Muslim woman, but never actually arrives entirely at an answer because desire fails at the point of total disclosure. Pleasure arises not from getting what one wants (rights) but rather from engaging with the *object a*.[86] This deferral is cogently detected in the call for the NATO to keep progress going because there are always violations to be addressed, more rights to be attained, more enjoyment (of possible wholeness) to be had.

The pursuit for rights sustains a fantasy that presents human rights society and the individual as complete with each right bringing one closer to ontological integrity.[87] The body, as Asad argues, is the locus of moral sovereignty in secular modernity. To deny its rights is a violation to the fundamentals of what it means to be human.[88] The body's integrity is presupposed in the discourse of rights. From Salecl's observations, Douzinas, we recall from the previous chapter, argues the law breaks the body down into functions and parts replacing its unity with rights, which symbolically compensate for bodily wholeness. Rights dismember the body: each part demanding different rights, different recognition to achieve wholeness.[89] This psychoanalytic reading of rights helps to explain why rights persist despite their paradoxes and theoretical and political pitfalls. It is because they allow the subject to desire and shield the body from the impossibility of wholeness.[90] In this vein, one can read the militant humanitarian intervention in Mali, Syria, Iraq and Afghanistan for human rights as an *intentional deferral of rights*: breaking down bodies in order to sustain the desire for rights. Douzinas' observation is apt: these interventions mark the paradox of human rights as ideologically dominant at a time of human rights' greatest violations.[91] In this mode, the call for the NATO to maintain progress professes the tension between the on-going progress of universalising rights and their on-going violations.

In Amnesty International's 2010 campaign "ignore us, ignore human rights", a similar civilisational demarcation is observed. The campaign, which won a Silver Lion in Press award at Cannes International Advertising Festival 2010, includes a collection of images of a crowd of people who have turned away from an execution, while someone is being beaten. While the beating appears to be in an African context, the executions and rebels are clearly set in Afghanistan and Pakistan. Nevertheless, in the fantasy scenario of saving women from *other* men—the conflation of geographies is intentional as the oppressive man is what Matua notes is representative of the "savage" culture that victimises and inspires heroism. The crowd of people have their backs turned away from a veiled woman who is about to be executed by two men presumed to be members of the Taliban. What is striking about this image is the western appearance of this crowd—consisting mostly of white men—representing the "international community" who are failing to address human rights violations in the country. The image invokes earlier incidents of Taliban executions of women in Afghan stadiums. These images were circulated in the build-up to the 2001 invasion and the earlier years of the war.[92] While the audiences of these executions were Afghans, it is not the Afghans that this campaign is addressing. Afghans are implicated in the violence against women, therefore, requiring an outside (western) intervention. This intervention is imaginatively represented by the presence of a western-looking crowd turned away from the victim. Whereas Afghan women are subject to the veil and stoning, connoting gender segregation, the bodies gathered together as witnesses are not segregated by gender nor entirely covered by the veil. Rights-bearers, it suggests, require uncovered desiring bodies. The image of the violated Muslim woman is a reminder of the subject's lack and the not-yet-fulfilled promise of human rights. The message "ignore us, ignore human rights" replaces the voice of the crouched woman who is about to be executed, thereby suggesting that her voice—her desire to escape her circumstances—is only barely audible, if she is even speaking at all, in the language of human rights.[93]

The violations perpetrated against Muslim women are presented as violations of her bodily integrity, denying recognition of her complete subjectivity, and bolstering her desire for human dignity and equality, which the fantasy of freedom imagines can be fulfilled only by rights. The possibility of rights failing to fulfil her desire and thus the possibility of not knowing what freedom is, is concealed by the imaging of her lack in a "seeing is believing" paradigm.[94] The power of this paradigm and the threat posed to rights being deferred or *taken away,* is brought to sharp relief in the frequently circulated black and white photograph of young Afghan women in short skirts, smiling, walking down a Kabul street in 1972.[95] This image has been circulated in social media over the past few years as "history in moments" (a history that we are often reminded) or to lament the loss of freedom Afghan women once had. A quick search on Twitter and Facebook reveals a curious commitment by the general public or political pages (far-right, women's rights, political atheists) to the brute truth of the photograph, as gestures of performative astonishment of how different the country was in the past. It is often depicted as a "before" and "after" with images of women in blue burqas and as a warning of Islam's political and cultural ambitions against the west's "way of life". The reproductive capacity of this image has transformed it into a meme, a dependable reference to condense western sentiments on Afghanistan as a place where once there was no Taliban and a reminder of what has been lost to the extremism that now the war on terror battles. The United Kingdom's chapter of Amnesty International used this image on the 25 November 2014 to illustrate to their followers of how much rights have been rolled back in Afghanistan since the 1970s, which they identify with the Soviet invasion and the subsequent civil war among different Afghan factions to be responsible. The 2001 invasion by the Coalition of the Willing, led by the United States is presented as an international force fighting to improve women's rights in the country. Like its 2012 NATO poster endorsing Operation Enduring Freedom, Amnesty International's use of this image is to vie with the forces that keep progress at bay for women and girls in Afghanistan. One celebrates progress and the arrival of freedom, the other laments the loss of freedom.

In August 2017, the image reappeared in mainstream media and went viral on social media. After initially calling for military withdrawal and describing the war as a "waste", the U.S. President Donald Trump declared his recommitment to the war in Afghanistan. It was reported that one of the reasons he had a change of heart was after being shown the image of unveiled Afghan women by national security advisor H. R. McMaster to persuade him. McMaster's strategy was to demonstrate that there was evidence of Afghanistan's capacity to receive western norms. If one can witness that it was present in the past, then the country was not a lost cause, and still had the capacity to desire freedom. So dominant was the image of the blue burqa-clad woman in reading Afghanistan, it had become a monstrous incarnation of all the bad things that are associated with the country and its failed state status. To think of an Afghanistan without the blue menace was a shock to the system and added to the excitement for the war effort. Trump's response to a singular image that marks a swift policy shift demonstrates how veiled and unveiled bodies of Afghan women are adequate reference for understanding the country's historical, political and cultural realities. It mattered little that the image is misleading, suggesting that all Afghan women dressed this way when they are the only representative of a minority urban elite, and that the burqa was widely worn at the time when there was no Taliban enforcing it.[96] The 1970s image is powerful because it is a visual guarantor for the moral vision of bringing freedom to the Muslim woman.

Factual truths are rendered secondary when the humanitarian pulse is racing with urgency that something must be done, and it must be done soon. In more recent years, the war to protect women has found a new front for humanitarian activists in Syria and Iraq. Stories of women enslaved by "extremists" under the label Islamic State of Iraq and Levant (or State) (ISIL/ISIS) have dominated western coverage of the conflict in Syria and the war in Iraq since the U.S.-led invasion in March 2003. The reporting of these stories is a telling insight to an empowered moral good in the unqualified and frequent condemnation by those that witness the gross human rights violations which were occurring. The judgement was swift and the desire for western intervention was revived by a similar coalition of the willing, galvanised by a common sense to protect women. The language that described the activities attributed to ISIS spoke of a desire for judgement in its hyperbolic, emotive and racialized wording: "medieval", "brutality", "extremist", "savagery", "terrifying", "horror". [97] The language appears to describe what it cannot bear to understand. It serves as an emotional barrier, piled on by layers of condemnation in a refusal to understand because barbarism is beyond comprehension. It is only to be recited as a gross violation to modern sensibilities. The danger of "this new enemy" provoked also a military response with Australia, the United States and the United Kingdom sending troops. The heightened security threat has also been raised by the online influence ISIS was having on young Muslims around the world, in particular in western countries. New counterterrorism laws have been declared to respond to this threat with passports of men with dual citizenship cancelled, further surveillance and criminal convictions.[98]

In this moral tale of rescue and the anxious atmospheric of new and hidden enemies, the details of actual events seemed to have become a secondary priority. The image in Fig. 3.1 was widely circulated on social media

Fig. 3.1 Women in black chador in south Lebanon participating in a Shiite theatrical performance. April 11, 2011 (Re-used with kind permission from Reuters)

and tabloid papers. The image is of women in black chador veils with chains, lined up and said to be enslaved women of ISIS. This image has been repeatedly used in online spaces such as far-right groups opposed to immigration to corroborate the dangers of Islamisation of the west; Zionists in their support for Israel's policies against Palestinians; as an expression of outrage at the violations of women's rights, and even used without reference in an academic blog when analysing gender and security.[99] The certainty of the moral outrage coalesces with the certainty of *what is believed is seen*. To be a witness is to gain moral knowledge of the world. Images of veiled women as we have seen already engender disquiet in western audiences, but veiled women in chains hasten the moral disgust felt in the covered body attributed to jihadism.

However, this image is not that of ISIS female prisoners, rather they are Shiite worshippers participating in a religious procession in Southern Lebanon in 2013.[100] The stark difference in fact from fiction is a remarkable insight into a contemporary crisis of ethical witnessing as vulnerable to political contamination.[101] In this case, it is not simply one of a reductive reading of an image but a *misrecognition* all together. The image is ominous and horrifying as it brings together the Fanonian phobogenic nature of the veil *as chains*—constraining the naturally secular body—and Islam as a contagion that appears as an imperilling mass. The overpowering sense of this image's affective effect operates as a symbolic knowledge in of itself. It reminds that the image embodies a way of seeing which requires narrative, language, a history, to give it intelligibility. In the secular language of rights and freedom, there is an absence of naming women who willingly wear heavy veils in chains to demonstrate in a religious ceremony.

In his study of disgust, William Ian Miller contends that any breach of human indignities and violations can be disgusting to behold,[102] here, expressed in the covered body as waste. Without identity or desire, the woman beneath, like Clérambault's heavily veiled Moroccan women, it is implied, is valueless—*wasted*. The violence of the other's being is imagined here as the wasteland of desire, of an identity that once was, an enjoyment that could be had, as the death of *jouissance* and with the absence of rights which promise permanent satisfaction, disappears. The veil, wrapped around her entire body, is imagined as a body wrapped up in the regressions of culture that denies enjoyment and bodily integrity. The veil instead "obliterates the expressive body".[103] There is nothing left but the "fact" of the crime scene, the pain—no traces of her rights; the spectator is recast as the criminal investigator, the purveyor of justice for "oppressed women" everywhere. The severity of her pitiable state, the emergency amplified to manic levels, the unfathomable inhumane conditions and the absolute desperation in escaping it, suggests a dream-like—*phantasmic*—dimension in the repetitiveness of the same image.

The theme of captivity persisted in April 2014 with the kidnapping of 276 Nigerian girls from their school in the town of Chibok in Borno State by the Nigerian militant group Boko Haram. In response, a global campaign #BringBackOurGirls was launched that recruited celebrities such as Michelle Obama, politicians, the Pope, Malala Yusufzai and other activists around the world, holding placards with the hashtag. The grainy still shot in Fig. 3.2 from the video of the captured girls released by the group accompanied much of the coverage of the global response. The girls, huddled together, wearing long blue scarves reminiscent of the Afghan blue burqa, stare back from their miserable state. The image tells us of a familiar horror story where young women and girls are vulnerable to dangerous men who have committed themselves to the idea that western education was a sin

Fig. 3.2 Still image from Boko Haram footage (Re-used with kind permission from AFP photo)

and would kidnap, rape and abuse to deliver this message. The theme of imprisonment also taps into old orientalist imagery of Muslim women as exotic captives of the harem and the veil. Captivity evokes high profiled critics like Ayaan Hirsi Ali who described the veil as "a mental cage" with its women trapped behind its mental bars.[104] Like the ISIS case, we are not only dealing with the captivity of Muslim girls but some of these girls were not of the same faith. In the imaginary scene of fragmentation, the state of crisis as the veil descends, imagines them all as Muslim girls.

Reflecting on the #BringBackOurGirls campaign, Ajisafe observes the intense media coverage of the incident and campaign and points to research showing how *The New York Times* between 1985 and 1995 published only seven stories pertaining to the region and four to any insurgency in the region. However, from 2009 to 2015, it published 453 stories on Boko Haram. What explains this sudden interest? Why do terrorist narratives capture global attention and lead to further indulging in the gory details of the violence done to bodies—the bloodshed, dismemberment, *the cutting*? Ajisafe concludes these stories exist to secure a hegemonic self who can be measured against a "troubling other": the disfigured African body where all kinds of violence are made possible and where the fight against terrorism is validated.[105] This is a body that is never whole, a non-human object or objects, drowning in traditions of impoverishment, conflict and excess violence—only to be recounted but rarely understood. The corporeal tour of unrestrained violence on captive bodies, crumbling with every affliction, sanctions the imagining of freedom's arrival via rights inscribed on the liberated secular body where violence is barred.

These images hint at the collusion of humanitarian concerns with the humiliation they contest. As Badiou reminds us, the need to emphasise the self-evidence of "evil" occurs in order for "public opinion" to pass its judgement and to respond with the "good" that human rights can offer.[106] Arguably, the suffering subject must first be exhibited, brutalised, humiliated, dehumanised and portrayed as deprived of human dignity, before the certainty of the violation, the judgment that follows, and its offer of rights can be fulfilled.[107] As an epistemic intrusion into the meaning of this suffering and experience, the images dismiss the possibility that these may not be translatable.[108] Like The Afghan Girl, the images are only communicable through western desire. The totalising nature of these representations suggests their purpose not as translating pain, but to present this pain as so crushing that it renders the women unable to speak for themselves. Thus, the viewer is the one who experiences pain. If, and when, she is finally granted agency and a voice to demand her rights and to articulate her pain, the veiled woman is strategically placed to demand further western intervention.

The veil as ontology of the Muslim woman evokes what Wendy Brown calls a suffering and injured body intelligible only through a discourse of cultural inflictions. In the fantasy of unveiling freedom, the veiled woman embodies these "injured" identities that seek protection from liberal states. She is a metaphor for the injured body.[109] Her haunting through the veil is represented by an inventory of repressive narratives from honour killings, stoning, acid-attacks, and mutilation of genitals, testifying the figure of the veiled woman. In this mode, the violence done to Muslim women's bodies manifests as visible and invisible symptoms of lack.

Observing that language often fails the one who experiences pain and injury, Scarry contends that a weapon and a wound can help attribute pain to a body and aid in expression.[110] The veil, similarly, occasions a way of imagining and expressing this pain. The veil's intimate proximity to the body makes language less ambiguous and knowledge of the other more certain.[111] Playing the role of both the weapon and the wound, the veil is a violence (the weapon) and the wound (cultural injury), gripping her body.[112] In the image of her beating, she is already an injured body (the veil) before the gun has gone off. Imagining her unveiling is the "language of agency", removing this weapon and healing her body.

Consuming Freedom

The circulation of the veiled woman as an emergency in these campaigns infers the natural condition of the unveiled body that enjoys freedom. Just as we have seen her image popularised in these campaigns that aim to popularise the dignity of all humans, stories on the wonders of unveiling have often followed. We have witnessed for instance the arrival of freedom in the painted faces of Afghan women who marked the "aesthetisation of women's bodies" in Afghanistan. In a country where the visible female body has been criminalised by the Taliban—who, it is reported, banned or restricted the wearing of heeled shoes, cosmetics, salons, fashion—these are faces of defiance, daring to display and enjoy their bodies. Similarly, for women heavily veiled by ISIS who are enslaved, forced to fulfil the desires of men. Such restrictions are narrated as dehumanising barbaric practices, which deny the "natural" human condition.[113]

Nevertheless, this unveiling of freedom is always a precarious one. Ellen McLarney identifies this in what was coined as a "lipstick revolution" where Afghan women rediscovered themselves through the enjoyment of their bodies. The aesthetisation of their bodies aimed more to rehabilitate Afghan women in the market from which they had been excluded by newly inscribing them with the signifiers of consumerism.[114] The unveiling of the Afghan female body became an untapped resource (the *real* resource being sought).[115] The commercialisation of the veiled woman continues this aestheticisation with the visibility and recognition of veiled Muslim women in entertainment and fashion industry increasingly tied to consumption.[116] The painted "visible" face, the body that enjoys, communicates familiarity through the universal signatures of choice, individualism and consumption. The veiled face, in contrast, seen through western eyes, is not just alienating, but also alien, abnormal and strange.[117]

Framing freedom as bodily aesthetics, the visibility of desire through the flesh, establishes the relationship between "being" human and the *consumption* of freedom. The biopolitical shaping of bodies—tweaking, dying, primping and painting, suggests a bodily subject to manage under neoliberalism's investment in new forms of enjoyment through the freely available unveiled secular body. Minoo Moallem argues that these "representational practices call upon Afghan women to take on the marks of white western femininity to become subjects".[118] Signs of consumption on the body have a universalising affect, evidencing the human. Thus, there is an untapped desire to be human under the veil; a desire that becomes articulable only through rights. The unveiled is imagined as a "natural condition" of *zoe*—a natural desire—in which these images are violent departures and fragments of the human. This is a desire interpellated as consumption viewed as a part of human nature and "adornment as a basic human right".[119] The rehabilitation of a primal self—that is, the legal activation of *zoe*—occurs through practices of consumerism, which gives them their humanity, control over their bodies and a wellness of being—a dignified wholeness. The *bios* of rights offers choices, individualism, autonomy and a "legal" desire to pursue multiple selves; "natural" human traits mirrored only through the "naturalness" of the flesh that exhibit them.

The burqa, McLarney observes, became "a dividing line between human and the inhuman, the person and the non-person, the normal and the abnormal". The unveiled face, we recall from Judith Butler, is "a condition of humanisation" that wars must be waged for.[120] But the promise of "wholeness" vis-à-vis the unveiling can only possess its power when veiled.[121] Like Aisha's cosmetic surgery, the enjoyment of freedom is only attainable when juxtaposed with the realisation that the painted face is vulnerable to being veiled again. In the politics of pity and the economy of desire in human rights campaigns, the Muslim woman is imagined as *always being veiled*. The veiled woman here is a screen, an ideological projection, for desires.[122] Just as the Orient comes into existence through a "systemic discipline of *accumulation*",[123] the veiled woman cannot be presented outside of this image as a stage of western imagining. She rarely speaks.

WHEN SHE SPEAKS

The case of 18-year-old Saudi Rahaf Mohamed Al-Qunun captured the world's attention in early January 2019 after she announced on social media that she had barricaded herself in a Bangkok hotel. She was refusing to leave with her family back to Saudi Arabia. She tweeted about her decision to renounce Islam, her abusive family, the oppressive conditions of Saudi women and the laws that sanction this abuse by denying her rights. Images of her flanked with white women accompanied reports of her arrival in Canada which had swiftly accepted her as a refugee rather than a claimant.[124] The story is remarkable at a time when millions of people from Syria and Afghanistan are seeking refugee status. The viral nature of the story demonstrates humanitarian intervention is one that is empowered by, what Shenila Khoda-Moolji contends is, an individual act of empowerment[125] which I have been tracing in the fantasy of unveiling the ideal, worthy rights-bearer, in the signature of a face among a sea of veils. This ideal appears most frequently in young vulnerable women victimised less by war and more by a "savage" culture of hostile irrational men she is daring to escape. Soon after her arrival in Canada, Rahaf Mohammed shed her family name "Al-Qunun" and Snapchat photos circulated in the media of her eating bacon for the first time, drinking Starbucks, and wearing a dress that showed her bare legs. Her unveiling is marked by the consumption of a once forbidden freedom and the body as witness to this new enjoyment.

However, one must not have to exit Islam and consume bacon to meet the conditions of recognition. Perhaps the most prominent example of the haunting presence of the veiled woman is Pakistani schoolgirl, Malala Yousufzai. Shot by the Taliban on 9 October 2012, Malala's ordeal has captured the world and galvanised global opinion. Approximately 100,000 people signed a petition for her to receive the Nobel Peace Prize and the United Nations declared a "Malala Day" in solidarity.[126] Heavily shrouded in her veil, appearing from the darkness but entering the light—summoning her unveiling to the world as a survivor of the veil, Malala appeared on *Time*'s front page as a runner-up in the magazine's Person of the Year contest in 2012. She has since been received by the former President of the U.S. Barack Hussein Obama, appeared on multiple talk shows[127] and written a book titled *I Am Malala* about her experience.[128] The attention Malala generated—dubbed as the "Malala phenomenon"[129]—raises the question of what it was about her that captured the western imagination? Malala is from the province of Waziristan, notorious as an area that is frequently droned by the United States, and killing up to 3000 civilians, of which 176 were children.[130] The attention she has received therefore, requires close attention.[131]

The interest in Malala has been impressive in its diversity. It has included feminists, policymakers, politicians, journalists, celebrities and NGOs. Much of the attention she has received has been carried through a narrative of strong emotions from shock, horror, anger, to compassion and admiration. The affective tone of the coverage of Malala has positioned Malala's story as an opportunity to alert the world to the threat of fundamentalism. western liberal feminists like Ida Lichter and the Former U.S. First Lady Laura Bush spoke out angrily about the shooting incident. They used the incident to speak about the continued challenges facing women in Afghanistan and the necessity to act.[132] Lichter warned feminists that Malala's experiences mark urgency, and stressed that feminists should not be "dallying while their Muslim sisters burn".[133] Talk shows like *The Ellen*

Show[134] and *The Daily Show with Jon Stewart*,[135] ritually expressed feelings of shock captured in the question: who could do this to a young girl? This was accompanied by expressions of admiration at her courage and determination, followed by frequent and rapturous audience applause. This reception elucidates how Malala is positioned in an economy of emotions that elicit a public desire to connect with a young girl from Pakistan as a "west" whose capacity to feel these emotions gives it a greater duty to the victims of human rights violations—to *being human*.

Like *Amnesty International*'s NATO poster, Malala's violent ordeal reminds her western audience of the young girl in red, seeking refuge and simply longing for the right to an education that has been denied by religious fundamentalism. By reducing her ordeal to that of a desire for education, the history of the Taliban and the geopolitical setting for its contemporary violence is erased. The bullet that entered Malala's head cemented, for many in the west, the violence that is inflicted on Muslim women. The bullet also silences voices of protest from the communities such figures hail from. Like the burqa, Malala is the visible case against the Taliban and against Islamic fundamentalism. Her body, reappearing in the theatres of western media, bears witness to the violations done to all women's bodies in her home country. Her injured body is all that needs to be known about the conditions in which Malala sought the universal right to education.

In addition to her campaign for universal education, Malala has also joined the campaign to eradicate female genital circumcision or "mutilation", as some call it—a tradition that is not well-known and rarely practised in Pakistan.[136] Malala's involvement in the anti-"FGM" campaign under the rationale of supporting *all* girls, thus conflating "FGM" with the right to education, strips away necessary complexities in the experiences of violence within an increasingly militarised Pakistan and couples it with long-held traditional practices in a host of countries with distinct histories and cultures. The cultural geographies of these bodies merge in a politics of emotions where feelings of shock, horror, anger, disgust and pity serve as social fact and *reasoned* reactions.

In the "new common sense", the war for the protection of Muslim women, third world women and girls like Malala are recruited as self-evidential victims of culture. Referring to dowry murders in India, Ratna Kapur notes how culture linked to violence occupies the popular imaginary because it essentialises and exoticises the other: the Indian Woman's body in flames, the African Woman being mutilated,[137] and I argue, the

Muslim woman being veiled. Culture as Sally Engle Merry observes, happens "over there"—in Indian villages, African huts, and the Muslim street—and not in UN offices and conference rooms. Culture, Merry continues, has historically been juxtaposed to civilisation, which continues to inform contemporary thought.[138] Through the cultural representation of suffering, the experience of "other" women is remade, thinned out and distorted.[139] Ultimately, their intimate and painful experiences are repackaged to sell the violence of "culture" whereby the others' lives become commodities for western consumption. The insistence on such limited representation is part of western demand for narrative, imagining an uncontested binary of "culture vs. civilisation" through the proximities of the veiled and unveiled.

Malala has a paradoxical role though as she is depicted as both victim and survivor. Behind her youth, beauty and innocence is The Afghan Girl. She is the little girl who NATO is asked to protect. She embodies the spirit of NATO's delivery of progress. She is Aisha surviving her ordeal thanks to the medical technologies of western doctors. The bodily affliction by the veil qua the bullet that entered her head, and managing to survive it, was her rebirth. She represents the modern child's turbulent coming of age. Received as a heroine in the west, she is projected as part of the unveiling tale whose fragile life was almost taken away. As a survivor, one can consider that she is still haunted by the veil in that her relevance does not extend beyond the original violence done to her.

The retelling of her experience and her hypervisibility as a return to the cathartic moment of her almost-fatal shooting and her emancipation produces Malala as a phenomenon. Through Butler's lens, we can interpret this phenomenon as the return to the violence, which brought Malala to the west's attention and mediates the value of her life and why it is worth preserving.[140] This original violence differentiates her from all the dead Pakistani children of American drones. It is a violence that classifies the Muslim woman's body as bearing the violence done by culture. Her body in crisis obeys the collective fantasy of a liberating west by allowing the expression of moral indignation, its promotion of human rights for women and children, and the extension of this offer to those who are deemed worthy. Thus, Malala's image comes alive. The complicity of proxy wars, political instability, the destruction of civil society and poverty is superimposed by her image and the imaginary that sustains it. Violence is attributed predominantly to Muslim "culture".[141] Her injuries are mobilised to perform the role of what Whitlock describes as "soft weapons"—autobiographies, memoirs, testimony, life narratives—generated for and appropriated by the war on terror.

The point here is not to present Malala as someone who lacks agency. Rather, it is to suggest that her activism (such as campaigning for education for all girls), in recent years, makes her politically valuable for not simply the Taliban, but also for western interests. Further, she has demonstrated her awareness of the complex factors contributing to violence in her home country, which she made sure to highlight in a meeting with the former U.S. President, when she raised the issue of drones in Pakistan. These details, however, are omitted as soft weapons, as part of the dissemination and consumption of certain categories of information.[142] Malala cannot be heard through the clamour of western discourses of freedom. She and the other young girls ground an arsenal of personal loss attributed to Islam—markers of difference that identify the bodies of (Asian, African, "Third World") female bodies to be saved by a benevolent and civilised west whose benign offer of rights unveils desire.[143]

Other Malalas

This ritual staging of lack and the fantasy of its possible or inevitable fulfilment is powerfully retold in the reappearance of The Afghan Girl in *National Geographic* a few years after her original image appeared. The later image is framed by a new "salvation narrative".[144] Instead of having Sharbat Gul (the Afghan Girl, now middle-aged) holding the photo, it is held instead by a woman in a burqa. The use of the veil here fuses two geopolitical themes from two different periods, and from two juxtaposing Afghanistans: the vulnerable Afghanistan of the Cold War as "our" allies who fought the Soviets and which The Afghan Girl came to embody, and the dangerous Afghanistan as a place of fundamentalism reflected in the burqa that descended—the Afghanistan "we" lost.

The significance of the veiled woman in the "recovering" of The Afghan Girl underlines a western impulse of *looking for the veiled woman in her*. Remaining veiled extends the anticipation of what has become of her, *of her unveiling*. Her presence invites the mission to find The Afghan Girl—who in this image represents the lost woman of Afghanistan, the one the west has loved and longs to see again. The journey to the East by Steve McCurry (the photographer who took Gul's photo in 1985), in search of her, became part of the spectacle of her consumption. The desire to "find" the girl that has haunted and captivated the west, gestures to the mysterious beauty of the Orient imagined beneath the veil and the harem. What beauty has always remained hidden beneath the veil? *Who is she?* The question was so persistent through the camera's lens that even though the team of journalists observed Gul was uncomfortable with being photographed, on both occasions, McCurry's team went ahead with it anyway. The camera's violation of Gul's privacy is captured in her returning glare in both images. Even her annoyance intrigued the journalists and allowed them to further explain her behaviour through cultural tropes of Pashtun gender customs.

We are also told that Gul remarkably never saw the photo of herself all these years, nor did members of her family. In contrast, this is an image that has an over-imposing presence in the west, including for those Afghans that live in it. The tension raises the question that all these images speak to: whose gaze is this image produced for if the locals never look upon it? The image of Gul was never intended for her but about possessing her. The desire to seize Gul through the image, is reflected in Sontag's observation of the image:

> To photograph people is to violate them, by seeing them as they never see themselves, by having knowledge of them that they can never have; it turns people into objects that can be symbolically possessed. Just as a camera is a sublimation of the gun, to photograph someone is a subliminal murder - a soft murder.[145]

Photographing her infers an objectification that resonates with the images of human rights campaigns that produce and circulate the Muslim woman for sanctioning an aggressive western imagination that demands to know. The word "Found" on the front cover of *National Geographic* further suggests the gaze for which this image was produced. There was no Gul, like there was no Malala, until she had been brought into existence through the concerns of her western interlocutors. Like the bullet intended for Malala, the camera similarly aims to erase them both.

The reference to "Found" impresses upon the viewer something that has been lost, *missing*, suggesting that something almost lost can finally be recovered. Recovery is enacted in the project of unveiling, imagined as bringing the Muslim woman into existence. However, as the analysis of these images show, the process of revealing the other by means of unveiling exists in conjunction with a prior process of veiling. Western "ecstasy over the righteousness" of the promise of unveiling forecloses any other reading, including the possibility of never recovering the lost object.[146] This foreclosure represents the limit of securing knowledge sanctioned by an Other that is never secured in its place; beyond her there is nothing, as Said's Orient deduces, because western knowledge is already skewed towards labelling, laying claim to knowing her and knowing what she needs.[147] The other's face is, to put it in Butler's terms, either "the spoils of war" or "the targets of war" but "in every instance, defaced".[148] These images of defacement repetitively announce the Muslim woman as always imagined veiled, always imperilled. The other's face names the violence against the Muslim woman to rationalise humanitarian concern, the war on terror, and the commodification of third world lives as "appropriate subjects for compassion".[149]

Conclusion

By examining images that posit her as the archetype of the human rights subject, this chapter has traced the imagining of the Muslim woman qua the veiled woman, as a symptom of violence. The veil, presented as both specular and non-specular imagery, inscribes violence on her body. The burqa-clad woman, Aisha, The Afghan Girl and Malala, each exemplify the "injured" body under a veil, which is always synonymous with violence. As an *object a*, these images have an imaginary dimension that is "always, by definition, perceived in a distorted way, because outside of this distortion, in itself, *it* does not exist, since it is nothing but the embodiment, the materialisation of this very distortion".[150] This distortion is the fantasy that disavows the nothing, and organises the symbolic register to imagine the veil but also who the veiled woman can potentially be, transposing her into a plaything cast in a light that causes the most excitement and pleasure.[151] Like Said's positional superiority,[152] the veiled woman is a narcissistic projection of the horrors that befall those outside the domain of rights, what Abu-Lughod has called "Islamland", a "mythical place" that "anoints the call to arms for women with transparent goodness", gaining moral capital and political support.[153] By thinking of the veil as an image that secures the violence done to Muslim women, Aisha, Rahaf and Malala are also productions of the veiled woman. If we peel back the material veil, there is always another aggression present, an Aisha, carrying some evidence of violation, some injury transforms into a cause for concern. The very violence of unveiling her in this imaginary—which misrecognises her—goes entirely unnoticed. Convinced by the seeing-as-believing truth of these images, unveiling becomes a cathartic undertaking assuring rights as the eventual promise to releasing the natural condition of the human body—its instincts for freedom. It is the cultural and political work performed by human rights imagery, the elision of any alternative that images provide and the responses it elicits, that reveal a story more about the salvation of western claims to universal selfhood than about the other's protection.

NOTES

1. Jean Baudrillard, *The Transparency of Evil: Essays on Extreme Phenomena*, trans. James Benedict (London and New York: Verso, 1993), 153.
2. See Wendy S. Hesford and Wendy Kozol, *Just Advocacy? Women's Human Rights, Transnational Feminisms, and the Politics of Representation* (New Brunswick: Rutgers University Press, 2005), 1–13.
3. Douzinas, *The End of Human Rights*.
4. Douzinas, *The End of Human Rights*, 9.
5. Joan Wallach Scott, *Sex and Secularism* (Princeton and Oxford: Princeton University Press, 2018), 149.
6. Scott, *Sex and Secularism*, 150.
7. Douzinas, *The End of Human Rights*, 336.
8. Lacan, *Ecrits: The First Complete Edition in English*, 2–3.
9. Douzinas, *The End of Human Rights: Critical Legal Thought at the Turn of the Century*, 320.
10. Abu-Lughod, *Do Muslim Women Need Saving?* 48.
11. Babajide Ishmael Ajisafe, "'All the Things We Could [Se]e by Now [Concerning Violence & Boko Haram], If Sigmund Freud's Wife Was Your Mother': Psychoanalysis, Race, & International Political Theory," *International Journal of Political Theory* 2, no. 1 (2017): 3.
12. Ajisafe, "All the Things We Could [Se]e by Now," 4
13. Yeğenoğlu, *Colonial Fantasies: Towards a Feminist Reading of Orientalism*, 15.
14. Makau Mutua, *Human Rights: A Political and Cultural Critique* (Philadelphia: University of Pennsylvania Press, 2002), 231.
15. Douzinas, *The End of Human Rights*, 320.
16. United Nations, "The Universal Declaration of Human Rights."
17. Douzinas, *The End of Human Rights*.
18. Salecl, *The Spoils of Freedom*, 112.
19. See Mutua, *Human Rights: A Political and Cultural Critique*.
20. See Gayatri Chakravorty Spivak, "Righting Wrongs," *The South Atlantic Quarterly* 103, no. 2/3 (2004): 523–581.
21. See Wendy Brown, "Suffering Rights as Paradoxes," *Constellations* 7, no. 2 (2000). Kapur critiques the neutrality, universality and the narrative of

progress that underpins human rights discourses. See Ratna Kapur, "Human Rights in the 21st Century: Taking a Walk on the Dark Side," *Sydney Law Review* 29, no. 4 (2006): 665–687.

22. See Asad, *Formations of the Secular: Christianity, Islam, Modernity.*
23. See Douzinas, *The End of Human Rights: Critical Legal Thought at the Turn of the Century.*
24. Wendy Brown, "Human Rights and the Politics of Fatalism," *The South Atlantic Quarterly* 103, no. 2/3 (2004): 253.
25. Wendy Brown, "Human Rights and the Politics of Fatalism," 452–453.
26. See Wendy Brown, *States of Injury: Power and Freedom in Late Modernity.*
27. Lynn Hunt, *Inventing Human Rights: A History* (New York: Norton Paperback, 2007), 32.
28. Daniel Lerner referenced in Zachary Lockman, *Contending Visions of the Middle East: The History and Politics of Orientalism*, 2nd ed. (Cambridge: Cambridge University Press, 2010), 138.
29. Yifat Hachamovitch cited in Young, *Judging the Image: Art, Value, Law*, 12.
30. Kennan Ferguson, *The Politics of Judgement: Aesthetics, Identity, and Political Theory* (Lanham: Lexington Books, 1999), 21.
31. Asad, *Formations of the Secular: Christianity, Islam, Modernity*, 111.
32. Susan Sontag, *On Photography* (New York: Rosetta Books, 1973), 3.
33. Sontag, *On Photography*, 14.
34. McClintock, *Imperial Leather: Race, Gender, and Sexuality in the Colonial Contest*, 59.
35. See discussion of Hugh Diamond's photographs of the asylum and how they emitted savagery, lack of consciousness and even unfamiliarity with the world around them, in John Illiopoulos, "Baudrillard and a Short History of Psychiatric Photography," *International Journal of Baudrillard Studies* 11, no. 1 (2014).
36. McClintock, *Imperial Leather: Race, Gender, and Sexuality in the Colonial Contest.*
37. Sherene Razack, "Stealing the Suffering of Others: Reflection of Canadian Humanitarian Responses," *Review of Education Pedagogy and Cultural Studies* 24, no. 4 (2007): 376.
38. Scarry, *The Body in Pain*, 6.
39. Gillian Whitlock, *Soft Weapons: Autobiography in Transit* (Chicago: University of Chicago Press, 2009), 9.
40. For example #bringbackourgirls—a 2014 campaign on Twitter against the kidnapping of Nigerian school girls by Nigerian fundamentalist group, Boko Haram.
41. For instance, the meme uses imagery, accompanied by a witty or catchy message—often for entertainment purposes, but increasingly, used to carry a political message—that informs, provides a particular social and political commentary, and aims to be memorable.

42. Hesford, *Spectacular Rhetorics*, 8.
43. Badiou, *Ethics: An Essay on the Understanding of Evil*, 8.
44. Referenced and discussed in Hunt, *Inventing Human Rights*, 19.
45. Lilie Chouliaraki quoted in Hesford, *Spectacular Rhetorics*, 7.
46. Sontag, *On Photography*, 131.
47. Abu-Lughod, *Do Muslim Women Need Saving?* 55.
48. Abu-Lughod, *Do Muslim Women Need Saving?* 83.
49. Mahmood, *Politics of Piety*, 197.
50. Mutua, *Human Rights: A Political and Cultural Critique*, 232.
51. Young, *Judging the Image: Art, Value, Law*, 12.
52. See Anne Orford, *Reading Humanitarian Interventions: Human Rights and the Use of Force in International Law* (Cambridge: Cambridge University Press 2003).
53. Saadia Toor, "Imperialist Feminism Redux," *Dialectical Anthropology* 36, no. 3/4 (2012): 147–150.
54. Stephen Sheehi, *Islamophobia: The Ideological Campaign Against Muslims* (Atlanta: Clarity Press, 2011), 77.
55. Irshad Manji, *The Trouble with Islam Today: A Muslim's Call for Reform in Her Faith* (New York: St. Martin's Press, 2007), 140.
56. She traces this vulnerable and abject African woman to the trans-Atlantic slave trade and the abolitionist movements, and how it legitimised a moral claim for intervention that continues today in human rights campaigns. Pamela Scully, "Gender, History, and Human Rights," in *Gender and Culture at the Limit of Rights*, ed. Dorothy L. Hodgson (Philadelphia: University of Pennsylvania Press, 2011), 17–31.
57. See for example Sheila Jeffreys, *Man's Dominion: The Rise of Religion and the Eclipse of Women's Rights* (Abington: Routledge, 2012).
58. Scully, "Gender, History, and Human Rights," 30.
59. See for example Mona Mahmood, "Double-Layered Veils and Despair… Women Describe Life Under ISIS," *The Guardian*, February 17, 2015. https://www.theguardian.com/world/2015/feb/17/isis-orders-women-iraq-syria-veils-gloves
60. Ajisafe, "All the Things We Could [Se]e by Now," 4
61. Sara Ahmed, "Affective Economies," *Social Text* 22, no. 2 (2004).
62. Mahmood, "Feminism, Democracy and Empire: Islam and the War on Terror," 82.
63. Spivak, *A Critique of Postcolonial Reason*.
64. Lacan, *Ecrits: The First Complete Edition in English*, 76–77.
65. See Fink, "Knowledge and Jouissance."
66. Jacques Lacan, *The Seminar of Jacques Lacan: Book IV the Object Relation 1956–1957*, ed. Jacques-Alain Miller, trans. L. V. A Roche (New York: W. W. Norton), 173–176.
67. Salecl, *The Spoils of Freedom*, 124.

68. Salecl, *The Spoils of Freedom*, 126.
69. Eric Santner, *The Royal Remains: The People's Two Bodies and the Endgames of Sovereignty* (Chicago: University of Chicago Press, 2011).
70. I could not obtain permission to include this image in the book. But the image can be seen here on Amnesty International USA website https://blog.amnestyusa.org/asia/we-get-it/. The website also includes a response from Amnesty International which clarified that they wanted to encourage the leaders of the summit to maintain the progress for women's rights. But this clarification reinforced the narrative the image was initially critiqued for and that is Amnesty International subscribing to the presence of NATO as a progressive force in the country.
71. Slavoj Žižek, *Looking Awry: An Introduction to Jacques Lacan Through Popular Culture* (Cambridge: MIT Press, 1992), 90.
72. Women's organisations like Revolutionary Association of the Women of Afghanistan, along with activists and female politicians like Joya have expressed criticism of the role of warlords, the Taliban and the occupation troops in the insecurities women face in the country. See Toor, "Imperialist Feminism Redux," 148.
73. Vienna Colucci, "We Get It" Amnesty International U.S., http://blog.amnestyusa.org/asia/we-get-it/.
74. Desmond Manderson, "From Hunger to Love: Myths of the Source, Interpretation, and the Constitution of the Law in Children's Literature," *Law and Literature* 15, no. 1 (2003): 94.
75. Laura Durkay, "'Homeland' Is the Most Bigoted Show on Television," *The Washington Post*, October 2, 2014.
76. "The adult, and even more the advanced child, demands something new in his activities, in his games. But this "sliding away" (glissement) conceals what is the true secret of the ludic, namely, the most radical diversity constituted by repetition itself. It can be seen in the child, in his first movement, at the moment when he is formed as a human being, manifesting himself as an insistence that the story should always be the same, that its recounted realization should be ritualized, that is to say, textually the same. This signifies that the realization of the signifier will never be able to be careful enough in its memorization to succeed in designating the primacy of the significance as such." Jacques Lacan and Jacques-Alain Miller, *The Four Fundamentals Concepts of Psychoanalysis*, ed. Jacques-Alain Miller, trans. Alan Sheridan (London: Karnac, 1973), 61.
77. See Anne McClintock, *Imperial Leather* for an analysis of the idea of "progress" and how it assumes a particular reading of history, time and space, and aligned with European biopower and imperial expansionist policies that exalted Europe as materially, culturally and spiritually developed than others who remained in "anachronistic space".
78. Young, *Judging the Image: Art, Value, Law*, 14.

79. For a broader analysis of the responsibility to protect in humanitarian interventions, see Anne Orford, *International Authority and the Responsibility to Protect* (New York: Cambridge University Press, 2011).

80. Juliet Rogers, "Unquestionable Freedom in a Psychotic West," *Law, Culture and the Humanities* 1, no. 2 (2005): 189.

81. Salecl, *The Spoils of Freedom*, 127.

82. Salecl, *The Spoils of Freedom*, 127.

83. Douzinas, *The End of Human Rights*, 320.

84. Salecl, *The Spoils of Freedom*, 127.

85. Jacques Lacan, *The Ethics of Psychoanalysis, 1959–1960*, 1st American Edition (New York: W. W. Norton, 1992), 14.

86. Henry Krips, *Fetish* (New York: Cornell University Press, 1999), 50.

87. Salecl, *The Spoils of Freedom*, 127–128.

88. Asad, *Formations of the Secular: Christianity, Islam, Modernity*, 84.

89. Douzinas, *The End of Human Rights*, 322.

90. Douzinas, *The End of Human Rights*, 317.

91. Douzinas, *The End of Human Rights*, 9.

92. See for example the 2001 award-winning documentary "Beneath the Veil" where, reporter Saira Shah, hid a camera under a burqa to film life for women under the Taliban. The film included footage of an execution and was circulated in the early years of the war. "Inside Afghanistan: Behind the Veil," *BBC*, January 27, 2001.

93. It is worth noting that I contacted the organisation for permission to include the image in this book, but my request was declined and was told the image was old and Amnesty International no longer aimed to communicate to the public about human rights in this way. However, 2010 is not so long ago which raises a question of the ethics of accountability in the production and circulation of such images that highlight the uncritical reception of popular images of a given political atmosphere.

94. Hesford, *Spectacular Rhetorics*, 29.

95. I was not able to obtain the license from the copyright holder due to printing restrictions. The image can be viewed at https://www.amnesty.org.uk/womens-rights-afghanistan-history.

96. Abu Lughod, Do Muslim women need saving? Also see, Rossalyn Warren "Are Old Photos of 'Westernised' Afghan Women Driving Trump's Foreign Policy," *The Guardian*, August 24, 2017, https://www.theguardian.com/commentisfree/2017/aug/23/photos-afghan-women-foreign-policy-trump-womens-rightsCNN, features a similar "past" and "present". See, Monica Sarkar, "Unveiled: Afghan Women Past and Present," *CNN*, June 5, 2015, https://edition.cnn.com/2014/06/05/asia/gallery/afghan-women-past-present/index.html.

97. "The Fundamental Horror of ISIS," *The New York Times*, October 2, 2014, https://www.nytimes.com/2014/10/03/opinion/the-fundamental-horror-of-isis.htmlDaniel. Hurst, "Tony Abbott Calls on

Western Nations to Consider Ground Troops in War on ISIS," *The Guardian*, December 10, 2015, https://www.theguardian.com/australia-news/2015/dec/10/tony-abbott-calls-on-western-nations-to-consider-ground-troops-in-war-on-isis.

98. "The Utility of Citizenship Stripping Laws in the UK, Canada and Australia," *University of Melbourne Law Review* 40 (2017), http://www5.austlii.edu.au/au/journals/MelbULawRw/2017/40.html.

99. Sara Meger, "Instrumentalising Women's Security in the Counter-Terrorism Agenda," Gender and War Project, July 17, 2018, http://www.genderandwar.com/2018/07/17/.

100. "False Images Used to "Prove" Slavery, Genital Mutilation Under ISIS," *The Observer*, August 12, 2014, https://observers.france24.com/en/20140812-slavery-genital-mutilation-collective-marriage-fake-isis-images.

101. Michal Givoni, "The Ethics of Witnessing," *Theory, Culture & Society* 31, no. 1 (2014): 123–142

102. William Ian Miller, *The Anatomy of Disgust* (Cambridge: Harvard University Press, 1997), 94.

103. Whitlock, *Soft Weapons: Autobiography in Transit*, 59.

104. See the use of "cage" in Ezra Levant, "Life in a Veil, Life in a Cage," *Toronto Sun*, July 11, 2011; and "imprisoning" in Tracy Clark Flory, "Is the Burqa a Prison?" *Salon*, June 23, 2009. See also Ayaan Hirsi Ali, *The Caged Virgin: An Emancipation Proclamation for Women and Islam* (New York: Atria Paperback, 2004) in which she describes the veil and the mindset that practices it as a "cage".

105. Ajisafe, "All the Things We Could [Se]e by Now," 4

106. Badiou, *Ethics: An Essay on the Understanding of Evil*, 9–10.

107. These "self-evident" visual depictions of excessive suffering offer an enjoyment to the one who is being called upon. This is what Carolyn Dean describes as pornographic imagery—an "eroticised objectification of pain", the reduction of human experience to commodities, and the freezing of any meaningful discussion. See Carolyn J. Dean, "Empathy, Pornography and Suffering," *A Journal of Feminist Cultural Studies* 14, no. 1 (2003): 91–93.

108. Spivak, *A Critique of Postcolonial Reason*, 309.

109. Wendy Brown, *States of Injury: Power and Freedom in Late Modernity* (Princeton, NJ: Princeton University Press, 1995), 7.

110. Scarry, *The Body in Pain*, 17.

111. Scarry, *The Body in Pain*, 17.

112. Scarry, *The Body in Pain*, 16.

113. See for example Mahmood, "Double-Layered Veils and Despair."

114. McLarney, "The Burqa in Vogue: Fashioning Afghanistan," 4.

115. McLarney, "The Burqa in Vogue: Fashioning Afghanistan," 2–3.

116. Rashmee Kumar, "Marketing the Muslim Woman: Hijabs and Modest Fashion Are the New Corporate Trend in the Trump Era," *The Intercept*, December 29, 2018, https://theintercept. com/2018/12/29/muslim-women-hijab-fashion-capitalism/?fbclid= IwAR3o7vAxBFf1AN1spLmJfTp5SvbGjwDgZQ5QIBPFjqKy_ YFGVt42hnbwwEA.

117. The humanising capacity of unveiling is discernable in media and socio-political discourses that link the "human" to storylines of "beneath the veil" and "unveiling the truth" and when journalists recognise the humanity of the women, they either interview or observe as their subject of analyses. Beneath the veil, as is often narrated, are desiring women whose bodily choices have been restrained.

118. Minoo Moallem quoted in McLarney, "The Burqa in Vogue: Fashioning Afghanistan," 5.

119. McLarney, "The Burqa in Vogue: Fashioning Afghanistan," 5.

120. Butler, *Precarious Life*, 141–142. Also cited in McLarney, "The Burqa in Vogue: Fashioning Afghanistan," 7.

121. Lacan, *Ecrits: The First Complete Edition in English*, 288.

122. Žižek, *Looking Awry*, 8.

123. A. L. Macfie, *Orientalism: A Reader* (New York: New York University Press, 2000), 107.

124. Shanifa Nasser, "Who Benefits from Rescuing Rahaf? Questions Linger After Whirlwind Story of Saudi Teen's Asylum," *CBC*, January 14, 2019, https://www.cbc.ca/news/canada/toronto/rahaf-al-qunun-canada-saudi-refugee-1.4976735.

125. Shenila Khoda-Moolji, *Forging the Ideal Educated Girl: The Production of Desirable Subjects in Muslim South Asia* (California: University of California Press, 2018).

126. Agence France-Press, "Malala's Wounded Friend Still Haunted," *Herald Sun*, November 10, 2012.

127. Elenor Goldberg, "How Malala, Teen Activist Shot by Taliban, Made Jon Stewart's Jaw Drop (VIDEO)," *The Huffington Post*, September 11, 2013.

128. Malala Yousafzai and Christina Lamb, *I Am Malala: The Girl Who Stood Up for Education and Was Shot by the Taliban* (London: Little, Brown, 2013).

129. Michael Edwards, "Assessing Malala's Legacy," *ABC*, October 13, 2013.

130. "Living Under Drones," http://www.livingunderdrones.org.

131. Especially if we consider on October 24, 2012, only two weeks after the attack on Malala, Nabeela Rehman, a 9-year-old girl from the same northern region of Pakistan almost died when hit by a drone while she was playing outside. Her grandmother, the only midwife in the village was, however, was killed. Rehman and her family travelled from their remote village to give their testimony at the Congressional Hearing of which only five representatives out of the 435 attended and largely dismissed. See Jihad Al Jabban,

"Nabila's Plea: The Case Against Congressional Apathy," *The Huffington Post*, May 11, 2013, https://www.huffpost.com/entry/congress-drone-strikes-hearing_b_4206793.

132. Laura Bush, "A Girl's Courage Challenges Us to Act," *The Washington Post*, October 1, 2012

133. Ida Litcher, "Feminists Dally While Islamic Women Die," *The Australian*, October 22, 2012.

134. "The Incomparable Malala Yousafzai," YouTube, The Ellen Show, 2015.

135. Goldberg, "How Malala, Teen Activist Shot by Taliban, Made Jon Stewart's Jaw Drop (VIDEO)."

136. Alexandra Topping, "Malala Yousafzai Backs Campaign Against FGM," *The Guardian*, February 25, 2014, https://www.theguardian.com/society/2014/feb/24/malala-yousafzai-backs-fgm-campaign.

137. Ratna Kapur, "The Tragedy of Victimisation Rhetoric: Resurrecting the 'Native' Subject in International/Feminist Post-Colonial Legal Politics," *Harvard Journal of Human Rights* 15, no. 1 (2002): 12–13.

138. Sally Engle Merry, *Human Rights and Gender Violence: Celebrating Transnational International Law into Local Culture* (Chicago: University of Chicago Press, 2006), 11.

139. Arthur Kleinman and Joan Kleinman, "The Appeal of Experience: The Dismay of Images: Cultural Appropriations of Suffering in Our Times," in *Social Suffering*, ed. Arthur Kleinman, Veena Das, and Margaret M. Lock (Berkeley: University of California Press, 1997), 2.

140. Butler, *Precarious Life*, 34.

141. It is a similar narrative which organisations like Women Living Under Muslim Laws produce by how their focus is on cultural violations, excluding structural and global interconnectedness. See Abu-Lughod, *Do Muslim Women Need Saving?* 143–172.

142. Whitlock, *Soft Weapons: Autobiography in Transit*, 54.

143. Razack, *Looking White People in the Eye*, 6–7.

144. Rogers, *Law's Cut on the Body of Human Rights*, 26.

145. Sontag, *On Photography*, 10.

146. Rogers, *Law's Cut on the Body of Human Rights*, 26.

147. See Said, *Orientalism*.

148. Butler, *Precarious Life*, 143.

149. Whitlock, *Soft Weapons: Autobiography in Transit*, 71.

150. Žižek, *Looking Awry*, 17.

151. Fink, *The Lacanian Subject: Between Language and Jouissance*, 60.

152. Said, *Orientalism*, 7.

153. Abu-Lughod, *Do Muslim Women Need Saving?* 68–79.

References

Abu-Lughod, Lila. *Do Muslim Women Need Saving?* Cambridge, MA: Harvard University Press, 2013.

Agence France-Press. "Malala's Wounded Friend Still Haunted." *Herald Sun*, November 10, 2012.

Ahmed, Sara. "Affective Economies." *Social Text* 22, no. 2 (2004): 117–139.

Ajisafe, Babajide Ishmael. "'All the Things We Could [Se]e by Now [Concerning Violence & Boko Haram], If Sigmund Freud's Wife Was Your Mother': Psychoanalysis, Race, & International Political Theory." *International Journal of Political Theory* 2, no. 1 (2017): 1–26.

Ali, Ayaan Hirsi. *The Caged Virgin: An Emancipation Proclamation for Women and Islam.* New York: Atria Paperback, 2004.

Asad, Talal. *Formations of the Secular: Christianity, Islam, Modernity.* California: Stanford University Press, 2003.

Badiou, Alain. *Ethics: An Essay on the Understanding of Evil.* Translated by Peter Hallward. London: Verso, 2001.

Brown, Wendy. *States of Injury: Power and Freedom in Late Modernity.* Princeton: Princeton University Press, 1995.

Brown, Wendy. "Suffering Rights as Paradoxes." *Constellations* 7, no. 2 (2000): 208–229.

Brown, Wendy. "'The Most We Can Hope For...': Human Rights and the Politics of Fatalism." *The South Atlantic Quarterly* 103, no. 2/3 (2004): 451–463.

Bush, Laura. "A Girl's Courage Challenges Us to Act." *The Washington Post*, October 1, 2012.

Butler, Judith. *Precarious Life: The Powers of Mourning and Violence.* New York: Verso, 2004.

Butler, Rex. "Baudrillard's Light Writing or Photographic Though." *International Journal of Baudrillard Studies* 2, no. 1 (2005): 1–21.

Dean, Carolyn J. "Empathy, Pornography and Suffering." *A Journal of Feminist Cultural Studies* 14, no. 1 (2003): 88–124.

Douzinas, Costas. *The End of Human Rights: Critical Legal Thought at the Turn of the Century.* Oxford: Hart Publishing, 2000.

Ferguson, Kennan. *The Politics of Judgement: Aesthetics, Identity, and Political Theory.* Lanham: Lexington Books, 1999.

Fink, Bruce. "Knowledge and Jouissance." In *Reading Seminar XX: Lacan's Major Work on Love, Knowledge and Feminine Sexuality*, edited by Suzanne Barnard and Bruce Fink. New York: State University New York Press, 2002.

Fink, Bruce. *The Lacanian Subject: Between Language and Jouissance.* Princeton: Princeton University Press, 1995.

Givoni, Michal. "The Ethics of Witnessing." *Theory, Culture & Society* 31, no. 1 (2014): 123–142.

Hesford, Wendy S. *Spectacular Rhetorics: Human Rights Visions, Recognitions, Feminisms.* Durham: Duke University Press, 2011.

Hesford, Wendy S., and Wendy Kozol. *Just Advocacy? Women's Human Rights, Transnational Feminisms, and the Politics of Representation.* New Brunswick: Rutgers University Press, 2005.

Hunt, Lynn. *Inventing Human Rights: A History.* New York: Norton Paperback, 2007.

Illiopoulos, John. "Baudrillard and a Short History of Psychiatric Photography." *International Journal of Baudrillard Studies* 11, no. 1 (2014).

Jeffreys, Sheila. *Man's Dominion: The Rise of Religion and the Eclipse of Women's Rights.* Abington: Routledge, 2012.

Kapur, Ratna. "Human Rights in the 21st Century: Taking a Walk on the Dark Side." *Sydney Law Review* 29, no. 4 (2006): 665–687.

Kapur, Ratna. "The Tragedy of Victimisation Rhetoric: Resurrecting the 'Native' Subject in International/Feminist Post-Colonial Legal Politics." *Harvard Journal of Human Rights* 15, no. 1 (2002): 1–37.

Khoda-Moolji, Shenila. *Forging the Ideal Educated Girl: The Production of Desirable Subjects in Muslim South Asia.* California: University of California Press, 2018.

Kleinman, Arthur, and Joan Kleinman. "The Appeal of Experience: The Dismay of Images: Cultural Appropriations of Suffering in Our Times." In *Social Suffering,* edited by Arthur Kleinman, Veena Das, and Margaret M. Lock. Berkeley: University of California Press, 1997.

Krips, Henry. *Fetish.* New York: Cornell University Press, 1999.

Kumar, Rashmee. "Marketing the Muslim Woman: Hijabs and Modest Fashion Are the New Corporate Trend in the Trump Era." *The Intercept,* December 29, 2018. https://theintercept.com/2018/12/29/muslim-women-hijab-fashion-capitalism/?fbclid=IwAR3o7vAxBFf1AN1spLmJfTp5SvbGjwDgZQ5QIBPFjqKy_YFGVt42hnbwwEA.

Lacan, Jacques. *Ecrits: The First Complete Edition in English.* New York: W. W. Norton, 2006.

Lacan, Jacques. *The Ethics of Psychoanalysis, 1959–1960.* 1st American Edition. New York: W. W. Norton, 1992.

Lacan, Jacques. *The Seminar of Jacques Lacan: Book IV the Object Relation 1956–1957.* Edited by Jacques-Alain Miller. Translated by L. V. A. Roche. New York: W. W. Norton.

Lacan, Jacques, and Jacques-Alain Miller. *The Four Fundamentals Concepts of Psychoanalysis.* Edited by Jacques-Alain Miller. Translated by Alan Sheridan. London: Karnac, 1973.

Litcher, Ida. "Feminists Dally While Islamic Women Die." *The Australian,* October 22, 2012.

Lockman, Zachary. *Contending Visions of the Middle East: The History and Politics of Orientalism.* 2nd ed. Cambridge: Cambridge University Press, 2010.

Macfie, A. L. *Orientalism: A Reader.* New York: New York University Press, 2000.

Mahmood, Mona. "Double-Layered Veils and Despair... Women Describe Life Under ISIS." *The Guardian*, February 17, 2015. https://www.theguardian.com/world/2015/feb/17/isis-orders-women-iraq-syria-veils-gloves.

Mahmood, Saba. "Feminism, Democracy and Empire: Islam and the War on Terror." In *Women's Studies on the Edge*, edited by Joan Wallach Scott. Durham: Duke University Press, 2008.

Mahmood, Saba. *Politics of Piety: The Islamic Revival and the Feminist Subject.* Princeton: Princeton University Press, 2005.

Manderson, Desmond. "From Hunger to Love: Myths of the Source, Interpretation, and the Constitution of the Law in Children's Literature." *Law and Literature* 15, no. 1 (2003): 87–141.

Manji, Irshad. *The Trouble with Islam Today: A Muslim's Call for Reform in Her Faith.* New York: St. Martin's Press, 2007.

McClintock, Anne. *Imperial Leather: Race, Gender, and Sexuality in the Colonial Contest.* New York: Routledge, 1995.

McLarney, Ellen. "The Burqa in Vogue: Fashioning Afghanistan." *Journal of Middle East Women's Studies* 5, no. 1 (2009): 1–23.

Meger, Sara. "Instrumentalising Women's Security in the Counter-Terrorism Agenda." Gender and War Project, July 17, 2018. http://www.genderandwar.com/2018/07/17/.

Merry, Sally Engle. *Human Rights and Gender Violence: Celebrating Transnational International Law into Local Culture.* Chicago: University of Chicago Press, 2006.

Mohanty, Chandra Talpade. "Under Western Eyes: Feminist Scholarship and Colonial Discourse." *Boundary 2* 12, no. 3 (1984): 333–358.

Miller, William Ian. *The Anatomy of Disgust.* Cambridge: Harvard University Press, 1997.

Mutua, Makau. *Human Rights: A Political and Cultural Critique.* Philadelphia: University of Pennsylvania Press, 2002.

Nasser, Shanifa. "Who Benefits from Rescuing Rahaf? Questions Linger After Whirlwind Story of Saudi Teen's Asylum." *CBC*, January 14, 2019. https://www.cbc.ca/news/canada/toronto/rahaf-al-qunun-canada-saudi-refugee-1.4976735.

Orford, Anne. *International Authority and the Responsibility to Protect.* New York: Cambridge University Press, 2011.

Orford, Anne. *Reading Humanitarian Interventions: Human Rights and the Use of Force in International Law.* Cambridge: Cambridge University Press, 2003.

Razack, Sherene. *Looking White People in the Eye: Gender, Race, and Culture in Courtrooms and Classrooms.* Toronto: University of Toronto Press, 1998.

Razack, Sherene. "Stealing the Suffering of Others: Reflection of Canadian Humanitarian Responses." *Review of Education Pedagogy and Cultural Studies* 24, no. 4 (2007): 375–394.

Rogers, Juliet. *Law's Cut on the Body of Human Rights*. New York: Routledge, 2013.

Rogers, Juliet. "Unquestionable Freedom in a Psychotic West." *Law, Culture and the Humanities* 1, no. 2 (2005): 186–207.

Said, Edward W. *Orientalism*. 1st ed. New York: Pantheon Books, 1978.

Salecl, Renata. *The Spoils of Freedom: Psychoanalysis, Feminism and Ideology After the Fall of Socialism*. London: Routledge, 1994.

Santner, Eric. *The Royal Remains: The People's Two Bodies and the Endgames of Sovereignty*. Chicago: University of Chicago Press, 2011.

Scarry, Elaine. *The Body in Pain: The Making and Unmaking of the World*. New York: Oxford University Press, 1985.

Scott, Joan Wallach. *Sex and Secularism*. Princeton and Oxford: Princeton University Press, 2018.

Scully, Pamela. "Gender, History, and Human Rights." In *Gender and Culture at the Limit of Rights*, edited by Dorothy L. Hodgson. Philadelphia: University of Pennsylvania Press, 2011.

Sheehi, Stephen. *Islamophobia: The Ideological Campaign Against Muslims*. Atlanta: Clarity Press, 2011.

Sontag, Susan. *On Photography*. New York: Rosetta Books, 1973.

Spivak, Gayatri Chakravorty. *A Critique of Postcolonial Reason: Toward a History of the Vanishing Present*. Cambridge: Harvard University Press, 1999.

Spivak, Gayatri Chakravorty. "Righting Wrongs." *The South Atlantic Quarterly* 103, no. 2/3 (2004): 523–581.

Toor, Saadia. "Imperialist Feminism Redux." *Dialectical Anthropology* 36, no. 3/4 (2012): 147–160.

Topping, Alexandra. "Malala Yousafzai Backs Campaign Against FGM." *The Guardian*, February 25, 2014. https://www.theguardian.com/society/2014/feb/24/malala-yousafzai-backs-fgm-campaign.

United Nations. "The Universal Declaration of Human Rights." http://www.un.org/en/universal-declaration-human-rights/.

"The Utility of Citizenship Stripping Laws in the UK, Canada and Australia." *University of Melbourne Law Review* 40 (2017). http://www5.austlii.edu.au/au/journals/MelbULawRw/2017/40.html.

Whitlock, Gillian. *Soft Weapons: Autobiography in Transit*. Chicago: University of Chicago Press, 2009.

Yeğenoğlu, Meyda. *Colonial Fantasies: Towards a Feminist Reading of Orientalism*. Cambridge: Cambridge University Press, 1998.

Young, Alison. *Judging the Image: Art, Value, Law*. New York: Routledge, 2005.

Yousafzai, Malala, and Christina Lamb. *I Am Malala: The Girl Who Stood Up for Education and Was Shot by the Taliban*. London: Little, Brown, 2013.

Žižek, Slavoj. *Looking Awry: An Introduction to Jacques Lacan Through Popular Culture*. Cambridge: MIT Press, 1992.

CHAPTER 4

The Woman Question

How could someone "be a woman" through and through, make a final home in that category without suffering claustrophobia - or hysteria? —Denise Riley[1]

INTRODUCTION

The imaginary assembling of veiled and unveiled bodies not only alludes to the desire for the unveiled complete human subject present beyond the frame, but also tells the story of who is a Woman and what does she desire. The little girl, accompanied by the unpromising presence of veiled women in humanitarian imagery, reappears in images like those by Boushra Almutawakel. Her precarious company heeding the warning of what would befall the little girl if—what critic of Islam and former Muslim Ayaan Hirsi Ali has called—the "Islamic curtain" descends on her and the future generation of women. Such warnings regarding women in states of crisis have amplified with the rise of a strong cultural sentiment around anti-immigration and anti-multiculturalism in the west, alongside a global war on terror, which have coalesced to diminish Muslims to a symbol of patriarchy and irreconcilable difference. The preoccupation with what is being done to women's bodies in a heightened security atmosphere has found

© The Author(s) 2020
S. Ghumkhor, *The Political Psychology of the Veil*,
Palgrave Studies in Political Psychology,
https://doi.org/10.1007/978-3-030-32061-4_4

powerful expression in concern about *other* women's bodies, namely Muslim women's bodies. Polygamy, female genital mutilation, honour crimes, forced marriage, and its most visible marker of injury, the veil, have united the political forces across the ideological spectrum in concern about Muslim women and what this means for "western" values like sexual progress and gender equality. Reflecting on Europe's contemporary racial politics, Eric Fassin contends this preoccupation with sexual and gender freedoms is a symptom of what he calls sexual democracy, which has become the "litmus test in Europe: it serves to justify, in democratic terms, the rejection of others".[2] Judith Butler similarly contends that sexual politics has become a way for Europe to produce distinct categories and identities within a temporal trajectory that identifies the west as the agent of secularism, modernity and freedom.[3] Sex, Michel Foucault reminds us, was essential to biopower as it gave life to the body and the means to understanding the origins of life itself.[4] The concept of the secular is critical to this expression of gender and sexual equality in its decreed triumph over the past and progressive vision for the future. If the secular is an unstable category but traceable through oppositions (reason/unreason, state/church, public/private),[5] the opposition between reason/sex, masculine/feminine, men/ women is also important to its workings which Joan Scott coins as "sexularism".[6] In these civilisational discourses, the troubling possibility of a universal Woman appears as an unstable identity. It is a category in which a "clash of civilisations" has been summoned to militantly affirm her ontological borders under a presumption of what Woman is and what she wants.

In this volatile climate, calls to unveil the Muslim woman are bolstered by the belief in what many feminists in the west have cautioned against—the erasure of women beneath the misogyny of the veil.[7] The veil is the Trojan horse of Afghanistan and Saudi Arabia, the creeping Sharia, entering the liberal sanctity of western borders and seeking to derail woman's identity and the desires of *all* women. As an "instrument of terror", the veil is imbued with Islam's patriarchal drive and "can hide a beard".[8] These often-fervent, and as this chapter will trace, even hysterical, demands to unveil the threat that the veil poses to women's bodies (wrapping them in patriarchal traditions that police their bodies for the desires of Muslim men), also bares the fragile basis for many western concerns. The presence of the veil in the west gestures to the limits of what the west can offer women.

The "natural" unveiled body is an invisible medium used to assess the bodily aspirations for universal status. Its secular contours coordinate with the desire for freedom and eventual liberation. The Muslim woman *is* all these different types of veil*ings*: symbolic pieces of the fragmented Woman, slowly disintegrating across a spectrum of veils—a collapsing akin to the biopolitical "destructive body".[9] The body here is a fragment that could be evidence of either bodily erosion or the formation of a new body. In either case, it is in parts. Each image announces a mourning of her missing parts—parts that must be put together—that have collapsed into the veil's intolerable and alienating void. This "putting back together", I argue, occurs through a desire to locate the Woman on this spectrum. The properties that identify her body as that of the Woman are not entirely recognisable *unless* the veil loosens its hold on her, makes visible her feminine bodily form. Hence, the veiled woman's proximity to the unveiled woman—the "real" Woman—is increased though the unveiled woman does not appear in the image. It is beyond the frame that the Woman, unveiled, announces herself. She is the missing image, or in other words, the very frame itself. She is the not-yet-visible place where Woman can be recovered and rescued from immanent loss as the veil descends on her. Examining western secular women's investment in the notion of a liberated body, this chapter examines the rescuing of the Woman's body from the veil of violence (lack) and what role it has in the phallic fantasy of the unveiled west. If bodies are made meaningful through the lens of a natural human progression in the desire for freedom through the secular body, how does this specifically affect sexed bodies in its regulation of men and women's *jouissance* within—what this book has been tracing—a *phallic* fantasy?

This chapter explores these questions through further unpacking the western fantasy of freedom by examining Lacan's schema for sexuation. This marks the impossibility of oneness, split into the subject who "has" access to whole (phallic) subjectivity ("man") or "to be" ("wom*e*n"), the latter who masquerades as whole within this fantasy. The fantasy of a free west relies on the phallic logic of whole, raising the issue of women's status within its borders. The chapter traces the fantasy this book has been examining by asking what imaginary underpins women's freedom in the west? What possibility does it offer women? As Saba Mahmood observes, "the desire for freedom and liberation is a historically situated desire whose motivational force cannot be assumed a priori but needs to be reconsidered in light of other desires, aspirations and capacities that inhere in a culturally and historically located subject".[10] The chapter will critically examine how this situated desire appears and is regulated in the production of sexed subjects and what political and epistemic implications it has had on the feminist imaginary: the vision for Woman's freedom and becoming.

This chapter contends that in a west which has claimed history's end, a universal Woman is made stable, visible, attainable and whole, through a phallic fantasy, which idealises her unveiled body, her ontological state of veils uncast. I explore how the relationship between freedom and the body exhibit certain truths about what it means to be a feminine whole. It is through the body that the fantasy frame of a universal free west constitutes secular bodies in the throes of unveiling as embodiments of sovereign flesh and makes freedom (political and sexual) a possibility. Similar to national discourses wherein women's bodies become cultural markers, inscribed with moral truisms, the nation, the "motherland", the home, the *volk* (the people),[11] the chapter contends that it is particularly through women's bodies that the west prescribes its liberal and secular values and the critical frontier of its civilisational claims.

I am also particularly concerned with how the image of unveiling is invested in the truth of women's ontology: what is it about the visibility of the Woman's body that announces her as a more recognisable and authentic Woman? What makes unveiling an intrinsic metaphor for women's liberation? The imagining of unveiling here takes on a "phantasm of control"[12] in the production of the Woman, traced through a specular body that anchors her in liberal secular truths of freedom and autonomy and protected from violence qua the veil. In this sense, I contend that retrieving and anchoring the Woman is pronounced through the partial representations of veiled or hidden bodies—that is, the veiling of the *other* woman to announce the natural uncontested condition of Woman: the (unveiled) liberated body. Unveiling, captured in the images I have examined, and reaffirmed in the popular consumption of Almutawakel's, signifies the integrity of a whole and recognisable body, the uncontested space around which fragments of womanness revolve. Cautioning loss, Almutawakel's image, despite her intentions, serves as a prescription for attaining the properties of the whole Woman. The more she unveils herself, the closer she comes to a natural *jouissance*—enjoyment of corporeal rights and desires. The more she unveils the more the teleology of womanness is obtained. This is a Woman who announces herself through the visibility of flesh that signifies desire excited by freedom. The specular image of the unveiled woman, however, is essentially an attempt at failed recognition of the Woman, concealed by the fantasy of the whole.[13] The call to defend women from the veil also pertains to an anxiety of the failure to represent the Woman. This failure is gestured to in Almutawakel's image: in the darkness of the veil, where the subject completely disappears, stands the abyss of the Other.

Feminism's (Im)possible Woman

Reflecting on cultural and political registers of the climate of security in post-9/11, Sunera Thobani argues that the war on terror has given rise to "new forms of invasions and occupations". Therefore, analysis must include how feminists in particular are theorising this new political terrain.[14] Just as the "The Woman Question" qua the veiled Oriental woman disguised the colonial incursions and the consolidation of European power in the Orient,[15] today the question has lent feminist credence to the imperial gestures that underpin the war against the west's enemies. Through the production of the imperilled Muslim woman, the western secular woman is posited at times as a vulnerable subject who has been offered the promises of democracy, sexual and gender equality, autonomy, modernity, and the right to pursue individual happiness[16]—secular freedoms that require constant policing from potential patriarchal threats. The incarceration, torture and murder of Muslim men occurs, as Thobani observes, in order for western women to feel the "paranoid imaginings" of herself and her society as threatened by a pathological violence at the hands of these men.[17] This paranoia has not only been expressed towards Muslim men but is part of a long history of racial anxiety about black men (Fanon 1968; Baldwin 1965; Marlon Ross 2004; Angela Davis 2017) exemplified in the Trump era when 53% of American white women and 45% of white college graduate women voted in the 2016 elections for a President who spoke of women needing to be "grabbed by the pussy", and campaigned for a Muslim ban and a wall to keep out immigrants.[18] It has also found contemporary expression in incidents of white women across the United States calling authorities on black, Muslim and other coloured members of the public on a perceived offense.[19]

In this paranoid state, we see that women have participated, reproduced and entrusted hegemonic discourses of militancy, jingoism, anxiety and claims of superiority that have characterised west-Islam relations in the post-9/11 epoch. The 2001 invasion of Afghanistan, the banning of the veil in France and calls to ban it elsewhere in the west have seen the voices of women visible as an identification with secularism, liberalism and the war on terror, in Europe, Australia and North America. Journalists, public intellectuals, politicians and activists similarly express their "concern" for Muslim women. Former U.S. Secretary of State Hilary Clinton and former First Lady Laura Bush reiterated their concern about women's rights in Afghanistan advising that if America turns away from the country women may be forced to retreat from classrooms, forced back into their homes, denied healthcare and participation in the running of the country.[20] Their concern echoed many leaders of western feminist organisations at the time, including Feminist Majority Foundation—one of the largest feminist organisation in the United States who supported the war under the rationale of their campaign to "Stop Gender Apartheid" in Afghanistan.[21] Further on the American right, we have seen intense opposition to Islam by a curiously high number of women, including Laura Ingraham, Ann Coulter and Pamela Geller.[22] The 2011 bombing of Libya by then U.S. President Barack Obama marked the first time in American history that military action was endorsed by a female-dominated diplomatic team, led by U.S. Secretary of State Hilary Clinton, U.S. ambassador to the United Nations Susan Rice and Multilateral and Human Rights director Samantha Power. In 2019, it was announced that women are now CEO of the four out of five American military contractors.[23] In 2014, former conservative Liberal Party senator Jacqui Lambie, a military veteran, linked the veil to a heightened security threat for Australia and saw Sharia as a threat to Australian culture.[24] In 2017, Australia's One Nation party leader Pauline Hanson appeared in Parliament in a burqa to theatrically reinforce Lambie's concerns about national security.[25] In Europe, we have seen frequent opposition from FEMEN, a European feminist organisation founded in Ukraine in 2008, known for using nudity as a form of protest. One of their campaigns have focused on international "Topless Jihad" day and protests outside mosques in Europe, calling for the right for Muslim women to make free choices, particularly in their appearances and behaviour, and not to be "slaves" to Islam.[26] Though coverage of their activism has waned internationally, their work for a radical image for women's rights continues. In France, prominent feminist philosopher Elisabeth Badinter was vocal in the call to ban the veil in France in 2011, recognising it as a symbol of gender oppression which has diffused throughout Europe.[27]

Observing the anti-Islam agenda through a cross-geographical mobilisation of women's rights in Europe, Sara Farris argues an alliance of European far-right nationalists, feminists and neo-liberals—a peculiar intersection she describes as "femonationalism"—have found common ground in a desire to emancipate Muslim women. These forces present Islam as Europe's other encompassing within it the exclusive place for sexism and patriarchy. Femonationalism has welcomed citizenship integration programs and fierce opposition to the burqa and niqab.[28] Farris's analysis is a critique of this commitment to gender equality in femonationalism, arguing like Dean

Spade and Sarah Lazare who point to the rise of women in the military industrial complex as an affront to feminist concerns,[29] how it has appropriated feminism to advance a neo-liberal and racist agenda. Although Farris's study examines France, the Netherlands and Italy, these alliances and political sentiments about Islam are discerned across the continent and as far as Australia. However, there is much more at work here than appropriation in the way western freedoms have been mobilised, and how modernism's forces of emancipatory discourses (secularism, liberalism, rights), nationalism and neo-liberalism have *instinctively* claimed feminism as their own.

It is this instinct that this discussion draws attention to. What empowers it? What are its ambitions? A place to begin thinking about this instinctual relationship with feminism appears in Australia's Q&A panel in 2017 when Muslim commentator and youth representative, Yassmin Abdel-Magied clashed with then Senator Jacqui Lambie, on the subject of Islam. Lambie, a vehement critic of the veil which she sees as symptomatic of the wider influence of Sharia law on Australian culture expressed her support for Trump's "Muslim ban" policy which would restrict people from Muslim majority countries from entering the U.S. Abdel-Magied defended Muslim women by declaring that "Islam is *the* most feminist religion". This statement did not sit well with Lambie and the wider public who were outraged over the public defense of Islam by a Muslim woman who was paraded as a success story for immigrants and Muslim women in Australia, now attributing some of that success to her faith. ABC was criticised for providing a platform for advocating Islam, with a petition by a right group garnering thousands of signatures calling for her to be fired. National cartoonist Bill Leak in *The Australian* drew her taking a selfie with a woman about to get stoned and Abdel-Magied forcing her to smile. Former Australian Prime Minister Tony Abbott insisted she must have been blindfolded during her tour to the Middle East.[30] The public response summoned an "essential woman"[31] who has been betrayed by Abdel-Magied's declaration placing her on the side of fundamentalism, misogyny and unfreedom. The backlash and the subsequent character assassination of Abdel-Magied reveal an *impulsive* identification with feminism as a western cultural possession— and what makes possible Femonationalism even while some of its forces actively undermine women's rights in other domains. The ideological and political contradictions within these forces are reconciled, or at least suspended, through their interrogation of Islam—not simply because of its perceived otherness, rather it provides confirmation of shared *secular* values which sexual freedom, above all, has come to be the founding premise of western secular democracy.[32]

The images, rhetoric, symbols and narratives that are mobilised to raise the Muslim Question through the Woman Question are part of the sticking hold of western positional superiority. Dipesh Chakrabarty's reading of how the modern and its universal and secular vision is intimately tied to its "silent referent": Europe and Europeanness, and how it reproduced "historicism"—reading non-European histories as a "not-yet" to somebody else—is useful here.[33] Chakrabarty argues that "political modernity", which is the rule by modern institutions of the state, bureaucracy, and capitalist enterprise, is impossible to think of anywhere in the world without invoking certain categories and concepts, the genealogies of which go deep into the intellectual and even theological traditions of Europe.[34] This conscious and unconscious turn to the origins of "concepts such as citizenship, the state, civil society, public sphere, human rights, equality before the law, the individual, distinctions between public and private, the idea of the subject, democracy, popular sovereignty, social justice, scientific rationality, and so on, all bear the burden of European thought and history".[35] Sara Ahmed similarly describes this burden as part of "histories of naming"[36] a naming that has residual effects that smothers other histories and modernities. This cultural schema, institutionalised, made manifest in speeches, policy, media coverage, and the everyday, identifies political modernity's persisting imagining across the political spectrum in a fantasy where the quicksands of the Woman[37] find stability in the *preservation* of her freedoms through the *secularisation* of her body. This is the modern body which promises having no lack. This fantasy announces itself in the encounter with Muslim women as objects that dispenses with ideological differences and transforms western political forces into women's rights activists. It is a fantasy that explains the prevailing belief in members of the public who know little about Islam yet know that Muslim women are oppressed and, at the very least, western women are always doing better. It empowers them to recite blanket statements about how grateful other women must be to have left their imagined persecution and found safety in the west. The role of women in this volatile terrain and the emergence of femonationalism, though varying in discursive and political composition, signals an overt vigilance of the west and secularity as a sanctuary for rights and the purveyor of freedom, and thus, a refuge from (feminine) alterity.[38]

Observing the possibilities that have been opened up to the "modern woman" in this universal secular vision, the contemporary world has, for Lacanian analyst Colette Soler, unleashed a "phallic rivalry" in the shadow of discourses of equality. Soler refers to men and women's claim to corporeal and ontological wholeness, through modernity's promise of freedom and the satisfaction of all desires. The modern woman is "hammered out by infinite numbers of mutual references from all sides of these studies, classifications and practices"[39]—that is, by modernity's claim to knowability. If women's *jouissance*, Soler contends, has failed to be reduced to the logic of unisex (oneness) because it is imagined uncontained and unlike men, she does not call for a complementary object of lack, the making of the modern woman has been tied to the cultural, political and epistemic production of the west and its promise to secure women's freedom. As such, this "phallic rivalry" is overcome by aligning oneself with western (phallic) *jouissance* and the object of lack in the *other* woman.[40] Entering the civilisational terrain (which pits rights and secular freedoms against cultural regression and "fundamentalisms") of phallic conquest, these women imitate a "white woman's burden" in support for wars being waged for women *over there*, and thus reformulating Spivak's saving brown women from brown men with the addendum using *our* men.

Retrieving Her in History

The feminist project in the west has emerged out of the tradition of Enlightenment and the pursuit for the light of reason and the rejection of unreason. Despite sharing enlightenment to critically look upon the social world as one that centres around the subject as masculine, feminist politics sits uncomfortably within the teleology of progressive time, what Julia Kristeva calls "masculine time", which is always "unfolding" and arriving.[41] Further, feminist analysis came to reveal the contradiction between Enlightenment's foundational assumptions of how to organise social life and the feminist project's specific aims of "insertion" in history as part of a "radical refusal".[42] This was a refusal that found expression in the body and what it meant for women, and what woman was—a tension contemporary feminism has not quite resolved nor settled on whether this is an objective to be pursued. But refusal is also an investment in the accusatory gaze that it intends to rebuke. As Wendy Brown[43] argues, feminism's reliance on the *intelligible* subject—be it identifying it as a masculine subject (Irigaray) or the discursive category of women as subject (Butler and Riley)—identifies an *attachment* to the cultural and political offerings of modernity.[44] This signifies political modernity that looks to Europe as the origins of emancipatory horizons (bodily integrity, autonomy as sovereignty, freedom as sexual desire) and their universal prescription. According to Joan Wallach Scott, the defining feature of the feminist project, despite its "isms", is critique: "our agency – our desire – is critique, the constant undoing of unconventional wisdom; the exposure of its limits for fully satisfying the goals of equality. It drives us to unforeseen places... critique as desire, provides no map".[45] Conceptualising this critique as agency, feminism has aimed to overturn patriarchy, breaking the oppressive chains of sexism, liberating women from the stereotypes that confine them, and bringing them onto the stage of history.[46] We have seen the dangers of privileging or seeking out certain values such as agency as the intelligible boundaries of the feminist subject as a political subject. Saba Mahmood warns us that feminist readings of Muslim women's religious lives have often looked to redeeming these women by seeking values that the women themselves may not pursue or identify with. As Mahmood has observed,

> Despite the many strands and differences within feminism, what accords the feminist tradition an analytical and political coherence is the premise that where society is structured to serve male interest, the result will be either neglect, or direct suppression, of women's concerns. Feminism, therefore, offers both a *diagnosis* of women's status across cultures and a *prescription* for changing the situation of women who are understood to be marginalised, subordinated, or oppressed.[47]

In diagnosing women's experience, feminism's conversations with history, its contemporary political praxis and epistemological charters, have been thoughtfully interrogated for their liberal and Eurocentric current.[48] The adoption or re-articulation of feminism by the non-western world, or the claim of indigenous feminist histories, must also contend with the epistemological, political and metaphysical disruption that comes with engaging with the world through its master narrative, or more disturbingly, the insistence on its naming.[49] How liberation is imagined, mapped symbolically, how desire is historically constituted, how critique has been secularised—conceiving a feminism in rebellion with the social and spiritual world—has left feminism's history open to accusations of colluding with imperial projects as a "handmaiden of empire"[50] or an epistemic violation that remodels history to match contemporary sensibilities. European women in history were subordinates to this history of freedom-making but were also constituted by it and active in the production of European imperial culture. Women participated in what Spivak has called the "soul-making" imperial project where the individualism and enlightenment of European women was used to identify the "not-yet-human-Other".[51] They, beneath their veils and in harems, were to be pitied. Or as we will examine, in the case of enslaved populations in America, a somatic colour line was patrolled to maintain their symbolic security as desired women. In the imperial fantasy, European women did not, however, fulfil the power fantasies of European men. They were portrayed as paragons of morality, parasitic and passive actors on the imperial stage, and rarely the object of European male desire.[52] European women exalted themselves in their encounter with the women of the Orient and deployed racial differences— Europeanness as a superior civilisation—to mark themselves from their Eastern female counterparts. British travellers like Lady Montagu (eighteenth century), Sophia Lane Poole (nineteenth century), Isabel Burton (nineteenth century) and American Edith Wharton (twentieth century) discovered in their travels in the Orient, freedoms almost equal to that of men.[53] Therefore, the social and political capital that imperial Europe bestowed upon its subjects had its own allure for European women. The appeal for recognition glazed over the question of who the Woman is and what she wanted and which *women* came to represent.

Despite feminism's different iterations, the tracing of the making of the west and feminism and exploring how they "instinctively" merge is analytically discerning when considering their intimate history. Riley measures this proximity in how the "volatility of "women" is so marked that the speed or slowness with which it is voiced may determine which alliances feminism makes".[54] In its encounters with Muslim women—a difference that challenges who and what woman is, feminism has been marked by the "speed" with which Woman has been announced and safeguarded. A speed discerned in the instinct of possessing feminism as a secular occupation, culturally sanctioned by western traditions.

If the Woman is a discursive category, as contemporary feminism has since increasingly committed to, women is historically and discursively constructed, always in relation to other categories. Third Wave feminism's intersectional approach has responded to these challenges, recognising the social, economic and political entanglement that women's experience with oppression are marked. These intersectional approaches have however slipped into problematic epistemological readings that emphasise certain categories of oppression over others so that it whitens intersectionality,[55] ignores the racial power divide of zones of being and non-beings[56] and relies on the primacy of subjecthood.[57] Notions of autonomy, agency, freedom, bodily integrity—the coordinates of modern *and* postmodern subjectivity suggests a persisting desire to master and manage the political, economic and the social experience.[58] These epistemic tensions warn of Riley's early concerns about the seduction of "the continuity of real women, above whose constant bodies changing aerial descriptions dance".[59] The rituals of practice and language of recognition in these feminist approaches also entrench a relationship between injury and self—what Brown cautions as "wounded attachments" that produce an injurious identity.[60] Taken to a global scene, these wounded attachments have a further constitutive effect on the "third world" and postcolonial experience. Scott, who has recently looked to psychoanalytic frameworks to push feminist critiques further, has similarly recognised this identification of Woman to be a fantasy with echoes and reverberations that can allow for identification across time, geographies and cultures, but encompasses its multiplicities and differences. As persuasive and profound these contributions have been, Europe's cultural, political and economic diffusion of power across the globe leaves reverberating trails—what Ann Laura Stoler describes as imperial debris[61] which raises the question: whose fantasy is echoed the furthest? Or in Abu-Lughod's framing, what are Muslim women being saved *from* and to *what*? As psychoanalysis reminds us, fantasy hinges on an exclusion—what is excluded in feminism's image of resemblance?

These interrogations also point to the relationship between knowledge and *jouissance* that governs how feminists "enjoy" by avoiding the discomfort of certain readings of lived experience. Spivak coins this avoidance as "translation as violation"[62]—the interpellation of the other's desires and experiences. Such translations in academic and political rationales for veiling often seek out the liberal subject—a pattern I turn to in the final chapter.[63] Western feminism's contemporary vision, or more precisely, its underlying fantasy of a politics grounded in a "logic of identification",[64] has however not escaped its history. This is a history informed by the demands of a social context that fought the darkness of lurking shadows. Despite feminism's aspirations to problematise the assumptions this Enlightenment paradigm has occasioned, Spivak insists that feminism must confront its complicity with the "institution within which it seeks its space".[65] It "must reckon with the possibility that, like any other discursive practice" feminism is "marked and constituted by", even as it constitutes, the field of its production.[66]

The history of feminism as one that is marred by its proximity to power—a collusion that has been recanted in the rise of humanitarianism and femonationalism as symptoms of political modernity—and women's ontology appears more fortified than unclaimed. What I want to tentatively propose is despite its different ideological and political manifestations feminism's pursuit for freedom and truth-making practices reveals an *imperial relation* to knowledge which is identified in its psycho-social attachment to how it imagines visibility and diagnoses through it. What "truth" can be ascertained is its reliance on "making visible" the experiences of women. That is, truth as something to uncover and reveal the hidden. The hidden, it contends, is how women's marginalisation or injury has been sustained.[67] The hidden is experienced as a not knowing. It is its linking of truth-telling through discovering that feminism's fantasy emerges within the scopic drive of modernity. The political imperative of uncovering and making women visible in history, Lamia Ben Youssef Zayzafoon suggests, invokes an Enlightenment metaphor of bringing light to darkness, "uncovering truth or identity".[68] Similarly, Meyda Yeğenoğlu links orientalist knowledge production on the veil in the colonial era with the Enlightenment notion of visibility as a "precondition for true knowledge".[69] Normalising western epistemology and modes of truth vis-à-vis clinical interventionism, feminist interventions to "speak out" and "breaking the silence", in a sense, *privilege the visible over the hidden*, the secular (as critique) over tradition (as belief), and the sovereign self over environmental constraints (cultural and religious). Put another way, the emphasis on making visible, is a secular expression of modernity and homogenising imaginary of seeing time and space through binaries of natural and supernatural, belief and reason.[70] This metaphysics is reflected in how from the sixteenth century, the verb *voiler* (to veil) in French discourse was not only erotised but became associated with "making less visible", "concealing", and "masking" light or truth.[71] This political intervention contains a suppressed universal desire for women's bodies to be liberated from the shadow of tradition, as part of the overall development of human history. Thus, feminist emphasis on critique as agency presupposes a *secular* agent desiring a "natural" freedom, whose political good is being critically engaged with its social context, shedding away the veil of tradition that conceals truth[72] and women's natural desires. Today, visibility has massive political, social and ethical purchase. To be visible is to be powerful, to be in control. To be hidden is to be repressed. Visibility in our social media age has heightened it as a virtue. The more visible you are the more it enables a progressive exploration and projection of one self.[73] To make oneself visible is to know oneself and the body is integral to its discovery. It also reveals an investment in the *integrity* of the secular body being unveiled by these practices of truth-telling.

The relationship between the secular and the unveiled, truth-making and visibility, if we recall from our previous discussion, is invested in modernism's imperial desire to discipline the body by naming—that is, discovering—it in language. Truth as uncovered and disrobed, is about possession—claiming knowability. However, knowability appears as a "pure surface", what Anne Ling Cheng recognises to be about possession by disciplining oneself from "regressive pleasures of ornamentation". That is, to identify progress as a process of removing the markers of "sexual and savage primitives"[74] which unveils truth in the mode of civilisation. Here, Cheng warns, we see the discourse of "becoming visible" which maintains progressive politics—whether racial and/or feminist—fails to address the tensions in the pursuit of "social visibility". This "remains inadequate to address the phenomenological social and psychical implications inhering in what it means to be visible".[75] This de-ornamentation, Asad has traced to the secular body which grooms a modern sensorium embodying habits, practices and desire for a self to reflect perceived secular traditions that are identified in opposition to religion. The body, taking up the secular, is an investment in the visible. To be visible is to be detectable, knowable, communicable, recognisable, to claim a knowledge which Foucault warns is a trap that masquerades as liberation when it's the hidden workings of power.

The universal impetus of the west and Feminism is entangled in cultural, political and economic power that deploys colonial and racialized dichotomies to continue "concealing the context out of which the western subject is comparing herself to its non-western counterpart".[76] Some truths, it seems, can remain invisible. The desire to critique with no historical map has been tied to a politics informed by an impulse that transforms those mobilised under the merging signifiers of the west and Feminism into political and desiring subjects. As such, they become subjects who make history.[77] The political freedoms attributed to the feminist subject as a normative practice of truth-making disavows how recognition requires its Other and therefore, can only occur "while standing on the back of someone else".[78] That someone, Sherene H. Razack reminds us, is always a woman.[79] Tracking this woman is also about understanding the vanishing of the feminine Other within Feminism's eclipsing pull qua "western feminism". It is why I have chosen to use "feminism" and not "western feminism" to avoid subduing this riddled past. It is a way of disavowing the injurious identity, by locating it in another body. Some women are to be the markers of ornamentation to be discarded. The role of western women in the fantasy of an unveiling freedom needs therefore to be carefully located, and not simply dismissed as "bad feminism", "liberal feminism", or what Susanna Mancini has called "populist-feminism".[80] My point here is not to present feminism as being hijacked by an imperial project. This would assume that democracy and feminism are "strangers to the project of empire-building".[81] Nor am I suggesting that western strands of feminism are mere masks of phallocentric European imperialism. Rather, I want to muddy the switch to *western feminism* to distance *feminisms* when considering feminist politics as a mode of imagining and organising desires—as imperialism's supplementary discourse *at the level of fantasy*.

The rescuing of the Woman qua Muslim women, as part of an imperial knowing of who the Woman is and judgement would she bring, manifests in an impulse to recover "loss" or the loss in origins of who she really is. For instance, the backlash against Abdel-Magied shows the partnership with freedom is formed in the place of excluding Muslim women who can be sacrificed in enunciation of women's freedom as Muslim women are always in the throes of violation, compromised by their religious beliefs, and only find guidance, relief, recognition in the offer of freedom. Abdel-Magied's eventual departure from Australia in the face of growing controversies on her political views became a ritual of *physical and symbolic* discarding of the other woman to maintain the untarnished national commitment to universal freedom for women. The phallic fantasy of unveiling truth qua freedom is recast here to retrieve an object of historical erasure.

This fantasy of knowing speaks from a particular "space", as Spivak has observed, and reads desire through secular critique[82] and not from a space of religious submission. In the fantasy of an unveiled subject, the critical subject *is* the desiring subject, and fantasy establishes the coordinates of desire, stifled only by a veil of tradition that has smothered women's natural desires. It is not only how feminists do history that has been transformed by this unearthing, as Joan Wallach Scott insists, but also how the body has been reconfigured and re-imagined in these changes. Women's sexual freedoms, autonomy and desire have, in other words, become a *culturally regulated way of being unveiled*. Through this lens, one may read the west' and feminism's unity through a return to history as a recovering of the fragmented women, locating her ontological status as that of the Woman, and rebelling against her psychic and epistemic condition of lack.

THE HYSTERIC'S QUESTION: THE MISTRESS/SLAVE GIRL

In this section, I examine how lack is overcome through a return to sexuation (the making of sexed subjects) and how it establishes the indeterminacy of identity through the practice of unveiling the whole body. Unveiling becomes the formula for "knowing Woman" by identifying the corporeal coordinates for satisfying her desire. Building on Sigmund Freud, Lacanian theory of sexuation shows us how identification with a subjectivity defined by "to have" the Symbolic phallus (or penis in Freudian parlance)[83] or "to be" (to behave like one has it)—both set a limit on how to engage the mOther. It is a differentiation between the subject who is "whole" and the subject who is "not-whole". Castration institutes this primordial loss of wholeness and the phallus comes to stand in for this loss in symbolic status, in language as such.[84] Hence, Lacan insists Woman struggles for recognition and ontological security as she's alienated from language that does not serve her desire. Sexuation addresses the very question: who am I? It also decides what *jouissance*—how one can experience pleasure—can be gained. All men, except one, the primordial father who limits enjoyment, is outside the law and has no limits to his *jouissance*[85]—are determined by phallic or symbolic *jouissance* representing ontological wholeness. I address the role of phallic *jouissance* in examining how pleasure is derived from pursuing wholeness, and in this context a pursuit of the wholeness of the Woman, and the role of the Other in seeking and claiming this pleasure—for both men and women.

The organisation of *jouissance* in this psycho-symbolic schema situates men's enjoyment in the symbolic fantasy of having the phallus (the all). This makes men agents in the order of being, that is of having. The phallic does not derive complete satisfaction but only promises it and men attach this promise to the body: of having and not-having knowledge (the phallus) and thus the promise of full pleasure. Women become the other—not-having (the not-all), enjoyed as an *object a*—a supplement of the lost object—by men as their lack holds the promise of full enjoyment, of possessing the (not-) all. Women in the symbolic world, where identities and self-other relations are constituted, have the supplemental *jouissance* of identifying with men but also another that is beyond the phallic, beyond the law. In other words, they do not entirely submit to the regime of phallic *jouissance*, whose enjoyment is not fully phallic but Other and thus inarticulable.[86] In addition, language fails to articulate the Woman whose *jouissance* falls in the realm of the Other.

The existential question at the heart of sexuation of what it means to be a sexual being is inherent to both sexes. Nevertheless, as there is no signifier for Woman in the Other, it is women who are left with more questions. In this mode of their feeling loss, the Woman remains an enigma that leads women to often ask "what am I as a woman"? Or *what is Woman?*[87] Where do I locate my *jouissance?* "What body do I incarnate?"[88] The question of not knowing who one is and seeking answers in the Other are the preoccupations of the hysterical subject who pursues an identity by demanding answers from the phallic Other (man) who is meant to have mastery over knowledge and therefore of the body. However, the response never satisfies. It always generates more questions. As Salecl contends, she does not have access to the object that man sees in her, so is always asking what is in her more than herself.[89] The psychoanalytic decentred body in hysteria, Jacqueline Rose observes, communicates its "inflection…*through* language in relation to the unconscious".[90] Breuer and Freud identify hysteria as a "*memory* of a trauma" which "acts like a foreign body which long after its entry must continue to be regarded as an agent that continues to work".[91]

Seeking refuge from the foreign body under a capitalised symbolic loftiness, the hysteric attempts to offer herself as Woman by deploying the body as a way of addressing the question of femininity.[92] The body, as the source of all knowledge, and thus the constitution of subjectivity, becomes both a tool of retrieval of (her) self and the barrier to her arrival. The hysteric however does not automatically mean a Woman but is more often presented in women who are fleeing from being an object—her sexed body as object.[93] The desire to know herself through the body correlates with Lacan's statement of Woman as a myth "Woman cannot be said (*se dire*). Nothing can be said of Woman".[94] She only exists under erasure because the phallus signifies man—the definite subject. Women's bodies in contrast are marked by symptoms that exceed language. Lacking the Symbolic phallus, Lacan contends, women only participate in the phallic structure by "virtue of its absence" thereby in some way to have it.[95] When Woman "speaks as an 'I' it is never clear that she speaks (of or as) herself and instead speaks in a mode of masquerade in imitation of the masculine phallic subject"[96] who she is led to believe has access to power and the means to recognition.

The conditions of recognition in this psycho-somatic scenario are fraught for women but are heightened if we consider it in a racial setting. What are the possibilities for feminine recognition vis-à-vis phallic *jouissance* if the racial marker has so forcefully already rendered the female slave's "unprotected flesh" as genderless, as Hortense Spiller observes?[97]

The "*memory* of a trauma" and repressed foreign is powerfully witnessed in the book *12 Years a Slave*, a rare direct account by Solomon Northup, a free black man from the New York state forced into slavery in the Deep South in 1841. It provides an insight into how women are haunted by the question of Woman and the hysteria that it can produce when confronted with the question of the *other* woman—a woman, if at all. Describing his life with a slave-owner Edwin Epps and his wife Mistress Mary Epps, Northup observes the hysteric in the Mistress who often appears in a state of uncertainty. She is preoccupied with maintaining the gaze of her husband who seems to always desire something else.[98] The figure of the young slave girl Patsey comes to embody this *else*—the object of desire. As a hysterical subject, the Mistress is haunted by identifying with the Other, her husband who as a white slave-owning man, orders her Symbolic world: one to which she adheres, where she is exalted, but then questions as to the success of adherence. Reflecting on the heightened sense of self which civilising missions invite, hysterics, Steve Marcus observes, "are excessively civilised persons".[99] She is haunted by questions: how can he desire this other woman? How can another woman be loved?[100] The hysteric identifies with the Symbolic security of civilisation and whiteness she believes phallic power can offer her in her challenge to men in the manner of the statements she addresses to Edwin Epps: "show me you are a man" in the sense of "Stand up and fight like a man".[101] Woman comes to being through these anxious demands. However, it is never clear what it is that the Mistress really wants—her husband's full desire? To be in the place of Patsey so she can be desired *like her*—something the Mistress assumes to know? Does she want to replace her husband as the phallic authority over women and slaves?

The inability to locate Patsey's desires drives both Edwin Epps and his wife mad with jealousy—each neurotically enthralled by their own racist fantasies of desiring Patsey as an object whose difference serves to secure their symbolic status *and* attempting to locate what her difference desires. Patsey is a tragic figure; she is caught up by two competing white fantasies that project onto her racialised body. Patsey's body is a site of continued realisation of Mr Epps' violent carnal fantasies. The violence of his preoccupation with Patsey drove Mr Epps into a fit of rage when Patsey went missing. He refuses to believe her after she returns and explains she had visited their neighbour Harriet for some soap to wash herself. The independent pursuit beyond the domestic domain was the result of being denied access to soap by the Mistress, rendering her body permanently unclean.

Keeping her body unclean is a feeble attempt on the part of the Mistress to punish Patsey by demanding that she embody her low social status, so she might control her husband's lustful gaze. Northup comments on the anxious disposition of the Mistress in her refusal to desist and with her chronic jealousy even when confronted with the truth of Patsey and Epps' relationship:

> I endeavoured to impress her with the truth that the latter was not responsible for the acts of which she complained, but that she being a slave, and subject entirely to her master's will, he alone was answerable. At length "the green-eyed monster" crept into the soul of Epps also, and then it was that he joined with his wrathful wife in an infernal jubilee over the girl's miseries.[102]

To confront this unknowable space in which Edwin Epps' desire is at once the only object to achieve and yet utterly elusive, Mistress Mary Epps would have to acknowledge that she is no different from Patsey. She has no control over her husband's gaze either.

The slave-owner's wife is also caught up in the violence of male-dominated white society in which the position of wife is secondary and even undermined when faced with her husband's desires. The category of "white family" includes her but with conditions: the white patriarch governs the family. The dynamics captured in Northup's account identifies a slave society modelled on white men's desires, phallic power, where white women and slaves are reduced to objects of desires and domination. The confrontation with this truth shatters the Mistress' fantasy of her own exceptionality as the Woman within white American slave-owning society. This fantasy had preserved the dignity of her social position, her appearance as a good wife—honourable, virtuous and desired for these things.[103] The figure of Patsey locates a repression in the vulnerability of the Mistress Epps' own position. She is reduced to one of *many women* and denied what she imagines as her "natural" position as Woman.

The hysteric believes wholeness—in the signifier of Woman—is attainable and the phallic subject—the Master—can deliver it, so as long the obstacle is removed. But the hysteric's persistent questions lead to an unsatisfying demand on the Master. The demand has a castrating affect that provokes the Master to secure "Truth"—in this case, to deliver on what whiteness guarantees. That is, her status as the only desired Woman. The hysteric is she who does not know who Woman is but prefers to be the being in the Other's desire (the phallic subject).[104] This privileging of the regulatory power of the phallus as the answer—albeit an unsatisfactory one—to the subject's ontological questions, has had some critical reception[105] and support from feminists. Lacan's controversial declaration "Woman does not exist" considers the centrality of the phallus in culture has also demoted women's Symbolic status, arguing that there is no signifier for Woman.[106] Lacan's aphorism of the nonexistence of the Woman is not to give legitimacy to Freud's phallocentrism (privileging the penis as Phallus). Rather, it is to concede to the logic of the Symbolic and its socio-linguistic law where the subjectivity of men takes prominence. As Juliet Mitchell and Jacqueline Rose highlight that Lacan reminds us how Freud had also acknowledged that sexuality was not entirely determined by the body, rather the assigned meaning and values we give it. Thus, sexuality was never secured through bodies and within the realm of a masquerade.[107] For my purpose though, I am interested in how the phallocentric fantasy of the unveiled interpellates the relations *between women*. Specifically, how the emancipatory feminist narrative of making women visible—addressing the very question of who am I that lies at the heart of feminist struggles—plays out in the fantasy of the unveiled west. As Kristeva asks of women who wish not to be excluded, but who are also dissatisfied with the function demanded of them, "what can be our place in the symbolic contract?"[108]

KNOWING WOMAN: A VEILED OR UNVEILED MASQUERADE?

In her Lacanian feminist reading of veiling as a Muslim practice, Ellie Ragland-Sullivan states that the veil is a desperate attempt to make Woman exist.[109] That is, the veil becomes the signifier for the Woman who is destined for a castrated/lacking representation outside the phallic formula of wholeness. Ragland-Sullivan argues that this phallic masquerade of normativity (of woman being the not-male) transposes the veil to whatever is in fashion, whatever fills up the lack in being, the not-having access to the phallus, the *not-all*. Women then mask their lack by "propping herself up" into the object of desire/phallus, and by pretending to be, in Lacan's words, what she does not have.[110] Here, she refers to Lacan's description of how the phallus can only play its role as long as it remains veiled.[111] For Ragland-Sullivan, this problem of what the Woman is plagues all people and all cultures. The veil is the complex Islamic solution to this problem: she exists by not being there, by signalling her invisibility, her exclusion from the Symbolic. Though she offers other possible readings, it is the reading of the Islamic veil as a supplement, what she calls a "veil of sorrow" at Woman's inexistence, that in the atmospheric of west-Islam relations has political purchase.[112]

Historically imbued with eroticism, exoticism and the hidden truth, in today's security and national discourses, the "veil of sorrow" appears in the form of Islam's cultural stain. This association identifies the stain as both threatening to women and to western freedoms, reflected in French feminist responses, within both the left and the right, who justified their support for banning the veil in 2011 because it was a signature of inequality and fundamentalism "whether consented or imposed".[113] In a more visual medium, the political impulse to tear off the veil of inexistence in the name of the feminine is discerned in a controversial viral advertisement in October 2018 for the Israeli company Hoodie under the tag "freedom is basic". It begins with a close shot of Israeli supermodel Bar Rafaeli wearing a black veil (in the niqab form) and the question: "Iran is here?" She then removes it to reveal her hoodie attire: a bright sweater and denim. She shakes her hair, dancing to lyrics of a song, "it's all about freedom, breaking the chains, costing my freedom". Rafaeli ends by repeating "freedom is basic. Hoodies". The advertisement was described as Islamophobic in the way it linked veiling with women's oppression. This concern was corroborated further by the timing of the release in the build-up to the Israeli elections which included anti-Palestinian/Arab and anti-Muslim messages—some which used the veil to highlight the cultural threat Islam posed, warning Israeli Jews that marrying Arabs and Muslims can result in one's daughter wearing it. Unveiling in these examples is projected as a triumph of the secular, and a prescription for women's liberation—a freedom that is so fundamental to being human, it is "basic". Unveiling activates an agency denied to Muslim women, who are imagined as wounded by Muslim men—or in the words of Femen, who "shroud their women in black sacks of submissiveness and fear, and dread as they do the devil the moment women break free to light, peace, and freedom".[114] The veil in these oppositional discourses is constructed as a phallic representation in that it is imagined conceding to patriarchal boundaries. The veil is what interrupts the teleology of the Woman with a body to prove it.

In the climate of security, these concessions are increasingly projected as *collusion* with patriarchy as part of a growing suspicion of Muslim women as conduits of radicalisation of which the veil has become its most radical symptom. In contrast to the humanitarian concerns about Muslim women as victims of the veil of violence, she is now an agent of dangerous ideas or "passive terrorism"[115]—the internalisation of women's lack who willingly wear the veil of lack. The feminist concerns for women's ontological insecurity corresponds and raises the stakes for the broader west's security concerns in times of terror, heightening the investment in women's unveiling. We see this theatrically displayed in August 2017 when Australia's One Nation's leader Pauline Hanson entered parliament wearing a burqa in a show of protest against the garb as a security threat. Removing it in a dramatic gesture almost identical to the Israeli advertisement, Hanson announced how glad she was to be free of it and called to have it banned on security grounds. Later she described wearing the veil as "really horrible and "more than uncomfortable… it's really hard to describe".[116] The lack of words to describe the experience of wearing the veil places the willingness to veil as beyond feminist or even human understandings—that is, beyond the realms of freedom. The obscenity of women covered up so completely evokes Copjec's reading of Clérambault images of Moroccan women and their "useless enjoyment".[117] Hanson's opposition to the veil as both a concern for women's rights and a national security threat is symptomatic of femonationalism's use of Muslim women's rights to achieve more conservative nationalist objectives against immigration, the "Islamification" of western culture and the obscenity of the Islamic body. Though she does not identify as a feminist, the gesture of unveiling is not possible without the imaginary of herself as having cast off the phallic veil.

Adhering to patriarchal codes of being, that is, the notion of covering over a lack, the veil appears as a masquerade of the phallus, a "masquerade-like-solution" to the question of what man is to woman and woman to man.[118] Reflecting on Lacan's non-existent Woman, Drucilla Cornell wonders if it is Lacan who is determined as "he's gotten to the bottom of her" and that "he knows Her" as a "lack" who is "just there",[119] at the same time he claims she cannot be known. Cornell insists that we cannot reduce women to lack simply because the feminine is unstable and the metaphors, such as her veiling, cannot capture her completely. Nor does this lack of separation from these metaphors mean that there is no truth to women's oppression. But it is precisely Lacan's own slippage into securing a truth through the Symbolic that warns of its compelling logic for both men and women. In the racist fantasy, where lack is doubly amplified, and the Symbolic—as we saw in Chapter 3—provides a "natural" refuge from alterity—both sexual and racial—this slippage takes on more urgency. We see the problematic of excluding race from sex in French feminist philosopher Luce Irigaray's interrogation of this sexual relation and its presupposition of the Lacanian One (Man). In her critical intervention, she prescribes a way for women to free themselves from the tyranny of the One and speak through the repressed feminine. Speaking against Lacanian phal-locentrism, Irigaray contends that the feminine is rendered invisible "be-hind a screen of representation" by the masculine self-same order, silencing women and forcing their exclusion. In this sense, women's "natural" body disappears into its representative function,[120] a phantom-like abstraction reduced to a commonality: phallic commodities.[121] Using Freud's exam-ple of the woman who weaves to compensate for her lack, Irigaray insists that if the woven veil sustains disavowal, one should on the contrary stop weaving and take off the veil in order to let down the disavowal and begin to see something else: woman's sex.[122]

"Unveiling" invoked in Irigaray is one of linguistic transformation: instead of using the French word for veil and maintaining its masculine meaning, she uses "envelope"—a space outside the masculine, not entirely "veiled" (concealed). However, as Anne-Emmanuelle Berger observes, Iri-garay then posits a woman who is naked without her envelope (her "nat-ural" body) and still seeking veils to cover herself.[123] Cornell's similarly suggests giving "body" to the feminine and speaking from an ideal—"the not-yet"—which could redeem the feminine from the shadow of obscurity: "We bring the feminine from the 'rere' to the 'front'". This bringing of "the not-yet" to the front is described in Cornell's account through the metaphors of "bring into light" from the "shadows",[124] "discovering" and "recovering", which not only slips back into the Symbolic, but the Imag-inary that makes possible the realisation of the Woman and knowing the Woman.

The veil in these feminist critiques appears as a phallocentric shadow, a symptom of mourning Woman's inexistence.[125] It conceals women's shame but its presence simultaneously reinforces the phallic logic of the Freudian lack, the Lacanian erasure of Woman, where she pretends to be what she does not have.[126] In other words, like Mistress Epps' hysterical demand to have her Symbolic status secured by policing Patsey's body, woman has to veil the best she can to conceal her "secret insufficiency".[127] By making herself up, showing off her "jewels" to increase her own value, the Woman is constantly trying to prove how priceless she is in the sexual economy.[128] The body here is fetishised and treated as a phallus.[129] In this mode of semblance, women submit to phallic pleasure by masquerading as the phallus.

Extending on Irigaray's feminist-Marxist narrative of the woman who conceals herself behind a screen—that is, who "weaves" to sustain the dis-avowal of her sex,[130] Svitlana Matviyenko suggests that woman "intensifies invention and the marketing of the endless opportunities in consumer culture which can produce her – always offering her new effective solutions to become such".[131] The veiled woman is then re-scripted in phallic logic as all women one way or another wear different forms of veils to conceal their lack. Highlighting other forms of veiling, Žižek adds that women in western consumer culture undergo extensive facial surgery and exhibit a "made up face which is no different from a face concealed by a burqa".[132] By presenting the body as "made up", what is intimated in these discourses of "weaving" is a belief in a "natural" body beneath racial shadows of lack—the veil—beyond the Symbolic meaning where women's bodies are identified.

Identifying the veil or its absence reveals a propensity in western feminist discourses to articulate politics and produce knowledge through the body. This body is both symbolically produced and brought into being through the imaginary. In the 1960s and 1970s second wave feminist activism in the United States and Europe heralded the body as a site of contestation through which women's identity could be announced. Feminism called for the liberation of women's bodies. Slogans like "our bodies, our selves", called for women to be unleashed from the burden of patriarchal/phallocentric signification imposed on their bodies; to *unveil* women's bodies in public space, culminating into a call for a broader sexual revolution. Through women's liberation struggles, women's *jouissance*, once confined, had opened up as part of the "unisex effect" and feminists contributed to the "unfinished human" that history was making. Women gained access to phallic *jouissance* through a process of phallic appropriation.[133] It is not that women have been deprived of this *jouissance*, but throughout history, they could only encounter it within the "limits of their destinies as wives and mothers".[134] Decades later, modernity has paved the way for unleashing all desires, and such the restriction is imagined as dissipated, conquered, for her to now enjoy as *Woman*. The unveiling of women's desire as an image of emancipation, and the announcement of the Woman in these political interventions in western tradition comes to be linked to "bared skin" and "flaunted sexuality", as a means of measuring women's freedom and equality.[135] Exposing (unveiling) and its liberating overtones also has a primal psychic relief in that it behaves as a feminine masquerade of full satisfaction, completion[136] beyond the confines of religion, culture, the "veil of sorrow" and the shame that it carries for women. In the Lacanian feminist framework, the veiled woman reinforces the lack-in-being, heralding the symbolic death of the fragmented woman. This lack makes possible the Woman known beneath her veil—pursuing (or in

Lacanian terms, a return to) the unveiled—by rejecting the assumption of her "castration".[137] The possibility of wholeness is imagined in the fantasy of her casting off her phallic veils.

Other Veils

The impulse to unveil corresponds with the western belief that unveiling is a universal good. As Zayzafoon observes, the metaphor of the "veiled phallus" in Lacan and the metaphor of the veil in French feminism, rely on a western tradition that favours visibility/presence over invisibility/absence, and truth/light over concealment/darkness. The veil in Muslim cultures was used for both men and women (the male *Tuareg* in the Sahara Desert). Thus, it was not necessarily always gendered. In the European setting, the veil was exclusively feminine and used to refer to brides, widows and nuns. In the nineteenth century, the veil became a marker of cultural difference.[138] It is, therefore, necessary to consider how the cultural and gendered components of the veil are understood by psychoanalysis in its deployment to connote femininity, and the anxiety of the other that possesses the phallus. Thus, the theory of the threat posed by women's excess sexuality is doubly threatening as it also an excess of difference.[139] This perceived threat of the veiled woman producing a "visor effect"—the a-reciprocal gaze which destabilised a western gaze—and in the context of this chapter, the idea that men are to look and women as objects are to be looked at.[140]

Within Muslim discourses veiling can be understood as a physical barrier to masculine fetishisation of women's bodies, thereby spoiling pleasure and pleasuring only for the women who wear it.[141] Berger offers a counter reading to the veil as lack. For her, it is less a means of covering up women's threatening sexual "difference" (that is, lack) from men, than it is a means of masking differences between Muslim women and overcoming the fragmenting of womaness.[142] The contemporary rise of veiling, perhaps unconsciously, ignores or negates sexual difference in the theological order by helping to define and assert a single, overarching Islamic identity—an identity perceived to be under threat—while affirming women's specific role. It is as though the particular invisibility of the veiled woman enables a visible Islam to stand in her place within the western symbolic secular space.[143] Veiling can be understood as a subtraction of particularities of womanness that are replaced with a singular Islamic identity for Muslim women.[144] This identity evokes fidelity to a transcendental Other—beyond the western universalist claims that her body is the origin of her true self and desires. The veil here announces the Woman by showing her to be feminine—a femininity that reconfigures what it means to make the feminine visible. In the west, this announcement is strengthened by identifying with the category of "Muslim women", looking at each other as a mirror image in which these women "see themselves reflected *as Muslims*".[145] These representations of womenness through the veil question the link between the veil and lack, by speaking to another possibility of an *Other feminine jouissance* one that extends beyond the regime of the veiled and unveiled that grip women's ontological status.

Announcing feminine identity as a successful masquerade of the phallus by veiled women, this identity gestures to a historical feminist refusal to accept the veil as an expression of anything other than a step backwards for women. Visibility is an ethical and *feminist* transgression. While this may explain an underlying western anxiety towards veiled women, it opens up the question of why the veil is not considered an option for the announcement of the Woman. Visibility is not only instituted through unveiling, but also becomes integral to women's identity; meanwhile other possibilities of representing or "being" "Woman" are subsumed by this unveiling imaginary.

Tracing the ambivalence in the Islamic veil, Henry Krips in *The Hijab, the Veil and Sexuation*, offers the possibility of the Woman beyond the hysteric that Jacques-Alain Miller attributed to "the postiche woman"—"the fake woman"—who is caught up in the feminine masquerade.[146] The Islamic veil, Krips contends, allows the possibility of the "true woman" whose access to feminine *jouissance*, allows her "beyond-of-pleasure"—disintegrating the symbolic order—and enjoying the varieties of womanness "*without leaving behind the body*". That is, finding womanness beyond a singularity.[147] In western social and political discourses this singularity operates in the mode of visibility and denies the existence of women behind the veil or the harem. However, it is precisely this possibility of a beyond singularity that the imagery of the veiled and unveiled, and its underpinning fantasy of an unveiling freedom, suppresses.

Rather than posing the question whether to unveil or not to unveil, which these readings imply, one might ask, "what is the veil and who is doing the unveiling?"[148] On the one hand, the veil regulates what is seen as excessive in the symbolic order as an *object a*. On the other, the invisibility of the veil in the non-Islamic world is the reason for an often false assumption about the Islamic veil and liberation from it. In this sense, western fixation on the veiled Muslim woman conceals the *masquerade* of the over-exposed body which is the master signifier of the unveiled and identified as the liberated body in the feminist imaginary, as just another form of veiling. With this paradox in mind, where do we place the so-called "unveiled" woman when sexuation demands she is also veiled in the desire of men? How does the west deal with its hysteric?

Fleeing the Veil of Lack

If we consider that the emergence of the Lacanian subject relies on exclusion—a failure of recognition that woman comes to represent[149]—the fantasy of unveiling freedom, suggests the unveiled is beyond sex and exclusion. Unveiling has political currency insofar as it reconfigures the symbolic phallic function that renders women as objects. If veiling reinforces women's lack, the act of removing the veil—exposing *a* woman—conveys an empowering alternative for (some) women. In the western feminist imaginary, unveiling is therefore a powerful political metaphor for women's dissent, signalling a refusal to participate in the logic of sexuation that codes women in the phallocentric structure of Woman as a lack-in-being. Like the governing presence of the phallus, the unveiled as a practice of the secular body is an escape from erasure for *the woman who unveils* and who is no longer burdened with carrying the signifier of castration.[150] The link between unveiling and freedom infers that phallic enjoyment *is not forbidden to all women.*

As a metaphorical expression of freedom, unveiling is imagined as going beyond the "respected masks" of sexual difference and transcending the demand on women to veil their lack in order to secure presence of the phallus. Through unveiling, the "phallic signifier is totally divorced from the penis" and becomes instead a "power-signifier" which covers up her lack.[151] Unveiling imagines locating the truth of Woman beyond lack by bringing into being her whole "natural" "pre-castrated" body. Peeling away the phallocentric symbolic, Irigaray's "natural" body is recovered, revealing that there is no lack; there is nothing to conceal. There is no shame attached to her body. This is the secular body that "does not blush".[152] The pursuit for wholeness, represented as something natural in the fantasy of unveiling, re-joins her with the phallic west not merely as a passive object for the look of others, but as an active agent flaunting her body with ontological certainty.

However, the performance of unveiling to be unveiled (nude) is not an activation of feminine *jouissance*, the *not-all.* Rather, it appears as the hysteric's strategy to masquerade as the Woman through its promise of overcoming the lack and fragmentation that women must veil. Western women's liberation movements have historically increased access to phallic wholeness under the banner of equality, but as Soler explains, this does not make women the Woman but an "appearance of the woman".[153] The unveiling of freedom, and the equality for both sexes it infers, only offers another feminine masquerade through a phallic west. Feminine *jouissance*, however, does not provide reassurance of "being" either. Since women cannot be the Woman as she does not exist, she chooses to become *one* woman, chosen by a man. She participates in a process of "phallicisation" or "playing the man"[154]—a masquerade where she props herself up in the insignia of western master signifiers: sexual freedom and autonomy. These "effective realisations"—goods, knowledge, power—in Lacanian parlance are imagined open to her.[155] Thus, Lacan's formulation of there being *a* woman—"since we cannot speak for more than one", is re-scripted in the west's fantasy of unveiling, from *one* woman to Woman: the one who is chosen. Almutawakel's image illustrates the constitution of this one woman as the Woman whose phallic approximation—an unveiled wholeness—is achieved through the imagining of *a* woman's body which constitutes the natural "human", made whole once the veil releases its suffocating grip. Each image represents the veil's incremental hijacking of woman's bodily parts, denying her control over her body; perversions of a "natural" bodily integrity. The increasing presence of the "veil of sorrow" slowly heralds the death of women's phallic *jouissance* in its symbolic dismemberment of Woman. Each image is a failure of the other women failing to repossess a body.

If women are unveiling to announce themselves, in the racist fantasy where freedom is realised in certain bodies, the exclusion of women occurs by transposing lack to the *other* women who remain veiled. Those who exalt the west's secular freedoms harvest the fragmentation of womanness in the other, like a prosthetic penis, to compensate for woman's lack.[156] It is the other woman who becomes burdened with shame, exhibits lack and is silenced by the imagined docility of the veil's presence in the west. The fantasy of a west that can "save" women from phallocentric erasure transposes the woman who veils into "the fake woman", the veiled masquerade for whom appearance is everything and who is reduced to an object for phallic/men's desires.[157] In contrast, the woman who unveils is free from shame and lack: the *complete* woman whose unveiling embodies her autonomy and sexual openness through a body which pursues what Elizabeth

Grosz observes as a "universal singular model" of the human, of the *feminine* human.[158]

For the hysteric, however, the demand for ontological certainty is never satisfied. It is difficult for her to be *a* woman and not the Woman, that is to say, to be one woman—meaning that there are others and that she is not unique.[159] This anxiety of the unstable status of the "*a* woman" is discernible in Mistress Epps's inability to tolerate the very presence of Patsey—the constant reminder of how she was not unique, and how she was not the only one chosen. Her relationship with Patsey is defined by anxiety and desire because the young slave girl served as a reminder of the shame of not being recognised as the only object of her husband's gaze— the only Woman. There is also another dimension to her shame: Patsey is not just another woman who attracts her husband's gaze. As well as being sexually desirable, she also contributes to his material wealth. Patsey, as the most efficient slave, gathers more cotton than the other slaves and this adds to her feminine allure.[160]

In contrast to Patsey, the Mistress, much like many women of her society, does not work. Her status and identity are tied to her husband and she has only her whiteness to secure her identity. Patsey's presence marks the limit of identifying with whiteness for women in American slave-owning society and reveals the Mistress to "the fake woman"[161] concealing a lack through a whiteness masquerade. The focus on Patsey's slave body throughout the story presents its *object a* qualities; it locates the source of her husband's sexual advances and stands in the way of respect the Mistress Epps' wants. It is also why Patsey's remaining presence, despite her Mistress' protests, is something that torments her. She is an impediment to her imagined status as the Woman. The constant return to her counterpart's feminine body[162] as something to be punished and contained, is how Mistress Epps' demands on her husband can finally be met, and where she finds solace and pleasure.

Witnessing her husband whipping Patsey, Mistress Epps' regains her pride and can announce that it is she who is in fact the chosen Woman. Each lashing reaffirms that it is Patsey who is nothing more than a masquerade and who needs to be reminded. Patsey's bloodied, whipped body locates the Mistress's desire to discipline the challenge she represents, but it is also the enjoyment in *punishing her husband* for failing to secure her symbolic status that whiteness promises. Race, as we recall from Seshadri-Crooks, offers the body total meaning: whiteness functions as an "illegal enjoyment of absolute wholeness", which is being denied her by her husband's lustful gaze. His taking the whip to Patsey's body becomes a way for her to make him desire her truth that she is the only Woman and is the only object of his desire. Patsey's bodily wounds offer relief, quelling the possibility of a desirable female slave body (and in turn, the Mistress' own lack) which allows her to enjoy her position as the Woman.

This racial dynamic can also be witnessed in "The Muslim Question" where "western women" have taken on the hysteric's role as an "activist for what does not exist"—the universal free Woman.[163] The peculiar concern for the Muslim woman calls on a west who is imagined as having the capacity to both liberate and guarantee woman as the Woman. She demands that the west announces to Muslim women, vis-à-vis its unveiling, the truth of the attainable Woman, who no longer needs to live in shame of her body. The west here is posited as one that can unlock woman's desires and her "true" self.

Veiling the Other

In the new era of Islamophobia, where images of violent fundamentalist men and over-bearing husbands and fathers dominate the western imaginary, patriarchy is increasingly represented as the exclusive domain of Islam.[164] Muslim women are reminded of the veil as a symbol of women's shame, inequality, subordination, humiliation and an intolerable discrimination. The veil is cast as demeaning,[165] rendering women to be seen only by her male authorities (father, brothers and husband).[166] The narratives of a veil as a violence here displaces patriarchy onto the body of the Muslim woman—a body constrained by unfreedom, denying unveiling as the gift of the phallus.[167] The other woman, reflected in Patsey and the Muslim woman, is burdened with the historical lack in order for freedom to be possible for women, and to perform their liberation from the veil as lack. In this sense, the west's (free) Woman shares in the phallic conquest of the other woman as the *object a*.

The scrutiny of the veil in the west also consigns the Muslim woman to reduced public visibility, amounting to her vanishing from public life and public debate. The concern for her "true" identity being denied by her bodily invisibility was discernible in the French National Assembly report on the veil in 2010 referring to the veil as an "assault on women's dignity and on the affirmation of femininity". Woman's identity, presence and dignity, is linked to the visible physical body.[168] Women's freedom to choose and exercise agency vis-à-vis the visible body became the evidence of Woman, who exercises this reason and autonomy *correctly* by not veiling. In contrast, the Islamic veil serves as a phallic fetishistic pleasure for male spectators.[169]

In her examination of the veil debate in France, Joan Scott contends that it was not the absence of women's sexuality but the *presence of sexuality*, and how it was being practiced outside of "normal" protocols of gender interaction, which unsettles.[170] The presence of the veil marks the failure of secularism to overcome (sexual) difference and reconcile it with gender equality, which Scott coins as "sexularism".[171] French feminist philosopher and supporter of banning the veil, Elisabeth Badinter, expressed this concern of invisibility and how it benefits men, differentiated nuns from Muslim women by claiming the former were asexual and have chosen to live that specific lifestyle whereas veiled women are "wives" and "mothers" interacting in the public sphere, were sexual subjects. Their sexual identities demand they interact with men according to western (universal) standards of gender relations. Mancini observes that there are a number of ways of reading this. It can mean that it is men who form women's identity by being able to *see* them as sexual beings.[172] It also suggests that women's bodies must always be offered to the Other. Not only is Badinter inferring that Woman is only recognised in the act of unveiling but she reduces women's identity and their sexuality to an exhibitionist body.[173] What bothers Badinter, and perhaps mobilises her activism against the veil, is that veiled bodies speak to a sexed experience that disrupts the symbolic reading of sexual identity already given it: women, like men, should express their sexuality *openly*—as part of what Scott calls an "open" culture.[174] The language of the body here is that of its accessibility to the other sex. Muslim women, in contrast, cover their sexuality because it is regulated by codes of modesty and honour—both bodily and mentally.[175] This exaltation of "open" culture forecloses any consideration of women's own gaze who see women under the veil. The emphasis on "openness", as signalling Woman's existence, is contingent on the gaze of men.

The more this free (unveiled) woman succeeds in the phallic conquest, however, the less she enjoys it. Her sense of instability grows because the question she fundamentally asks about her essence, as the Woman, can never be answered because it speaks to the heart of sexual difference.[176] In order for the hysteric to enjoy—that is, to attain an identity—in her phallic conquest, the claim to being the Woman can only occur by offering the other woman some protection. The protection of Muslim women—whether by sending troops to countries where she is imperilled—or through legal proclamations—positions western men's gaze as fulfilling women's desire. This finally answers the hysteric's question by guaranteeing their symbolic status as satisfied free women.

The Muslim woman stands in for the category of "women"—the fragmented bodies seen in Almutawakel's image—as the insurance, the comparison, the glitch in the assembling of Woman, that turns the other into the representation for difference. The hysteric's question of "who is the Woman?" is addressed by a series of negations. If women are free in the west, there are other men—a patriarchal violent figure who is always prepared to sell, veil or kill his daughter/wife to guarantee their enslavement.[177] Thus, it is "our" men who must prove they are not like them by liberating Muslim women. In this demand, the Lacanian erasure of Woman is overridden.

Imagining themselves in this continuum of negation, western critics of the veil identify with the fantasy of unveiling freedom. They imagine themselves as having fought for their bodies and reclaimed them as unconstrained, desiring and visible. Unveiling connotes the shift in defining respectability from that of containing sexuality—as it was understood in the past—to openly enjoying one's body and sexuality,[178] and exerting women's agency. These distinctions do not mean that feminists in the west have not been critical of the focus on women's bodies as a "sexual exhibitionism", reducing women to a sexed body. However, as Scott observes, these concerns have been set aside in the ideological confrontation with Islam. Differences that are put aside to protect the identity of a "west" whose civilisational wholeness is asserted in its encounter with others. Equality is equated with the visibility of the female body as the only acceptable expression of being the Woman.[179] The unconscious identification with the west in uncovering the body to retrieve the (free) Woman also reveals, paradoxically, the very visibility of sexual difference. This revelation occurs through women's bodily difference as marketed, desirable and enjoyed by both women *and* men.

CONCLUSION

Unveiling as a mode of hysteria is a defense mechanism against the impossibility of the Woman who polices her boundaries. It is a state of distress over the possibility of a woman that exceeds veiling and unveiling, and that the Woman can only exist in the epistemic confines of uncovering herself to speak. But this speaking is always a form of ventriloquism, where the other woman's voice is animated by intervention. Behind the alarm for the helplessness of the Muslim woman is the frightening confrontation with the unstable nature of the identity that confers the liberated unveil woman's proclamation that fleshly freedom is intrinsic to knowing and being the Woman. That is, there are no essential characteristics of the Woman and that activating her in the post-9/11 epoch does not guarantee universal inscription, and thus the west's security of self. As Seshadri-Crooks notes, the possibility of whiteness—the unveiled—not fulfilling its objective arouses an anxiety of the terror of sameness: that the unveiled Woman is no different from other women; the unveiling performance is a masquerade of the veil; or even the possibility that the western fantasy is also bolstered by her being its *object a*. The racist fantasy of an unveiled (liberated) subject saves her from ontological disintegration, but it anxiously relies on veiling another: the not altogether woman.

Sensitive to the tense climate of the war on terror and the visibility of western women in their concern for Muslim women, this chapter reassesses Lacan's controversial announcement that Woman does not exist within the context of racist fantasies and their prominence in the pronouncement of the free west today. The discussion entailed a closer examination of how the imagery of the veiled and unveiled is a medium in defining relations between western women and the other woman that shapes the progressive politics of a feminist imaginary. Through this lens, Lacan's formula for sexuation and the unveiling fantasy of the unveiled west, provides a shortcut to "saving" the unveiled woman who positions herself as the one who is recognised against the lack in recognising the Woman. This chapter contends that the reoccurring image of the Muslim woman qua the veiled woman in the unveiling fantasy arranges unveiled (white) western female bodies against oriental/veiled bodies for the imagining of a Muslim that threatens the freedoms that have been gained for women. The constitution of this relationship is plugged into a fantasy of bodies arranged—like in Almutawakel's image—according to how freedom is to be consumed. The veiled woman becomes a spectral underside to a progressive imaginary of bodily typologies of freedom and unfreedom, and an overcoming of the Lacanian lack.

Notes

1. Denise Riley, *'Am I That Name?' Feminism and the Category of 'Women' in History* (London, UK: Palgrave Macmillan, 1988), 38.
2. Erin Fassin, "Sexual Democracy: The New Racialization of Europe," *Journal of Civil Society* 8, no. 3 (2012): 288.
3. Butler, "Sexual Politics, Torture, and Secular Time," 2.

4. Michel Foucault, *The Will to Knowledge: The History of Sexuality I*, trans. Robert Hurley (London: Random House, 1978).
5. See Asad, "Thinking About the Secular Body, Pain and Liberal Politics."
6. Joan Wallach Scott, *Sex and Secularism* (Princeton and Oxford: Princeton University Press, 2018).
7. British Labour party politician and former Culture Secretary Tessa Jowell linked the visibility of the body to identity, arguing that the identity of women is "obscured to the world, apart from their husband." Cited in Nahid Afrose Kabir, *Young British Muslims: Identity, Culture, Politics and the Media* (Edinburgh: Edinburgh University Press, 2010), 146.
8. Scott, *The Politics of the Veil*, 133.
9. Butler, "Foucault and the Paradox of Bodily Inscriptions," 603.
10. Saba Mahmood, *Politics of Piety: The Islamic Revival and the Feminist Subject* (Princeton, NJ: Princeton University Press, 2005), 45.
11. Seyla Benhabib referenced in Susanna Mancini, "Patriarchy as the Exclusive Domain of the Other: The Veil Controversy, False Projection, and Cultural Racism," *International Journal of Constitutional Law* 1, no. 2 (2011): 412.
12. Butler, *Bodies That Matter: On the Discursive Limits of 'Sex'*, 48.
13. Juliet Rogers, "Making the Crimes (Female Genital Mutilation) Act 1996, Making the 'Non-mutilation Woman'," *The Australian Feminist Law Journal* 18, no. 1 (2003): 100.
14. Sunera Thobani, "White Wars: Western Feminisms and the 'War on Terror'," *Feminist Theory* 8, no. 2 (2007): 170.
15. See Ahmed, *Women and Gender in Islam: Historical Roots of a Modern Debate*.
16. Thobani, "White Wars," 174.
17. Thobani, "White Wars," 183.
18. Lynn Stuart Parramore, "White Females from Hell," *Lapham's Quarterly*, August 2, 2017. https://www.laphamsquarterly.org/roundtable/white-females-hell.
19. Jessica Guynn, "BBQ Betty, Permit Patty and Why the Internet Is Shaming White People Who Police People 'Simply for Being Black'," *USA Today*, July 18, 2018. https://www.usatoday.com/story/tech/2018/07/18/bbq-becky-permit-patty-and-why-internet-shaming-white-people-who-police-black-people/793574002/.
20. Shushannah Walshe, "Hillary Clinton, John Kerry, Laura Bush Rally for Afghan Women," *ABC News*, November 15, 2013.
21. "Special Message from the Feminist Majority on the Taliban, Osama bin Laden, and Afghan Women," press release, *Feminist Majority Foundation*, September 18, 2001. https://www.feminist.org/news/pressstory.asp?id=5802.
22. Mark Potok and Janet Smith, "Women Against Islam," *Intelligence Report*, June 10, 2015. https://www.splcenter.org/fighting-hate/intelligence-report/2015/women-against-islam.

23. Dean Spade and Sarah Lazare, "Women Now Run the Military-Industrial Complex: That's Nothing to Celebrate," *In These Times*, January 12, 2019. http://inthesetimes.com/article/21682/women-military-industrial-complex-gina-haspel-trump-feminism-lockheed-martin.

24. Lizzie Dearden, "Parents Who Force Their Children to Wear a Burqa Should Be Jailed, Says Australian Senator," *Independent*, October 29, 2014. https://www.independent.co.uk/news/world/australasia/parents-who-force-their-children-to-wear-a-burqa-should-be-jailed-says-australian-senator-9825696.html.

25. Katherine Murphy, "Pauline Hanson Wears Burqa in Australian Senate While Calling for Ban," *The Guardian*, August 17, 2017. https://www.theguardian.com/australia-news/2017/aug/17/pauline-hanson-wears-burqa-in-australian-senate-while-calling-for-ban.

26. Alan Taylor, "Femen Stages a 'Topless Jihad'," *The Atlantic*, April 4, 2013. https://www.theatlantic.com/photo/2013/04/femen-stages-a-topless-jihad/100487/. In addition, there is Laura Bush, Feminist Majority, feminist Ida Lichter, Conservative American commentator Anne Coulter and British critic Melanie Philips.

27. Marie Gilbert, "France's 'Battle of the Veil'," *Open Democracy*, April 8, 2011.

28. Sara Farris, *In the Name of Women's Rights: The Rise of Femonationalism* (Durham: Duke University Press, 2017). Alism.

29. Dean Spade and Sarah Lazare, "Women Now Run the Military-Industrial Complex: That's Nothing to Celebrate," *In These Times*, January 12, 2019. http://inthesetimes.com/article/21682/women-military-industrial-complex-gina-haspel-trump-feminism-lockheed-martin.

30. Ben Winsor, "ABC Has No Plans to Cut Yassmin Abdel-Magied, Despite Campaign," SBS News, February 20, 2017. https://www.sbs.com.au/news/abc-has-no-plans-to-cut-yassmin-abdel-magied-despite-campaign.

31. As opposed to "inessential" women who are not white and middle class as argued in Elizabeth V. Spelman, *Inessential Woman: Problems of Exclusion in Feminist Thought* (Boston: Beacon Press, 1990).

32. Scott, *Sex and Secularism*.

33. Dipesh Chakrabarty, *Provincialising Europe: Postcolonial Thought and Historical Difference* (Princeton and Oxford: Princeton University Press, 2000).

34. Chakrabarty, *Provincialising Europe*, 8.

35. Chakrabarty, *Provincialising Europe*, 8.

36. Sara Ahmed, Affective Economies, *Social Text* 22, no. 2 (2004): 131.

37. Scott, *The Fantasy of Feminist History*, 36.

38. Soler, *What Lacan Said About Women: A Psychoanalytic Study*, 185.

39. Riley, *Am I That Name?* 41.

40. Soler, *What Lacan Said About Women: A Psychoanalytic Study*, 170–171.

41. Julia Kristeva, "Women's Time," [Alice Jardine and Harry Blake.] *Journal of Women in Culture and Society* 7, no. 1 (1981): 17.

42. Kristeva, "Women's Time," 20.

43. Wendy Brown, *States of Injury: Power and Freedom in Late Modernity: Power and Freedom in Late Modernity* (Princeton: Princeton University Press, 1995).

44. Brown, *States of Injury*, 40.

45. Joan Wallach Scott, *The Fantasy of Feminist History* (Durham: Duke University Press, 2011), 43.

46. Scott, *The Fantasy of Feminist History*, 25.

47. Mahmood, *Politics of Piety*, 10.

48. See, for example, Spivak, *A Critique of Postcolonial Reason*; Lila Abu-Lughod, "Orientalism and Middle East Feminist Studies," *Feminist Studies* 27, no. 1 (2001).

49. I have in mind Islamic studies scholar Asma Barlas' concerns about her work being labelled as "Islamic feminist" by historian Margot Badran. She argues she has never identified her work as feminist and would prefer to work outside of it. See Asma Barlas, "Secular and Feminist Critiques of the Qur'an: Anti-hermeneutics as Liberation?" *Journal of Feminist Studies in Religion* 32, no. 2 (2017): 111–121.

50. Ahmed, *Women and Gender in Islam: Historical Roots of a Modern Debate* (New Haven and London: Yale University Press, 1992), 229.

51. Ahmed, *Women and Gender in Islam*, 122.

52. McClintock, *Imperial Leather: Race, Gender, and Sexuality in the Colonial Contest*, 213.

53. See Barbara Hodgson, *Dreaming of East: Western Women and the Exotic Allure of the Orient* (Vancouver: Greystone Books, 2007).

54. Riley, *Am I That Name?* 37.

55. Sirma Bilge, "Intersectionality Undone: Saving Intersectionality from Feminist Intersectional Studies," *Du Bois Review: Social Science Research on Race* 10, no. 2 (2013): 405–424.

56. Ramón Grosfugel, Lecture on Intersectionality, University of South Africa, August 19, 2016. https://www.youtube.com/watch?v=FMEhyKqMWmA.

57. Jasbir Paur, *Terrorist Assemblages: Homonationalism in Queer Times* (Durham and London: Duke University Press, 2007).

58. See Meyda Yeğenoğlu, *Colonial Fantasies: Towards a Feminist Reading of Orientalism* (Cambridge: Cambridge University Press, 1998) and Saba Mahmood, *Politics of Piety: The Islamic Revival and the Feminist Subject* (Princeton, NJ: Princeton University Press, 2005).

59. Riley, *Am I That Name?* 39.

60. Brown, *States of Injury*, 134.

61. Ann Laura Stoler, "Imperial Debris: On Ruins and Ruination," *Cultural Anthropology* 23, no. 2 (2008): 191–219.
62. Spivak, *A Critique of Postcolonial Reason*, 164.
63. Mahmood, *Politics of Piety*.
64. Kristeva, "Women's Time," 19.
65. Spivak, *A Critique of Postcolonial Reason*, 147.
66. Spivak, *A Critique of Postcolonial Reason*, 147.
67. Brown, *States of Injury*, 41.
68. Lamia Ben Youssef Zayzafoon, *The Production of the Muslim Woman: Negotiating Text, History, and Ideology* (Lanham, MD: Lexington Books, 2005), 66.
69. Yeğenoğlu, *Colonial Fantasies*, 116.
70. See Asad, *Formations of the Secular: Christianity, Islam, Modernity*.
71. Zayzafoon, *The Production of the Muslim Woman*, 65–66.
72. Scott, *The Fantasy of Feminist History*, 24.
73. Rafia Zakaria, *Veil* (New York and London: Bloomsbury Academic, 2017), 6–7.
74. Cheng, *Second Skin*, 24.
75. Cheng, *Second Skin*, 167.
76. Mancini, "Patriarchy as the Exclusive Domain of the Other," 427.
77. Scott, *The Fantasy of Feminist History*, 43. There have been numerous studies done on the role of whiteness as an agent of power. See Anne McClintock, *Imperial Leather*, which examines the role of whiteness staging European superiority in a time of colonial conquest. On the psychopathology of the colonial condition and whiteness as integral to colonial violence, see Frantz Fanon, *Black Skin White Masks* (London: Pluto Press, 1986).
78. Razack, *Looking White People in the Eye*.
79. Razack, *Looking White People in the Eye*, 30.
80. Mancini, "Patriarchy as the Exclusive Domain of the Other," 414.
81. Mahmood, "Feminism, Democracy and Empire: Islam and the War on Terror," 82.
82. Talal Asad, *Is Critique Secular? Blasphemy, Injury, and Free Speech* (Berkeley: Townsend Center for the Humanities, University of California Press, 2009), 9.
83. See Sigmund Freud and James Strachey, *Three Essays on the Theory of Sexuality* (New York: Basic Books, 2000).
84. Elizabeth Grosz, *Jacques Lacan: A Feminist Introduction* (New York: Routledge, 1990), 73.
85. Fink, *The Lacanian Subject: Between Language and Jouissance*, 110.
86. Soler, *What Lacan Said About Women: A Psychoanalytic Study*, 178.
87. Colette Soler, "Hysteria and Obsession," In *Reading Seminar I and II: Lacan's Return to Freud*, ed. Richard Feldstein, Bruce Fink, and Maire Jaanus (New York: State University New York Press 1999), 272–273.

88. Ellie Ragland, "The Hysteric's Truth," in *Reflections on Seminar XVII: Jacques Lacan and the Other Side of Psychoanalysis*, ed. Justin Clemens and Russel Grigg (Durham: Duke University Press, 2006), 81.

89. Renata Salecl, "Love Anxieties," in *Reading Seminar XX: Lacan's Major Work on Love, Knowledge, and Feminine Sexuality*, ed. Suzanne Barnard and Bruce Fink (New York: State University of New York Press, 2002), 94.

90. Jacqueline Rose, *Sexuality in the Field of Vision* (London and New York: Verso Books, 1986), 38.

91. Cited in Megan Macdonald, "Sur/veil: The Veil as Blank(et) Signifier," in *Muslim Women, Transnational Feminism and Ethics of Pedagogy: Contested Imaginaries in Post-9/11 Cultural Practice*, ed. Lisa K. Taylor and Jasmine Zine (New York: Routledge, 2014). In this powerful critique, Macdonald too identifies the role of hysteria in the surveillance of Muslim women's bodies and situates it in colonial history and its postcolonial reoccurrences.

92. Florincia Farías, "The Body of the Hysterical Woman—The Feminine Body," April 2010. http://www.champlacanien.net/public/docu/2/rdv2010pre5.pdf.

93. Soler, *What Lacan Said About Women: A Psychoanalytic Study*, 52.

94. Barnard and Fink, *Reading Seminar XX, Lacan's Major Work on Love, Knowledge, and Feminine Sexuality*, 2.

95. Jacques Lacan, *The Seminar of Jacques Lacan, Book IV: The Object Relation 1956–1957*, ed. Jacques-Alain Miller, trans. L. V. A. Roche (1956–1957), 170.

96. Grosz, *Jacques Lacan: A Feminist Introduction*, 72.

97. Hortense J. Spillers, "Mama's Baby, Papa's Maybe: An American Grammar Book," *Diacritics* 17, no. 1 (1987): 66–67.

98. Solomon Northup, *12 Years a Slave: Narrative of Solomon Northup, a Citizen of New-York, Kidnapped in Washington City in 1841, and Rescued in 1853*, ed. David Wilson, Electronic ed., 1997 vols. (Chapel Hill, NC: Documenting the American South, University of North Carolina, 1853).

99. Cited in Macdonald, "Surveil," 30.

100. Soler, "Hysteria and Obsession," 260.

101. Soler, *What Lacan Said About Women: A Psychoanalytic Study*, 52.

102. Northup, *12 Years a Slave*, 254.

103. Krips, *Fetish*, 49.

104. Soler, "Hysteria and Obsession," 273.

105. See, for example, Anne McClintock, "Psychoanalysis, Race and Female Fetishism," in *Imperial Leather* (New York: Routledge, 1995).

106. This "masculine" and "feminine" for Lacan are not to be conceived as anatomical differences but psychic differences that can have cross—sociological and biological differences. Henry Krips, "Hijab, Veil and Sexuation," *Psychoanalysis, Culture and Society* 13, no. 1 (2008): 38.

107. For more details on what psychoanalysis through Freud and Lacan can offer feminist conversations see introduction in Jacques Lacan, Juliet Mitchell, and Jacqueline Rose, *Feminine Sexuality: Jacques Lacan and the école freudienne* (New York: Pantheon Books, 1982).

108. Kristeva, "Women's Time," 23.

109. Ellie Ragland, "The Masquerade, the Veil, and the Phallic Mask," *Psychoanalysis, Culture and Society* 13, no. 1 (2008).

110. Anne-Emmanuelle Berger, "The Newly Veiled Woman: Irigaray, Specularity, and the Islamic Veil," *Diacritics* 28, no. 1 (1998): 97.

111. Lacan, *Ecrits: The First Complete Edition in English*, 699.

112. Ragland, "The Masquerade, the Veil, and the Phallic Mask," 10–11. Renata Salecl has similarly described female genital cutting as a "mark" in *Perversions in Love and Hate* (New York: Verso Books, 1998).

113. Sirma Bilge, "Beyond Subordination vs. Resistance: An Intersectional Approach to the Agency of Veiled Muslim Women," *Journal of Intercultural Studies* 31, no. 1 (2010): 29.

114. Statement from FEMEN published in Louise Pennington, "Femen's International Topless Jihad Day," *Huffington Post*, April 4, 2013.

115. Kalia Abiade, "Passive Terrorism: CVE Blames Muslim Women and Puts Us at Risk," *Huffington Post*, March 7, 2016. https://www.huffingtonpost.com/kalia-abiade/cve-blames-muslim-women_b_9370672.html.

116. Primrose Riordan, "Hanson Wears Burqa in 'Appalling' Senate Stunt," *The Australian*, August 17, 2017. https://www.theaustralian.com.au/nation/politics/pauline-hanson-wears-burka-in-senate/news-story/cd29b0ac7e07bab761004381e3a42882.

117. Copjec, *Read My Desire*, 106.

118. Ragland, "The Masquerade, the Veil, and the Phallic Mask," 19.

119. Drucilla Cornell, "Doubly-Prized World: Myth Allegory and the Feminine," *Cornell Law Review* 75, no. 3 (1990): 674.

120. Luce Irigaray, *The Sex Which Is Not One*, trans. Catherine Porter and Carolyn Burke (New York: Cornell University Press, 1985), 186.

121. Irigaray, *The Sex Which Is Not One*, 175.

122. Berger, "The Newly Veiled Woman," 99.

123. Berger, "The Newly Veiled Woman," 115.

124. Cornell, "Doubly-Prized World," 698.

125. Ragland, "The Masquerade, the Veil, and the Phallic Mask," 12.

126. Berger, "The Newly Veiled Woman," 97.

127. Grosz, *Jacques Lacan: A Feminist Introduction*, 133.

128. Berger, "The Newly Veiled Woman," 99.

129. Grosz, *Jacques Lacan: A Feminist Introduction*, 133.

130. Quoted in Berger, "The Newly Veiled Woman."

131. Svitlana Matviyenko, "The Veil and Capitalist Discourse: A Lacanian Reading of the Veil Beyond Islam," *(Re)-Turn: Journal of Lacanian Studies* 6 (2011): 7.

132. Slavoj Žižek, "The Neighbour in Burka," *The Symptom* 11 (2010).
133. Soler, *What Lacan Said About Women: A Psychoanalytic Study*, 67.
134. Soler, *What Lacan Said About Women: A Psychoanalytic Study*, 159.
135. Wendy Brown cited in Abu-Lughod, *Do Muslim Women Need Saving?* 19.
136. Fink, *The Lacanian Subject: Between Language and Jouissance*, 194.
137. Grosz, *Jacques Lacan: A Feminist Introduction*, 7.
138. Zayzafoon, *The Production of the Muslim Woman*, 67.
139. Zayzafoon, *The Production of the Muslim Woman*, 72.
140. Annelies Moors, "The Dutch and the Face-Veil: The Politics of Discomfort," *European Association of Social Anthropologists* 17, no. 4 (2009): 405–406.
141. Henry Krips, "The Hijab, the Veil and Sexuation," *Psychoanalysis, Culture & Society* 13 (2008): 42.
142. Berger, "The Newly Veiled Woman," 105.
143. Berger, "The Newly Veiled Woman," 104.
144. Matviyekno, "The Veil and Capitalist Discourse," 14.
145. Berger, "The Newly Veiled Woman," 112. It is worth noting that in many Muslim cultures such as in Afghanistan, most of the Arab world, Somalia and Iran, women who do not cover their hair are often described as staging their unveiling. In Pashto, she is *"zan laghar kele de"* she has made herself naked, which privileges the agent who is unveiling, and suggests it being done for another's gaze.
146. Jacques-Alain Miller, "The Relation Between Sexes," in *Sexuation*, SIC 3, ed. Renata Salecl (Durham: Duke University Press, 2000).
147. Krips, "The Hijab, the Veil and Sexuation," 45–46.
148. Matviyekno, "The Veil and Capitalist Discourse," 19.
149. Lacan, *Ecrits: The First Complete Edition in English*, 114.
150. Soler, *What Lacan Said About Women: A Psychoanalytic Study*, 78.
151. Krips, "The Hijab, the Veil and Sexuation," 43.
152. Jelle Wiering, "There Is a Sexular Body: Introducing a Material Approach to the Secular," *Secularism and Nonreligion* 6, no. 8 (2011): 1–11.
153. Soler, *What Lacan Said About Women: A Psychoanalytic Study*, 81.
154. Soler, *What Lacan Said About Women: A Psychoanalytic Study*, 38.
155. Soler, *What Lacan Said About Women: A Psychoanalytic Study*, 159.
156. Soler, *What Lacan Said About Women: A Psychoanalytic Study*, 67.
157. Matviyekno, "The Veil and Capitalist Discourse," 8.
158. Grosz, *Volatile Bodies: Toward a Corporeal Feminism*, 19.
159. Soler, "Hysteria and Obsession," 279.
160. Northup, *12 Years a Slave*, 199.
161. Matviyekno, "The Veil and Capitalist Discourse," 8.
162. Krips, *Fetish*, 50.
163. Soler, *What Lacan Said About Women: A Psychoanalytic Study*, 161.
164. Mancini, "Patriarchy as the Exclusive Domain of the Other," 427.

165. Theodore Darlymple, "Civilised Society Should Not Draw a Veil Over the Niqab," *The Telegraph*, September 14, 2013.
166. Julie Bindel, "Why Are My Fellow Feminists Shamefully Silent over the Tyranny of the Veil, Asks Julie Bindel," *Daily Mail*, September 17, 2013. https://www.dailymail.co.uk/debate/article-2424073/Why-fellow-feminists-shamefully-silent-tyranny-veil-asks-JULIE-BINDEL.html.
167. Lacan, *The Seminar of Jacques Lacan: Book IV the Object Relation 1956–1957*, 157.
168. Mancini, "Patriarchy as the Exclusive Domain of the Other," 420.
169. Krips, "The Hijab, the Veil and Sexuation," 42–43.
170. Scott, *The Politics of the Veil*, 154.
171. Scott, *The Fantasy of Feminist History*, 93.
172. Scott, *The Politics of the Veil*, 156. Also referenced in Mancini, "Patriarchy as the Exclusion Domain of the Other," 421.
173. Mancini, "Patriarchy as the Exclusive Domain of the Other," 421.
174. Scott, *The Politics of the Veil*, 167.
175. Scott, *The Politics of the Veil*, 155.
176. Soler, *What Lacan Said About Women: A Psychoanalytic Study*, 53.
177. Razack, "Imperilled Muslim Woman, Dangerous Muslim Men and Civilised Europeans: Legal and Social Responses to Forced Marriages," 152.
178. Mancini, "Patriarchy as the Exclusive Domain of the Other," 422.
179. Scott, *The Politics of the Veil*, 156.

References

Abu-Lughod, Lila. *Do Muslim Women Need Saving?* Cambridge: Harvard University Press, 2013.

Abu-Lughod, Lila. "Orientalism and Middle East Feminist Studies." *Feminist Studies* 27, no. 1 (2001): 101–113.

Ahmed, Leila. *Women and Gender in Islam: Historical Roots of a Modern Debate.* New Haven: Yale University Press, 1992.

Ahmed, Sara. "Affective Economies." *Social Text* 22, no. 2 (2004): 117–139.

Asad, Talal. *Formations of the Secular: Christianity, Islam, Modernity.* Palo Alto, CA: Stanford University Press, 2003.

Asad, Talal. *Is Critique Secular? Blasphemy, Injury, and Free Speech.* Berkeley: Townsend Centre for the Humanities, University of California Press, 2009.

Asad, Talal. "Thinking About the Secular Body, Pain and Liberal Politics." *Cultural Anthropology* 26, no. 4 (2011): 657–675.

Baldwin, James. *Going to Meet the Man.* San Francisco, CA: Vintage Books, 1965.

Barlas, Asma. "Secular and Feminist Critiques of the Qur'an: Anti-Hermeneutics as Liberation?" *Journal of Feminist Studies in Religion* 32, no. 2 (2017): 111–121.

Barnard, Suzanne, and Bruce Fink. *Reading Seminar XX, Lacan's Major Work on Love, Knowledge, and Feminine Sexuality.* New York: SUNY Press, 2002.

Berger, Anne-Emmanuelle. "The Newly Veiled Woman: Irigaray, Specularity, and the Islamic Veil." *Diacritics* 28, no. 1 (1998): 93–119.

Bilge, Sirma. "Beyond Subordination vs. Resistance: An Intersectional Approach to the Agency of Veiled Muslim Women." *Journal of Intercultural Studies* 31, no. 1 (2010): 9–28.

Bilge, Sirma. "Intersectionality Undone: Saving intersectionality from Feminist Intersectional Studies." *Du Bois Review: Social Science Research on Race* 10, no. 12 (2013): 405–424.

Brown, Wendy. *States of Injury: Power and Freedom in Late Modernity: Power and Freedom in Late Modernity.* Princeton: Princeton University Press, 1995.

Butler, Judith. *Antigone's Claim: Kinship Between Life and Death.* New York: Columbia University Press, 2002.

Butler, Judith. *Bodies That Matter: On the Discursive Limits of 'Sex'.* Oxon: Routledge, 2011.

Butler, Judith. "Foucault and the Paradox of Bodily Inscriptions." *The Journal of Philosophy* 86, no. 11 (1989): 601–607.

Butler, Judith. "Sexual Politics, Torture, and Secular Time." *The British Journal of Sociology* 59, no. 1 (March 2008): 1–23.

Chakrabarty, Dipesh. *Provincialising Europe: Postcolonial Thought and Historical Difference.* Princeton and Oxford: Princeton University Press, 2000.

Cheng, Anne Anlin. *Second Skin: Josephine Baker and the Modern Surface.* Oxford and New York: Oxford University Press, 2011.

Copjec, Joan. *Read My Desire: Lacan Against the Historicists.* Cambridge, MA: MIT Press, 1994.

Cornell, Drucilla. "Doubly-Prized World: Myth Allegory and the Feminine." *Cornell Law Review* 75, no. 2 (1990): 644–699.

Davis, Angela. *Policing the Black Man: Arrests, Prosecution and Imprisonment.* New York: Pantheon Books, 2017.

Fanon, Frantz. *Black Skin, White Masks.* London: Pluto Press, 1986.

Farías, Florincia. "The Body of the Hysterical Woman—The Feminine Body," April 2010. http://www.champlacanien.net/public/docu/2/rdv2010pre5.pdf.

Farris, Sara. *In the Name of Women's Rights: The Rise of Femonationalism.* Durham: Duke University Press, 2017.

Fassin, Erin. "Sexual Democracy: The New Racialization of Europe." *Journal of Civil Society* 8, no. 3 (2012): 285–288.

Fink, Bruce. *The Lacanian Subject: Between Language and Jouissance.* Princeton: Princeton University Press, 1995.

Foucault, Michel. *The Will to Knowledge: The History of Sexuality I.* Translated by Robert Hurley. London: Random House, 1978.

Freud, Sigmund, and James Strachey. *Three Essays on the Theory of Sexuality*. New York: Basic Books, 2000.

Grosfugel, Ramón. Lecture on Intersectionality, University of South Africa, August 19, 2016. https://www.youtube.com/watch?v=FMEhyKqMWmA.

Grosz, Elizabeth. *Jacques Lacan: A Feminist Introduction*. New York: Routledge, 1990.

Grosz, Elizabeth. *Volatile Bodies: Toward a Corporeal Feminism—Theories of Representation and Difference*. Bloomington: Indiana University Press, 1994.

Guynn, Jessica. "BBQ Betty, Permit Patty and Why the Internet Is Shaming White People Who Police People 'Simply for Being Black'." *USA Today*, July 18 2018. https://www.usatoday.com/story/tech/2018/07/18/bbq-becky-permit-patty-and-why-internet-shaming-white-people-who-police-black-people/793574002/.

Hodgson, Barbara. *Dreaming of East: Western Women and the Exotic Allure of the Orient*. Vancouver: Greystone Books, 2007.

Irigaray, Luce. *The Sex Which Is Not One*. Translated by Catherine Porter and Carolyn Burke. New York: Cornell University Press, 1985.

Kabir, Nahid Afrose. *Young British Muslims: Identity, Culture, Politics and the Media*. Edinburgh: Edinburgh University Press, 2010.

Krips, Henry. *Fetish*. New York: Cornell University Press, 1999.

Krips, Henry. "The Hijab, the Veil and Sexuation." *Psychoanalysis, Culture & Society* 13, no. 1 (2008): 35–47.

Kristeva, Julia. "Women's Time." [Alice Jardine and Harry Blake.] *Journal of Women in Culture and Society* 7, no. 1 (1981): 17.

Lacan, Jacques. *Ecrits: The First Complete Edition in English*. New York: W. W. Norton, 2006.

Lacan, Jacques. *The Seminar of Jacques Lacan: Book IV the Object Relation 1956–1957*. Translated by L. V. A. Roche and Edited by Jacques-Alain Miller. New York: W. W. Norton, 1956–1957.

Lacan, Jacques, Juliet Mitchell, and Jacqueline Rose. *Feminine Sexuality: Jacques Lacan and the école freudienne*. New York: Pantheon Books, 1982.

Mahmood, Saba. "Feminism, Democracy and Empire: Islam and the War on Terror." In *Women's Studies on the Edge*, edited by Joan Wallach Scott. Durham: Duke University Press, 2008.

Mahmood, Saba. *Politics of Piety: The Islamic Revival and the Feminist Subject*. Princeton, NJ: Princeton University Press, 2005.

Mancini, Susanna. "Patriarchy as the Exclusive Domain of the Other: The Veil Controversy, False Projection, and Cultural Racism." *International Journal of Constitutional Law* 1, no. 2 (2011): 411–428.

Matviyekno, Svitlana. "The Veil and Capitalist Discourse: A Lacanian Reading of the Veil Beyond Islam." *(Re)-Turn: Journal of Lacanian Studies* 6 (2011): 7.

McClintock, Anne. *Imperial Leather: Race, Gender, and Sexuality in the Colonial Contest.* New York: Routledge, 1995.

Miller, Jacques-Alain. "The Relation Between Sexes." In *Sexuation*, SIC 3, edited by Renata Salecl. Durham: Duke University Press, 2000.

Moors, Annelies. "The Dutch and the Face-Veil: The Politics of Discomfort." *European Association of Social Anthropologists* 17, no. 4 (2009): 393–408.

Northup, Solomon. *12 Years a Slave: Narrative of Solomon Northup, a Citizen of New-York, Kidnapped in Washington City in 1841, and Rescued in 1853.* Edited by David Wilson, Electronic ed., 1997 vols. Chapel Hill, NC: Documenting the American South, University of North Carolina, 1853.

Parramore, Lynn Stuart. "White Females from Hell." *Lapham's Quarterly*, August 2, 2017. https://www.laphamsquarterly.org/roundtable/white-females-hell.

Paur, Jasbir. *Terrorist Assemblages: Homonationalism in Queer Times.* Durham and London: Duke University Press, 2007.

Potok, Mark, and Janet Smith. "Women Against Islam." *Intelligence Report*, June 10, 2015.

Ragland, Ellie. "The Hysteric's Truth." In *Reflections on Seminar XVII: Jacques Lacan and the Other Side of Psychoanalysis*, edited by Justin Clemens and Russel Grigg. Durham: Duke University Press, 2006.

Ragland, Ellie. "The Masquerade, the Veil, and the Phallic Mask." *Psychoanalysis, Culture and Society* 13 (2008): 8–23.

Razack, Sherene. "Imperilled Muslim Woman, Dangerous Muslim Men and Civilised Europeans: Legal and Social Responses to Forced Marriages." *Feminist Legal Studies* 12 (2004): 129–174.

Razack, Sherene. *Looking White People in the Eye: Gender, Race, and Culture in Courtrooms and Classrooms.* Toronto: University of Toronto Press, 1998.

Riley, Denise. *'Am I That Name?' Feminism and the Category of 'Women' in History.* London, UK: Palgrave Macmillan, 1988.

Riordan, Primrose. "Hanson Wears Burqa in 'Appalling' Senate Stunt." *The Australian*, August 17, 2017. https://www.theaustralian.com.au/nation/politics/pauline-hanson-wears-burka-in-senate/news-story/cd29b0ac7e07bab761004381e3a42882.

Rogers, Juliet. "Making the Crimes (Female Genital Mutilation) Act 1996, Making the 'Non-mutilation Woman'." *The Australian Feminist Law Journal* 18, no. 1 (2003): 93–113.

Rose, Jacqueline. *Sexuality in the Field of Vision.* London and New York: Verso Books, 1986.

Ross, Marlon. *Manning the Race: Reforming Black Men in the Jim Crow Era.* New York and London: NYU Press, 2004.

Salecl, Renata. "Love Anxieties." In *Reading Seminar XX: Lacan's Major Work on Love, Knowledge, and Feminine Sexuality*, edited by Suzanne Barnard and Bruce Fink. New York: State University of New York Press, 2002.

Salecl, Renata. *Perversions in Love and Hate.* New York: Verso Books, 1998.

Scott, Joan Wallach. *The Fantasy of Feminist History*. Durham: Duke University Press, 2011.

Scott, Joan Wallach. *The Politics of the Veil*. Princeton: Princeton University Press, 2007.

Scott, Joan Wallach. *Sex and Secularism*. Princeton and Oxford: Princeton University Press, 2018.

Soler, Colette. "Hysteria and Obsession." In *Reading Seminar I and II: Lacan's Return to Freud*, edited by Richard Feldstein, Bruce Fink, and Maire Jaanus. New York: State University New York Press 1999.

Soler, Colette. *What Lacan Said About Women: A Psychoanalytic Study*. Michigan: Other Press, 2006.

Spelman, Elizabeth V. *Inessential Woman: Problems of Exclusion in Feminist Thought*. Boston: Beacon Press, 1990.

Spillers, Hortense J. "Mama's Baby, Papa's Maybe: An American Grammar Book." *Diacritics* 17, no. 1 (1987): 64–81.

Spivak, Gayatri Chakravorty. *A Critique of Postcolonial Reason: Toward a History of the Vanishing Present*. Cambridge: Harvard University Press, 1999.

Stoler, Anna Laura. "Imperial Debris: On Ruins and Ruination." *Cultural Anthropology* 23, no. 2 (2008): 191–219.

Thobani, Sunera. "White Wars: Western Feminisms and the 'War on Terror'." *Feminist Theory* 8, no. 2 (2007): 169–185.

Wiering, Jelle. "There Is a Sexular Body: Introducing a Material Approach to the Secular." *Secularism and Nonreligion* 6, no. 8 (2011): 1–11.

Yeğenoğlu, Meyda. *Colonial Fantasies: Towards a Feminist Reading of Orientalism*. Cambridge: Cambridge University Press, 1998.

Zakaria, Rafia, *Veil*. New York and London: Bloomsbury Academic, 2017.

Zayzafoon, Lamia Ben Youssef. *The Production of the Muslim Woman: Negotiating Text, History, and Ideology*. Lanham, MD: Lexington Books, 2005.

Žižek, Slavoj. "The Neighbour in Burka." *The Symptom* 11 (2010).

CHAPTER 5

The Postcolonial Veil: Bodies in Contact

Yet the edges and blank spaces of colonial maps are typically marked with vivid reminders of the failure of knowledge...The failure of European knowledge appears in the margins and gaps of these maps in the forms of cannibals, mermaids and monsters... —Anne McClintock[1]

INTRODUCTION

The west's preoccupation with the veil has taken us on a journey through the body (both imaged and imagined) and the investment in its anatomical truth telling. This venture also revealed that the body is a map of the ruins of our "postcolonial" world, history strewn throughout its corporeal terrain. The body confesses where modernism, knowledge, universalism and subjectivity have failed to conquer its ambivalent crevices, stumbling on its inert existence. The chapters so far have demonstrated the limits of this epistemological enterprise through a succession of impossibilities and tensions. It has made us cognisant of how the preoccupation with the veil is a preoccupation with the body as a testimony for the success of political projects, and their underpinning fantasies and anxieties. This book has examined how we imagine the body as constrained and its release from obstructions through the fantasy of freedom, a fantasy that makes

© The Author(s) 2020
S. Ghumkhor, *The Political Psychology of the Veil*,
Palgrave Studies in Political Psychology,
https://doi.org/10.1007/978-3-030-32061-4_5

Woman and the western secular subject, conceivable and attainable. In this chapter, I want to attend to the fantasy that defends these identity formations from the impossibilities of not knowing. I want to expand my analysis to the broader relationship between knowledge and power as it appears in the discourses of orientalism and Islamophobia. This chapter aims to elucidate the unravelling of contemporary self/other relations as the postcolonial condition through the psychoanalytic approach I have undertaken. The "post" in the postcolonial more ambivalently announces the end of colonialism and its deployment across different academic and political conversations. It is a prophylactic symbol of departure from a history that was mediated through imperial violence and domination. Despite its dubious spatiality (was colonialism experienced in the same way?) and problematic temporality (did it begin and end at once?)[2]; the postcolonial locates a way of thinking about power through language and the body, and the way in which the desire for knowledge (of the body, of the Other) is still driven by conscious and unconscious desire for mastery.

In the contemporary liberal west, the "post" imagines an end to history's shortcomings and the arrival of universalisms such as human rights and democracy. It claims to have dissolved geographical and cultural boundaries through the migration of freedom and consensual economic and political relations. The flattening of experiences through the dissolving of borders of East–West, North–South, Islam and West, has not meant a departure from the rigid civilisational demarcations of the past. Mary Louise Pratt has called these new encounters "contact zones of imperialism", the new frontiers which reverse the geographical boundaries of *over there* to *here*.[3] Writing as early as 1970s, Edward Said observed these intimate encounters when he states:

> If the world has become immediately accessible to a western citizen living in the electronic age, the Orient too has drawn nearer to him and is now less a myth perhaps than a place crisscrossed by western, especially American, interests. One aspect of the electronic, postmodern world is that there has been an encroachment of the stereotypes by which the Orient is viewed... This is nowhere more true than in the ways by which the Near-East is grasped.[4]

This proximity to otherness is more intensified in a world saturated by images due to the emergence of dynamic digital technologies. This book has examined so far how images are a new mode of knowledge production, a "regime of truth", that shape the world we live in.[5] Nevertheless, it is not just any image that circulates, but certain images are repeatedly circulated and often centred around *other bodies*. The production of the Muslim woman through the image of the veil exemplifies this repetition. In this chapter, I want to re-situate the discussion by looking at the pre-occupation with the veil and the body—both imaged and imagined as a precarious condition of the postcolonial. The veil, once far away in an Orient that only appeared to the west in distant writings and images, fuelled by western fantasies for the exotic, has now arrived in the space of civilisation and freedom. Psychoanalysis offers possible answers to understand the crisis triggered by this "civilisational proximity"[6] and the ways it is coped. Rather than examining the racialisation of otherness and discursive representations, this chapter identifies how power persists through the hidden psychosocial practices, ideas and images, into the "post" era, connecting us to the past.

The present anxious times are also paranoid times[7] where the preferred language is one of uncovering conspiracies, hidden enemies and what the presence of others—immigrants, refugees, Muslims, Chinese—means *to us*. The paranoid state, Lacan observes, is an obsession with oneself through an encounter that is experienced as disturbance, a suspicion of the other, and therefore subject to interpretation. Paranoia is therefore illusory and runs through subjectivity as a growing presence that haunts its acquisition of knowledge.[8] This chapter attends to the impulse to both expel *and* cling to difference in this encounter—a deferral that reveals the postcolonial impasse as one of paranoia: the liberal west's failure to universalise its moral vision of freedom and secure itself as the arbiter of all knowledge. This crisis has produced a hypochondriac-like phobia manifested in Islamophobia of the "foreign" body, of *all* bodies, which both secure and disrupt the fantasy of always knowing. If hysteria is one of seeking validation in the Other, hypochondria is an embodied hysteria which presents itself in Islamophobia as a perpetual interrogation of the Muslim. That is, Islamophobia is the hysterical questioning of one's standing with the Other. Islamophobia as a hypochondria of the body politic is a paranoid condition of what Jacques Derrida, when diagnosing the events of 11 September 2001 and its reception, describes as the west's autoimmune disease. Autoimmunity, Derrida observes, is when "a living being, in quasi-suicidal fashion, "itself" works to destroy its own protection, to immunise itself against its own immunity".[9] This biological metaphor is useful to think about the imagining of the post-9/11 threat as both foreign (infiltrating "our" borders) and domestic (hidden enemy), and the blurring of the "inside/outside, friend/enemy, native/alien, literal/figurative" relations.[10]

The hypochondriac condition is often a paranoia of the body, experiencing it as alien, which leads to a *misdiagnosis*. If we think about the western post-9/11 condition as a continuous misreading by pursuing dangerous phantasms to secure the body politic, the hypochondriac state is a hysterical obsession. It is western narcissistic attachment to an unveiling freedom that both misreads the geopolitical motivations of terrorism as a nonstate violence against "our freedoms" *and* compounds its insecurities by eroding said freedoms through the war on terror's Islamophobic surveillance of all bodies. This chapter contends that Islamophobia's preoccupation with bodies exhibits a western hysteria in demanding to know the threat in a state of paranoid questions: how another can enjoy without it? How the body can be anything but ours? In this hysterical state, the postcolonial body is burdened with "autoimmunitary terrors"[11] by appearing as a riddle that requires immediate answers.

The "post" carries with it such riddles in the form of historical loss, anxiety and trauma for not just victims of colonialism and imperialism—something that is often the subject of postcolonial theory—but its agents. For Europe and its western counterparts whose identity, desire and knowledge production has been vastly shaped by a colonial legacy, the "post" is also about coping with the loss of meaning, the limits of knowledge and the failure of naming. Loss has been a reoccurring theme throughout the chapters of this book leaving its traces on the body as both imaged and imagined. For a west whose dominion has been knowledge, truth and universality, the postcolonial has brought with it a crisis of knowledge and identity in the breaking down of the "rules of recognition".[12] Who are you? What am I to you? What do you want? *Che Vuoi?*[13] The desire for a recognised Other is accompanied by the anxiety of there being no satisfying answer: of not knowing. With this question in mind, this chapter's purpose is to reflect on what the veiled woman can reveal about how racism is sustained in the "new" postcolonial world. The chapter contends that a discursive analysis leaves "unchecked", what psychoanalytic theorist Derek Hook insists are, the "pernicious (bodily, sexual and unconscious) facets of postcolonial racism".[14] The psychic mechanics of racist discourses need to be considered to better understand the cyclical repetitions of images as a symptom of acting out these contact zones.

The persistence of racialising discourses in the mode of orientalism and Islamophobia, and the accompanying images and imaginaries of the veiled and unveiled, are understood as symptoms of a crisis of knowledge. Orientalism's presentation of otherness through negations is not simply about binary oppositions of a homogenised west and an equally homogenised and misrepresented Islamic otherness, as an array of post-9/11 literature on Muslims suggest.[15] Rather, it is a dialectical scene of western subjectivity. Tracing the psychic investment in representation, the structural repressions of knowledge—what constitutes its subjectivity—psychoanalytic lens reveals not a means of "interpreting the image, but shows how the image interprets the complexities of subjectivity to us".[16] A psychoanalytic reading invites to a deeper analysis of the power of language as discourse, text, image, and their conditions of their arrival and reception. Through this lens, we can read this reception through both a symbolic register (that of language and discourse) and the imaginary, the domain of the subject's identification with the image.

Paranoid Knowledge: The Other's Question in the Muslim Question

What is more than just a woman beneath the veil is a symptom of a "nervous condition" impelled by colonial and postcolonial tensions in self/other relations.[17] In the past few decades, the demand to know what lies beneath the veil has appeared more broadly in the form of the "the Muslim question" in the west. This is a question that is about the proximity of the other and the danger it poses to western culture and identity. Edward Said, in *Orientalism*, describes European fixation on Islam throughout the colonial period and the postcolonial era as a "lasting trauma".[18] This trauma, Said contends, was triggered by Islam's lurking dangerous presence as an "Ottoman peril" at the edges of Europe until the seventeenth century.[19] Far from being a disinterested knowledge, western orientalism is a knowledge production that aims to cope with the questions at the heart of its own subjectivity. Imperial narratives of superiority over others not only emerge from economic and political motivations but also from unconscious investment in the dialectic of European self-other relations. Orientalism links *desire for/and knowledge* in the question: what is the Orient to itself and to me?

Knowledge, Jacques Lacan observes, is paranoid. The Other's question at the heart of subjectivity is one that is a knowledge that is persecutory because it can never be guaranteed, even terrorising as it threatens to invade the subject. Paranoia emerges when the imaginary ego which is based on a primordial misrecognition in which the displaced subject attempts to affirm its self-image through the Other. The subject's pursuit for knowledge to secure its completeness places it in a vulnerable state of dependency. This contingent relationship for recognition produces increased frustration, alienation and aggression as the subject competes for reaffirmation and its realisation of this contingency.[20] Paranoia emerges from this desire for recognition and not having it validated. Paranoia identifies what is alien to the subject, its opposite—an other that desires and therefore has other knowledge. The subject's dependency is then disavowed in an illusion of autonomy and freedom.[21] The subject's desire is therefore characterised by incompleteness and lack and its fantasy of completeness is a defence against fragmentation anxiety.[22]

Knowledge is also has a proximity to enjoyment.[23] The desire for knowledge, the Other's question: "what does the Other want?" builds a link between discourse and desire, a means of *jouissance* and the constitution of the subject. This is an enjoyment however that maintains a defensive state of being which keeps persecutory knowledge, a knowledge that cuts away at the subject's imagined boundaries, at bay. Built into this pursuit for knowledge is an unconscious desire not to know.[24]

In the contemporary postcolonial world where the other has arrived through multiple channels, there has been a disruption to the boundaries of a west whose margins have been closely policed through the expulsion of others, through the binaries that have sustained its identity. The static Orient that Said wrote about, and enjoyed by Europeans for centuries from afar, is now animated by mobilised masses, militancy and "religious fervour", giving credence to historical fears and new paranoia. Western viewers are now exposed to an East that is no longer discreet, exotic and a distant place with an "aura of apartness".[25] Incidents of gratuitous or "terrorist" violence involving Muslims convey the "return of Islam",[26] perceived as a civilisational threat to western traditions of secularism, democracy, human rights and freedom. Since the Cold War, these traditions have been exalted with the declaration of an end of history.[27] Islam, in these geopolitical calculations, is imagined as what Derrida describes as "the other of democracy".[28] Muslims, Yasemin Yildiz, observes, have now become "*internal* Others", a position once held by Jews.[29] The new civilisational and psychic tension are inflated by both the past (a historical trauma) and the post (the possibility of cultural contamination and loss). They mirror the question of the west's agony over its identity, its symbolic status as a universal truth, when it is confronted by the possibility of another's *jouissance*, what Slavoj Žižek has called the "theft of enjoyment".[30]

As a knowledge production that produces an Islam and Muslims for European consumption, paranoia about Islam's growing presence in the west has given orientalism new political traction in the mode of Islamophobia. Islamophobia contains an "unfounded hostility towards Muslims, and therefore fear or dislike of all or most Muslims".[31] The "unfounded" dimension of Islamophobia is relevant (and curious) to understanding the *paranoid* delusions that drive it and make it immune to rational engagement. Western paranoia is captured by polls and studies of what the western public think of Muslims and Islam who are often imagined as a cultural menace.[32] Despite the varying descriptions and explanations of Islamophobia, it adopts both the discursive foundations of orientalism and the fantasy of *knowing the Other*. The act of unveiling, so crucial to liberating the Afghan woman in recent years, serves what Joan Wallach Scott describes as a "symbolic gesture" that allows the west to act out "tremendous anxiety not so much about fundamentalism, but about Islam itself".[33] This anxiety, I contend, manifests itself in the "terrifying ambiguities"[34] of the Muslim stranger in our midst who enjoys differently—that is, who eats, dresses and believes something else—and as such, triggers a desperation to know the Other's desire. Islamophobia appears to be a more *localised* phenomenon focusing on the Muslim within "our" borders, whereas contemporary (and traditional) orientalism is more internationalised.[35] Once conquered in lands far away, Islam as an unruly dangerous foe is imagined as now within "our" midst. It needs to be domesticated lest it spills over, contaminates and extinguishes, what former U.S. President George W. Bush coined, "our freedoms", and "our way of life".[36] In this sense, Islamophobia speaks about Muslims *over here* as potential sites of contamination and leakages for generalised orientalism *over there*.

The localised nature of Islamophobia, and the preoccupation with what the presence of Muslims can mean, is evident in Anne Norton's description of "the Muslim question" as,

> The concerns the West directs at Muslims maps sites of *domestic anxiety*… faced with continued questions about the status of women, sexuality, equality and difference, faith and secularism. They are fuelled by *anxieties of the past and the direction of the future* [my emphasis].[37]

The "domestic anxiety" about Muslims in the west also attests to the localised nature of the phenomenon where Muslims are subject to over-policing, manifesting as "hostility" and "violence", and particularly, sustained accusations, "distrust", "rejection", "exclusion" and "discrimination".[38] Islamophobia is motivated by the trope of the "enemy within" suggesting the orientalist confidence in *knowing* the Muslim and the apprehension the Muslim's arrival has caused.

Behind the need to know persist questions about Muslims: What is Islam? Who are Muslims? Why do they hate us? Why are they here? These paranoid questions are driven by unease, suspicion and fear. Demanding in tone, they require immediate answers that must offer relief. That these questions are asked in 2019 about a 1400-year-old Abrahamic religion with long histories in the west and followed by 1.6 billion people, suggest that the questions have a more troubling and phobic basis, which clearly no answer can satisfy.[39] At the base of these questions is the haunting ontological tension: *Che vuoi?* Tell me who you are? What do you want from me? What am I to you? Islamophobia materialises through these questions as an exaggerated fear about racial proximity (for example, the anti-halal campaign and mosque building in Australia) fearful of foreign bodies ("Female Genital Mutilation", veiled women), which attempts to make sense of these questions by how the contact with other bodies "convinces of a civilisational clash will be inevitable and all-consuming".[40]

EMBODIED ISLAMOPHOBIA

The "domestic anxiety" of Islamophobia draws attention to the location of bodies and their proximity to "us". While much has been written on the subject of Islamophobia,[41] with the exception of the veil, little attention has been given to the extent to which the body features in its mood of paranoia, anxiety and fear of this cultural menace. The salience of bodies in racism, as we saw in Chapter 2, is imperative to imaging and imagining the racialised hierarchy whiteness produces. The body also features in nations and nationalisms as a mode of mapping imagined identities and communities. Scholars on nationalism like Ernest Gellner[42] and Benedict Anderson[43] have argued the nation is imagined as a passive agent that is naturally present. Gendered readings have revealed the nation's passivity and natural conditioning is unimaginable without women's bodies that reproduce and secure its future and authentic moral vision.[44] The nation is made *familiar* with shared experiences, desires, memories and a belief in sameness.

The body is a pre-discursive reference and mediator to imagine the universal sameness of the secular notion of the human. The fantasy of unveiling freedom is mobilised by western feminism as part of a femonationalism to escape *from* castration *to* bodily integrity and ontological wholeness, by projecting the veil of lack on to Muslim women. The Muslim body has been central to the rationale for the surveillance technologies of the last two decades and the veil of violence ever-present on Muslim women's bodies, has been its most productive strategy, bringing together historical tropes of women as cultural markers and hidden threats. "Surveil", as Megan Macdonald observes, combines the "gaze-as-surveillance and also locating it, when the word is split: sur/veil, *on* the veil". Surveillance, is about keeping watch over an (other).[45] The nation appears as a surveiller, an integrationist if not an assimilationist project that watches and disciplines Muslim men whose perceived treatment of Muslim women is a danger to the secular values (sexual desire, gender equality, bodily autonomy) of western society thus determining the conditions of recognition. Those who disrupt the nation's gaze for sameness, in turn, are seen as unnatural, contaminating, foreign and dangerous. Thus, the "natural" body becomes a way of marking cultural boundaries, policing the imagined community or to ensure the purity and *possibility* of the nation's becoming.

But just as the nation can be imagined as a unified biological body, it can also be imagined as a political body subject to fragmenting—threatened by enemies, cultural menaces and outsiders. Paranoia is always about proximity and the body is central to measuring this. In anxious times such as the climate of a war on terror, biological figures—the darker forboding bearded man or the veiled woman—*the religious body*—become the language in which security of the body politic is rationalised. There is always a return to the body to "sing the nation-state".[46] Reflecting on Derrida's immunity metaphor, Timothy Mitchell contends how the theory of immunity is,

> riddled with images of socio-political sphere—of invaders and defenders, hosts and parasites, natives and aliens, and of borders and identities that must be maintained. In asking us to see terror as autoimmunity, then, Derrida is bringing the metaphor home at the same time he sends it abroad, stretching it to the limits of the world. The effects of the bipolar image, then, is to produce a situation in which there is no literal meaning, nothing but the resonances between two images, one biomedical, the other political.[47]

Islamophobia, which narrates Muslims as a problem, deploys this bipolar image in its targeting of Muslim cultural practices as suspicious, fearful and requiring surveillance. The calls to stop the "Islamisation" of western society throughout Europe, North America, Australia and New Zealand, targets Muslims as cultural agents, infecting the national body that will weaken it for its eventual replacement. The anxiety over being replaced is rooted in "the great replacement" formula propagated by the far-right such as France's Le Pen party, Netherland's Geert Wilders of the Party For Freedom, Australia's scattered but ever-present far-right groups, the manifesto of Anders Breivik who murdered 77 people in Norway, neo-Nazis who in 2017 marched in Charlottesville, Virginia chanting "you will not replace us", and in the title of a manifesto written by Australian Brenton Tarrant before he shot dead 50 Muslims in two mosques in Christchurch, New Zealand.[48] The manifesto expresses concern about Muslim *invasion* and capacity to *out-breed* and *over-populate* western countries eventually replacing them and bringing on a "white genocide". Not only is the image of the Muslim riddled with the existentialist threat of a biological weapon, there is a curious admission of the peril being named a "replacement"—a word that designates lack, desire for something else other than "us"— *a rejection*. In a disenchanted world where communities are increasingly defenceless against the necropolitics of biopower that Agamben warns us of in its production of political life (*bios*), the feeling of being replaced is a symptom of the blurring conditions of postcolonial recognition.

The body is central to the management of this replacement anxiety. It is where foreign enemies are pronounced, borders are established, and triumphs are avowed. We have become familiarised with the body so far as an instrument through which knowledge is both challenged and safeguarded, in an effort to address the fundamental tension at the heart of sexuation and thus subjectivity: *what do these bodies mean?*[49] Bodies legitimise the universal and intrinsic value of political projects, fasten truths and ground identities. They are also sites of deep repression requiring constant management. Seeing as nationalist, racist and feminist imaginaries have attempted to make intelligible bodies in order to secure their political projects, the body manifests in Islamophobia as under siege by cultural disease that will result in an existential crisis. It is the location on which the shrill cry against inauthentic others, whose foreignness must be cast out, is most cogently heard. Consider how often Islam is described as a "disease". In 2017, One Nation Party's leader Pauline Hanson when talking about Islam declared "we have a disease—we need to vaccinate ourselves against it".[50] Former

National Security Advisor to U.S. President Donald Trump, Michael Flynn described Islam as "a "malignant" and "vicious cancer in the body of 1.7 billion people and has to be excised".[51] In the United Kingdom, leader of the right-wing party UKIP in 2017 described Islam as a "cancer within our society".[52] Most recently far-right online personality Laura Loomer, who has been banned on Twitter for her anti-Muslim accusations against American-Somali Ilhan Omar—one of two first Muslim women elected to U.S. Congress in 2018, took to Instagram to continue her attack on Omar and described Islam as a "cancer".[53] These are worrying bouts of a sick body politic, bloated by religious ailment, attributed to the menacing presence of Islam's growing visibility "within". The secular body as the natural prescription for human desire—protected and disciplined by secular democratic traditions—is now imagined presenting with symptoms of cultural regression threatening to devour its fleshly triumphs and rational surfacing.

The concern about the sick body politic apprehends the postcolonial condition as a "nervous" one. In biomedical parlance, the postcolonial intimacy of bodies in an atmosphere of post-9/11 insecurity, has shaken the west's nervous system which has become depressed, anxious, panic-stricken, provoking psychosis, hallucinations and paranoid fantasies that has in turn disrupted the immune system in the mode of legal and political traditions.[54] The body as the mediator of nation-building becomes a site of terror, a nervous preoccupation whose symptoms are unrecognisable, signalling a deeper ailment: a crisis of knowledge of the future of the body politic, the nation, "our way of life". Islamophobia's demanding questions to know the Muslim and their location to "us" suggest not only its phobic dimensions but the hysteric's dissatisfaction in the response. This frustration further suggests the failure of knowledge of western security and its capacity to protect the body, wrestling with the historical hauntings of a vision of freedom that was never guaranteed nor uniformly interpreted. The anxious preoccupation with the body in the paranoid imaginings of Islamophobia is a form of what, Julia Barossa and Caroline Rooney who examine neurosis in racism and nationalism, call a "collective hypochondria".[55] If we think about the symptoms of hypochondria, they exhibit a hysterical preoccupation with the health of the body, a terror of the invisible that lurks in it, and a dissatisfaction with knowledge. It does not matter how many medical professionals the hypochondriac visits, there is always an element of doubt that follows: a "yes, but what if...??" It is both a certainty that something is wrong in one's own body and uncertainty about whether this danger to the body has been fully *discovered* and treated through a secular "critical act of unmasking".[56] The fantasy of the west as always knowing is both consolidated (who the question is ultimately posed to—not the Muslim but the Other) and pushed to its limits in the hysterical demand for more knowledge (what if?). Hypochondriac symptoms manifest in the perception of the body as a question that refuses to disclose all its answers. It is potentially contaminated, *potentially foreign*, not to be trusted and thus, must be vigilantly monitored. As Barossa and Rooney explain, "the body manifests itself as precisely a body through its occasion of foreignness, and it is the body of the other that is the fantasmatic carrier of certain unease and potentially disease".[57] Hypochondria, Anne Anlin Cheng argues, is about the *perception* of the world and one's body in respect to social relations.[58] Centred on the body, hypochondria manifests in Islamophobia as a national anxiety about one's location to Muslims. Here modernism's preoccupation with unveiled/bare surface coincide with post-9/11 paranoia of the undetectable risk in the unseeing and therefore, unknowable body.

Hypochondria also drives a paranoia that entails a fixation on who Muslims are, what Muslims do or are doing, driven by delusions of being attacked, and the fear of the proximate. It is a narcissism that is present in knowing the west is the target of the attack and the threat to one's *jouissance*. Hypochondria, as a mode of hysteria, is also about the search for absolute knowledge, witnessed in the demand for the other to announce themselves through unveiling and the constant surveillance of others. This is perhaps why the questions, which sustain Islamophobia, resist answers— *diagnosis*. It is because they are incalculable.[59] Why, for instance, when Muslims condemn terrorism they need to, in the words of former Prime Minister of Australia, "mean it" because the correct condemnation is in its felt experience, in the impossibility to *know*.[60] Or when the insistence on the "moderate Muslim" heightens anxiety about the "true" intentions of Muslims who supposedly practice *taqiyya* and aim to deceive by hiding their true ambitions to "Islamicise" western society.[61] But it is the western hysteric's question as a racial paranoia that continually misreads the body's symptoms, real or imagined—that enables the west to speak as a unified bodily self, confronted by the threat of its national fragmentation, *of being infected*.

The Contaminated and Contaminating Body

We can see the symptoms of a hypochondriac Islamophobia in the anti-halal campaign that began in 2014 in Australia. The campaign has included Federal Member of Parliament Luke Simpkins, Liberal MP Cory Bernardi, Former One Nation leader Pauline Hanson, far-right movements like Reclaim Australia and Restore Australia, aiming to protest companies that are "halal-certified". Halal-certification identifies the absence of any traces of pork, blood or alcohol so Muslims can consume it.[62] Despite a 2015 Senate Inquiry into third-party certification of food that was called by anti-halal critics,[63] the campaigners continue their paranoia that insists the profits from halal-certification fund terrorism, halal-certified products are more costly on non-Muslim consumers, and the industry enables Sharia to operate in the country. The movement's most vocal representative, Kirralie Smith who describes herself as a "concerned mother of three", explained her objection to halal-certification: "Islam won't need all out violent jihad to dominate the world. It is being done by stealth and you and I are funding it every day with our grocery purchases". Positioning her as an everyday mother with children gives legitimacy to the concern about halal funding jihad, evoking images of violence and domination and threaten the sanctity of the nation qua the family.[64] The link to jihad is also about the *fear of contagion*, the body potentially being lost to jihad—a body that turns against itself.

Carrying this infection, the body becomes foreign and "we" participate in our own self-destruction. The consumption of halal as something that can potentially "take over" the body is more directly admitted by former Liberal MP Luke Simpkins' warning of halal certification: "By having Australians unwittingly eat Halal food, then we are one step down the path of conversion, and that's a step we should only make with full knowledge and not imposed upon us".[65] Halal products, like viruses, invisibly infect the bodies that have consumed them, inferring the loss of control of the nation qua the body and its meaning. This loss felt forces a confrontation with the question of who we are if we are without our (imagined) "whole" bodies. Considering the little evidence for any of the conclusions made by the movement, the reference to "full knowledge" is only imaginable in the absence of knowledge: the "uncontaminated" body (full knowledge) is only obtained by fixating on its contamination (the loss of knowledge). But the desire for full knowledge is more performative in that no knowledge can satisfy because in the hypochondriac's approach to "knowing", knowledge is something perpetually lamented rather than attained.

Only the removal of halal-certification, campaigners suggest, can guarantee the purity of food. Such investment in the body suggest the extent to which campaigners ponder the possibilities of what uncontaminated food can invite. It deploys the uncontaminated body that is visible, slim and attractive, to invoke a sense of disgust at the halal diet, which is associated with poor health and modern excess. Like the person whose racism is manifested in their "ethnic" neighbours' bodily presence who are too noisy, dress funny and eat smelly food,[66] halal diet is similarly identified as the too-much-ness of the foreign. The biopolitical policing of the body, as we saw in the previous chapters, is here *unveiled* as an ideal body, the "natural" body, whose desires can only be realised once the foreign and "grotesque" (bodies) are abjected.[67] Invoking modern concerns about health and ideal body image, the foreign not only contaminates but also responsible for the decline in the health of the nation.

Radicalised Symptoms

The foreign that potentially contaminates fuels the politics of fear in terrorism. With the emergence of Al-Qaeda and Islamic State of Iraq and Levant (ISIS), the western public have been fixated on the suicide attacks and potential beheadings of westerners.[68] Unable to identify the enemy within, there has been a fixation on the safety and identity of bodies in the confrontation with the *embodied violence* of terrorists. The suicide bomber in the western imaginary has marked a transgression of modern sensibilities on the integrity of the body, the valuing of life and secular reason as the privileged site of political engagement.[69] The horror of suicide bombing is not simply the shock at someone's willing self-destruction but what Lauren B. Wilcox describes as the merging of victim and perpetrator, blurring bodily boundaries. The suicide bomber whose alleged contempt for life is the body that randomly explodes its inside/outside, destroying and contaminating those that are in close proximity. The suicide bomber "within" is the most potent expression of the west's autoimmunity—the return of the repressed as an internal aggression against the faux boundaries of civilian/military, civilisation/barbarism, reason/unreason, religion/secularism. The explosive body breaches political identities, bodies "we" have given meaning and protection to, and that which constitutes subjectivity.[70] For a west that imagines the body as whole, the suicide bomber is a contaminating force that undermines the illusory markers of the body, rendering them completely meaningless. The biopolitical investment in the production of life returns as a destructive body whose death drive disintegrates others in its path. In other words, the suicide bomber pierces the veil of the skin and exposes the abject inside.

Pierced skin and exposed flesh gesture to other kinds of dangers. In the months following the suicide attacks on the World Trade Centre, a team of medical examiners went through the painfully slow process of identifying the bodies of victims.[71] The task was near impossible considering the small bodily fragments found due to the power of the explosions. The families of the victims had not only been urgent in their request to have the victims identified *but also that of the hijackers*. The families of the victims did not want the bodies of their loved ones having any traces of the hijackers' DNA. Such traces were described as a continued affliction—a contamination of the victims and the perpetrators. Only 300 "whole" bodies were recovered from the 2974 victims and 21,743 fragments were analysed. Only 12,595 victim parts and 9 of the 10 hijackers have been identified.[72] Locating the missing flesh was critical to finding out what happened to them, their bodies as evidence of their victim and grieve-able status. The need to identify and separate body fragments had urgency because of the continued proximity of the perpetrators with the victims, presenting a sustained violation.[73] Recovering their loved ones suggested an end to their ordeal and reuniting with their loved one. The two-year project, the millions of dollars that went into such efforts, and the national memorials set up in their name, indicate the pieces of flesh of the nation whose symbolic boundaries had been shattered and desired restoration. By identifying and putting together the uncontaminated flesh, the national body imagined as whole could be restored. In contrast, none of the families of the hijackers claimed their bodies, or the country of their origins, as if to communicate they were foreign to all.

The biopolitical policing of bodies as a way to manage and locate the foreign within is most vigilant in the use of surveillance technologies and border protection policies to identify, predict and contain the threat of terrorism, and more recently, "radicalisation", in the post-9/11 era. If bodies are continuously inscribed with cultural codes and meaning such as race and gender, as discussed in Chapters 2 and 4, the body in Lacanian parlance is never ours but always Other. The body must be brought into meaning through the Symbolic. Surveillance, Foucault has observed, was about the regulation and disciplining of bodies so they become bodies that are intelligible and subject to discursive inscriptions.[74] The bodies of Muslims, in the climate of Islamophobia and security, are symbolically inscribed as potentially threatening, "radicalised", disloyal and a cultural menace needing to be surveilled. Muslim bodies carry necessary information (skin tone, names, dress, nationality), becoming sources of data (knowledge), dissected and assembled through racial profiling, coded into different degrees of risks.[75] These are bodies that leave traces of data, traces of the foreign, that can be located, diagnosed and *deradicalized* by secular practices of more "restrained" ways of expressing politics. The undisciplined bodies of young Muslims, mainly men but increasingly women, are constructed in deradicalised narratives as bodies that are susceptible to external codes of meaning such as receiving radical ideas of jihad from abroad (ISIS and Al-Qaeda) or travelling to conflict zones such as Iraq and Syria, and then "groomed" into acting on these violent ideas in their western "host" country. This radicalisation has also *spread* to young "white" Australian men like Jake Bilardi who was "radicalised" online, converted to Islam, joined ISIS in Iraq and reported to have orchestrated a suicide attack in Iraq's Anbar province.[76] Or charismatic preacher Musa Cerantonio for spreading ISIS propaganda who was arrested in 2016.[77] The paranoia of the Muslim as the Trojan horse, destroying from within, reaches an anxious tone in this story as "our" body that is contaminated, foreign and blurring geo-cultural boundaries, indicated in the title of Bilardi's manifesto: "From Melbourne to Ramadi".[78] In the hypochondriac logic, his journey does not only involve contact with the foreign but that Bilardi's radicalisation also provokes the likelihood (what if?) of what the journey "From Ramadi to Melbourne" could involve.

"Radicalisation" also has another symptom undetected: how it can incite extreme reactions to cure it. In response to the Christchurch shooting, Australian Senator Fraser Anning whose maiden speech called for a Muslim immigration ban as part of a "final solution", linked the violence to the "growing fear within our community, both here and in New Zealand of the increasing Muslim presence".[79] Compared to the irrational violence of the Muslim as a suicidal entity that terrorises within, the fear of being replaced turned violent, appears as a defence, a rational inevitability to contain the disease where it is most concentrated: their place of worship and community such as the mosque. Driving these racialising practices of surveillance, policing and even eradication is the desire to stabilise social boundaries, secure the missing flesh that will unify the national subject of whose knowledge of what it means to be part of an Anglo-Euro tradition, marks the body *as ours.* Observing the new orientalist grammar as an Islamophobic anxiety over Muslim women's transgressive body in the possibility of their participation in terrorism, Magnet and Mason argue that surveillance technologies such as backscatter X-rays further the colonial preoccupation with making visible Muslim women's bodies as a way of policing the Muslim community.[80] The impetus to ban the veil as an issue of security and corporeal citizenship[81] is a way of concealing the underlying antagonism in western societies that have yet to reconcile the relationship between freedom and the body. The casting out of Muslims from strategies of deradicalization, "Muslim ban" legislation, to "final solutions" is symptomatic of a narcissistic tendency of the inherent aggressivity in the western subject's failure to reconcile with its self-image—here, manifesting as western self-destruction qua jealously protecting law, civil liberties, human rights, freedom as such.

Muslim Women's Bodies

If the body (and therefore the nation) is imagined as whole, we have seen throughout the chapters that this corporeal totality is made possible in a fantasy of freedom. Like the body, freedom in the west is never something to be parted from. Like the body, it is something not thought, but something already possessed.[82] Therefore the relationship between the "whole" body and freedom is bound. The body's boundaries and unthinkingness of freedom is, however, brought into question by the presence of women wearing the veil. The concealed body suggests a foreign enjoyment of freedom, or possibly the lack of desire for freedom, as not "ours". The veiled body compels the west to *think* about freedom proclaimed within its borders and thus, question the "whole" body that receives and experiences it. In the politics of Islamophobia, freedom is in jeopardy—"they hate us for our freedom"—and this paranoia is mapped on to the body now imagined in a critical condition as it makes contact with bodies with symptoms of unfreedom. In Islamophobia, the reassembling of a narrative of Islam's cultural regression and political violence dissembles her body as symptoms of affliction needing another to put her together. As Sherene H. Razack writes,

> The Muslim woman's body is used to articulate European superiority. We cannot forget for an instant the usefulness of her body in the contemporary making of white nations and citizens. Her imperilled body has provided a rationale for engaging in the surveillance and disciplining of the Muslim man and Muslim communities.[83]

Islamophobia has not simply invoked the imperilled body but oscillated between two images of Muslim women: the orientalist image of her imperilled, and increasingly, as *imperilling*: a symbol of excessive difference, fundamentalism, violence, threat and a cultural menace.[84] We saw her imperilling capacity in the nation-wide search for those involved in the attacks on Paris in November 2015. Media widely reported a suspect who may have been involved as Hasna Ait Boulahcen and described her as "Europe's first female suicide bomber". An image circulated of the 26-year-old woman of Moroccan background in hijab, her face partially covered, posing for the camera. Since then, we have seen several of these women in contrasting photographs of their "western" lives and appearances and transformed into menacing veiled entities. The juxtaposing imagery is often surveillance footage of them at transport stations and airports exiting and their reappearance in Syria wearing heavy black veils, now wives, mothers and even soldiers holding weapons. Reports tell the story of these young women who lived seemingly "normal" lives but were increasingly disturbed and incited by the Islamic State's propaganda.[85] With the growing defeat of the Islamic State in Syria, many of these women and their children now remain in refugee camps, some like British citizen Shamima Begum, who want to return to their western host country with their children. But this has provoked intense debate on whether these women should be able to return. In addition to a desire to punish their disloyalty, coverage has also been dominated by the potential threat the women pose and preventative measures that need to be taken. In the case of Begum, preventive measures have come with the stripping of her citizenship, ushering the very bedrock of political recognition—citizenship—and is destabilised in the desire to cast out the dangerous body. Returning to the ominous image of Boulahcen, this time the image of the dangers of "radicalised" Muslim women did not circulate alone and accompanied with details of her dismembered body, scattered on to the street after she self-detonated when authorities arrived. This body, bloated by propaganda, could have been any "jihadi bride" returning "home". It was reported that Boulahcen "lured" police in by screaming, "help me, help me, help me" before she detonated the explosives.[86] Later, less circulated corrections claimed that her body had remained intact and that she may not have been wearing an explosive belt after all.

The invocation of a dangerous Muslim woman's body is not new to France. Fanon had reflected on France's encounter with her in the Algerian woman who refused to unveil triggering violent sexual fantasy of conquest.[87] I return to the Algerian woman in the next chapter but for now I want to highlight how her refusal marked a *jouissance* that is *feminine*, one that cannot be symbolically accounted for, exceeding the western (phallic) subject. As Colette Soler writes of the feminine, "she has a desire that is quite foreign to any interest in having but is not a demand for being either. It is defined as an equivalent, if not to a will, at least to an aim of *jouissance*".[88] Boulahcen's reported calls for help, and the subsequent explosion of her body, mobilises the imperilled ("help me") and imperilling (bodily detonating) Muslim woman, in a way that blurs their meaning. She denies the "having" of the body all together and instrumentalises it as a weapon.

Boulahcen's exploded body left traces of this unknown invading *jouissance*, with reports providing as much gruesome details as possible. The details of her bloodied body on the street, her head rolling down the street, pieces of her spine landing on a police car, echoing that of Almutawakel's image of veiled fragments, suggests a preoccupation with locating her body. The ghastly scene triggers revulsion in the possibility of contamination. Like a field of landmines in war, the street is imagined littered with pieces of infected "foreign" blood and flesh. Muslim women's bodies are already bodies that are not entirely known, imagined infected (by the excesses of culture, fanatical ideologies), and breaking apart. This fragmentation is imagined as a dangerous contagion, potentially leaking into the illusory boundary of our public spaces, into "our" bodies.

This preoccupation with women's bodies as contagion is also mirrored in the discussions of gender segregation, female genital cutting, forced marriages, "honour crimes"—widely diverse practices and experiences that serve as "data" of veiled fragments with jarring edges that can disfigure the body politic. These symptoms of the body become the most reliable source for critics for evidencing the charges made against Islam and Muslims. The examples present her body as restricted, denied access (gender segregation), mutilated and sexually controlled ("FGM" and "honour crimes"), sexual object with reproductive capacity (forced marriage and "jihadi" brides). The body's natural desires are denied through such constraining and injurious practices. The chapters identified these bodily violations as a veil of violence. In the paranoid imaginings of Islamophobia, the veiled body—real and imagined—fuels the hypochondria of foreign bodies concealing phantom threats. It is the imaged and imagined veil that produces such oscillations of bodies imperilled and imperilling. I want to stress here that such oscillations speak to the book's underpinning tension: the veil signals a repressed condition in the west that the body *has yet to be domesticated* by the symbolic domain where language fastens itself to its corporeal contours. The body cannot be entirely known for the biopolitical regulation to take its docile effect, no matter what meanings are attached to it. The veil of unfreedom located within the west—a west that has freedom and access to universal knowledge—indicates the *failure of knowledge*.

What is elided in the emphasis on representational distortions of Muslim women is the west grappling with the "extra-discursive"—the traumatic reals of the body. That is, the loss of what fails to be captured by symbolic or discursive meaning.[89] The desire for what needs to be known, and for which orientalism has fantasised answers for centuries, is a desire to give meaning to the "extra-discursive" which appears here as the neighbour's *jouissance*. Behind the discourse of Islamophobia and its fervent calls to ban the veil, is the gaze that marks the Other's hidden *jouissance* that "we" cannot name, producing questions about where it stands in relation to "our" *jouissance*? "our" laws, *our body*? Our Other? During a parliamentary consultation in April 2008 amid a national debate on the veil, a representative of the Sociality Party in the Netherlands which introduced a partial ban of the veil in public areas captures this discomfort in the failure to see oneself in the Other:

> I live in Amsterdam and there I have encountered once, and only once, a woman in a niqab in a park. I felt uncomfortable. There was someone who did not want to make contact with me and with whom I could not make contact. We do not belong to the same city. We do not belong together.[90]

For contact to be possible bodies have to be visible, known and seen. Bodies that are seen are those that define the boundaries of who we are and what we are not. Those who call for the veil ban display a hysterical condition of not knowing, of rejection—what is the stranger concealing? What does she really desire? Why is she not desiring me? A "me" that is itself a nothing, which requires affirmation, is brought into being by being desired by a perceived other. The abstraction at the heart of my being, which can potentially be affirmed in the form of a further question: If she is free here, why does she not unveil? We see this unbearable question during the national debate on France's decision to ban the face veil in 2010, French MP Jacques Myard's, one of the main advocates of the ban, defended the move in an interview with ABC's *Foreign Correspondent*, with a rather personal note: "When you hide your face... I am the victim. I am—because you refuse [to let me see] who you are and this is not acceptable".[91] To refuse the gaze is to make the visibility of European flesh exposed to the Other's persecutory gaze, which haunts with the question that identifies the hypochondriac digging into flesh as the search for recognition.

In July 2009, French feminist philosopher Elisabeth Badinter, named in a 2010 French poll as the country's "most influential intellectual", and a vocal opponent of both the headscarf (hijab) and veil, wrote a rebuke raising this very question. The article, titled "To those who voluntarily wear the burqa" in *Le Nouvel Observateur*, demonstrates a freedom presumed to be already possessed through the question:

> Why don't you move to Saudi Arabia or Afghanistan where nobody would ask to see your face, where your daughters would be veiled too and where your husband would be polygamous and repudiate you whenever he wants?[92]

For Badinter, freedom is something without interference, the natural condition of the body, a freedom that is secularised by fleshly agency, exteriorised and as an individualised embodied performance.[93] The proximity to another body that does not exhibit freedom is a body that does not desire—that is, does not enjoy freedom. This triggers an anxiety of all bodies, including our own, without secure boundaries, as foreign and not ours. The body has potential to showing symptoms of social disintegration—a lack of freedom, or more alarming, *not knowing* freedom. For Badinter's feminist concerns, Muslim women's bodies must embody Womanness and a sexuality that is unhindered, in order to secure the fantasy of absolute knowledge of what Woman is and what she desires. To not desire this freedom is a symptom of madness brought on by illness that has gripped some women's bodies. In 2010, Badinter turns to the disease metaphor to describe the condition of Muslim women who veil, "I think we are dealing with very sick women [i.e., full-veiled Muslim women] and I do not think we have to be determined according to their pathology".[94] Embedded in this distancing statement is a cultural anxiety about the spread of this pathology that threatens not only the ontological being of women and the question of freedom, but what constitutes boundaries of the western subject. The possibility of freedom being rejected shatters the narcissistic image of the western giver,[95] and of losing control over the veil's meaning. To keep such cultural anxiety at bay, the demographic (over) presence of the veil as a menace is projected on to the image of the Muslim woman who is always imagined veiled by violence—that is, *riddled by disease*. Her repetitive circulation, I explain in the following section, is a means of coping with the feeling of being overwhelmed, of not securing knowledge of *and* in the body. The image becomes crucial to the production of knowledge of containing the body due to its capacity to condense and apprehend meaning.

THE *CIRCULATING* IMAGE: "HYPERVEILING" ISLAMOPHOBIA

In the wake of Australia's largest counter-terrorism raid on 18 September 2014, attention was soon drawn to the veil, as both a "shroud of oppression" and a concern for "national security", by Liberal senators Jacqui Lambie and Cory Bernardi.[96] Calling for an immediate and public ban of the burqa, Lambie posted an image on Facebook on 19 September 2014.[97] It is a photograph of a woman wearing a burqa with a raised hand holding a gun. This image was captioned—"Terror attack level: Severe—an attack highly likely. For security reasons it's now time to ban the burqa". The image had been first published by far-right group Britain First and widely circulated. The image links the localised phenomenon of Islamophobia and its fear as a cultural menace, with the global war against terrorism.

This image of the woman in a blue burqa was not unfamiliar to many. As I discussed in the introduction and elaborated in Chapter 3, it has been popularised since the events of 9/11 and the subsequent war in Afghanistan. The burqa has become the symbol of Islam, fundamentalism, terrorism, the oppression of women, as well as the war in Afghanistan. Nevertheless, removed from the frame of this familiar image are the women like Malalai Kakar who wear it. Beneath the veil is Kandahar's first female police officer and head of the city's department for crimes against women. The Taliban killed Kakar outside her home in 2008. The original photo reappears now overlaid with alarmist words such as "terror attack" and "security".[98] The use of an image of a victim of the Taliban by a member of government from a country involved in combat in Afghanistan against the Taliban, to suggest the danger beneath the veil, throws a puzzling light on the image. This is an image that also invites the possibility of an Afghan woman protecting herself as opposed to needing protection. However, the veil's presence trumps any possibility that extends beyond the oscillations of her either being a victim (of fundamentalism) or perpetrator (of fundamentalism), imperilled and imperilling. Importantly, this image is not about fundamentalism "over there" but about its proximity "here", and why Lambie sees in the veil a symptom of an invisible danger that she has named.

Lambie's use of the image needs to be situated in not just the discursive lens of orientalism and Islamophobia. Doing so would mean an epistemological focus that analyses the image as exemplary of the kind of misinformation and disinformation the current climate has produced. What this empirically based critique elides is the original image did not receive the same kind of attention and circulation. Nor does it account for why the "fact" of Kakar did not contain the image's meaning and suffice as a counterpoint that disrupts the politics that connects the veil with the enemy within. The image's ocular epistemology—"this is what happened here"—as discussed in human rights campaigns in Chapter 3, reveals not simply its mode of realism, but its meaning cannot be contained on its own, it needs to be aided by something else.

Images, we have observed earlier, are produced and disseminated by new technologies such as social media (Facebook, Twitter, Instagram) as well the traditional Entertainment industry (Hollywood, video games, music videos). Others around the world inundate our daily lives through these modern mediums. The proliferation of the image means that we can no longer limit the other in imposed zones. Writing about the excess of the image Julia Kristeva notes,

> we are inundated with images. Some of which resonate with our fantasies, and appease us but which, for lack of interpretive words, do not liberate us. Moreover, the stereotype of those images deprives us of the possibility of creating our own imagery, our own imaginary scenarios.[99]

The veiled and unveiled imagery I have traced so far demonstrates the "fixing" of the imaginary, and the ways in which knowledge and freedom are interpreted through its epistemic and political weight. Akin to Foucault's discursive formations, the image is highly situated and interested.[100] The ocular epistemology of the image is accompanied by the imaginary that drives its circulation and meaning. Its circulation today is "like a contagion, growing more pervasive, and destroying rival or competing images to convey a competing or rival truth".[101] It is not simply enough for the image to communicate its meaning (this is what happened) but overcome all other meanings through its repeated circulation. Lacan reminds us that repetition "is turned towards the ludic, which finds its dimensions in the new". Repetition imagines the subject's connection with the lost object (*object a*) at the same time it misses it.[102] Like the child who plays *Fort! Da!* to cope with the mother's absence, repetition allows the subject to enjoy—that is, imagine the possibility of being in control (united with the mOther)—by losing a piece of themselves and have it return.[103] In a world where the image is increasingly becoming a source of our daily knowledge, the image of the veiled woman is repeatedly recruited for western viewers, who have been habituated in the post-9/11 climate to link security with *securing* knowledge over Islam, Muslims and the Muslim woman. Whereas the colonial image was a more controlled and contained representation of the exotic were at a distance, the postcolonial image is more pervasive, intense and mobile. The postcolonial image is about the domestication of difference through the repetitive and pervasive circulation of certain images.

The contact between bodies as a provocation of boundaries being blurred is given momentary relief for the west's hypochondriac Islamophobia by determining meaning of the body in the repeated image as complete knowledge of the body. On the one hand, Lambie's image demonstrates the hypochondriac paranoia of international threats localised in the image of the veiled woman as the hidden enemy, of the other. On the other hand, Lambie offers answers to the question of who and what is the Muslim and its relationship to "us". By condensing complex geopolitical events in a single image, enables the naming of the enemy within, the establishing of (bodily) boundaries by locating the enemy and offering a remedy through increasing security. Security threats, as we know, are about containing and extracting the threat by surveillance, torture, racial profiling, veil bans and other ways of policing Muslim (foreign) bodies. The potential hidden enemy feeds the fantasy of always knowing in the mode of diagnosing the threat by positioning Lambie as the one who will unveil and neutralise the danger.

This naming (and containing) the enemy was taken to an extreme in 2017 when One Nation Party's leader Pauline Hanson wore it in the Australian National Senate in August to protest the dangers the veil poses to Australia's national security in a symbolic gesture of entering enemy territory—to go beneath the veil—and to report back on its dangers. In a dramatic casting off the veil, adjusting her outfit and fixing her hair, Hanson declares she is "quite happy to remove this because this is not what should belong in this Parliament".[104] What does it mean for someone who has described Islam as a "disease" that requires a vaccination to express such an intimate form of protest? Hanson's populist support base would read such "high risk" efforts as a testament to her heroism. Her unveiled/secular body put on the line performs the naming of the bodily ailment in donning the veil as a correct diagnosis for national crises, and in the literal casting off its most dangerous symptom. It is to *re-establish* the boundaries of the secular body that is visible and therefore, recognisable. There is also a deeper stake in turning to the veil: the possibility that *she too* could be engulfed by the power of not so much by its intelligible visible difference but by its unintelligible *invisible sameness.*

What we have here is the parading of the enemy vis-à-vis the veiled woman as an example of what Neil Macmaster and Toni Lewis describe as a "hyperveiling". Identifying a contemporary investment in the veil, Macmaster and Lewis found that whereas nineteenth-century European discourse of orientalism was focused on the erotic images of unveiling, the "Scheherazade syndrome" of discovering the forbidden, in the postcolonial context, there is now focus on "hyperveiling". This shift to emphasise "complete forms of covering", seen in Lambie's image, aims at widening the difference between Islam and the west and "maximize the danger" to the nation.[105] Hyperveiling signals that

> Veiling and concealment are always inherently sinister, as with masking in general, and always lurking behind the figure of the veiled woman is the shadowy fundamentalist, the fanatical bomber who manipulates her.[106]

Hyperveiling carries with it the historical figure of the Algerian woman who carried concealed weapons beneath her veil.[107] Now, the veil has crossed western borders giving visible credence to the phobic dimensions of "the Muslim question". Scott observes that during the "foulard affair" (the debate on the headscarf in schools) the term "*voile*" took over and the subject of debate became the face veil, invoking fundamentalisms of Iran, Afghanistan and Saudi Arabia.[108] While Macmaster and Lewis also focused on France, hyperveiling appears in the Netherlands, Australia and the wider west where the "burqa" (full face veil) has become the ubiquitous term to describe all face veiling.[109] The hidden body is "intolerable", "uncomfortable", "not acceptable", and in the words of former Australian Prime Ministers Julia Gillard of the Labour party and Tony Abbott of the Liberal party, "confronting". Despite such alarm, hyperveiling ensues. This suggests that Lambie's use of the image and Hanson's donning of the veil, is not merely a misrepresentation brought on from Islamophobic hysteria but like unveiling (the desire to know juxtaposed with the anxiety of what will be known) is an *enjoyment* in this image and how it organises desire (what is she hiding?) at the same time it induces anxiety (what if?). In other words, it identifies western *jouissance* in the economy of the veiled (desire) and unveiled (anxiety).

We are reminded here of Clérambault's Moroccan photographs as a form of hyperveiling that marks off the wasted body, what Copjec argues is a useless enjoyment that served no functional purpose in the modern world.[110] We hear a similar concern for the niqab and burqa as having no place in the modern secular world, and how impractical it is for participating in public life, such as one's productivity through being employable.[111] The veiled body is the obscene religious body. But as know from Clérambault's veiling efforts, the naming of the veiled body as undesirable, masks a deeper anxiety about the other's knowledge of the body. In the logic of Islamophobia as a hypochondriac's "yes, but what if?", hyperveiling seeks out absolute knowledge of the other through naming it while not entirely satisfied with the naming ever. By circulating the image in the mode of hyperveiling, the hypochondriac can enjoy proximity to knowledge but also following it with the question of "what if...?". The veil is a means of perpetual discovery. Hyperveiling must therefore be repeated as an image of abjection.

The hyperveiling image of the Muslim woman transposes her into an object of fear beyond politics. Heavily veiled, her absolute difference means she is outside of social engagement and beyond accommodation because we can only approach her with condemnation, surveillance and calls to expel her. She is what Jeffrey Stephenson Murer calls a toxic image that,

> is no longer a question of a "false" or "true" representation of reality, for the imagery is no longer "true" or "false". Rather all of this is simultaneous true, representing simultaneous and multiple truths, while at the same time creating whole new realities by joining these truths together in a single image.[112]

Hyperveiling the object of fear enables western desire to access knowledge of what or who is the enemy. *Che vuoi?* But only in the repetition of the image is there satisfaction (if there is any at all) of imagining an answer. The image, put differently, is a way of diagnosing the body through the other and offering temporary remedies to relocate its secular and religious boundaries.

The spectre of the veiled face, as opposed to the veiled head, is both the visible difference of the Muslim qua the veil, and the invisibility of its locality to "us" qua what lies beneath it. Like Žižek's Jew in anti-Semitism, the veiled woman is a "master signifier"—both an empirical designation (like the image) and an unrepresentable signifier (beyond representation). She stands in for the void from where the figure of the Muslim as terrorist, disloyal and cultural menace names the difference. In this vein, the Muslim is the Lacanian *object a*, the "hidden ground"—what lies beneath the veil—that which comes to mark and "explicate" any representation of the Muslim's strangeness.[113] The *object a* is the non-specular, what Žižek calls "the leftover of every signifying operation, a hardcore embodiment of horrifying jouissance, enjoyment and an object which simultaneously attracts and repels—which *divides* our desire".[114] It is an object that draws the links between discourses through provoking desire for knowledge. This knowledge can appear by the very circulation of the image, which like surveillance technologies, registers the Muslim woman.

In the fantasy of a west with freedom, the certainty of *object a* sustains the precarious knowledge of the Muslim in the figure of the veiled woman. Located at the nexus of the gaze and "the nothing", fear is produced by a difference that is evident qua the veil and thus, a persisting desire (to know) for what is hidden. Like in hypochondria, the material (imaged) veiled woman triggers an unknown symptom on the body that further activates the compulsion to explain it before it engulfs. The fear is more fundamental than the veil itself. The veil as *object a* momentarily secures knowledge, dispels fundamental fear of loss and locates it in a cultural symbol of difference which the west can collectively identify as threatening. However, hyperveiling is another veil of violence that triggers more "yes, but what if?", inviting fantasy narratives—here in the mode of un-integration, sur*veil*lance and violence against Muslim women's bodies. Even when she was confronted by the photographer Lana Šlezić who had taken the photo of Kakar, Lambie insisted that the image was done in her honour: "If there was a reason why this brave woman was shot, my guess is that it was because she chose to defy the Sharia extremists and submit to their threats—and dressed without their burka".[115] Lambie's "guess" is the very "what if" that erases Kakar's life by deploying the (toxic) image of the veiled woman which "abbreviates" the hidden threat of radicalisation, home grown terrorism, building of mosques, terror plots, raids, halal certification, Sharia law, etc., and the very figure that explicates the threat.[116] She appears as both *materialised and imagined*, foregrounding the discursive production of the "Muslimwoman" as a radical difference, and is the very condition of her possibility. The debate on veiling is about the invisible face of Islam—the *object a*—as an other, more than itself (beyond its empirical details) that masks the impossibility of unifying the postcolonial body.

Conclusion

The image is a means of enjoyment for Lambie who is not interested in the veil beyond that which allows her to draw the link between Islam and terrorism. This aggressive knowledge that appears reductive, repetitive, is part of a fascination brought on by the confrontation with deeper ontological disruptions to the question of who "we" are. This chapter aimed to understand the nature of knowledge in the contemporary world we live in where knowledge is increasingly accessible and consumable through the image. While discursive readings are an important insight into the political, ideological and historical makeup to understanding the fixation on the veil, this chapter demonstrated that they do not adequately deal with postcolonial tensions and the new modes of knowledge because they still pursue the real without ever really harnessing it.

This chapter examined the image's capacity to exceed its content by identifying the limits of discursive analysis. The focus on epistemology to examine the phenomenon of Islamophobia only reproduces its existing premises, entertains its phobic imaginary, because they are invested in perceiving Islamophobia as about misrecognition that can be dispelled by correct representations. Even after the fact that these images are a misrepresentation, they do not explain the continuing and consistent nature of representing the Muslim woman as imperilled (orientalism) and imperilling (Islamophobia). They do not bridge the politics, history and psychoanalytic vocabularies to address the unconscious investment, and even fascination, in these representations by the west. This chapter's purpose was not to understand Islamophobia as a mode of racism, but to understand it as an "unmediated mode of response that pre-empts or overrides discursive responses".[117] By linking psychoanalysis to the politics of Islamophobia, the pattern of repetition and the emotional investment in the hidden face/threat can be better understood as a failure of knowledge.

Sidestepping the epistemological focus, we can better appreciate the encounter with the veil is about the crisis of knowledge through the contact with other bodies. If we take into consideration the conclusions of the previous chapter that the body has been central to securing the fantasy of western truths, in a world where we are exposed to all kinds of bodies—both demographically and in images—how can knowledge be secured? How does the west deal with the very question of its own limit? The postcolonial condition has brought on a hypochondriac response in the mode of Islamophobia as a politics and a knowledge production needing to police other bodies by a paranoid imaginary that sees potential foreign contamination; borders that have been compromised. Bodies that are veiled trigger an anxiety of not only experiencing the body differently but about one's *own body as foreign, unknown.* To repress the trauma of one's own limit, the repeated circulation of the image as a naming of the threat, of imagining ways of locating the bodies that carry hidden dangers, gives momentary relief.

The initial encounter with difference signals the arrival of a fantasy that enables the west to come to terms with the other's destabilising difference and itself, in the lingering shadow of this encounter. As Said writes, the Orient "vacillates between the west's contempt for what is familiar and its shivers of delight in—or fear of—novelty".[118] The psychic dimensions of this dynamic assist in considering not only how the metanarratives, like the desire about who is Aisha, and the desire to rescue, are produced and received, but these desires are the hidden drives of these representations. If unveiling is a way of disciplining knowledge of the Orient, hyperveiling in the postcolonial era is a mode of unveiling as inoculating the body.

NOTES

1. McClintock, *Imperial Leather*, 28.
2. Ella Shohat, "Notes on the 'Postcolonial'," in *The Preoccupation with Postcolonial Studies*, ed. Fawzia Afzal-Khan and Kalpana Seshadri-Crooks (Durham: Duke University Press 2000), 130.
3. Mary Louise Pratt, *Imperial Eyes: Travel Writing and Transculturation* (New York: Routledge, 2008), 7.
4. Said, *Orientalism*, 26–27.
5. Michel Foucault and Colin Gordon, *Power/Knowledge: Selected Interviews and Other Writings, 1972–1977* (Brighton, Sussex: Harvester Press, 1980), 109–133.
6. Chetan Bhatt, "The Times of Movements: A Response," *The British Journal of Sociology* 59, no. 1 (2008): 25–33.
7. Writing about paranoia, David Trotter describes it as a "delusion of magical power" whose symptoms emerge in the nineteenth century with western elites who were coming to terms with modernism's "messes" as political,

economic and social disruption to their symbolic status. *Paranoid Modernism: Literary Experiment, Psychosis and the Professionalisation of English Society* (Oxford: Oxford University Press, 2001), 7.

8. Jon Mills, "Lacan on Paranoiac Knowledge," *Psychoanalytic Psychology* 20, no. 1 (2003).

9. Jacques Derrida, "Autoimmunity: Real and Symbolic Suicides—A Dialogue of Jacques Derrida," in *Philosophy in a Time of Terror: Dialogues with Jurgan Habermas and Jacques Derrida*, by Giovanna Borradori (Chicago: University of Chicago Press, 2003), 92.

10. Timothy Mitchell, "Picturing Terror: Derrida's Autoimmunity," *Critical Inquiry* 33 (2007): 281.

11. Derrida, "Autoimmunity: Real and Symbolic Suicides."

12. Neil Larsen, "Determination: Postcolonialism, Poststructuralism, and the Problem of Ideology," in *The Preoccupation with Postcolonialism Studies*, ed. Fawzia Afzal-Khan and Kalpana Seshadri-Crooks (Durham: Duke University Press, 2000), 146.

13. Lacan, *Ecrits: The First Complete Edition in English*, 690.

14. Hook, *A Critical Psychology of the Postcolonial: The Mind of Apartheid*, 6.

15. See, for example, Open Society Foundations, "Unveiling Truth: Why 32 Muslim Women Wear the Full-Face Veil in France," *At Home in Europe Project* (2011); Abdullah Saeed and Shahram Akbarzadeh, ed., *Muslim Women in Australia*, Islamic Studies Series (Sydney: UNSW Press, 2010).

16. Pollock, *Psychoanalysis and the Image: Transdisciplinary Perspectives*, 26.

17. See Jean Paul Sartre's preface in Frantz Fanon, *The Wretched of the Earth* (New York: Perseus Books Group, 2007).

18. Said, *Orientalism*, 59.

19. Said, *Orientalism*, 59.

20. Mills, "Lacan on Paranoiac Knowledge," 35.

21. Yeğenoğlu, *Colonial Fantasies: Towards a Feminist Reading of Orientalism*, 6.

22. Mills, "Lacan on Paranoiac Knowledge," 36.

23. Ragland, "The Hysteric's Truth," 69.

24. Mills, "Lacan on Paranoiac Knowledge," 43.

25. Said, *Orientalism*, 229.

26. Edward W. Said, *Covering Islam: How the Media and the Experts Determine How We See the Rest of the World*, Rev. ed. (New York: Vintage Books, 1997), 1.

27. See Fukuyama, *End of History and the Last Man*.

28. Jacques Derrida, *Rogues: Two Essays on Reason* (Palo Alto, CA: Stanford University Press, 2005), 25–41.

29. Yasemin Yildiz, "Governing European Subjects: Tolerance and Guilt in the Discourse of 'Muslim Women'," *Cultural Critique* 77 (2011): 75–77.

30. Slavoj Žižek, *Tarrying with the Negative: Kant, Hegel and the Critique of Ideology* (Durham: Duke University Press, 1993), 201–205.
31. The Runnymede Trust: Intelligence for a Multi-Ethnic Britain, *Islamophobia: A Challenge to Us All* (London, 1997). Though it was reported in use during the revolution in Iran to describe Iranian hostility towards religion—an origin that deserves closer examination but one that lies beyond the scope of this book—Islamophobia was first mentioned in the west in 1991 in a Runnymede Trust Report. Referenced in Christopher Allen, *Islamophobia* (Farnham, Surrey: Ashgate, 2010), 5.
32. Salman Sayyid, "Racism and Islamophobia," in *International Centre of Muslim and Non-Muslim Understanding* (Adelaide: University of South Australia, 2011), 1.
33. Joan Wallach Scott, "Symptomatic Politics: Banning Islamic Head Scarves in French Public School," in *Postcolonialism and Political Theory*, ed. Nalini Persram (Lanham and Plymouth: Lexington Books, 2007), 197.
34. McClintock, *Imperial Leather*, 184.
35. Allen, *Islamophobia*, 142.
36. George W. Bush, "Speech Transcript of President Bush's Speech," *CNN*, September 21, 2001.
37. Norton, *On the Muslim Question*, 4.
38. Dekker and Van Der Noll, 2009, quoted in Apetroaie, "The Trembling Veil: Issues of Gendered Islamophobia and Intolerance Towards Veiled Muslim Women, Current Issues of Islam," 4.
39. For example, western demands on Muslim communities in the west to condemn terrorism involving Muslims. The call for condemnation is often accompanied by the accusation that Muslims do not condemn enough and are often quiet when these events take place, suggesting they approve of such activities. Meanwhile, official Muslim bodies routinely condemn acts of violence committed by Muslims and clarifying Islam's official position.
40. Peter Gottschalk and Gabriel Greenberg, *Islamophobia: Making Muslims the Enemy* (Lanham, MD: Rowman & Littlefield, 2008), 3.
41. Some view it as a historically situated prejudice, which resides deeply in the western consciousness and can be traced to the origins of Islam. Others theorise that latent forms of anti-Muslim and anti-Islam anxieties and fears are endemic to European and western societies. These manifest when incidents involving Muslims take place. See Allen, *Islamophobia*, 14–15. Building on Edward Said's work, others have looked at it as a 'Cold War' between the west and Islam, particularly in the 1990s. See Emran Qureshi and Michael A. Sells, "Introduction," in *The New Crusades: Constructions of the Muslim Enemy*, ed. Emran Qureshi and Michael A. Sells (New York: Columbia University Press, 2003).
42. See Ernest Gellner, *Nations and Nationalism* (New York: Cornell University Press, 1983).

43. See Benedict Anderson, *Imagined Communities* (London: Verso, 2006).
44. See, for example, Sita Ranchod-Nilsson and Mary Ann Tetreault, *Women, States and Nationalism: At Home in the Nation?* (New York: Routledge, 2000); Zayzafoon, *The Production of the Muslim Woman*.
45. Megan Macdonald, "Sur/Veil," 39.
46. Judith Butler and Gayatri Chakravorty Spivak, *Who Sings the Nation-State? Language, Politics, Belonging* (Kolkata: Seagull Books, 2007).
47. Mitchell, "Picturing Terror: Derrida's Autoimmunity," 282.
48. Nick Miller, "'The Great Replacement': An Idea Now at the Heart of Europe's Politics," *The Sunday Morning Herald*, March 19, 2019, https://www.smh.com.au/world/europe/the-great-replacement-the-racist-idea-now-at-the-heart-of-europe-s-politics-20190319-p515cc.html.
49. Joan Wallach Scott, *The Fantasy of Feminist History* (Durham: Duke University Press, 2011).
50. Amy Rameikis, "Pauline Hanson Says Islam Is a Disease Australia Needs to 'Vaccinate'," *The Sunday Morning Herald*, March 24, 2017, https://www.smh.com.au/politics/federal/pauline-hanson-says-islam-is-a-disease-australia-needs-to-vaccinate-20170324-gv5w7z.html.
51. Andrew Kaczynski, "Michael Flynn in August: Islamism a 'Vicious Cancer' in Body of All Muslims That 'Has to Be Excised'," *CNN*, November 22, 2016, https://edition.cnn.com/2016/11/22/politics/kfile-michael-flynn-august-speech/index.html.
52. "London Attack: Nuttall Says Cut Out Radical Islam Cancer," *BBC*, March 23, 2017, https://www.bbc.com/news/uk-politics-39367928.
53. Kelly Weill, "Instagram Stands by Laura Loomer Calling Ilhan Omar's Islamic Faith 'Cancer'," *The Daily Beast*, April 11, 2019, https://www.thedailybeast.com/ilhan-omar-death-threats-surge-online-after-911-comments?fbclid=IwAR0OZJ7xHtdu2-ACNVo6WlGOe1ifWHbEs4QETrtHhHbE3xxuHkBLPhBRCRs.
54. Mitchell, "Picturing Terror: Derrida's Autoimmunity," 285.
55. Julia Barossa and Caroline Rooney, "Fortress Hypochondria: Health and Safety," in *Nationalism and the Body Politic: Psychoanalysis and the Rise of Eurocentrism and Xenophobia*, ed. Lene Austead (London: Karnac, 2014), 13.
56. Talal Asad, "Thinking About the Secular Body, Pain and Liberal Politics," *Cultural Anthropology* 26, no. 4 (2011): 659.
57. Barossa and Rooney, "Fortress Hypochondria," 13.
58. Cheng, *The Melancholy of Race*, 69.
59. Rooney, "Fortress Hypochondria: Health and Safety," 8.
60. For example, Australian Prime Minister Tony Abbott's response to national security insisted that Muslim leaders be more genuine in their condemnation of extremism. "I've often heard western leaders describe Islam as a

'religion of peace'. I wish more Muslim leaders would say that more often, and mean it". What Muslims really mean is always in question. Knowledge of the other is always unsatisfying. See Shalailah Medhora, "Tony Abbott Urges Muslim Groups 'to Get with the Program' and Condemn Extremism," *The Guardian*, February 24, 2015.

61. Ishmael N. Daro, "'Taqiyya': How an Obscure Islamic Concept Became an Obsession of Anti-Muslim Activists," *Buzzfeed News*, April 12, 2018, https://www.buzzfeednews.com/article/ishmaeldaro/taqiyya-explained.

62. "Halal" is the Arabic word for what constitutes as lawful for Muslims to consume in accordance with Muslims scripture. Concerned with products that are consumed, it includes food products, meat, cosmetics, personal care products, pharmaceuticals and food ingredients. For more details on the dietary standards of Muslims, particularly in Australia, see the public announcement on halal products from The Islamic Council of Victoria, "What Is Halal? A Guide for Non-Muslims," http://www.icv.org.au/index.php/publications/what-is-halal.

63. Will Ockenden, "No Direct Link Between Halal Certification and Islamic Terrorism, Senate Inquiry Told," *ABC*, September 24, 2015, https://www.abc.net.au/news/2015-09-24/senate-inquiry-no-direct-link-between-halal-certification/6801968; Caitlin Drysdale, "Flyer Linking Halal Certification to Terrorism Circulates Southern Brisbane," *The Courier Mail*, August 12, 2015, https://www.couriermail.com.au/questnews/southeast/flyer-linking-halal-certification-to-terrorism-circulates-southern-brisbane/news-story/ae1cbea1efc7d7cf52ea619a0dff6629?sv=cb4b2254c748d411e0d963d150fd94f6.

64. Max Chambers, "Welcome to the Strange Logic of Kirralie Smith, Anti-Halal Truther," *New Matilda*, September 21, 2014.

65. David Gear, "We Are Unknowingly Being Converted to Islam, Says Cowan MP Luke Simpkins," *Perth Now*, November 25, 2011.

66. Rooney, "Fortress Hypochondria: Health and Safety," 13.

67. The abject is the "thing" that the hidden threatens to overwhelm, that induces disgust at the thought of it escaping and contaminating, is what Kristeva describes to be a symptom of that which is rejected and needs expunging. The social is always something to be policed and preserved. Society, through its processes of "civility" identifies and encourages the expulsion of certain elements that it deems impure (vomit, blood, incest, etc.). This is a process of abjection. It is not simply bodily excess that needs to be "cast out, or away" but to whatever lack has been politically attributed: the feminine (women), death (the uncontrollable drives that exceed the subject's fantasy) and the foreigner (the stranger within us). See Julia Kristeva, *Powers of Horror: An Essay on Abjection* (New York: Columbia University Press, 1982).

68. For example, under Tony Abbott, the Liberal government in Australia frequently spoke about terror threats, mainly from what he called the "death cult" of ISIS as "likely" or "imminent" despite the admission "there is no specific evidence of a terror plot". Daniel Flitton, "Tony Abbott's Muddled Message on Terrorism," *The Sydney Morning Herald*, September 13, 2014.

69. Talal Asad, *On Suicide Bombing* (New York: Columbia University Press, 2007).

70. Lauren B. Wilcox, *Bodies of Violence: Theorising Embodies Subjects in International Relations* (New York: Oxford University Press, 2015), 89–90.

71. Eve Conant, "Terror: The Remains of 9/11 Hijackers," *News Week*, February 1, 2009.

72. Stuart Winter, "Exclusive: Remains of 9/11 Killers Found," *Sunday Express*, January 11, 2009.

73. Conant, "Terror: The Remains of 9/11 Hijackers," *News Week*.

74. See Foucault, *Discipline and Punishment: The Birth of the Prison*.

75. Although not specifically dealing with the Muslim community, Yasmin Ibrahim examines the construction of bodies in surveillance societies as part of new technologies and counter-terrorism policies. See Yasmin Ibrahim, "Commodifying Terrorism: Body, Surveillance and the Everyday," *Journal of Media and Culture* 10, no. 3 (2007).

76. "Jake Bilardi: Blog Believed to Belong to Australian Teenager Details Journey Behind Radicalisation," *ABC News*, 2015.

77. Adam Cooper, "Jail Term Awaits Islamic 'Wunderkind' Over Doomed Travel Plot," *The Sydney Morning Herald*, March 15, 2019, https://www.smh.com.au/national/jail-term-awaits-islamic-wunderkind-over-doomed-travel-plot-20190315-p514m6.html.

78. Cooper, "Jail Term Awaits Islamic 'Wunderkind'."

79. Jen Kirby, "Far-Right Australian Senator Blames New Zealand Attack on Muslim Immigrants," *Vox*, March 15, 2019, https://www.vox.com/2019/3/15/18267077/australian-senator-new-zealand-attack-muslims-immigrants.

80. Shoshana Magnet and Corinne Lysandra Mason, "Of Trojan Horses and Terrorist Representations: Mom Bombs, Cross-Dressing Terrorists and Queer Orientalisms," *Canadian Journal of Communications* 39, no. 2 (2014): 193–209.

81. Magnet and Mason, "Of Trojan Horses and Terrorist Representations."

82. Rogers, "Unquestionable Freedom in a Psychotic West," 187.

83. Sherene H. Razack, *Casting Out: The Conviction of Muslims from Western Law and Politics* (Toronto: University of Toronto Press, 2008), 168–169.

84. Anne Aly, "Media Hegemony, Activism and Identity: Muslim Women Representing Muslim Women," in *Beyond the Hijab Debates: New Conversations on Gender, Race and Religion*, ed. Tanja Dreher and Christina Ho

(Newcastle: Cambridge Scholars, 2009), 20. See also Gholam Khiabany and Milly Williamson, "Veiled Bodies—Naked Racism: Culture, Politics and Race in the Sun," *Race and Class* 50, no. 2 (2008): 71.

85. Nabeelah Jaffer, "The Secret World of ISIS Brides: 'U dnt hav 2 pay 4 ANYTHING if u r wife of a martyr'," *The Guardian*, June 24, 2015, https://www.theguardian.com/world/2015/jun/24/isis-brides-secret-world-jihad-western-women-syria.

86. Sarah Ann Harris, "Paris Attacks: Europe's First Female Suicide Bomber Named as Hasna Ait Boulahcen," *The Huffington Post*, November 19, 2015.

87. Nadia Aitia describes these initial reports as a "fixation on the Muslim woman's body" which has a long history. See "Your Fascination with Muslim Women's Bodies Has a Long Misogynistic History," *Media Diversified*, December 17, 2015.

88. Soler, *What Lacan Said About Women: A Psychoanalytic Study*, 105–106.

89. Hook, *A Critical Psychology of the Postcolonial: The Mind of Apartheid*, 52–60.

90. Moors, "The Dutch and the Face-Veil: The Politics of Discomfort," 400.

91. Jacqui Pavey, "The Burqa or the Ban: Which Is Worse?," *Right Now*, February 14, 2011.

92. "The Background to the French Parliamentary Commission on the Burqa and Niqab," in *European Race Audit* (Institute of Race Relations, 2010).

93. Mahmood, *Politics of Piety*, 29.

94. Translation from Sara Farris, *In the Name of Women's Rights: The Rise of Femonationalism* (Durham: Duke University Press, 2017).

95. Butler, *Precarious Life: The Powers of Mourning and Violence*, 24.

96. Cory Bernadi, "For Australia's Sake, We Need to Ban the Burqa," *The Sydney Morning Herald*, May 6, 2010.

97. The photographer did not permit the use of this image as she did not want Malailai Kakar's life and identity further associated with the story.

98. Lisa Visentin, "Senator Jacqui Lambie's Anti-Burqa Post 'Desecrated' Image, Photographer Says," *The Sydney Morning World*, September 20, 2014.

99. Francis L. Restuccia, "Kristeva's Intimate Revolt and Thought Specular: Encountering the (Mulholland) Drive," in *Psychoanalysis, Aesthetics and Politics in the Works of Julia Kristeva*, ed. Kelly Oliver and S. K. Keltner (New York: SUNY Press, 2009), 68.

100. Foucault and Gordon, *Power/Knowledge: Selected Interviews and Other Writings, 1972–1977*.

101. Jeffrey Stevenson Murer, "Toxic Images or Imaging the Other," *Open Democracy*, March 22, 2013.

102. Lacan and Miller, *The Four Fundamentals Concepts of Psychoanalysis*, 61.

103. Fink, "The Real Cause of Repetition," 228–229.

104. Amy Rameikis, "One Nation Leader Pauline Hanson Wears Burqa in Senate Question Time Stunt," *The Sydney Morning Herald*, August 17, 2017, https://www.smh.com.au/politics/federal/one-nation-leader-pauline-hanson-wears-full-burqa-in-senate-question-time-stunt-20170817-gxyd5d.html.
105. Macmaster and Lewis, "Orientalism: From Unveiling to Hyperveiling," 122–130.
106. Macmaster and Lewis, "Orientalism: From Unveiling to Hyperveiling," 130.
107. See Frantz Fanon, "Algeria Unveiled," in *Decolonisation: Perspectives from Now and Then: Rewriting Histories*, ed. Prasenjit Duara (London: Routledge, 2003).
108. Scott, *The Politics of the Veil*, 23.
109. Moors, "The Affective Power of the Face Veil: Between Disgust and Fascination," 285.
110. Copjec, *Read My Desire*, 69.
111. In addition to her opposition to the burqa as a security threat and not suited for a modern society, Pauline Hanson also calls for its ban because it makes women unemployable. Joe Kelly, "Hanson Labels Feminists Pathetic on Burka-Ban," *The Australian*, September 13, 2018, https://www.theaustralian.com.au/nation/politics/pauline-hanson-labels-feminists-pathetic-on-burka-ban/news-story/370cc98ad66e0d9f2ab69cac412f0a81.
112. Jeffrey Stevenson Murer, "Toxic Images or Imaging the Other," *Open Democracy*, March 22, 2013.
113. Rex Butler, *Slavoj Žižek: Live Theory* (New York: Continuum, 2005), 50.
114. Slavoj Žižek, *The Sublime Object of Ideology* (London: Verso Books, 1989), 180.
115. Bridie Jabour, "Jacqui Lambie Says Criticism Over Burqa Post is a 'Gross Overreaction'," *The Guardian*, September 21, 2014.
116. Butler, *Slavoj Žižek: Live Theory*, 49–50.
117. Hook, *A Critical Psychology of the Postcolonial: The Mind of Apartheid*, 70.
118. Said, *Orientalism*, 59.

References

Allen, Christopher. *Islamophobia*. Farnham, Surrey: Ashgate, 2010.
Aly, Anne. "Media Hegemony, Activism and Identity: Muslim Women Representing Muslim Women." In *Beyond the Hijab Debates: New Conversations on Gender, Race and Religion*, edited by Tanja Dreher and Christina Ho. Newcastle: Cambridge Scholars, 2009.
Anderson, Benedict. *Imagined Communities*. London: Verso, 2006.

Apetroaie, Vladiana. "The Trembling Veil: Issues of Gendered Islamophobia and Intolerance Towards Veiled Muslim Women, Current Issues of Islam."

Asad, Talal. *On Suicide Bombing*. New York: Columbia University Press, 2007.

Asad, Talal. "Thinking About the Secular Body, Pain and Liberal Politics." *Cultural Anthropology* 26, no. 4 (2011): 657–675.

Barossa, Julia, and Caroline Rooney. "Fortress Hypochondria: Health and Safety." In *Nationalism and the Body Politic: Psychoanalysis and the Rise of Eurocentrism and Xenophobia*, edited by Lene Austead. London: Karnac, 2014.

Bhatt, Chetan. "The Times of Movements: A Response." *The British Journal of Sociology* 59, no. 1 (2008): 25–33.

Butler, Judith. *Precarious Life: The Powers of Mourning and Violence*. New York: Verso, 2004.

Butler, Judith, and Gayatri Chakravorty Spivak. *Who Sings the Nation-State? Language, Politics, Belonging*. Kolkata: Seagull Books, 2007.

Butler, Rex. *Slavoj Žižek: Live Theory*. New York: Continuum, 2005.

Cheng, Anne Anlin. *The Melancholy of Race: Psychoanalysis, Assimilation, and Hidden Grief*. New York: Oxford University Press, 2000.

Derrida, Jacques. "Autoimmunity: Real and Symbolic Suicides—A Dialogue of Jacques Derrida." In *Philosophy in a Time of Terror: Dialogues with Jurgan Habermas and Jacques Derrida*, by Giovanna Borradori. Chicago: University of Chicago Press, 2003.

Derrida, Jacques. *Rogues: Two Essays on Reason*. Palo Alto, CA: Stanford University Press, 2005.

Fanon, Frantz. "Algeria Unveiled." In *Decolonisation: Perspectives From Now and Then: Rewriting Histories*, edited by Prasenjit Duara. London: Routledge, 2003.

Fanon, Frantz. *The Wretched of the Earth*. New York: Perseus Books Group, 2007.

Farris, Sara. *In the Name of Women's Rights: The Rise of Femonationalism*. Durham: Duke University Press, 2017.

Fink, Bruce. "The Real Cause of Repetition." In *Reading Seminar XI: The Four Fundamental Concepts of Psychoanalysis*, edited by Bruce Fink, Richard Feldstein, and Marie Jaanus. Albany: State University of New York Press, 1995.

Foucault, Michel. *Discipline and Punishment: The Birth of the Prison*. Translated by Alan Sheridan. New York: Random House, 1995.

Foucault, Michel, and Colin Gordon. *Power/Knowledge: Selected Interviews and Other Writings, 1972–1977*. Brighton, Sussex: Harvester Press, 1980.

Fukuyama, Francis. *End of History and the Last Man*. New York: Free Press, 2006.

Gellner, Ernest. *Nations and Nationalism*. New York: Cornell University Press, 1983.

Gottschalk, Peter, and Gabriel Greenberg. *Islamophobia: Making Muslims the Enemy*. Lanham, MD: Rowman & Littlefield, 2008.

Hook, Derek. *A Critical Psychology of the Postcolonial: The Mind of Apartheid*. London: Psychology Press, 2012.

Ibrahim, Yasmin. "Commodifying Terrorism: Body, Surveillance and the Everyday." *Journal of Media and Culture* 10, no. 3 (2007).

Kelly, Joe. "Hanson Labels Feminists Pathetic on Burka-Ban." *The Australian*, September 13, 2018. https://www.theaustralian.com.au/nation/politics/pauline-hanson-labels-feminists-pathetic-on-burka-ban/news-story/370cc98ad66e0d9f2ab69cac412f0a81.

Khiabany, Gholam, and Milly Williamson. "Veiled Bodies—Naked Racism: Culture, Politics and Race in the Sun." *Race and Class* 50, no. 2 (2008): 69–88.

Kristeva, Julia. *Powers of Horror: An Essay on Abjection.* New York: Columbia University Press, 1982.

Lacan, Jacques. *Ecrits: The First Complete Edition in English.* New York: W. W. Norton, 2006.

Lacan, Jacques, and Jacques-Alain Miller. *The Four Fundamentals Concepts of Psychoanalysis.* Translated by Alan Sheridan. Edited by Jacques-Alain Miller. London: Karnac, 1973.

Larsen, Neil. "Determination: Postcolonialism, Poststructuralism, and the Problem of Ideology." In *The Preoccupation with Postcolonialism Studies*, edited by Fawzia Afzal-Khan and Kalpana Seshadri-Crooks. Durham: Duke University Press, 2000.

Macdonald, Megan. "Sur/Veil: The Veil as Blank(et) Signifier." In *Muslim Women, Transnational Feminism and Ethics of Pedagogy: Contested Imaginaries in Post-9/11 Cultural Practice*, edited by Lisa K. Taylor and Jasmine Zine. New York: Routledge, 2014.

Macmaster, Neil, and Toni Lewis. "Orientalism: From Unveiling to Hyperveiling." *Journal of European Studies* 28, no. 1 (1998): 122–130.

Magnet, Shoshana, and Corinne Lysandra Mason. "Of Trojan Horses and Terrorist Representations: Mom Bombs, Cross-dressing Terrorists and Queer Orientalisms." *Canadian Journal of Communications* 39, no. 2 (2014): 193–209.

Mahmood, Saba. *Politics of Piety: The Islamic Revival and the Feminist Subject.* Princeton, NJ: Princeton University Press, 2005.

McClintock, Anne. *Imperial Leather: Race, Gender, and Sexuality in the Colonial Contest.* New York: Routledge, 1995.

Mills, Jon. "Lacan on Paranoiac Knowledge." *Psychoanalytic Psychology* 20, no. 1 (2003): 30–51.

Mitchell, Timothy. "Picturing Terror: Derrida's Autoimmunity." *Critical Inquiry* 33 (2007): 277–290.

Moors, Annelies. "The Affective Power of the Face Veil: Between Disgust and Fascination." In *Things: Religion and the Question of Materiality*, edited by Digit Houtman and Birgit Meyer. New York: Fordham University Press, 2012.

Moors, Annelies. "The Dutch and the Face-Veil: The Politics of Discomfort." *European Association of Social Anthropologists* 17, no. 4 (2009): 393–408.

Norton, Anne. *On the Muslim Question*. Princeton: Princeton University Press, 2013.

Pollock, Griselda. *Psychoanalysis and the Image: Transdisciplinary Perspectives*. Malden, MA: Blackwell, 2006.

Pratt, Mary Louise. *Imperial Eyes: Travel Writing and Transculturation*. New York: Routledge, 2008.

Qureshi, Emran, and Michael A. Sells. "Introduction." In *The New Crusades: Constructions of the Muslim Enemy*, edited by Emran Qureshi and Michael A. Sells. New York: Columbia University Press, 2003.

Ragland, Ellie. "The Hysteric's Truth." In *Reflections on Seminar XVII: Jacques Lacan and the Other Side of Psychoanalysis*, edited by Justin Clemens and Russel Grigg. Durham: Duke University Press, 2006.

Ranchod-Nilsson, Sita, and Mary Ann Tetreault. *Women, States and Nationalism: At Home in the Nation?* New York: Routledge, 2000.

Razack, Sherene H. *Casting Out: The Conviction of Muslims from Western Law and Politics*. Toronto: University of Toronto Press, 2008.

Restuccia, Francis L. "Kristeva's Intimate Revolt and Thought Specular: Encountering the (Mulholland) Drive." In *Psychoanalysis, Aesthetics and Politics in the Works of Julia Kristeva*, edited by Kelly Oliver and S. K. Keltner. New York: SUNY Press, 2009.

Rogers, Juliet. "Unquestionable Freedom in a Psychotic West." *Law, Culture and the Humanities* 1 (2005): 186–207.

Saeed, Abdullah, and Shahram Akbarzadeh, ed. *Challenging Identities: Muslim Women in Australia*. Islamic Studies Series. Sydney: UNSW Press, 2010.

Said, Edward W. *Covering Islam: How the Media and the Experts Determine How We See the Rest of the World*. Rev. ed. New York: Vintage Books, 1997.

Said, Edward W. *Orientalism*. 1st ed. New York: Pantheon Books, 1978.

Sayyid, Salman. "Racism and Islamophobia." In *International Centre of Muslim and Non-Muslim Understanding*. Adelaide: University of South Australia, 2011.

Scott, Joan Wallach. "Symptomatic Politics: Banning Islamic Head Scarves in French Public School." In *Postcolonialism and Political Theory*, edited by Nalini Persram. Lanham and Plymouth: Lexington Books, 2007.

Scott, Joan Wallach. *The Politics of the Veil*. Princeton: Princeton University Press, 2007.

Shohat, Ella. "Notes on the 'Postcolonial'." In *The Preoccupation with Postcolonial Studies*, edited by Fawzia Afzal-Khan and Kalpana Seshadri-Crooks. Durham: Duke University Press 2000.

Soler, Colette. *What Lacan Said About Women: A Psychoanalytic Study*. New York: Other Press, 2006.

Trotter, David. *Paranoid Modernism: Literary Experiment, Psychosis and the Professionalisation of English Society*. Oxford: Oxford University Press, 2001.

Wilcox, Lauren B. *Bodies of Violence: Theorising Embodies Subjects in International Relations*. New York: Oxford University Press, 2015.

Winter, Stuart. "Exclusive: Remains of 9/11 Killers Found." *Sunday Express*, January 11, 2009.

Yeğenoğlu, Meyda. *Colonial Fantasies: Towards a Feminist Reading of Orientalism*. Cambridge: Cambridge University Press, 1998.

Yildiz, Yasemin. "Governing European Subjects: Tolerance and Guilt in the Discourse of 'Muslim Women'." *Cultural Critique* 77 (2011): 70–101.

Zayzafoon, Lamia Ben Youssef. *The Production of the Muslim Woman: Negotiating Text, History, and Ideology*. Lanham, MD: Lexington Books, 2005.

Žižek, Slavoj. *Tarrying with the Negative: Kant, Hegel and the Critique of Ideology*. Durham: Duke University Press, 1993.

Žižek, Slavoj. *The Sublime Object of Ideology*. London: Verso Books, 1989.

CHAPTER 6

The Confessional Body

We are nothing but foils, instruments of white vanity. —Houria Bouteldja[1]

INTRODUCTION

In the early twentieth century, 20-year-old Druze woman Nazira Zain al-Din diagnosed the condition of her society by pointing to a visible marker of difference between Europe and the East:

> I have noticed that the nations that have given up the veil are the nations that have advanced in intellectual and material life. The unveiled nations are the ones that have discovered through research and study the secrets of nature and have brought the physical elements under their control as you see and know. But the veiled nations have not unearthed any secret and have not put any of the physical elements under their control but only sing the songs of a glorious past and ancient tradition.[2]

The seductive power of the imagery of the veiled and unveiled abstracts meaning and placates questions, at the expense of the intricacies and unpredictabilities of varying histories, cultures, politics and economies. The unveiled, in Zain al-Din's vision, invites knowledge, material progress and advances into the future, whereas the veiled body, oppresses knowledge and is preoccupied with traditions of the past. The unveiled gestures to

© The Author(s) 2020
S. Ghumkhor, *The Political Psychology of the Veil*,
Palgrave Studies in Political Psychology,
https://doi.org/10.1007/978-3-030-32061-4_6

discovery, while the veiled remain in the Platonic cave of ignorance. These cultural and political observations were certainly not exceptional, and were echoed by her Arab compatriots such as the nineteenth century Egyptian legal theorist Qasim Amin who, reflecting on European success, asked the question "do you think such people would have abandoned veiling after it had been in use among them if they had seen any good in it"?[3] These existential musings accompanied the Arab and Islamic Orient's encounter with a Europe that professed to know the "secrets of nature", claimed civilisational dominion over universal truths and history, and produced a new age of modernity where freedom came to be associated with certain things and in modes of adorning the body that one cannot not want. Therefore, the contemporary veiled and unveiled imagery has a much longer history, establishing a fault line in the East–West experience as markers of arrival or departure from an imagined modernity where freedom can only be had in the unveiled. The agent of this universalist project was a west that animated desire towards progress and "organised the world"—and, I argue, bodies—"endlessly to represent it".[4] This chapter turns to this worlding of colonial modernity and how it has shaped Arab and Muslim responses.

For European colonialists of the nineteenth and early twentieth century, the veil was an indictment of a society's unwillingness to progress. It represented a visible symptom of cultural inferiority, signalling "the degradation of women" and Islam's "complete failure" as a cultural system.[5] Philosophically, the veil embodied the Hegelian charge against "Mohammedans" for their "enthusiasm for the abstract" and its propensity for an irrational absoluteness as an unnatural reversion from history. Taking up Zain al-Din civilisational diagnosis in announcing her commitment to women's rights, in 1923 Huda Sha'arawi, an Egyptian feminist activist, publicly removed her face veil after returning from a women's conference in Europe. This act of unveiling, a refusal to no longer wear the veil, shifted the national, and later the postcolonial imaginary, in a way that cannot be underestimated: it carved a reading of history as progressive—*dynamic* in the act of uncovering. It imagined freedom as cumulative and intrinsic to truth-making. The refusal to veil locates modernism's search for transparency and investment in the visibility of bare surface on which it announces its naked truth. The historical moment heralded modernity's arrival in Egypt in the guise of a new political subject—the "native" whose desires were made visible and enthused history forward, to shed the veil of tradition, literally and metaphorically.[6]

This identitarian knowledge, projected on to bodies, signals what Edward Said discerned in "imperialism as an export of identity".[7] This new subject was characterised by the pursuit of autonomy, freedom and the exercise of a "new" secular liberal agency marked by this refusal. Nadia Fadil describes this refusal as a modern aesthetic that announces an "ethical self-fashioning" through the "problematisation" of the veil.[8] Unveiling came to be internalised as an expression of desire, knowledge, freedom and truth, much of which took the European experience as its moral imperative to move history forward. Reflecting on the contemporary discursive landscape, Yasemin Yildiz highlights, "The active participation of 'Muslim women' in a dichotomous civilizational discourse is indeed one of the most visible innovations in the current moment".[9] In the following discussion, I aim to unpack the contemporary politics of activism by performing unveiling and the desires and fantasy that exist between women of a Muslim background and the west.

In the fantasy of unveiling freedom, the one who unveils is the liberal, liberated, and liberat*ing* subject. In Chapter 4, we saw more explicitly the phallic nature of this fantasy and how it opens opportunities for "western women" to acquire a form of secular subjectivity signalling modernity's claims to know and attain the universal through unveiling. The previous chapter examined the emphasis on the secular body as a source of postcolonial *jouissance* by identifying its relationship to *secu(la)ritising* knowledge. In this chapter, I ask—if unveiling is the acquisition of knowledge and a means to discover a natural condition of freedom for men and women who situate themselves within the secular confines of the west, is a similar fantasy available to unveiled women of Muslim backgrounds? If hypochondria is about the way one imagines and locates one's body to other bodies which are made to bear the fear of contamination, I take Anne Anlin Cheng's cue by examining how this fear impacts those racialised subjects of racism, or specifically in this case, Islamophobia.[10] While the postcolonial has been experienced in the west as a desire to *sur (veil)*[11] these contact zones, for former colonised subjects, the post has similarly meant dealing with the residues of collapsed and collapsing identities, repudiation and projection,[12] but with the corrective of what subjectivity is possible under the shadow of assimilationist demands. I explore the connection of fantasy with unveiled bodies triggered in these "other" bodies. How do those whose body is the source of sickness, always plagued by questions, respond?

What is depicted in Zain-al-Din's representational framing is not only a loss of autonomy over the representation of oneself but for a west invested in the representation and the governance of the Other, this is an affirmation of desire for freedom in moments that identify a rupture that "awakens" desire for specific subjects. What this rupture promises is treating symptoms of societal failure and training the body to discover and preserve the "secret" knowledge to liberating desire. It is the genealogy of this rupture that this chapter traces through two scenes of this fantasy: unveiling and confession, and the body in which both scenes would not be conceivable without.

Scenes in the psychoanalytic sense is a fantasy that defends against castration—the fragmentation of one's imagined wholeness and ontological certainty.[13] The first scene of rupture is the more familiar scene of the imperial desire to unveil Muslim women, echoed in Zain-al-Din's diagnosis of the unveiled state of truth. It is the scene this book has traced through the imaging and imaging of the body, human rights campaigns, the production of the Woman and Islamophobia. In the colonial context, the veiled and unveiled was a libidinal economy of securing control, governance and fantasising domination. For French colonialists in Algeria and British colonialists in Egypt, *mission civilisatrice* as a mission to bring the "native" under the fold of civilisation was impossible to fulfil in the presence of the refusing veil. The veil's stubborn denial to see the body challenged what can be known and Europe's vision of modernity as a claim of discovery to know the universal body. "Giving up" the veil was perceived to be unnatural qua—an *undesirable* state that violated the conditions of civilisation and humanisation.[14] In the contemporary climate, the presence of the veiled face *in the west* amplifies this anxiety which becomes "intolerable" for blurring the geographical and civilisational boundaries. The *mission civilisatrice* qua unveiling, however, has a paradoxical function: the mission to "modernise" qua civilise is also invested in the failure of this mission because it was salient to the procurement of civilisational boundaries that constituted what it meant to be French and European, and the *rationale for domination*.[15] If the colonial and postcolonial scene of unveiling as a "natural" state of modernity is inherited with this contradiction, what knowledge does unveiling intend to expose?

One can find a stable response to this question in the second scene of this rupture which appears in modernity's culture of confession. Writing about the politics of truth, Michel Foucault argues, in *The History of Sexuality*, confession has become an integral part of modern power, and "one of the main rituals we rely on for the production of truth".[16] Like Lacan, sexuality, truth and power are interlinked and reproductive in Foucault's account of the confession. In the previous discussion, unveiling revived the historically displaced universal Woman through femonationalism's instinctual relationship to freedom to emancipate Muslim women by releasing them from the veil of violence. The discussion that followed examined the paranoid imaginings of the continued presence of the veil *on* and *in* the body politic that unsettles western universalist truths. This chapter explores the politics of confession—confessing practices of the other through the lens of veiling and unveiling, tracing the desire to confess by those of an Arab or Muslim background who are hailed as *desiring* secular subjects. These secular "insider" critics of the Muslim community are unveiled affiliates of the west and considered "neutral" interlocutors, whose own desire for freedom through their own unveiling show the promise of liberating the native's repressed body. As new "Muslim" subjects, they enact a secular "critical act of unmasking"[17] which detects bodily sickness, casting a critical gaze over any shadows on the body, and look to western truth-making practices for resolutions. The chapter examines confession as an internalised hypochondria, which collects knowledge to western interrogations of the Muslim, through the experiences of women whose personal struggles have become the post-9/11 diet on Islam. These interlocutors, often in alliance with femonationalist forces, offer personal narratives and "unique" insights to their culture in which the Muslim body in crisis is central to this experience. Their public interventions are part of a politics of confession on how one survived—and at times, "survives" (like an instruction manual)—"Islamland", a "mythical place" where women's rights activists activate their sense of virtue and moral capital.[18] These confessional narratives serve as the wanting of the west by identifying Islam's lack, evidencing the desire to give up what is seen as the embodiment of Islamic *jouissance* and in so doing, guaranteeing the knowing of Islam. Their subversive commentary adopts a language of agency, thereby evoking a perpetual reinstalment of the fantasy of unveiling *through confession*.

In other words, there is always a veil (of violence) that identifies the potential of (self) discovery. The unveiled critic's (coded as Muslim) body ushers what Joseph Massad observes as empire's crusading sexual identarian impulses, assimilating identities, practices and bodies, into a "translation… that the west can recognise and tolerate".[19] Most saliently, unsuccessful translation is judged as evidence of failure of a society and culture[20] and diagnosed as an ailment. As I hope this book has made clear, I am not discounting that women in these communities face violence or that being unveiled positions one as an apologist for imperial discourse. Women face violence, sometimes it is specific in its forms and sometimes universal.[21] Rather, I am interested in how the concern for Muslim women is arranged in these discourses, how "violence against women" is translated with a universal certainty that can only speak of this violence and Muslim women at the level of fantasy. This chapter is situated in the book's broader concern with fantasy's libidinal impulses of "uncovering of truth", the desires it generates, and for whom. These confessional tales, like hyperveiling, is incitation to discourse, managing phantom threats through perpetual diagnosis of symptoms of the body, for things certain but unlocalisable. Thus, the rituals of concern for the Muslim become the occasion for (paranoid) knowledge and must identify what can and cannot be considered as social ailment to prescribe treatment.

Unveiling and confession not only function as disciplinary modes of control and governance but also as knowledge production of the body. The body functions as a material security that can source fundamental truths (because it can be scientifically studied and "known"). Talal Asad contends, the body is imperative to the teleology of modernity and the heralding of the emancipated human of history whose pain is replaced with pleasure through freedom.[22] Unveiling and confession, confession as unveiling, this chapter argues is the productions of truth, as *scenes of revelation*—from forced unveiling to a willing unveiling vis-à-vis confession—which carry a modern imaginary of releasing the body and its *natural/universal* desire for freedom. Confession becomes a means of unveiling and a prophylactic for the symptoms diagnosed as the origins of one's failure.[23]

Modernity as Rupture

The story of modernity is told as a rupture, a separation from the premodern,[24] and the explosion of knowledge which gave way to the cumulative growth of freedom. A rupture suggests something compressed and a pressure that has built up suddenly bursting energetically. A genealogy of modernity is beyond the scope of this chapter, but what I want to consider here, and what I have been attempting to trace throughout this book, is the discursive workings of the modern and how it imagined "an unfolding of time" centred around an agent of freedom,[25] rising up from the ashes of tradition—the site of a kind of rupture where human agency is realised in a dynamic transformative process of discovery and Enlightenment. Modernity, Daniel Lerner contends produces a "mobile personality" which is characterised by dynamism and is receptive to change.[26] To be modern is to be, what John F. Wilson observes, new and innovative, as opposed to settled, ancient and traditional.[27] While it stressed the dynamism of this rupture, modernity organised the world in a singular narrative across time, culture and space. It was a force that portends a freedom in the throes of departing *from* tradition, the Church, monarchical rule, and even the state. With the rise of liberalism, rationality, science and secularism, the dynamism of modernity enabled access to knowledge and truth as something disclosed, and unconcealed. Every discovery was a rupture that enlightened one towards a freedom that Judith Butler observes, "must always be increasing".[28] Its ruptures are made possible in the binaries it constructs for itself—reason/unreason, religion/state, private/public, freedom/unfreedom—and defines itself through organising history, epistemology and bodies in oppositional frameworks as preconditions for an emancipatory future. This is a freedom whose *telos* marches history forward, migrating globally as it detects constraint and gives expression to suppressed desires. Modernity, it is foretold in this western mythology, uncovers a human agency that is divorced from the constraints of belief, tradition, irrational passions and aspiring to a secular totality the future promises. This teleology towards a satisfied future in Lacan's terms is "a phallic attempt to make knowledge adequate to the One"[29]—something satisfied and *whole without fracture*. By this, Lacan meant the underlying fantasy of modern discourses is to aspire to complete pleasure and thus, knowledge without ambivalence and without question. The agent of knowledge was the "unfinished person" of the future whose *consumption of freedom* fulfils modernity's prophecy.

Nevertheless, all desires, including the desire for freedom, in psychoanalytic parlance, are to keep anxiety at bay from the ontological lack that signals the impossibility of freedom's guarantee. Anxiety, if we recall, coincides with not the lack but what is beyond the *object a*, the Symbolic when fantasy starts to disintegrate.[30] How this anxiety appears in western modernity is the crushing uncertainty of what freedom promises: a *phallic jouissance* qua the subject's ontological integrity and the body that received it. In a west where freedom has already arrived, the possibility of this desire for freedom as either not fulfilled, denied or rejected, raises the uncertainty of the west's relationship to its master signifiers of truth, universalism and freedom, in which all knowledge is measured and where its power thrives. This active discovery, authored by an always-knowing west, deserves closer consideration because it mediated the experiences of Europe with its others.

Theories of modernity often begin and end in the west. Michel Foucault's genealogy of European modernity is traced to the production of disciplinary bodies, space and movement in institutions like prisons, clinics and asylums as part of the "political economy of populations", which he located in Europe and not where we see their first appearance—in the non-European world. Reflecting on this disappearance, Timothy Mitchell contends modernity was not defined in Europe but formed through its imperial and colonial projects in the colonies where the west discovered itself in a new image of *being modern*.[31] The encounter with the non-European world provoked a desire to fix difference as a self-homogenising "integral totality" along the axis of modernity/tradition. The assertion of Europe and all others—the not-yet—was an assertion of knowledge in response to experiencing the potential mixing of races, genders, cultures and classes. These "new forms of disorders" were not only about anxieties of contamination but the witnessing of an unfamiliar *jouissance*, of experiencing the body as unknown, and the paranoia over the possibility of the "theft" of *jouissance* and thus, the loss of knowledge. The "discovery" of the non-European world signalled what Anne McClintock calls a "poetics of ambivalence"—the failure of European knowledge, and the "politics of violence"—the domination of the other, to quell "the implacable rage of paranoia".[32] What incites paranoia in knowing is an opposition, something that is perceived to be alien to the self which then "torments, persecutes, *cuts*" in its dissatisfaction of fulfilled meaning.[33] We recognise this paranoia played out in the hypochondriac state of the west's preoccupations in the war on terror where the presence of the veiled Muslim provoked national hysteria of cultural and corporeal contamination in all other bodies.

On the question of freedom, the Other can always challenge with their own claims to knowledge with a cutting question: why must freedom be expressed *this* way? Why must unveiling be the main register of the modern political subject? How has this epistemic claim shaped those who are named not modern enough? The modern imaginary represents answers to these questions through scenes of rupture *from* difference, *from being cut*. If hyperveiling is about the hysterical management of the potentially contaminating body and the slippages of civilisational differences, the contemporary call to unveil Muslim women's bodies through legal bans, deradicalization and surveillance are nervous detectors of shadowy wounds on the body and tracking their retreat as the body's unveiling. The discarding of the veil as a denunciation of the veil of violence assimilates the unveiling body into modernity's long-held determination of an ocular epistemology.

SCENE ONE: COLONIAL UNVEILING

Much of this book has traced the paranoid obsession with the postcolonial veil to contend with this cutting question—*che vuoi?*—from the Other who does not believe. But we must turn to a familiar colonial scene to appreciate the psycho-somatic nature of this disorder. Writing about the veil ban in France, Joan Wallach Scott observes it is a "symbolic gesture" that allows the west to act out "tremendous anxiety not so much about fundamentalism, but about Islam itself" that has deep colonial origins. European paranoia finds consistent expression in Europe's experience with the most visible site of this difference: the veiled woman of the Orient.

Building on Said's observations of the veil's over-presence in the colonial imaginary, Meyda Yeğenoğlu adds, the Orient was intrinsically "feminine, always veiled, seductive, and dangerous".[34] These seductive qualities were given more specificity in the intimate observations by Martinique psychiatrist Frantz Fanon during his service in French-occupied Algeria. Fanon invites us to understand the French fixation on the veiled Algerian woman whose veiled body denied the right to know the hidden "secrets" of the nation, provoking an aggressive fantasy of control and domination of the gaze that looked back. Much has been written on the veil in the colonial period, so I do not intend to rehash it here, but I want to emphasise how the veil as a marker of difference was not simply about fixing difference but about the fear of losing control over difference, of fearful bodies, racial proximity and confronting the limit to naming the body. What Fanon reveals about French colonial anxiety in Algeria is what Derek Hook calls the "psycho-visceral" reactions to the other.[35] This "psycho-visceral" response is visible in the French encounter with the veiled woman who "sees without being seen", a visible limit to the other's enjoyment, provoking frustration, paranoia and violent aggression in the French.[36] The Other's body appears here as another mode of organising, experiencing and enjoying the body which radically differed from modernity's imaginary of freedom as universally realised and experienced in unveiled flesh. The veil was a barrier that denied access to the "secrets" of Algeria. Thus, unveiling was a *disciplining* tool to domesticate Algeria through claiming control over the representation and knowledge of the body. Unveiling, became a strategy of securing the difference that sustained *la mission civilisatrice*, and not the erasure of difference by the removal of the veil.

In modernity's scopic gaze, the veiled body appears as a lack, an injury, concealing the secrets of the body's natural desire. Unveil*ing* the body offered new horizons of knowledge and a source of empowerment for European colonialists, as long as Europe was the agent of this unveiling. Europe's "flexible positional superiority" in which the Other is brought into meaning[37] portends to organising knowledge as a practice of *disavowing* its own limit. Thus, it was not enough that this unveiling occurred on its own but these "test-women" needed to be staged for the consumption of Europe. A ceremonial unveiling in 1958, Algeria saw an assertion of French cultural (and military) superiority over Algeria as some generals gathered Algerian male villagers and had French women stage the public unveiling of a group of Algerian women.[38] In 1960, this need to see was further enforced through surveillance policies which implemented photo ID cards forcing Algerian women to remove their veils for identification.[39] Fanon writes of the "atmosphere of newness" and the sense of "victory" that the bared face incited in Europeans upon seeing the visible signs of conversion, even if momentarily.[40] Notwithstanding, such interventions did not satisfy the paranoiac gaze that insisted on the visibility of knowledge: "Every rejected veil disclosed to the eyes of the colonialists the horizons until then forbidden, revealed to them, piece by piece, the flesh of Algeria *laid bare* [my emphasis]".[41] The baring of flesh qua the unveiling body, modernity's "bare surface"—where knowledge of the Algerian woman could be had—needed to be discovered, disciplined, by being made visible in postcards and paintings where she was shown unveiled and therefore knowable. Staging Muslim women's unveiling fulfilled the fantasy of unveiling the Other's desire—a desire imagined as the *wanting of Europe*. Curiously, the veil's presence in these images sometimes remained, often as a sheer veil, reminding of what is being cast off. The continued threat of being engulfed by the darkness of the margins thereby fuelled the desire for *more* knowledge. The consumption of these images heightened the awareness of the edges of the colonial map where veiled shadows appeared in the forms of "hybrids (mermaids and monsters)" and "prehistoric zone of dervishes, cannibals and fetish-worshippers".[42]

While the persistence of the veil despite these efforts was the cause of much unease, the terror of what Algerian women's bodies could do reached new proportions during the Algerian struggle for Independence (1954–1962). Algerian women willingly unveiled to disguise themselves and with their "very Europeanised" "appearances" joined the battle because they were not suspected and therefore, able to pass necessary weapons in their suitcases and purses. As unveiled enemies, they became the embodiment of the veiled gaze that can "see without being seen". When this strategy failed, the veil became another strategy where women behaved like a "fatma"—what Fanon identifies as the coy passive Algerian woman in a veil, in order to conceal her true identity and the weapons she carried. While the unveiled body had to be disciplined, slim and attractive, this veiled body had to entirely disappear, squashed into a "shapeless" form.[43] Veiled or unveiled, Algerian women's bodies violated the modern imaginary at the same time they performed the difference that sustained its economy. These were not bodies that exhibited a difference that was "almost the same but not quite" that Homi Bhabha has recognised as a terrifying sameness[44] but a difference that was radically Other. Veiled or unveiled, this was a body that experienced a *jouissance* that the European gaze could not detect nor control by frames of its own reference: the unveiling body that enjoys freedom—an intrinsic freedom expressed through desiring European modernity. This was a dynamic body whose *jouissance* was unsettling because it desired both or something beyond.

Scene Two: Confessions of a Native Informant

In this paranoid climate where Muslims are increasingly perceived as a suspicious and hostile community, the demand to know the veiled woman is ultimately a demand for the Other's confession. What are you hiding? *Che Vuoi?* Reflecting on the shift in modern power and the reconfiguration of truth-making practices, Foucault argues that the drive to confess, to tell the truth about sexuality, to reveal your crime before the law, is a key aspect of biopower as a mode of organising bodies.[45] With the advent of modernity, the state of perpetual rupture was expressed as an explosion of knowledge and the emergence of these new governing technologies transported bodies into a tool of governance where knowledge of the body was recorded and disciplined into a regime of truth.

Confessing your inner desires, the body's secrets, was a means of *uncovering truth* in the making of modern western subjectivity. Confession is speaking about what can only be spoken. The most intimate experiences, desires, illnesses, uneasiness and guilt are articulated in public in the presence of an authority who judges, punishes and forgives or consoles the confessor.[46] For Foucault, sex undergirds all confession and it is through women that techniques of confession occurred, committing sex to a "shadow existence" that must always be talked about while rendering it "*the* secret".[47] What was always private is made public, politicised and a source of knowledge and truth once it is confessed. In this vein, it is not a coincidence that post-9/11 discussions about refugees, immigrants and the Muslim question has focused on as "sexual democracy" (Fassin 2012) and "sexual politics" (Butler 2008) as contemporary measure for recognition and exclusion. Sexual desire has become the original principle for *becoming* secular and modern. Like South Africa's apartheid pencil tests for racial classification, how a Syrian refugee confesses their feelings about a photo of a homosexual couple kissing or a woman wearing a bikini, identifies the truth of who they are (as Muslims), locate their desire and the degree to which they have socially evolved to earn an European status. Truth for Foucault is lodged in our secret nature and demands only to surface; that if it fails to do so, is because a constraint holds it in place, the violence of a power weighs it down and it can be articulated at the price of a kind of liberation. Confession frees, but power reduces one to silence; truth does not belong to the order of power but shares an original affinity with freedom.[48]

Like Lacan, the pursuit of truth for Foucault is one of liberation but it is also about the truth of pleasure, of knowing, discovering, exposing, seeing and telling truth, while generating the other's interest in it.[49] If freedom is instinctual then truth-telling is human nature. The individual, who reveals the desires of the flesh, where truth is realised, is "exonerated, redeemed, purified" and liberated by the promise of salvation. The one who confesses who they really are, is for Foucault caught up in power relations, tying the capacity to desire with docility. What is confessed, and the desires, obsessions, images, pleasures that accompany it, are *given meaning*, socially constituted and disciplined by an epistemic privilege that sanctions what is permissible and what is not.[50] The confessional subject who announces their desires cannot, however, authorise its meaning. Instead, the confession emanates from the body, and the confessor who defines it is the speaker of the confession.[51] Nevertheless, what the subject knows and desires is not entirely of its own making, as it is performative, requiring the Other. Confession is about disciplining the body into meaning, determining the standards of pleasure and thus, constructing knowledge qua sexuality.[52] For the one who confesses, it is one of cathartic relief, a discarding of epistemic weight in exchange for recognition.

While Foucauldian confession is a process of interpellation and a production of power, in psychoanalysis confession can be considered a form of psychic liberation and a cure offered by the phallic paternal authority to the confessor.[53] Confession, in psychoanalytic terms, capitalises on the anxieties of the subject and enables a path to resolving the fundamental question at the heart of subjectivity: who am I? what does this body mean?

It potentially brings solace to the uncertainty of subjectivity through the act of recognition by an Other who attempts to fill the ontological lack. In both Foucault and psychoanalysis, the confessor is the one who pre-scribes meaning to the confession. Confession is always mediated by the Other—a submission to a moral authority, whether the state, psychiatrist, or the modern gaze. In other words, there is always a desire for and towards which the act of confession is directed. For Lacan, the Other is necessary to the subject's formation: what it knows needs reaffirmation and recognition. Within the psychic gratification or political subversion of confession lies the technology of obedience and disciplinary power.[54]

As part of the democratisation of power today—that is, society as judge—the act of confession, the revealing of truth, is given excep-tional validity. Critically reflecting on confessional stories, an article by Jia Tarantino in *The New Yorker* in May 2018 declared "the personal-essay boom is over", referencing the explosion of stories written by women about their lives which seem to dominate the early years of social media.[55] Responding to the piece, Lorraine Berry is reminded of an earlier but sim-ilar declaration by the celebrated writer Virginia Woolf who wrote in 1905 that there is a saturation of personal writings which have deadened the art of writing the personal, which has become more performative, mechanical and superficial.[56] Like a Heideggerian idle speak, contemporary personal stories appear to be renditions of women's speech that have lost their pur-pose. However, one kind of confessional tale is not over and that is the personal stories of women from Muslim backgrounds.

In anxious times where security is the dominant paradigm for political transaction, confession is a desire for truth not so much by Muslims them-selves, but a western hysterical demand to totalise one's understanding of the Muslim other who must reveal everything: from terrorist plots, sleeper cells, abuses against women, to sexual desires. Confession, like torture, is a coercive uncovering of what western beliefs already believe is the "true" Muslim self. In other words, the speaking subject as confessional subject, "draws on the language of domination and/or authority *as* the language of freedom"[57] Confessional practices by those of a Muslim background perform the romance of resistance that Abu-Lughod critically reflects in her own work,[58] and Mahmood in *Politics of Piety* (2005) more force-fully problematises, as a precondition for the political subject who must subscribe to liberal notions of agency, autonomy and choice. That is, the confessional Muslim subject is one that is always in defiance of her commu-nity and cultural norms. A voyeuristic gaze (beyond the veil) and a war on terror (surveillance, the demand for Muslims to perpetually condemn terrorism, etc.) demands perpetual confession from Muslims who are willing to condemn their own, denounce certain interpretations of their religious text, to evidence their capacity to critique their religion—to be able to step outside of it. Such integrationist requirements measure—or even monitor—Muslim capacity for secular modernity as a practice of freedom in the name of security. This stepping outside of the community is often embodied in the gesture of unveiling—in the refusal to veil—both physically and metaphorically, which their personal stories recount versions of and are framed within the political economy of the veiled and unveiled, veiling and unveiling. The point here is not to collapse a Muslim woman's refusal to veil or even the undetermined state of being "unveiled" with the unveiling political act that the book has been tracing. We already see an alternative possibility to the unveiled Muslim/Arab woman in the earlier example of the Algerian women's resistance—expressed both as veiled and unveiled—to French colonial power. Rather, *how* this refusal is rationalised identifies a wider discursive and embodied practice that assumes the secular modern condition to be the natural state of the body.

Confessions of Terror

In the current political climate, the desire to confess and the desire for confession manifests most powerfully in the dissenting voices of insiders. These confessions focus on addressing taboo issues to unveil the "truth" of Islam, the plight of its women and the threat that it bares to the modern era. While the colonial and political scene of unveiling recognises a coercive move that demands to know who the Muslim woman is, these insiders are *willing* subjects of confession whose words document abuses of their community. In the intimidating mood of Islamophobia, this willing confession has immense political purchase. Autobiographical genres and testimonials have attended to Islamophobic preoccupations in the fallout of the events of 2001.[59] As Mahmood observes, these insiders secure "judgement that Islam's mistreatment of women is a symptom of a much larger pathology that haunts Islam, namely, its propensity to violence". Despite their differences, we saw that Femonationalism signals the increasingly shared belief in Islam's oppression of its women and the need for reform in Islam, bringing together progressives, liberals and conservatives.[60] In addition, despite describing Muslims as lagging in "enlightened thinking, tolerance and knowledge of other cultures"[61]—something difficult to imagine being said of any other community—it is the west's emancipatory model and desire for liberal freedoms that mobilises this array of supporters.[62] In the tradition of confession, these individuals are often women whose concerns frequently touch on themes of sexuality, the secrets of the flesh and violence that brings about its fleshly wounds. Disclosing the traumas of their communities through the transmission of authentic human experiences, their confessions are always and inevitability partial. What is not confessed is important, if not more telling, than what is confessed. What is not confessed frames the confessions, marking the boundaries of the confessable.

Hamid Dabashi highlights the rationalisation for the recent phenomenon of what he calls the modern "native informant", a figure who produces a knowledge that they do not in fact have,[63] and serves as a "cover of legitimacy" to western interests in the Muslim world. Unlike colonial accounts that revealed the suffering of the native woman, or the staged unveiling scenes of colonial Algeria, it is now the native herself who provides the "ethnographic grist for this bloodied imagination, lending a voice of authenticity to the old narrative that a liberal ear, raised on a critique of colonial literature, can more easily hear and digest".[64] Said's observations of a knowledge production centred on European "positional superiority" is offered here to the native—in today's lexicon a type of a "good Muslim"—who can be relatable but has the "indigenous knowledge" on what it is about his or her community that needs announcing. This announcing occurs in the form of what Mayanthi L. Fernando describes as an autobiography doubling up as an ethnography, which describes the life of women in their communities, replacing sociological expertise with personal experience.[65]

The native informant's insider accounts confirm conclusions that are already presupposed by the west[66]—a west that incessantly demands to have its knowledge reaffirmed. She provides the ideological fodder to sustain the fantasy of a west as the source of, and impetus for, all knowledge. As a political subject whose agency is one of refusing what is assumed to be culturally sanctioned practices against women, the native informant imitates the mission to civilise (unveil) and criminalise resistance to western domination.[67] In Lacanian parlance, she is the "subject-supposed-to-believe", masquerading as a "true believer". This is the subject who makes it known that the Other—as the designator of law, language, the symbolic[68]—as not an unearthing of "new"/threatening knowledge but the reaffirmation of the west's symbolic identification as a universal knowing subject.

This is a west that is imagined as the agent of freedom, of one's unveiling. In this sense, the native informant is a figure who continues to orientalise the imagined other for the west's world of meaning, and the agency for this other's unveiling. The native informant believes in the obsessive acquisition of knowledge vis-à-vis the possibilities of freedom qua unveiling,[69] thus shoring up the fantasy of securing the west's ontological claims. This need to "believe" in what the native informant provides is illuminated in the rapid recognition of these authoritative voices.[70] Their expertise is often discerned in the only relevant "fact" of them being Muslim (or ex-Muslims), from Muslim-majority countries or in their brown bodies. In addition, it stems from an imagined sense of their illicit voice as women about taboo subjects like violence against women and sexual desires.

Representing themselves as free souls under fundamentalist constraints, lamenting the loss of freedom under the veil of constraint, the native informant stages escape, implicitly or explicitly, through and to, a secular liberal west. This is manifest in their personal accounts of the Muslim community's shortcomings, retold through the frames of women's rights, human rights and civil rights and how they were denied them.[71] These courageous figures offer dissenting narratives told through the tropes of freedom, democracy and gender inequality.[72] Preoccupied with the plight of Muslim women, these insider critics, Yildiz argues, reformulate Spivak's critique of the saviour fantasy to "brown women saving brown women from brown men". While both are "brown" women, they are distinguished by one being subjects of agency and the other as victims without agency.[73] western critiques derive further authority in the expert testimonies of these women as critical agents by claiming their privileged access to the backstage of oppressive cultures. In this sense, they are instrumental to providing a veneer of legitimacy to surveillance of Muslim communities, militarised foreign policy, as part of the unveiling of Islam, so that it is (made) "known" and "knowable". Honourable in their courage and determined in their reform, they lay the problems of the community at the door of a barbaric, violent and misogynistic Islam. In other words, they impute lack, where they may just as easily discuss difference.

A snapshot of this rise of Muslim and former Muslim critics of Islam in the past two decades include: the veterans Somali-born Ayaan Hirsi Ali, an atheist renowned for her criticism of Islam; Syrian-American Wafa Sultan, a member of *Stop Islamisation of America*; Canadian journalist and author Irshad Manji whose *Moral Courage Project* was an Oprah "Chutzpah" Winner for "boldness" which called for Islam to be reformed and in her most recent book *Don't Label Me* (2019) criticised "dishonest diversity" and "call out culture"[74]; journalist Asra Nomani whose work focuses on the harms done to women in the name of Islam including FGM, veiling and gender segregation[75]; Maryam Namazie who leads the *Council of British Ex-Muslims*, Gita Sahgal founder of *Women Against Fundamentalism* and executive director of *Centre for Secular Space* which opposes fundamentalism and promotes secularism. Then, there are the more recent critics who have joined these expressions of cultural anxiety about the Muslim question: Somali-British activist Nimco Ali, an activist against "FGM" (female genital "mutilation") and forced veiling of children in the UK[76]; former wife of an al-Qaeda member now atheist, Yasmine Mohammed whose project *Confessions of an Ex-Muslim* has her sharing platforms for secularists and atheist podcasts and YouTube channels, and speaks of her departure from Islam as the removal of the veil; Masih Alinejad runs the *My Stealthy Freedom* Facebook page where Iranian women send photos of their unveiling. She is also the author of *The Wind in My Hair* (2018) which is about her personal journey as a dissident; London-based Kenyan-Tanzanian ex-Muslim and secular activist Zara Kay who founded "Faithless Hijabi" which aims to work "towards normalising the path from indoctrination to freedom" for Muslim and non-Muslim women[77]; and Mona Eltahawy, a writer who is often given a platform to speak through distinguished papers as The Guardian, The New York Times and Foreign Policy—the latter which published a controversial essay in April 2012 titled *Why Do They Hate Us?* She later published an extended version titled *Headscarves and Hymens: Why the Middle East Needs a Sexual Revolution* (2015). These figures can be placed within the broader discourse of confessional culture, what Gillian Whitlock calls "life narratives"—memoirs and testimonies that often tell of experiences of violence, trauma, heroism and risk. These confessions by survivors, heroes or victims, function as exotic commodities, emphasising transformation, showcasing selves in imagined and constructed ways.[78] The circulation of their personal anguish to their western audiences in Europe, North America and Australia, shapes the "new common sense" where going to war for women, and the fantasy which gives force to a desire to deliver women's rights, become the desired end.[79] They are exemplary of the normative political subject whose agency is modelled on the liberal binary of subordination (practicing) or subversion (not practicing), confessing freedom as its political ideal.[80]

   In the fantasy of freedom qua unveiling, unveiled western women use their bodies as an act of liberation and often of knowledge and access to phallic power—phallic, in the psychoanalytic sense, as a totality of knowledge where there is no lack[81]—by dressing their bodies as having *already* been liberated, representing freedom in the form of *unveiled indigeneity*. As such, in the western imaginary women's ontological and bodily integrity, knowing what Woman is and what she wants, is invested in the performance of releasing oneself from lack, shedding tradition from her body. While this impulse could be considered as a response to Sigmund Freud's contention of women lacking a phallus and therefore, veil their lack by defiantly confessing there is no lack beneath the veil,[82] in the racial dynamic between women, a different kind of confessional act (unveiling) occurs by women of an Arab/Muslim background. Theirs is an unveiling staged and compulsively performed as verification of refusing the veil, of their desire for freedoms and unveiled wholeness that only can be attained from a position of marginality and resistance. For these women, the unveiled operates as a natural condition of being free, of being a woman, beyond cultural constraint into the realm of the secular as a truth-making practice of self-discovery. The new native informant performs a desire for this unveiled condition through the *masquerade of repetitive confession* of the other's lack and "natural" desire in the evidencing of cultural constraints, which continue to veil her. In her refusal to veil—that is, rejecting the normative demands of her community—she positions herself as an unveiled neutral rational critic, not subject to indoctrination, bias, false consciousness. Rather, she is one who embodies a secular normativity.[83] She represents herself as the example of becoming, of the subject whose lack of freedom allows one to imagine this lack fulfilled, and this fantasy is utilised by confessional subjects to attain freedom in performing the always-veiled Muslim woman losing it. By performing as secular insiders who divulge the hidden body of the Muslim woman—what has been done to it and what's being done to it—the native informant is the figure that eases western paranoid symptoms of the Other's desire.

Confessions of Hate

Exemplifying this politics of confession in the "post-9/11-post-Arab-Spring" era is Egyptian-American journalist Mona Eltahawy who came to prominence during the first year of the Egyptian revolution in 2011 when she was arrested reporting on a protest. She accused Egyptian authorities of physical and sexual assault during the incident. Eltahawy has since become a visible critic of the Mubarak regime, the Muslim Brotherhood and the condition of women in the Arab and broader Muslim world. It is her assessments on the latter that has given her a platform to speak through distinguished papers. In 2011 and 2012, she wrote and appeared in debates expressing her support for the banning of the face veil in France and elsewhere, describing it as the "disappearance of women" and a symbol of the "Muslim Right".[84] Her feminist concerns for women in Arab society and in Islam are expressed in a controversial and widely circulated article in April 2012 for Foreign Policy magazine, titled *Why Do They Hate Us?* A scathing critique of what she describes as rampant misogyny in Arab societies, the article generated heated debate in the media and on social networking sites, splitting the feminist community, both Arab and western, as well as the wider Muslim community.

Other female critics of Muslim background have endorsed Eltahawy's claims albeit with different style and rhetorical tactics. Their language is more directly racist, silent on the impact of neo-liberalism on women in less fortunate communities, silent on American foreign policy on Iraq and Afghanistan and elsewhere, and support Israel and its occupation of Palestine. Eltahawy, however, demonstrates nuance in her political worldview because she problematises America's role in the Arab world, condemning and protesting the actions of organisations like *Stop Islamisation of America* or *American Freedom Defense Initiative*. She spray-painted a poster of theirs in New York that equated Muslims with "savages" and was subsequently arrested.[85] Nevertheless, her feminist concerns for women's rights, as we will see, have a political tone and texture comparable with those articulated through orientalist tropes of the imperilled Muslim woman, the violent and misogynistic Muslim man and an unchanging static Arab and Islamic culture that must be reformed. As Saadia Toor contends, the late period of the war on terror has seen the emergence of more of an array of feminist critics who do not automatically subscribe to neoconservative arguments but share similar discourse and policy prescriptions.[86] Islamophobia's capacity to collapse the political spectrum is evident in Eltahawy's politics that are underpinned by an unproblematic consensus that the west has "got it right" despite some of its shortcomings. *Women Living Under Muslim Laws* also subscribes to an uncritical account of *culturally specific* forms of violence by Islam against women.[87]

Whether speaking from the right or the left, these insider perspectives are increasingly framed, shaped and implicated in a broader post-9/11 climate that sees such cultural exchanges within a "clash of civilisation" thesis that expresses alarm about the cultural threat of Islam and a perpetual war on those that embody it. With this in mind, the "truth" of violence, harm and emotional pain, which Eltahawy provides in her media profile, needs to be accompanied with the question Abu-Lughod asks, "what bodies are breathed into life" or what lives are brought into view in her insider tales?[88] In other words, who is doing the confessing?

Eltahawy frequently tells of how at the age of fifteen she was "traumatised into feminism" through her experiences of living in Saudi Arabia.[89] Through the difficulties in dealing with a fundamentalist regime that restricted her movement and capacity to dress, she often shares her journey of removing the hijab in her broader criticism of religious and cultural misogyny.[90] Hirsi Ali similarly equates the veil to being caged and views it as "a constant reminder to the outside world of a stifling morality that makes Muslim men the owners of women and obliges them to prevent their mothers, sisters... from having sexual contact".[91] Her counterparts have their own stories of escape which echo stories we often find in literature of "pulp non-fiction"[92] that are narrated through binaries of modernity versus tradition–domestic violence (Hirsi Ali), terrorist violence (Sultan, Mohammed), indoctrination (Manji). These stories are characterised as sites of agency, first denied and then unearthed in a self-fashioned triumph of survival and struggle, critique, intense emotions, presenting an Islam that is all-too familiar to a western imaginary—denied any nuance of its own, always presented as a problem to either escape or wage a battle with. Once their oppressed culture has been shed, they are the proof of what is possible for Muslim women whose inner desires reveal they are just like us. As Said's Orientalism reminds us Islam *is not perceived* in misrepresentation *but conceived* into being.[93]

The title of Eltahawy's widely circulated article invokes George W. Bush's speech in response to the events of 2001: "Why Do the Hate Us?"; and more broadly, British-American historian of Oriental Studies Bernard Lewis's declaration that the fundamental difference between Arab culture and the west is its treatment of women.[94] The question positions Elthawy as knowing the source of civilisational tensions—the Other's desire which can finally be disclosed. The question locates this desire in Eltahawy's own concerns as part of a western discontent and apprehension about or towards the Arab and Muslim man's mysterious/irrational hate, stating "They [Arab men] don't hate us [Arab women] because of our freedoms, we have no freedoms because they hate us". By appropriating the language of the war on terror, one could say that if Bush essentialised Arab and western differences over the issue of freedom, Eltahawy's pathologises the difference: "They hate our freedoms because they hate us". Arab/Muslim women come to be located in the civilisational narrative as "one of us" and "they"—the "brown" men that oppress and threaten— and must be fought, or in the war on terror logic: Muslim men whose hate for the civilised world and commitment to terrorism must be fought.

The use of sensational post-9/11 lexicon is also reproduced in the titles and works of: Lebanese critic of Islam Brigitte Gabriel Christian's *Why They Hate: A Survivor of Islamic Terror Warns America*; Hirsi Ali's books *Infidel*, *The Caged Virgin* and *Nomad: From Islam to America: A Personal Journey Through the Clash of Civilisations* relying on a Manichean analysis; Sultan's title *A God Who Hates: The Courageous Woman Who Inflamed the World Speaks Against the Evils of Islam* warns of the cultural threat; Manji's *The Trouble with Islam* (2004 edition) *Today* (added to the 2005 edition) and *Faith Without Fear* which constructs an individual struggling to survive in a religion that denies her sexuality and free-thought. Each author, drawing on a civilisational discourse, covers the familiar themes of hate, trauma, victimhood, fear, risk, violence, survival and heroism.

Eltahawy's article begins with a provocative fictional scene by novelist Alifa Rafaat on the intimacy between a husband and wife. Like the beginning of a Hollywood film, western readers are immediately introduced to a Muslim setting by its dominant signifiers: religion and sexuality— a husband, sexually satisfied, deprives his wife of an orgasm and upon hearing the *adhan* (Muslim call to prayer), uses it as an opportunity to leave.[95] Islam and Muslim men are conceived here as disruptive violators of women's desires, enabling Eltahawy to assert that "We have no freedoms because they hate us"—a hate that saps any "natural" human (and in this case sexual) experience. The story, in Eltahawy's reading, exemplifies what is at stake for women in the revolutionary upheavals, their sexual freedoms, which will be sacrificed in a revolution that will ultimately exclude them.

I'm not talking about sex hidden away in dark corners and closed bedrooms. An entire political and economic system — one that treats half of humanity like animals — must be destroyed along with the other more obvious tyrannies choking off the region from its future. Until the rage shifts from the oppressors in our presidential palaces to the oppressors on our streets and in our homes, our revolution has not even begun.[96]

Eltahawy's call for a sexual revolution incites the exposure of "the secret" that which has been (sexually) repressed, concealed and denied.[97] Sexual freedoms are subsumed by religious practice and are the tools to what would identify and resolve the problems facing women in the region. Straddling the relationship between sex and secularity—"sexularism", Eltahawy performs the virtues of an unveiled freedom that prescribes sexual equality, but this is a freedom, as we will see below that is mediated through the veiled woman.[98] The remainder of Eltahawy's article is perforated by similar themes of deprivation in which the insatiable sexual drives of Arab men not only deny women sexual pleasure but fulfil their own through sexually harassing women, child brides, denying women to drive and forced veiling, and "female genital mutilation". Attributing these issues to an innate hate of women by Arab men, Eltahawy represents what Fernando calls a "carceral emancipation" wherein Muslim women are only saved by punishing Muslim men. Observing the neo-liberal logic of carcerality, Fernando contends that it criminalises these practices through emphasising "free choice" by individuals she does not explore it through structural problems such as high unemployment, poverty or political repression. Moreover, these choices are retold through a "cultural pathology" which explains this violence.[99] In Eltahawy's prognosis, women's problems are the result of a culture of hate.

The culture of hate is identified further through anecdotes and statistics such as that of the World Economic Forum's 2012 Global Gender Gap Report stating that not a single Arab country was ranked in the top 100.[100] Each violation enumerates the case for how Arab/Muslim men hate women, sexually pathologising and criminalising their assumed pattern of conduct. The word "hate" features ten times in cataloguing the case against Arab men and forewarning the reader of what is at stake for women in the region. Each detail is an offering of the others' experiences—what Sherene H. Razack contends is "stealing the pain of others"[101] which is repackaged in Eltahawy's political strategy by making the Muslim woman qua the Arab woman known through cultural lacks.

In an interview discussing the impact of Eltahawy's article, historian Leila Ahmed challenged her generalisation of the Arab world and her interpretation of Alifa Rifaat's opening scene between a husband and wife, which Ahmed contends was about the woman's love for her religion, and not sublimation through religion. Eltahawy explains that her strategy was to "go for the jugular", to highlight uncomfortable truths that needed addressing.[102] Her emotive account rearranges details and occludes the gradations of social practices and incidents of violence. There is no critical perspective offered on reports that deal with "human development" and gender gaps that Abu-Lughod has described as "pathologising" cultures in the region, exhibiting a middle class liberal reading of what constitutes modernity and progress.[103] Nor is there a consideration of the limits of right's frameworks and the necessity to factor in global economic and political forces that impact on their lives[104] and is the context within which culture is produced. The most striking feature of the article is its accompanying images of women covered entirely in black paint except for their eyes. The images remind Eltahawy's largely western audience whose imaginary has likely been moulded by mass-marketed imagery of veiled women. In such images, her imperilled state is paraded on the cover of books with personal tales of struggle reflected in the dramatic titles: *Burned Alive, Married by Force, My Forbidden Love.*[105] The coupling of victimhood and veiling appears as stock orientalism, reducing experience to caricature, to bolster and illustrate her case.

The articulation of "uncomfortable truths" through the passive image of the veiled woman at a time when Arab societies were politically engaged, protesting on the streets of Egypt, is confounding. Eltahawy renews pernicious orientalist imagery at the same time they are being tested by protesting women—veiled or unveiled, from all classes and social backgrounds.

The images include dark female figures in different passive poses: one slouched as if tending to a wound on her arm; another looking directly at the camera with her hands over her mouth, her gaze looking elsewhere suggesting she is being prevented from speaking; the other looking away from the camera as if ashamed. Each image of the darkness of the veil, in Foucauldian parlance, renders the "secret" at the same time as it calls for its disclosure through the insistence to "blaspheme", dismiss "political correctness", refuse silence and declare Arab men's hate. Such subversive language injected throughout the article positions Eltahawy as the heroine willing to violate cultural taboos and be a witness to its violations. The black backdrop merges with the paint on the woman's body enveloping her in a way that she is barely visible akin to Almutawakel disappearing women and child beneath the veil. The image realises Eltahawy's defense of France's 2011 ban on the veil and her charge that women are disappearing beneath the veil.[106] "Speak!" Eltahawy seems to be saying before the veil of hate descends and devours what is left of women. The visible departure of Muslim women is expressed in each statistic and anecdote, carried on her imprisoned body. If there is uncertainty about the corporeal contours of the religious body and secular body, Eltahawy's sexual revolution, as an unveiling of Arab women's desires attempts to locate the secular by identifying the veiled body as one bloated by a data of injuries and hate.

Muslim women's bodies presented here as a drowning in religious burdens, a spectacle of lack, humiliation and violence, is reminiscent of Theo Van Gogh and Hirsi Ali's 2004 film *Submission* which tells the story of forbidden love, forced marriage, domestic violence and rape. In *Infidel*, Hirsi Ali describes how these women are representatives of the "hundreds of thousands" of Muslim women who are subject to violence justified by Islam.[107] The veil embodies the truth of all Muslim women and presents it as sinister, exotic and seductive.[108] In the first scenes we are introduced to the Muslim Woman, her body covered in a sheer veil that appears as a menacing shadow as she prays and laments her forbidden love. Her naked body, visible through her veil, implies an arrested freedom, thinly veiled behind the oppressive letters of the Quran. The narrative is punctuated by the sound of lashings accompanied by the presence of her nude body lying on the dark floor. With a weak light shining on her, enough to see the verses of the Qur'an imprinted on her bare skin, the lashings suggest her body is reclaimed by another veil, even when it has escaped the veil. What is evoked is the terror of the veil, sanctioned by a brutal Islam, and its oppressive demands on her body. The cultural inscriptions on her body appear as each lashing pierces the skin and cuts away at the flesh. Like colonial paintings of Muslim women half-naked and half-veiled, Muslim women's bodies in the film are not downtrodden but seductive, eroticised and exoticised,[109] confessing (sexual) desire for the (western) fulfilling gaze. The veil's overpowering claim on her body is evident in the black backdrop that threatens to entirely engulf what is left of her body. Her body straddles seduction *and* terror. The figure of the veiled woman is presented in the film as standing in for the Muslim woman, whose injured body marks her difference, and identifies it as one in need of saving.

Eltahawy's intervention similarly depicts the veil as a visible evidence of the hate men have for women, shrouding every part of her body and confining her. Like a toxic oil spill, the veil is a hate that is contaminating the natural habitat of women's bodies. The veil reappears containing her sexual freedoms, her universal right to drive cars, smothering her "real" identity, and her *capacity to desire*. The remarkable disconnect in the use of this imagery and the realities unfolding in Egypt returns us to the underlying tension of this thesis: the veiled woman always appears as a figure to fulfil a freedom that one cannot not want, a return to a natural pre-discursive unveiled self, which the dynamicity of unveiling can promise. Muslim women's bodies become mere avatars of missing freedoms. In the climate of revolution, the imagery of "unveiling" is crucial here to imagining a desire for women's rights and whose visible body in public space retrieves their voices.

By heavily veiling Muslim women's bodies, Eltahawy apprehends the western imaginary of the imperilled women of this region and allows her to anchor the array of violent experiences she uses to build her case. The veil's appearance encapsulates the theme of "confessing" the hidden. Eltahawy's question of *Why?* positions her as the one committed to revealing—*confessing*—the "secrets" of Arabs and Muslims, historically concealed by the veil and the harem. The veil sets a mood of danger, with Eltahawy urgently collecting evidence for her case. This urgency is reminiscent of the women who used a hidden camera under their veil and smuggled footage of the public execution of burqa-clad Zameena by the Taliban in 1999.[110] Under the shadow of the veil, Eltahawy similarly smuggles out the evidence of violations and misogyny.

In an unusual contrast, the article is accompanied by an iconic image of a veiled female protestor being dragged by Egyptian soldiers, her veil over her head revealing her bright blue bra. It is not only the violence of the Mubarak regime that is captured in this image of her half-naked body being brutalised and dragged away but the framing of this moment also exemplifies for Eltahawy the undeniable misogyny of Arab society. The placing of this image as a case against Arab men is surprising in several ways. During the protests, the same, if not worse, violence was inflicted on young men, many of whom were beaten, arrested and murdered in an attempt to intimidate activists.[111] In her challenge to Eltahawy's reading, Ahmed contends, it was the denial and ridicule at the plight of a poor Tunisian man and his subsequent self-immolation, which set the scene for the protests in the country and throughout the region. "They", in Eltahawy's narrative, become all men—revolutionaries (Liberal, Socialist and Islamist), the army and Mubarak's supporters—who follow the same cultural script and remind "us" of those who must be pursued in the war on terror.[112]

Including in the article the image of a woman being dragged by Egyptian soldiers denies the details of who this woman was and what role she and others like her had in the revolution. The image frames the "fact" of the violence—the violence done to Arab women—while silencing the context of what produced the violence and the perpetrator. The woman in the image is Hend Badawi, a 23-year-old master's student who came from a pro-Mubarak family but who supported the revolution, a stance that got her severely beaten and tortured by Mubarak's police. She later released a video detailing her ordeal and denounced the government and police repression against any act of dissent.[113] Also leading the opposition was Asmaa Mahfouz, the founder of the "April 6 Youth Movement", and the first person to make a call to protest in Tahrir Square after four incidents of self-immolation in protest against the Mubarak regime.[114] These women, beyond the frame, reflect the key role women took in the revolutions throughout the region. Along with their male counterparts, they intervened against a culture of corruption, repression, economic deprivation, and in their revolutionary calls, demanded a new national vision. Veiled or unveiled women of different classes and social backgrounds joined these voices and indeed were proponents of women's rights but saw it as part of a nation-building project. These women did not articulate their politics through their individual bodies but through the social body of a revolutionary mass opposed to a life not corrupted by authoritarian repression, economic uncertainty and political stagnation, rather than framing their protest against "Arab culture". Eltahawy's depiction of women of the region as victims of hateful men attaches the Arab Spring upheavals onto women's bodies: visible symptoms of violence. This is a violence, which Slavoj Žižek describes as a visible and "irrational" violence that horrifies with a "lure which prevents us from thinking" about the non-violent standard it assumes.[115]

Under the mystifying lure of cultural hate, the image of the blue bra and bare skin accompanying the veiled bodies, is crucial to the confessional politics Eltahawy manipulates into the image by taking her viewers on a titillating tour of the corporeal terrain of Muslim women's bodies. Like The Afghan Girl and Aisha's mutilated face, confession here appears as a desire for the Other: the native informant's self-orientalisation offers knowledge of the body beneath the veil in exchange for recognition, to be desired. The colour blue reminds the western viewer of the blue burqa that terrorises the Afghan woman: this is a fragmented body reduced to a single symptom— an ontological lack qua the veil. The image lays bare the violent fantasy which underpins Eltahawy's own confession: positioning herself as *the one removing the veil*—both the metaphorical one of the nation and the material one wrapped around women's bodies.[116]

The positioning of Muslim women's bodies as imperilled at a time when women mobilised in revolutionary protest, raises the questions about Eltahawy's vision of women's empowerment. What is she saving women from if the violence they are subjected to appears as irrational? In her 2015 book based on the article, she gives us the answer in her call for a "sexual revolution" embodied in the front cover of the book which has a red veil in the throes of removal with a white backdrop. This gesture of defiance, the dynamism of discovering one's desires, matches the fierce language of Eltahawy's words of confession. The secular progressive politics underpinning her confession ignores the presumption of superiority she adopts. It assumes the right to speak for the women of this region, what she identifies as social ills, the solutions she offers and what she is "saving them for".[117] It is no surprise that the backlash against her was intense—not so much from men, but Arab and Muslim women—many of whom accused her of reducing complex issues to simplistic and historically-based racist binaries by reconstituting Arab/Muslim women as third world victims.[118] The orientalist imagery and the secular liberal logic of her readings reproduce western truths, and what the west had always imagined of the Orient's hidden secrets, its confession. Eltahawy situates herself as intimately aware of the conditions in the region but through orientalist clichés she attempts to create a distance between herself and cultural realities. Her vilification of Arab culture (s) omits other possibilities of assessment by shrouding Arab and Muslim women in orientalist imaginings, overdosing on statistics, case studies and anecdotes. These omissions assist in staging the confessional for a west that already imagine Muslim women cloaked under a veil.

Unveiled, Eltahawy's own worry serves as a confession premised on the promise of freedom, agency and consciousness which unveiling one's desires can bring, and she is exemplary as a "modern" successful Arab female writer. She speaks because she has survived the veil. As a victim of the veil and the practices that it sanctions, she presents herself as *heroically unveiling*, and in doing so, attaining the capacity to speak, and confess the plight of women in the region. This is perhaps why Eltahawy frequently recounts her experiences of wearing the veil. The veil plays a salient role in Eltahawy's confession because it enables her to retell her own heroism of escaping what it marks: the impending Islamist threat and the hijacking of the revolution where women are to be cheap bargaining chips. The metaphor of the veil of constraint is also reproduced in Hirsi Ali's description of Muslim women as "caged virgins" and her own escape from this cage by entirely rejecting Islam's barbarism through atheism.[119]

Eltahawy wrote the article to provoke debate among Arabs, yet her critique is delivered through a western paper with largely western readers and written in English. She directly addresses her western audience forewarning them of the criticism that will follow: "you—the outside world—will be told that it's our 'culture' and 'religion' to do X, Y or Z to women. Understand that whoever deemed it as such was never a woman". The reference to woman suggests that it is she who knows what Woman truly is, thus playing the role of the native informant as Other—the one who can offer universal knowledge to a phallic west obsessed with securing a question of its being and its female hysterics (demanding an answer to the question of am I a Man or a Woman?). Eltahawy's performance of knowledge appears as a lustful bearded fundamentalist patriarch with a rootless and irrational rage against Woman.

The medium in which she delivers her castigation suggests that despite the Arab world undergoing its massive changes, it is through the western gaze that its inadequacies will be overcome and her conversation with the Arab/Muslim world is being played out before a western audience. Like the unveiling of Afghan women's bodies by human rights emancipation, reforming Arab society is linked to unveiling women's bodies. Deploying the language (hate, misogyny, violent), imagery (veiled bodies) and tropes (oppressed women and angry misogynistic Arab/Muslim men) of the war on terror, Eltahawy's "insights" offer a knowledge of the Muslim most desired in the west.

Confessions of Freedom

The unveiling body as a paragon of desire and freedom, a site of confessional truths, has also appeared in the protesting body of Muslim women, many of whom are "ex" Muslim women. In 2011, we saw Egyptian Alia Almahdy, who posted a nude photo of herself on her blog, "Diary of a Rebel". Wearing nothing but red shoes and thigh-high black stockings and a red flower in her hair, she declared a sexual revolution through her nudity. The blog was viewed by millions of people and she has posted dozens more since. In an interview, Almahdy attests that her transgressions via nudity are an "expression of her being" and an "artistic representation".[120] Inspired by FEMEN's activism, a European feminist organisation that has participated in nude protests in the name of women's rights, in March 2013, 19-year-old Tunisian activist Amina "Tyler" Sboui posted two nude images of herself. The first image she loaded was in English "fuck your morals" and the second in Arabic "My body belongs to me, and is not the source of anyone's honour". She later allegedly scrawled "FEMEN" on a cemetery wall near Kairouan's main mosque. Both acts angered conservatives and liberals in the country and led to her being detained for four months. The response to Sboui's images was more severe and internationalised: in addition to a Global Topless Jihad Day being declared in support of her, she received support from high profile figures like outspoken critic of religion, Richard Dawkins who signed a petition for her to be released.[121] Middle Eastern feminists expressed their disapproval of Sboui's strategy, however, arguing it was naïve and discredited the historical grassroots work women's rights activists and could endanger the projects and discourses they had developed.[122] In an interview, she explained that it was her way of "making Tunisian women's voices heard" and "protecting them from suppression". In another interview, she defended her style of protest by emphasising it as a choice, "everyone has the right to express themselves in their own way and I chose my way of doing so in the Femen way".[123] But as Judith Butler reminds us, the body is never entirely ours, even when it is naked it is subject to a gaze, a violence, and thus, remains vulnerable.[124]

Like the orientalist art that exhibited Muslim women's nude bodies as a triumph over the veil, the nude bodies of Sboui and Almahdy remain vulnerable to other meanings. Staged before an international public, these bodies are confessions of the veil: what it *really* means for women and what it has always repressed. The historical removal of the face veil by Sha'rawi in the turn of the twentieth century and the "unveiling" of Almahdy and Sboui are unalike in that both are symbolic acts of dissent enthused by a desire to uncover an "authentic" truth—and thereby escape the veil of lack. The discarding of the veil demonstrates a desire to self-fashion a secular liberal subject whose individuality, autonomy and agency is discovered in a politics of refusal. Both not only sought encouragement from European feminist imaginings, but whose defense of a secular "good" is underpinned by a belief that "bare skin and flaunted sexuality" represents, if not measures, women's freedom and equality.[125] These protesting bodies, taken up in international space, are interpellated as confessional *Muslim women's* bodies—atheist or not—whose nudity, is scripted as the contours of the secular with a refusal to submit to a religious order that deprives them of bodily integrity. The story their bodies can confess is the authentic witness. Like her European counterparts of FEMEN, nudity is accompanied by slogans on their body, containing bodily testimony and the body as witness to the political statements. The visibility of breasts is not so much to offend but to imbue these feminine symbols with anything other than a "lack"—a reclaiming of a body splintered by tradition, culture, Islamism: the veil of violence. Their bared bodies confess the "truth" of what Muslim women desire is the flesh of freedom or *freedom as flesh*.

Like FEMEN's women, Sboui and Almahdy do not simply unveil their liberated bodies but also aesthetically present them, leaving "humanising" traces—desire in the form of choice and bodily enjoyment. This is evident in Almahdy's choice to wear stockings and red shoes, and Sboui's red lipstick, black eyeliner and smoking. Both display elements of consumer chic and sexy, in addition to the allure of rebellion. These well-placed and aesthetically presented images echo their European counterparts who also present their bodies as desirable. In this mode, there is a performance of bodies as screens projecting FEMEN's ideology to validate an already European unveiling masquerade. More precisely, their bodies are displayed for a panoptic gaze—the desire for modernity—and uncritically embedded in a patriarchal mode of marketing Woman as a commodity and saturated in choice. By adopting the language of agency, which unveiling claims, the subversive acts of young Muslim (or those coded as Muslim) women disrobing—as a personal narrative and using their bodies to retrieve their voices— become uncritical embodiments of secular and neo-liberal norms, reconstituting a corporeal space for secular consumption. Choice and agency are, for instance, "linked to consumption and the auto-sexualisation of the body".[126] Nudity here is depicted the reclaiming of the *desiring* body and concurrently an expression of renouncing Islam/religion which she holds responsible for shackling women's body under a repressive veil, smothering their rights and capacity to choose how to express their individuality and sexuality.

Like women who identify with the signifier of west, unveiling here is represented as a *shedding of symbolic violence on women's bodies* and confessing a universal mode of "being" beneath the symbolic mirage. This *hyper-unveiling* is the reverse of Clérambault's Moroccan women whose obscene difference were depicted and contained in the anxious gestures of veiling their bodies.[127] The "naked" body, performing an obscene defiance against all veils, appears as the other extreme in a hysterical quest for the secular body through hyper-unveiling.

This shedding of symbolic cuttings has gained traction beyond FEMEN's activism and increasingly present on social network sites. In recent years, the unveiling "other" (Muslim) woman has been revived again in confessing the horrors of ISIS and Iranian religious tyranny. The liberation of women in Eastern Syria from ISIS control in 2017 was visibly marked by the circulation of images and videos of women removing their veils, burning them, amid celebrations by surrounding crowds.[128] Many remembered the veiled bodies in chains (real or imagined) amid stories of sexual violence, female enslavement and other horrors under the impending Caliphate. Their liberation through the symbolic gesture of removing the veil combined with western media awe over female Kurdish fighters who participated in defeating ISIS served as a powerful symbol of confessing women's true desires and an immediate prophylactic against the violence of war and its political contradictions.

The confessional body via unveiling has dominated stories of Iranian women's struggles against the government. The unveiling body as a paragon of desire, agency and freedom is indicated by social network campaigns by Masih Alinejad, an American-based Iranian journalist. The campaign began on a Facebook page, My *Stealthy Freedom*, as a site for unveiled women throughout Iran to post photos as an act of subversion against a "forced hijab" as part of a "White Wednesday" campaign—white, symbolising opposition to the darker chadors and hijab expected by the state. It is also a curious reminder of the "white revolution"—the national development project of the Pahlavi regime in the 1960s and 1970s which grew unpopular and contributed to the 1979 revolution. Alinejad presents her protest project as an instinctual response to being free. To express herself, she posted a photo of herself in Iran without any head covering and wondered if other women had similar photos where they "enjoyed their freedom in secret".[129] Iranian women have made similar protests beyond this page, leading to several arrests. Images of women standing on Iranian streets holding their headscarves away from them—a pose that echoes the images of women removing their veils in Syria after ISIS was defeated—have appeared on Instagram, Twitter and other social media platforms. The White Wednesday campaign has garnered international attention, including from the Trump administration by then Secretary of State Mike Pompeo who met with Alinejad to express support for Iranian women's rights.[130] Alinejad's page has a million followers on Facebook. She has received a human rights award in Geneva[131] and in 2019, was featured in *The Guardian* where she provided insights on women's struggles in Iran with images of women in the throes of removing their veil.[132] Alinejad wrote a book soon after further reflecting on her personal experience in Iran and the motivation for the project. The title *The Wind in My Hair: My Fight for Freedom in Modern Iran* (2018) is accompanied by a photo of her with her long black curly hair surrounding her face like a mane, lifted and animated by wind of freedom. The book is dedicated to the "brave women" who have participated in the "White Wednesday" campaign. Her website has amassed hundreds of photos and videos of unveiled women in parks, grassy plains, beaches, and in their cars. These images have been accompanied by statements such as "It was a wonderfully pleasant experience to walk on city sidewalks feeling unchained and free", and "Here is my stealthy freedom in nature… Together with nature, I want to defend my natural right, which is freedom. I am tying a not [sic] with the grass (An an [sic] ancient Persian New Year tradition) with the hope that one day justice could be established in this country". While many of the women on the page oppose forced veiling, these statements, for their western audience, couple unveiling with freedom and the capacity to choose. Unveiling here activates an inner "natural" or "true" self who, burdened by tradition, has yet to announce itself and realise those choices. The statements express a yearning for the right to self-expression, desire and freedom, punctuated by references to nature, beauty, hair flowing in the breeze, choice and natural rights.[133] Once the veil is removed, experience becomes "actual" experience—the beach is enjoyed as a beach, the breeze can truly be felt, grass can finally be touched, and one can finally reconnect with nature—suggesting to those who transact in the language of western truths and the body that carries them, there is no enjoyment unless the body is witness to it through making itself visible. There is no knowledge without the (unveiled) body as witness. There is no confession (knowledge) without the veiled body inviting discovery. The more uncovered, the more alive the body, and the more it can experience all human senses, and intimately connect to the world by witnessing its pleasures. It is the dominant schema in which women's struggles in Iran, as it has been for Afghan women, is told through the veil as a visible detector of freedom and unfreedom. In these freedom confessions, we do not hear from the women who support veiling yet are critical of the government, nor the women who may share the vision of the state. These are women who have yet to discover their "true" selves.

Alinejad's project is not the only online anti-veiling campaign. A similar campaign has also been launched on Tumblr for "ex-hijabis" to document themselves wearing the veil and removing it with a short story about their journey from veiled constraint to bodily freedom. What is noteworthy about the project is that it has been set up by an ex-Muslim woman called Mara, who wanted the site to be a place for Muslim women (and men) who believe in having control over the representation of their bodies. The images capture human stories of women—smiling, posing in fashionable attire, and celebrating their sexuality—who, it is inferred, have survived to tell their story. Though the site is dedicated to ex-hijabis, many of the stories are about the authors' departure from Islam, which is represented as an unfreedom that is oppressive, indoctrinating, superstitious, physically constraining and emotionally crippling. One commentator talks about her entire experience of leaving Islam through what she describes as escaping the "suppression of bodily control". Having worn a hijab from the age of eight until 23, she reflects on how her body, smothered by the discipline" of "ritual and now owned by her. Again, we see the positioning of insider perspectives as knowing what the Woman really is beyond the tyranny of culture, with bodily integrity, all the while mobilising the fantasy of freedom. Her reflections describe a struggle for her to come to terms with her free body after years of training it to be less visible.[134] The "natural" must be learnt and cultivated. The other entries similarly describe journeys of self-discovery through their unveiling (both physically and metaphorically). The ambiguity of the site's appellation becomes clearer in that the role of unveiling here (being ex-hijabi) has a double meaning: it is a revelation of both bodily honesty (learning how to desire) and renouncing Islam—for one without the *other* is unimaginable. Akin to the phallic logic that announces a universal subjecthood, the protesting body here signals a dispensing with the veil that shames through the internalisation of lack. In this sense, the site is dedicated to confessional subjects who seek recognition by unveiling their cultural transgressions and their inner desires to discover who they really are. These layers of contradictions in the confessional subject coded as Muslim are wiped away in the stories of the veil as compulsion and its removal as the prophylactic to Iranian women's social, political and economic ordeals.

The Veil in Solidarity

If unveiling has become a powerful symbol of agency and a normative liberatory practice for "secular" women fleeing the veil of lack or the veil of terror, this imaginary and imagery of freedom's arrival was destabilised by the public veiling of New Zealand's Prime Minister Jacinda Ardern as a gesture of solidarity with the Muslim community after the massacre in two mosques in Christchurch on 15 March 2019. The emphatic act was also repeated a week after the shootings by women around New Zealand who wore it in solidarity with the New Zealand's Muslim community. Ardern described it as an "obvious decision" as she comforted the Christchurch's Muslim community. It was also a way to support women who wear hijab to feel a sense of security.[135] The striking image of the highest representative of a secular state, a white secular woman, willingly wearing a scarf over her head incited protests from different sections of the global community. One of the most circulated and vocal critics was Masih Alinejad who expressed disappointment that New Zealand's women used a "visible symbol of oppression for Muslim women" around the world as an empathetic act.[136] One can respond to this criticism with the obvious point that the veil can mean oppression or liberation, depending on one's experience. There is a weighted value in highlighting empirical truths which does not take away from the experiences of women who have positive and negative experiences with the veil. Nevertheless, this uprooting of the veil to that of a shifting signifier is underpinned by the very liberal secular truth-claims that legitimises and delegitimises the wearing and not wearing the veil. The veil as a religious requirement that transcends this binary of resistance/oppression is erased in these sociological explanations that privilege the individual as interlocutor. More curiously, critics like Alinejad who would rather privilege a reading of the veil that captures Muslim women's experience as oppressive insist on injecting the abstract "abused Muslim woman" into contemporary western discourse on Islam and Muslims for political expediency. Muslim women are "neither the subject nor the object of these discourses, but rather their vehicles".[137] In the racial economy of the veiled and unveiled bodies, Alinejad's resolve requires Ardern's "secular" body to *remain* unveiled to bolster her claim against a freedom lost. White women's bodies as the pre-discursive measure of all other bodies authenticate her truth-claims and give political credence to confessional tales that rely on the veil as an ominous presence in their lives. Muslim women in New Zealand (and elsewhere) who wear hijab/veil without state imposition, however, do not provide the assurance that the veil is an embodied Muslim practice beyond the political dealings of the state.

REDEEMING THE VEIL: THE UNVEILED-VEILED MUSLIM WOMAN

I want to briefly explore another possibility of how such refashioning of the secular self can be taken up in the paranoid preoccupation with Muslims. What the examples so far have examined is how confession, like unveiling, is a political and epistemic practice of maintaining western knowability through a performance of freedom that must be made visible. If unveiling and confession trades in an ocular epistemology that privileges visibility as a truth-making practice, today's new technologies invite new ways of being visible. Over the past few years, there has emerged another kind of desirable Muslim subject who also suggests that unveiling is not simply a material uncovering of corporeal truth, but one that trades in the racial politics of confession: the hijab-wearing Muslim "cool girl" in the west. This is a Muslim subject whose sole preoccupation is not with disclosing the horrors of Islam and her community but with redeeming the hijab for a western audience by verifying its liberating qualities. We have seen a proliferation of the increasing visibility of Muslim women in entertainment, popular culture and general public life. These hijab-wearers appear to be in a perpetual state of "dispelling", "shattering", "challenging", "breaking", *rupturing stereotypes* which often frames their pursuit in sports, fashion, magazine covers, rapping, singing and other activities deemed non-stereotypical of hijab-wearing Muslim women. Like the unveiled confessional subjects discussed earlier, they accrue social capital by positioning themselves, or are positioned in media coverage, as exceptional voices. Their talent, self-empowerment, uniqueness *and visibility* are also invested in the stereotype of the veiled Muslim woman. In the paranoid gaze of the Muslim question, their efforts aim to *humanise* Muslim women, to educate the world of Islam's relatability (and therefore, compatibility) as a religion of peace and individual empowerment. To be human is to be visible, transparent and have nothing to hide.

We have seen the making of the "human" is a fraught process subject to biopolitical calculations that Agamben, using Foucault, warns reduces bodies to political life (*bios*). In the confessional demands of the post-9/11 security state, confession also masquerades as a language of freedom to make one visible for its inevitable judgement. In the empowering discourse of the modern hijab-wearer, to confess is not only to make one visible but to have, in the feminist psychoanalytic sense, *no shame*. To be human is to be more visible, transparent, progressive—modern. An example of this Muslim mode of confession includes popular American website such as *Muslim Girl* which aims at normalising the word "Muslim" by "taking back the narrative" for "modern Muslim women" to tell their own stories in a more honest conversation. Although they do not exclude non-hijab-wearing young Muslim women, the project emphasises on the modern Muslim woman who isn't bound by her hijab, conservative constraints, openly expresses her desire and explores herself through fashion, beauty, identity, sexuality and other taboo subjects. While the stories are diverse, there is an emphasis put on visibility as salient to Muslim women's normalisation and humanisation. This visibility is discerned in their appearance in media, beauty and fashion. Take for example, how Muslim Women's Day 2019 was marked by the website which listed the "very best" conversations that depict the "strength and resilience that Muslim women had to offer... centred around the lives and daily realities of Muslim women". All 14 selected articles focus on the need for representation but the majority centre on appearance, fashion, wellness, beauty and celebrity, as the "reality" of Muslim women's lives.

The strategy of humanising through visibility at a time when Muslim visibility—veils, mosques, halal-certification—has been a provocation is a curious one. Muslims are indeed visible and even hyper-visible. So, what kind of visibility is being pursued here? What is being "taken back" and reintroduced as normal? What kind of body does this "modern" veiled woman have? Muslim women's announcement and empowerment is contingent on her desire and capacity to consume. Like the confessional bodies of Sboui and Almahdy, the "modern" veiled woman carries with her the signature of freedom, the signs of consumption. Afghanistan's "lipstick revolution" as a "beauty without borders", is reassured in the corporeal reception of the *unveiled-veiled* Muslim woman. If unveiling and confession are a biopolitical policing of the knowable body to manage the Other's question, the regulation of *jouissance* through fleshly freedom, the unveiled-veiled Muslim woman whose veiled body confesses it *still* belongs to everyone—to paraphrase Alain Badiou's critique of the French veil ban, she still shows what she has to offer, to always be hinting of undressing, to participate in the market's circulation of woman.[138] These women, adorned in the latest fashion, beautiful, polished, their skin glistening by brushes of makeup, resemble modernism's "pure surface" as a "residue of synthetics",[139] an enlightened corporeal surface that has witnessed disciplining. The unveiled-veiled woman is an unveiling of the Muslim woman's knowable body.

The shift to a consuming, and therefore consumable, veiled Muslim subject is difficult to apprehend without considering how this palatable image has been narrated in a liberal language that stresses choice, freedom and individuality. Initiatives like World Hijab Day, which began on 1 February 2013 is an example of Muslim women speaking back, reclaiming the narrative by defending the hijab and inviting non-Muslim women to experience it as a form of education. The day has grown in popularity and is marked by almost 190 countries every year. Through liberal offerings, non-Muslim women are invited to participate in veiling, reassured that like Muslim women, this is a veil of choice, one that preserves freedom and an expression of individuality. What non-Muslim women (including Ardern's gesture of solidarity) are invited to defend and participate in, is the canonical liberal truths through which the day finds purpose. One must wonder if the day would have the same resonance if the reasons for wearing the veil are emphasised as fundamentally a religious obligation. Erased from the consumerist narrative is a belief in submitting oneself to the transcendental that could potentially destabilise the liberal defenses surrounding the sovereign individual. If the unveiled-veiled Muslim woman signals a body that is normalised, relatable and consumable, what is the difference that is being celebrated? Are we witnessing the sinking of the religious body into secularism's tenacious mandate on bodily integrity? Entangled in the racial and racialising regime of the veiled and unveiled, zones of being and non-being, the production of the Muslim woman is one of an embodied Muslim, fixed within racial markers, entangled within its discursive possibility.

CONCLUSION

The secular liberal progressive politics underpinning confessional narratives, where agency is located in the pursuit of an unquestioned desire for freedom, not only highlights the circumscribed form in which the Muslim woman is present in political discourse, but also reveals the presumption of superior knowing adopted by critics. This belief in the goodness of universal solutions and reasoning within its framework manifests in both outsiders and secular progressives within the Muslim world who are obsessed with "constraint", most visible in the persistent worries about the veil.[140] These examples of conviction in the promise of unveiling bodies enhance the capacity for choice and autonomy, and veiled bodies constrain and discipline, neglect to appreciate what Wendy Brown argues is "the extent to which all choice is conditioned by as well as imbricated with power, and the extent to which choice itself is an impoverished account of freedom".[141] Liberal values of freedom from Islamism, religion and hateful men, come to be the only way we conceptualise women's experiences and our attention is taken away from the many covert ways in which we are regulated.[142] The unveiling of Muslim women's bodies levels difference, erases the complexities of these discourses and how they are enacted. There is also not much reflexivity or consideration of the debates that are currently being waged about what constitutes "morals" and "honour" confidently sprawled on the protesting body as the body that problematises the veil. These confessional bodies carry the currency of freedom, choice, autonomy which are concepts, according to Razack, "that impose a particular kind of order, a structure that violently suppresses those details that do not fit" such as the details of the form of domination that occurs, hierarchies that are reproduced in the unveiling of oppression,[143] and the limitations of extracting bodily confessions.

Muslim women's bodies are produced within confessional narratives as remaining under a veil of violence by always pointing to the violence. Like images, confessional narratives order the way bodies are read and produce knowledge of Islam and Muslims in the post-9/11 world around themes of violence and pain, and the threat that this can pose to the natural body. In this chapter, I traced the phallic fantasy in the "personal testimonies" of secular critics of Muslim background, identifying unveiling in the political arrangement their confessions appear. I argued the insider perspectives of these critics of Islam and Arab culture who confess the moral perversions of their society and the threat that it poses. Dissenters are accounts of the native informant—a figure who speaks for a community deemed speechless to answer the west's questions of who Muslims are. Situating herself as a courageous figure who confronts this threat, and divulges Islam's lack, the new native informant performs a heroic unveiling through confession of the desires of the flesh beneath the veil. These are confessions that shed light on the shadows on the body that historically, and continue, to provoke western hysteria. These figures represent articulations of intact bodily substance, the "truth" of the hidden. Unveiling not only performs her liberation, staged for western approval, but realises the "natural body" in the language of western secular and liberal truths.

This chapter identified these confessional subjects as situating themselves having the authentic insider perspectives on their communities which rely on unveiling bodies that refuse the veil as a confessional performance. Like their western counterparts, both invoke the image of the veil of violence (the symptom of lack) through a heroic triumph of fleeing it through unveiling, but these women of the "East" perform unveiling through repetitive insider confession of the other's veiled lack and thus, knowledge of bodily truths. The shedding of lack through confessions appear as both—identifying lack and desiring to be free from it. Arab and Muslim women's lack in the feminist interventions of these critics capitalise on the image of unveiling—both through the imagined body (Eltahawy) and material body

(FEMEN/Iranian anti-hijab activists)—as bodies *receiving* freedoms. The reception of freedom also extends to the body of the woman who continues to cover, reminding that the unveiling body is one that shows itself to be a conduit of freedom, veiled *or* unveiled in the problematisation of the veil that defies secular liberal sensibilities.

NOTES

1. Houria Bouteldja, *Whites, Jews and Us: Towards a Politics of Revolutionary Love* (Los Angeles, CA: Semiotext(e), 2016), 84.
2. Quoted in Katherine Bullock, *Rethinking Muslim Women and the Veil* (Herndon, VA: International Institute of Islamic Thought, 2003), 8.
3. Amin quoted in Leila Ahmed, *Women and Gender in Islam: Historical Roots of a Modern Debate* (New Haven: Yale University Press, 1992), 46.
4. Timothy Mitchell, *Questions of Modernity* (Minneapolis and London: University of Minnesota Press, 2000), 15–17.
5. Lord Cromer, British Consul to Egypt quoted in Leila Ahmed, *Women and Gender in Islam: Historical Roots of a Modern Debate* (New Haven: Yale University Press, 1992), 152–153.
6. What is questionable about this historically recognised act of "indigenous" female agency is Sha'arawi's own alienating experience. She was raised by a European feminist, Eugenie Le Brun, who inducted young Muslim women into a colonial understanding of the veil echoing Cromer's belief in it being a barrier to Egypt's progress. See Margot Badran, *Feminism in Islam: Secular and Religious Convergences* (Oxford, MI: Oneworld, 2009), 73.
7. Said cited in Éwanjé-Épée, Félix Boggio, and Stella Magliani-Belkacem, "The Empire of Sexuality: An Interview with Joseph Massad," *Jadaliyya*, March 5, 2013, https://www.jadaliyya.com/Details/28167/The-Empire-of-Sexuality-An-Interview-with-Joseph-Massad.
8. Nadia Fadil, "Not-/Unveiling as an Ethical Practice," *Feminist Review* 98, no. 1 (2011): 83–109.
9. Yasemin Yildiz, Governing European Subjects, 77.
10. Anne Anlin Cheng, *The Melancholy of Race: Psychoanalysis, Assimilation, and Hidden Grief* (New York: Oxford University Press, 2000), 68.
11. Megan Macdonald, "Sur/Veil," 39.
12. Cheng, *The Melancholy of Race*, 68.
13. Rogers, *Law's Cut on the Body of Human Rights*, 10.
14. See Judith Butler, "Sexual Politics, Torture, and Secular Time," *The British Journal of Sociology* 59, no. 1 (2008).
15. Joan Wallach Scott, *The Politics of the Veil*, 88.
16. Michel Foucault, *The Will to Knowledge: The History of Sexuality I*, Translated by Robert Hurley (London: Random House, 1978), 58.
17. Asad, "Thinking About the Secular Body, Pain and Liberal Politics".

18. Abu-Lughod, *Do Muslim Women Need Saving?*, 69.
19. Joseph Massad, *Islam in Liberalism* (Chicago: University of Chicago Press, 2015), 233.
20. Asad cited in Massad, *Islam in Liberalism*, 237.
21. For example: Judith Herman, *Trauma and Recovery: The Aftermath of Violence—From Domestic Abuse to Political Terror* (New York: Basic Books, 1997); Adrian Howe, *Sex, Violence and Crime: Foucault and the 'Man' Question* (New York: Routledge, 2008).
22. Talal Asad, *Formations of the Secular: Christianity, Islam, Modernity*, 68.
23. Cheng, *The Melancholy of Race*, 69.
24. Mitchell, *Questions of Modernity*, 18.
25. Mitchell, *Questions of Modernity*, 8.
26. Daniel Lerner referenced in Zachary Lockman, *Contending Visions of the Middle East: The History and Politics of Orientalism* (New York: Cambridge University Press, 2004), 138.
27. See John F. Wilson, "Modernity and Religion: A Problem of Perspective," In *Modernity and Religion*, edited by William Nicholls (Waterloo, ON: Wilfrid Laurier University Press, 1987).
28. Butler, "Sexual Politics, Torture, and Secular Time," 6.
29. Suzanne Barnard, "Introduction," In *Reading Seminar XX: Love, Knowledge and Feminine Sexuality*, edited by Susan Barnard and Bruce Finks (New York: State University Press, 2002), 11.
30. For a closer psychoanalytic reading of anxiety, see Jacques Lacan, *Anxiety. The seminar of Jacques Lacan: Book X*, edited by Jacques-Alain Miller and translated by A.R. Price (Cambridge: Polity Press, 2014). For Lacan anxiety emerges when fantasy breaks down and desire loses its coordinates, exposing the subject to the object that remains in the place of lack.
31. Mitchell, *Questions of Modernity*, 3.
32. McClintock, Imperial Leather, p. 28.
33. Ross Mills, "The Confession as a 'Practice of Freedom': Feminism, Foucault and 'Elsewhere' Truths," *Law, Text, Culture* 2, no. 1 (1995), 93.
34. Meyda Yeğenoğlu, *Colonial Fantasies: Towards a Feminist Reading of Orientalism* (Cambridge: Cambridge University Press, 1998), 11.
35. Derek Hook, *A Critical Psychology of the Postcolonial: The Mind of Apartheid* (London: Psychology Press, 2012).
36. Frantz Fanon, *A Dying Colonialism* (New York: Grove Press, 1965), 44.
37. Said, *Orientalism*, 7.
38. Scott, *The Politics of the Veil*, 2007.
39. Megan Macdonald, "Sur/Veil: The Veil as Blank(et) Signifier," in *Muslim Women, Transnational Feminism and Ethics of Pedagogy: Contested Imaginaries in Post-9/11 Cultural Practice*, edited by Lisa K. Taylor and Jasmine Zine (New York: Routledge, 2014).
40. Fanon, *A Dying Colonialism*, 42.

41. Fanon, *A Dying Colonialism*, 42.
42. McClintock, *Imperial Leather*, 227.
43. Fanon, *A Dying Colonialism*, 60–63.
44. Homi Bhabha, *The Location of Culture*, 1994 (2012 ed.) (New York: Rout-ledge, 2012).
45. Foucault, *The Will to Knowledge*, 77.
46. Foucault, *The Will to Knowledge*, 19.
47. Foucault, *The Will to Knowledge*, 35.
48. Foucault, *The Will to Knowledge*, 60.
49. Foucault, *The Will to Knowledge*, 71.
50. Foucault, *The Will to Knowledge*, 61–63.
51. Susan David Bernstein, *Confessional Subjects: Revelations of Gender and Power in Victorian Literature and Culture* (Chappel Hill, NC: University of North Carolina Press, 1997), 17.
52. Bernstein, *Confessional Subjects*, 18.
53. Bernstein, *Confessional Subjects*, 15.
54. Jean-Michel Landy, "Confession, Obedience and Subjectivity: Michel Foucault's Unpublished Lectures on the Government of the Living," *Telos* 146 (2009): 111–123.
55. Jia Tolentino, "The Personal Essay Boom Is Over," *The New Yorker*, May 18, 2017, https://www.newyorker.com/culture/jia-tolentino/the-personal-essay-boom-is-over.
56. Lorraine Berry, "Virginia Woolf: There Are Way Too Many Personal Essays Out There," Literary Hub, May 24, 2017, https://lithub.com/virginia-woolf-there-are-way-too-many-personal-essays-out-there/.
57. Mills, "The Confession as a 'Practice of Freedom'," 101.
58. See Lila Abu Lughod, "Romance of Resistance: Tracing Transformation of Power Through Bedouin Women," *American Ethnologist* 17, no. 1 (1990): 41–55.
59. Hamid Dabashi, *Brown Skin, White Masks* (London: Pluto, 2011), 15.
60. Saba Mahmood, "Feminism, Democracy and Empire: Islam and the War on Terror," In *Women's Studies on the Edge*, edited by Joan Wallach Scott (Durham: Duke University Press, 2008), 83.
61. Mahmood, "Feminism, Democracy and Empire," 87.
62. Mahmood, "Feminism, Democracy and Empire," 84. For example, Irshad Manji sat down with civil rights activist and scholar, Cornel West. Despite being a staunch critic the war on terror and Israel's occupation and severe treatment of the Palestinians endorsed by Manji—much of the conversation was spent on praising and congratulating Manji for her work. "What Do You Stand For? An Evening of Moral Courage with Cornel West and Irshad Manji," New York University, April 16, 2013, accessed 3 August, 2016, http://www.nyu.edu/reynolds/speaker_series/past_ss/1213/west_manji.html.

63. Hamid Dabashi, *Brown Skin, White Masks* (London: Pluto, 2011), 12.
64. Mahmood, "Feminism, Democracy and Empire," 84.
65. Mayanthi L. Fernando, *The Republic Unsettled: Muslim French and the Contradictions of Secularism* (Durham: Duke University Press, 2014), 194.
66. Dabashi, *Brown Skin, White Masks*, 23.
67. Dabashi, *Brown Skin, White Masks*, 16.
68. Jacques Lacan, *The Four Fundamental Concepts of Psychoanalysis*, translated by Alan Sheridan (London: Karnac, 2003), 232.
69. Slavoj Žižek, *The Plague of Fantasies* (London: Verso, 1997), 107.
70. Stephen Sheehi, *Islamophobia: The Ideological Campaign Against Muslims* (Atlanta: Clarity Press, 2011), 93.
71. Abu-Lughod, *Do Muslim Women Need Saving?*, 17.
72. Mahmood, "Feminism, Democracy and Empire," 82.
73. Yasemin Yildiz, "Governing European Subjects," 2011.
74. See her discussion of "ijtihad"—the Islamic concept of independent thinking, which she argues is a responsibility of all Muslims. Her claim departs from the traditional use of itjihad by those trained in the Islamic tradition. Manji, *The Trouble with Islam Today: A Muslim's Call for Reform in Her Faith*.
75. See Nomani's controversial article she co-authored with Hala Arfa, calling on supporters for "Wear Hijab Day" to not wear it as it sanctions the policing of women's bodies and sexuality. https://www.washingtonpost.com/news/acts-of-faith/wp/2015/12/21/as-muslim-women-we-actually-ask-you-not-to-wear-the-hijab-in-the-name-of-interfaith-solidarity/?utm_term=.dde86fbe77bd.
76. Sahgal also headed Amnesty International's Gender Unit but had a falling out with the organisation in April 2010 after she contended that it had partnered with a "Taliban supporter", Moazzem Begg, as part of its campaign against human rights violations at Guantanamo. Sahgal saw this partnership as a betrayal of Afghan women despite Begg's denial of ever supporting the Taliban. The Centre of Secular Space emerged as a result of this incident, and Toor notes how Sahgal has been received well by a feminist community (including many from the Global South) as standing up to fundamentalism and "naïve human rights organizations". Toor, "Imperialist Feminism Redux," 153.
77. Zara Kay, "Faithless Hijabi," https://www.faithlesshijabi.org/?fbclid=IwAR38gYeL3cAM9iTIp0yhW5ztB8BBxphdwUAHv1ZCB2uuwMrzakC3NEX6Xb4.
78. Gillian Whitlock, *Soft Weapons: Autobiography in Transit* (Chicago: University of Chicago Press, 2009), 3.
79. Abu-Lughod, *Do Muslim Women Need Saving?*, 69.
80. Mahmood, *Politics of Piety*, 14.

81. Bruce Fink, "Knowledge and Jouissance," in *Reading Seminar XX: Lacan's Major Work on Love, Knowledge and Feminine Sexuality,* edited by Susanne Barnard and Bruce Fink (New York: State University New York Press, 2002).

82. See Sigmund Freud and James Strachey, *Three Essays on the Theory of Sexuality* (New York: Basic Books, 2000).

83. Fadil, "Not-/Unveiling as an Ethical Practice," 90.

84. Mona Eltahawy, "From Liberals and Feminists: Unsettling Silence on Rending the Veil," *Washington Post,* July 17, 2010, http://www.washingtonpost.com/wp-dyn/content/article/2010/07/16/AR2010071604356.html.

85. Amanda Holpuch, "Activist Mona Eltahawy Released After Arrest in New York Subway Protest," *The Guardian,* September 27, 2012, https://www.theguardian.com/world/2012/sep/26/mona-eltahawy-released-new-york-subway.

86. Toor, "Imperialist Feminism Redux," 150.

87. Abu-Lughod, *Do Muslim Women Need Saving?,* 157.

88. Abu-Lughod, *Do Muslim Women Need Saving?,* 9.

89. Mona Eltahawy, "Why Do They Hate Us?," *Foreign Policy,* April 23, 2012, https://foreignpolicy.com/2012/04/23/why-do-they-hate-us/.

90. See her discussing her experience in Saudi Arabia with journalist Mehdi Hassan where she describes her move there "like the lights were being turned off." "Head to Head: Do Arab Men Hate Women?," (*Al Jazeera,* 2014).

91. Preface in Ayaan Hirsi Ali, *The Caged Virgin: An Emancipation Proclamation for Women and Islam,* 1st Free Press ed. (New York: Free Press, 2006).

92. Dohra Ahmad refers to "pulp-nonfiction" as the cultural production of the sub-genre of "first-person" stories centred around the "oppressed Muslim woman' trope which produces sympathy in American audiences at the same time it decontextualises oppression. Dohra Ahmad, "Not Yet Beyond the Veil: Muslim Women in American Popular Literature," *Social Text* 99, no. 2 (2009): 105–106. See also, Lila Abu Lughod, *Do Muslim Women Need Saving,* 81–113.

93. Said, *Orientalism,* 32.

94. Sheehi, *Islamophobia: The Ideological Campaign Against Muslims,* 90.

95. The evocation of Muslim women serving men's sexual desires is not new, however. The history of orientalist representations of the harem and the veil has already conveyed this, but it is also deployed in media coverage of the conflicts following the "Arab Spring". For instance, stories linking jihad, sex, forced marriages and incest in the conflict in Syria appear randomly

but with little context and detail and disappear with no or little follow up—
entrenching orientalist ideas of Arab and Muslim men's perverted sexuality
and women as sexual captives.

96. Eltahawy, "Why Do They Hate Us?".
97. An example of these frequently referenced "secrets" in the media. See: "Sex Jihad Raging in Syria, Claims Minister," *The Telegraph*, September 20, 2013, https://www.telegraph.co.uk/news/worldnews/middleeast/syria/10322578/Sex-Jihad-raging-in-Syria-claims-minister.html.
98. Scott, *The Fantasy of Feminist History*.
99. Susan Terrio cited in Fernando, *The Republic Unsettled: Muslim French and the Contradictions of Secularism*, 198–200.
100. Eltahawy, "Why Do They Hate Us?".
101. Razack, "Stealing the Suffering of Others: Reflection of Canadian Humanitarian Responses," 376.
102. Melissa Harris Perry Show, "Misogyny in the Muslim World" (2012). Saba Mahmood similarly debated Eltahawy on her cultural framing. https://www.youtube.com/watch?v=ee8MomymrOU&list=PLNXY-YQrxZv3qgvbnXptjJ4QeTsiUdjld.
103. Lila Abu-Lughod, "Dialects of Women's Empowerment: The International Circuitry of the Arab Human Development Report 2005," *International Journal of Middle Eastern Studies* 41, no. 1 (2009): 97.
104. Abu-Lughod, "Dialects of Women's Empowerment," 192.
105. These titles encapsulate the personal experiences of survivors of honour killings, forced marriage and those who have been denied the right to experience universal love.
106. Mona Eltahawy and Stephen Street, "Is France Right to Ban Wearing the Burka in Public," *The Guardian*, March 21, 2010.
107. Ayaan Hirsi Ali, *Infidel* (New York: Free Press, 2007), xxi.
108. Theo Van Gogh and Ayaan Hirsi Ali, "Submission" (2004).
109. Moors, "The Affective Power of the Face Veil: Between Disgust and Fascination," 293.
110. British-Afghan journalist Saira Shah provided this footage for Channel 4 and became part of a film titled "Beneath the Veil" which was repeatedly shown in the United Kingdom and American in the period of the initial invasion of Afghanistan in 2001. "Inside Afghanistan: Behind the Veil."
111. A reported example of the violence male protestors were subjected is reflected in Human Rights Watch's recording an incident in May 2012 where 350 protestors arrested were tortured and abused by authorities. From this group 334 were men and 16 were women. Human Rights Watch 2013, Events of 2012, https://www.hrw.org/world-report/2013/country-chapters/egypt#.
112. Abu-Lughod, *Do Muslim Women Need Saving?*, 105.

113. John Lloyd, "Getting Away from the Arab Street," *Reuters*, November 19, 2012, https://www.reuters.com/article/lloyd-arab/column-getting-away-from-the-arab-street-idUSL1E8MJOOP20121119?type=companyNews&feedType=RSS&feedName=companyNews.
114. "Asmaa Mahfouz and the YouTube Video that Helped Spark and Egyptian Uprising" (*Democracy Now*, 2011). https://www.youtube.com/watch?v=1JW3m8uwcL4.
115. Žižek, *Violence: Six Sideways Reflections*, 2–3.
116. It is also worth noting that the violent unveiling of Badawi in this image has been reanimated by the regime of General Abdel-Fatah El-Sisi, which overthrew elected president Mohammed Morsi in July 2013. In a climate of paranoia, the language of the war on terror has seeped in which links beards and veils to the Muslim Brotherhood, other Islamist opponents and radicalisation. These conflations of terrorism and religious practice have also resulted in the call for women to publicly unveil.
117. Abu-Lughod, *Do Muslim Women Need Saving?*, 47.
118. See a collection of these responses on The Stream, "Article on Women in the Middle East Triggers Debate" (*Al Jazeera*, 2012).
119. Hirsi Ali, *The Caged Virgin: An Emancipation Proclamation for Women and Islam*, 21–22.
120. Mohamed Fadel Fahmy, "Egyptian Blogger Alia Almahdy: Why I Posted Naked," *CNN*, November 20, 2011.
121. Emily Greenhouse, "How to Provoke National Unrest with a Facebook Photo," *The New Yorker*, April 8, 2013.
122. Rania Salloum, "Tunisian Feminist Leader: 'Femen, Please Leave Us Alone'," *Spiegel (International)*, June 13, 2013.
123. "Opinions in Tunisia Divided Over Topless Feminist Amina," *The Daily Star*, June 6, 2013, http://www.dailystar.com.lb/News/Middle-East/2013/Jun-06/219575-opinions-in-tunisia-divided-over-topless-feminist-amina.ashx.
124. Butler, *Precarious Life: the Powers of Mourning and Violence*, 26.
125. Abu-Lughod, *Do Muslim Women Need Saving?*, 19.
126. O'Keefe, "'My Body Is My Manifesto': Slutwalk, FEMEN and Feminist Protest." This is not to say that nudity cannot be a subversive act in a non-western context. In the past century, there have been successful examples of nude protests by Nigerian women against colonial power; and in more recent years, Nigerian women have used their bodies as a way to express their fundamental opposition to the violence of the Nigerian state and multi-national oil companies. See Sokari Ekine, *Blood Sorrow and Oil: Testimonies of Violence from Women of the Niger Delta* (Oxford: Centre for Democracy and Development, 2001).
127. Joan Copjec, *Read My Desire: Lacan Against the Historicists* (Cambridge, MA: MIT Press, 1994).

128. Lucy Pasha-Robinson, "Women Liberated from ISIS in Syria Take Off Face Veils and Burn Them," *Independent*, February 23, 2017, https://www.independent.co.uk/news/world/middle-east/women-liberate-isis-syria-burn-veils-burqa-hijab-take-off-islamist-jihadis-state-deir-ezzor-a7596116.html.

129. Masih Alinejad, "My Stealthy Freedom" (Facebook Page, 2014).

130. Azadeh Moaveni, "How the Trump Administration Is Exploiting Iran's Burgeoning Feminist Movement," *The New Yorker*, July 9, 2018, https://www.newyorker.com/news/news-desk/how-the-trump-administration-is-exploiting-irans-burgeoning-feminist-movement.

131. Saeed Kamali Dehghan, "Iranian Woman Wins Rights Award for Hijab Campaign," *The Guardian*, February 24, 2015, https://www.theguardian.com/world/2015/feb/24/iranian-woman-wins-rights-award-hijab-campaign.

132. Helen Elston, "Behind the Veil: Iranian Women Cast the Hijab—In Pictures," *The Guardian*, January 7, 2018, https://www.theguardian.com/artanddesign/gallery/2018/jan/06/behind-the-veil-iranian-women-cast-off-their-hijabs-in-pictures?fbclid=IwAR2P_duIhbCSdbp0PsXkZNgjaYtyNJ3lj1TuvGqUrHhsVNk59JJlZV9DB2g.

133. Masih Alinejad, "My Stealthy Freedom." See also, report by Heather Saul, "Iranian Women Discard Their Hijabs for 'Stealthy Freedom' Facebook Page," *The Independent*, May 13, 2014, https://www.independent.co.uk/news/world/middle-east/iranian-women-discard-their-hijabs-for-stealthy-freedom-facebook-page-9361388.html.

134. See post "Life and Love Post-Hijab," *The Ex-Hijabi Photo Journal*, *The Ex-Muslim*, June 16, 2014.

135. Karen Ruiz, "'My Job Is to Make People Feel Safe': Jacinda Ardern Says It Was an 'Obvious Decision' to Wear a Hijab as She Grieved Following the Massacre of 50 Muslims," *The Daily Mail*, March 25, 2019, https://www.dailymail.co.uk/news/article-6846915/New-Zealand-Prime-Minister-Jacinda-Ardern-said-wearing-hijab-obvious-decision.html.

136. "Iranian women's rights activist says NZ hijab display after Christchurch shooting is 'heartbreaking'," *NZ Herald*, April 2, 2019, https://www.nzherald.co.nz/nz/news/article.cfm?c_id=1&objectid=12218679.

137. Yildiz, "Governing European Subjects," 80.

138. Miri Davidson, "Alain Badiou, 'The Law on the Headscarf Is a Pure Capitalist Law'," *Verso* (blog), June 4, 2015, https://www.versobooks.com/blogs/2025-alain-badiou-the-law-on-the-headscarf-is-a-pure-capitalist-law.

139. Cheng, *The Melancholy of Race*, 7.

140. Abu-Lughod, *Do Muslim Women Need Saving?*, 17.

141. Wendy Brown quoted in Abu-Lughod, *Do Muslim Women Need Saving?*, 19.

142. Abu-Lughod, *Do Muslim Women Need Saving?*, 19.
143. Razack, *Looking White People in the Eye*, 31.

REFERENCES

Abu Lughod, Lila. "Romance of Resistance: Tracing Transformation of Power Through Bedouin Women." *American Ethnologist* 17, no. 1 (1990): 41–55.

Abu-Lughod, Lila. *Do Muslim Women Need Saving?* Cambridge: Harvard University Press, 2013.

Abu-Lughod, Lila. "Dialects of Women's Empowerment: The International Circuitry of the Arab Human Development Report 2005." *International Journal of Middle Eastern Studies* 41, no. 1 (2009): 97.

Ahmad, Dohra. "Not Yet Beyond the Veil: Muslim Women in American Popular Literature." *Social Text* 99, no. 2 (2009): 105–113.

Ahmed, Leila. *Women and Gender in Islam: Historical Roots of a Modern Debate.* New Haven: Yale University Press, 1992.

Ali, Ayaan Hirsi. *Infidel.* New York: Free Press, 2007.

Ali, Ayaan Hirsi. *The Caged Virgin: An Emancipation Proclamation for Women and Islam,* 1st Free Press ed. New York: Free Press, 2006.

Asad, Talal. "Thinking About the Secular Body, Pain and Liberal Politics." *Cultural Anthropology* 26, no. 4 (2011): 657–675.

Asad, Talal. *Formations of the Secular: Christianity, Islam, Modernity.* California: Stanford University Press, 2003.

Badran, Margot. *Feminism in Islam: Secular and Religious Convergences.* Oxford, MI: Oneworld, 2009.

Barnard, Suzanne. "Introduction." In *Reading Seminar XX: Love, Knowledge and Feminine Sexuality,* edited by Suzanne Barnard and Bruce Finks. New York: State University Press, 2002.

Bernstein, Susan David. *Confessional Subjects: Revelations of Gender and Power in Victorian Literature and Culture.* Chapel Hill, NC: University of North Carolina Press, 1997.

Bhabha, Homi. *The Location of Culture,* 1994 (2012 ed.). New York: Routledge, 2012.

Bouteldja, Houria. *Whites, Jews and Us: Towards a Politics of Revolutionary Love.* Los Angeles, CA: Semiotext(e), 2016.

Bullock, Katherine. *Rethinking Muslim Women and the Veil.* Herndon, VA: International Institute of Islamic Thought, 2003.

Butler, Judith. "Sexual Politics, Torture, and Secular Time." *The British Journal of Sociology* 59, no. 1 (2008): 1–23.

Butler, Judith. *Precarious Life: The Powers of Mourning and Violence.* New York: Verso, 2004.

Cheng, Anne Anlin. *Second Skin: Josephine Baker and the Modern Surface.* Oxford and New York: Oxford University Press, 2011.

Copjec, Joan. *Read My Desire: Lacan Against the Historicists.* Cambridge, MA: MIT Press, 1994.

Dabashi, Hamid. *Brown Skin, White Masks.* London: Pluto, 2011.

Davidson, Miri. "Alain Badiou, 'The Law on the Headscarf Is a Pure Capitalist Law'." *Verso* (blog), June 4, 2015. https://www.versobooks.com/blogs/2025-alain-badiou-the-law-on-the-headscarf-is-a-pure-capitalist-law.

Hook, Derek. *A Critical Psychology of the Postcolonial: The Mind of Apartheid.* London: Psychology Press, 2012.

Ekine, Sokari. *Blood Sorrow and Oil: Testimonies of Violence from Women of the Niger Delta.* Oxford: Centre for Democracy and Development, 2001.

Eltahawy, Mona. "Why Do They Hate Us?" *Foreign Policy*, April 23, 2012.

Éwanjé-Épée, Félix Boggio, and Stella Magliani-Belkacem. "The Empire of Sexuality: An Interview with Joseph Massad." *Jadaliyya*, March 5, 2013. https://www.jadaliyya.com/Details/28167/The-Empire-of-Sexuality-An-Interview-with-Joseph-Massad.

Fadil, Nadia. "Not-/Unveiling as an Ethical Practice." *Feminist Review* 98, no. 1 (2011): 83–109.

Fanon, Frantz. *A Dying Colonialism.* New York: Grove Press, 1965.

Fernando, Mayanthi L. *The Republic Unsettled: Muslim French and the Contradictions of Secularism.* Durham: Duke University Press, 2014.

Fink, Bruce. "Knowledge and Jouissance." In *Reading Seminar XX: Lacan's Major Work on Love, Knowledge and Feminine Sexuality*, edited by Susanne Barnard and Bruce Fink. New York: State University New York Press, 2002.

Foucault, Michel. *The Will to Knowledge: The History of Sexuality I.* Translated by Robert Hurley. London: Random House, 1978.

Freud, Sigmund, and James Strachey. *Three Essays on the Theory of Sexuality.* New York: Basic Books, 2000.

Herman, Judith. *Trauma and Recovery: The Aftermath of Violence—From Domestic Abuse to Political Terror.* New York: Basic Books, 1997.

Howe, Adrian. *Sex, Violence and Crime: Foucault and the 'Man' Question.* New York: Routledge, 2008.

Human Rights Watch 2013, Events of 2012. https://www.hrw.org/world-report/2013/country-chapters/egypt#.

Kay, Zara. Faithless Hijabi'. https://www.faithlesshijabi.org/?fbclid=IwAR38gYeL3cAM9iTIp0yhW5ztB8BBxphdwUAHv1ZCB2uuw MrzakC3NEX6Xb4.

Lacan, Jacques. *The Four Fundamental Concepts of Psychoanalysis.* Translated by Alan Sheridan. London: Karnac, 2003.

Lacan, Jacques. *Anxiety. The seminar of Jacques Lacan: Book X.* Edited by Jacques-Alain Miller and translated by A.R. Price. Cambridge: Polity Press, 2014.

Landy, Jean-Michel. "Confession, Obedience and Subjectivity: Michel Foucault's Unpublished Lectures on the Government of the Living." *Telos* 146 (2009): 111–123.

Lockman, Zachary. *Contending Visions of the Middle East: The History and Politics of Orientalism.* New York: Cambridge University Press, 2004.

Macdonald, Megan. "SUR/VEIL: The Veil as Blank(et) Signifier." In *Muslim Women, Transnational Feminism and Ethics of Pedagogy: Contested Imaginaries in Post-9/11 Cultural Practice*, edited by Lisa K. Taylor and Jasmine Zine. New York: Routledge, 2014.

Mahmood, Saba. "Feminism, Democracy and Empire: Islam and the War on Terror." In *Women's Studies on the Edge*, edited by Joan Wallach Scott. Durham: Duke University Press, 2008.

Mahmood, Saba. *Politics of Piety: The Islamic Revival and the Feminist Subject.* Princeton: Princeton University Press, 2005.

Manji, Irshad. *The Trouble with Islam Today: A Muslim's Call for Reform in Her Faith.*

Massad, Joseph. *Islam in Liberalism.* Chicago: University of Chicago Press, 2015.

McClintock, Anne. *Imperial Leather: Race, Gender, and Sexuality in the Colonial Contest.* New York: Routledge, 1995.

Mills, Ross. "The Confession as a 'Practice of Freedom': Feminism, Foucault and 'Elsewhere' Truths." *Law Text Culture* 2, no. 1 (1995): 100–117.

Mitchell, Timothy. *Questions of Modernity.* Minneapolis and London: University of Minnesota Press, 2000.

Moors, Annelies. "The Affective Power of the Face Veil: Between Disgust and Fascination." In *Things: Religion and the Question of Materiality*, edited by Digit Houtman and Birgit Meyer. New York: Fordham University Press, 2012.

Razack, Sherene H. *Looking White People in the Eye: Gender, Race, and Culture in Courtrooms and Classrooms.* Toronto: University of Toronto Press, 1998.

Razack, Sherene H. "Stealing the Suffering of Others: Reflection of Canadian Humanitarian Responses." *Review of Education Pedagogy and Cultural Studies* 24, no. 4 (2007): 375–394.

Rogers, Juliet. *Law's Cut on the Body of Human Rights.* New York: Routledge, 2013.

Said, Edward W. *Orientalism*, 1st ed. New York: Pantheon Books, 1978.

Scott, Joan Wallach. *The Fantasy of Feminist History.* Durham: Duke University Press, 2011.

Scott, Joan Wallach. *The Politics of the Veil.* Princeton: Princeton University Press, 2007.

Sheehi, Stephen. *Islamophobia: The Ideological Campaign Against Muslims.* Atlanta: Clarity Press, 2011.

Toor, Saadia. "Imperialist Feminism Redux." *Dialectical Anthropology* 36, no. 3/4 (2012): 147–160.

Whitlock, Gillian. *Soft Weapons: Autobiography in Transit*. Chicago: University of Chicago Press, 2009.

Wilson, John F. "Modernity and Religion: A Problem of Perspective." In *Modernity and Religion*, edited by William Nicholls. Waterloo, ON: Wilfrid Laurier University Press, 1987.

Yeğenoğlu, Meyda. *Colonial Fantasies: Towards a Feminist Reading of Orientalism*. Cambridge: Cambridge University Press, 1998.

Yildiz, Yasemin. "Governing European Subjects: Tolerance and Guilt in the Discourse of 'Muslim women'." *Cultural Critique* 77 (2011): 70–101.

Žižek, Slavoj. *The Plague of Fantasies*. London: Verso, 1997.

Žižek, Slavoj. *Violence: Six Sideways Reflections*. London: Profile Books, 2008.

CHAPTER 7

Conclusion: The Final Veil

...the final veil, the insurmountable veil that drops when we think all veils have been torn down. —Jean Baudrillard[1]

No, my body does not belong to me. My mother continues to exercise sovereignty over it. But I am a conscious accomplice. I share the reins to my life with her, with my entire tribe. In any case, even if I had removed them, it would have been to hand them over to white people. I'd rather die. I would rather deal with it... And play it by ear. Racism is perverse. It is a devil. —Houria Bouteldja[2]

As I began to reflect on the images of activists at protests and the debate on the role of the nude body in articulating feminist politics, I pondered the effects of including uncensored images of members of my family and community. At what expense should the authenticity of the image's purpose be included? Was there anything authentic being conveyed through the naked body? What would be the intellectual exercise being pursued in including these images? It occurred to me that these questions were already flirting with the epistemic terrain of the veiled and unveiled that I have traced in this book, as markers of possibilities and impossibilities, the symbolic and pre-symbolic. Confronted with my desire to conceal the body and to preserve the hidden in some way, I was faced with the question of my own social relations. This was not due to some innate affront to seeing women

S. Ghumkhor, *The Political Psychology of the Veil*,
Palgrave Studies in Political Psychology,
https://doi.org/10.1007/978-3-030-32061-4_7

bare, but rather to question the flesh as a site of our symbolic and imaginary meaning and self-construction.

The veiled and unveiled become ways of managing our relationship with flesh as an endless supply of knowledge-making and desire. Yet, bodies continue to defy us as they become the limits of our attempts to know. My concern over the personal implication of an uncovered body reflects my analyses in that it considers the symbolic world in which we are situated, wherein I as a Muslim am positioned, as the source of everyday social meaning. Thus, I was faced with my own limit: Do I play the role of the native informant, in the sense of internalising a "unique *jouissance*" which would compel me to perform the "endless truths" of the flesh? Do I pursue the "something else" that women can be saved to when the final veil is removed?

Would removing the final veil somehow elevate the body of the Woman in the form of Amina Sboui or Alia Almahdy, whose defiance is announced on their bare breasts with protesting messages. What exactly is being staged in this final scene? The selling of freedom as an unquestioned truth qua unveiling is powerfully captured on this defiant body. Yet, this is a body that is not entirely unveiled: but it is *covered* by written messages. There is an over-emphasis on the need to proclaim freedom vis-à-vis unveiling the body. It is after all these gestures that the body *still* cannot stand alone in delivering on its promise. The protesting body's proclamation displays the horror of confronting the bare body as a failure of one's ideal *jouissance*— the truth of the body not obtaining total freedom—or as Jacques Lacan states, not knowing what the Other wants from me.[3]

Like Aisha's unveiled face that incites anxiety in the western viewer who sees in her the failure of freedom, the protesting body as an unveiled body might never be unveiled enough. The more she unveils and exposes her nude body, the less she can assume her status of freedom. This is a cycle that seems to maintain desire through deferral through which the masquerade of unveiling *to be unveiled* circulates. The political slogans plastered over the protesting body confess an anxiety at their ontological status of the *gestalt*, an anxiety of their nude bodies as *just womenness*, in fragments. Like Frantz Fanon's reflections of unveiled Algerian women as "fragmented", transposing revealed flesh to a "cultural coding" of the colonial enterprise—just another veil,[4] the unveiled status designates their split ontology, suggesting the final veil can never be disrobed because it proposes a relieving unity.

This book has traced the corporeal leak, the flicker of symbolic fragments that emanates from the unveiled body's failure to secure meaning in the prophylactic fantasy of unveiling the universal body beneath. The west's preoccupation with the veil is, in this sense, a preoccupation with the body as a site of knowledge and its limit. This book traced this symptom of loss for the west absorbed by the question of the Other, permeated in the body that refuses to confess. In the encounter with the veiled face is a brush with the Other whose covered body portends to the possibility of enjoying differently. The book concludes that the unveiled body confesses the impossibility of knowledge, of securing the *jouissance* of the "whole" body, still being put back together by its political slogans. It has contended that the historical and contemporary fascination with the veiled woman is not simply about the fixing of difference but the anxiety about loss: the possibility of not knowing and experiencing the Other's desire as *not ours*. This book posits that the return to the veiled woman is about the failure of western epistemological and ontological truths: freedom, rights, universalism and the unveiled "natural" body as its final domain. The veil's reoccurrence seduces the western subject into the possibility of recovering the loss which the Other marks.

This book identified the west in the image of the Muslim woman qua the veiled woman by examining the psychic and political economy of the veiled and unveiled that has historically interpellated the west's relationship with Islam and Muslims through a claim of knowing who the Muslim woman is. The image of the Muslim woman tells the story of the west as an imaginary that assumes an evolutionary continuum wherein an economy of the veiled and unveiled are produced. The veiled and unveiled are powerful metaphorical expressions and coordinates of agency, autonomy and freedom in a post-9/11 world of national security, multiculturalism, human rights and women's rights. I unpacked not simply the epistemic (mis)representation of such imagery, but the psychic and libidinal investment in the imaginary boundaries that it polices and where meaning is produced. The relationship between the veiled and unveiled is one that disciplines cultural encounters, corrupting other possibilities of assessment, and is crucial to the building of a narrative of progress which spans from unfreedom to freedom, and the psychic and ontological landmines it may involve.

The fantasy of knowing the corporeal and epistemological boundaries of freedom and unfreedom is mapped onto and anchored in the image of the (veiled) Muslim woman. Her reoccurring image is more about the story of making the west—the "gaze that does not look back on itself"[5]—than it is about the Muslim woman and Islam. Yet, more intimate examination of her reoccurrence reveals her capacity to destabilise this gaze whose existing normative praxis of western liberalism with its universal notions of freedom, identity, agency and self, are never questioned. As a repetitive symptom, she requires a response from the subject she helps constitute through unveiling a west, who has freedom, rights and the capacity to activate a "natural" and universal desire. The book's contribution lies in how it has demonstrated that the discourse on the Muslim woman needs to shift the focus away from women who are recipients of its violence—whether this focus is to search and make visible a "truth" in the lived experiences of these women, or how these women live with this racist violence—in an effort to decentre and dissuade orientalist and Islamophobic ideas of her and her community. This is not simply a case of racial fixing but one that reveals western paranoiac and obsessive desire for knowledge of the Other, the desire to make intelligible the unknown. That is, to make visible the invisible. This is a question of what the Other wants. *Che vuoi?* The veiled and unveiled emerge as a mode of governing the Muslim to offer answers in a strategy of managing the experiences with and of difference. The veiled and unveiled as markers of progress, modernity and civilisation, cordons off the violent fantasy of these demarcations with such persuasive simplicity that freedom cannot be desired nor imagined in any other way.

I have argued that at the level of the imaginary, the Muslim woman *is* the veiled woman—the master signifier who foregrounds the discursive construction of who and what the Muslim woman is. The Muslim woman cannot be divorced from the veiled woman because she exists within an imaginary that is invested in constituting a Muslim woman as a symptom of violence. The shadows of a symbolic fragmentation that can destabilise the fantasy of unveiling freedom are kept at bay by the imaginary appeal to the veil in the mode of the Muslim woman as always tormented by the veil of violence. In Freudian parlance, the hysteric's fantasy of an other who deserves her misfortune speaks to a desire to punish and be punished by an authority[6]; it is along these lines that the Muslim woman is imagined as always being punished by patriarchy. There is always "a bearded Muslim man carrying knives"[7] behind her. The veiled woman remains a reoccurring metaphorical image of the Muslim woman—fixed in the image of violence.

Positioning her as always veiled by violence and needing rescue invites the constant discovery of a western subject, the attaining and enjoyment of freedom, of a fantasy of freedom not yet discovered and thus, the possibility of retrieving bodily unity beneath the shadows of the veil. These are shadows that invite corporeal discovery, conviction in unlimited knowledge—*the tearing away of all veils*—on corporeal terrains. This disrobing manifests in the proclamation of a universal, pre-discursive, natural, unified body of the human, who freely constitutes and perpetuates its own freedom. What makes possible an "unveiling" "human" through the retrieval of the "natural" body, also leaves the possibility of proclaiming the universal Woman in the west. The Lacanian lack of women as fragmented and never represented is disavowed by projecting on to the Muslim women—as "the fake woman"—[8] who submits to patriarchy and the veil.

The veil as lack reveals itself in images of Muslim women as bodies in a state of emergency: traumatised, mutilated, stoned, humiliated, constrained and veiled by violence. In the "new common sense" where women's rights today are an unquestioned political good[9]—even trumping the very lives of women with the increasing propensity for militarised humanitarianism (Afghanistan, Iraq, Nigeria, Syria, Libya and Mali) that must be offered and preserved for all—she is the quintessential subject of human rights. The image of her human rights violations fulfils the promise of freedom by sustaining a fantasy of attaining freedom by accumulating more rights. The veiled and unveiled activate this desire through the exchange of *veiling* and *unveiling*, as markers of violations (veiling) and attaining rights (unveiling). The absence of rights becomes the precondition to imagining the possibility of total knowledge and full satisfaction through the attainment of more rights.

If we return to the image of Aisha that I introduced at the beginning of this book, we saw how her disfigured face, her missing flesh, is a piece of revealed truth: the Other's question as permanently unanswered, a desire dissatisfied. Confronted by the Other's question, this book revealed how the veiled woman serves as a discursive hidden space through which possible answers are projected and fantasised. She is a primary witness to the litany of charges against Islam—veiling, female genital mutilation, forced marriages and honour crimes—and its modes of violence while permanent racial shadows mark her body. In the climate of the war on terror, the Muslim woman's body becomes witness to the violence of fundamentalism, a violence that "we" can imagine will spill out and inflict, or rather, *infect our bodies.*

The postcolonial debates on multiculturalism and integration, security and surveillance and anti-immigration are often centred on the veiled woman. This preoccupation is not simply because of her status as a visible other, but because she reveals the blurring of bodily boundaries which further reveal the limits to knowing and securing knowledge of the body. In this vein, the veiled and unveiled are strategies of managing knowledge over the body that can be both foreign and "ours". I argued that Islamophobia's hysterical questioning of the Muslim among "us" is preoccupied with the body like a collective hypochondria that demands to know all bodily symptoms. This fixation is driven by a commitment to knowing the universal "natural" body whose boundaries can be secured through unveiling (knowing of) the body. In the fantasy of freedom, it is only in the repetition of the image of the veiled woman, who circulates as the foreign identified and contained as an image, that exists a substitute for absolute knowledge over the body by offering momentary relief. A form of hyperveiling—complete forms of covering[10]—occurs as a new mode of knowing the Muslim and therefore, proclaiming new knowledge of the unveiling universal body. If freedom cannot be guaranteed—that is, a freedom that may be rejected—freedom must be deferred through the imaging and imagining of veiling as a fixing of bodily boundaries between us and them.

This imagining and securing of freedom/knowledge through flesh is deployed in the question of the other woman and her escape from the veil. Internalising the hypochondriac response to other bodies, the other woman in the form of the secular "unveiled" Muslim woman, subjects her body to self-scrutiny to produce a knowledge that can secure her freedom. By identifying the symptoms of cultural regression and constraints, she overcomes woman's bodily lack by unveiling in heroic narratives that confess the "truth" of Islam, the ordeals of experiencing bodily (sexual) constraints and surviving the violence of the veil. In other words, her confessions through her body are attempts to answer the Other's question.

Veiling is transformed from a strategy of internationalising the new humanitarian crusade and domesticating difference to enable the naming of violence and thus, the disavowal of cultural lack as part of unveiling to both universalise the human and overcome bodily difference. The economy of the veiled and unveiled modern "native informants" similarly performs an unveiling but as part of a confession of the "truth" of her culture which centres around a Muslim woman always constrained by the veil. Such heroic escapes from the veil can only be broadcasted with the backdrop of (hyper) veiling, witnessing Muslim women's bodies in crisis.

What veiling reveals in these discussions is that the fantasy of freedom, the discovery of the universal body that can finally be known, is only secured not by unveiling but by clinging to the final veil—the one that allows the imagining and naming of the violence on Muslim women's bodies. This is the veil that maintains the symbolic shield, the fantasy that sustains desire for the "something else". In this mode, this book concludes that the repeated image of the veiled woman in western socio-political discourse is a process of disciplining and containing knowledge of the Other—an *Islamic jouissance*—as the shadow on the body that gestures to the undesirability of liberal freedom as a universal prescription.

The anxiety and over-determining force of the veiled body, which the international and domestic settings highlight, is about the imagining and fantasising of the universal body, the experience of the flesh as one that witnesses the enjoyment of freedom *that one cannot not want*.[11] Western investment in the veiled woman is, therefore, about modernity's claims to truth and knowledge, secured through the visible body: the source of truth, of one's identity and one's humanisation. The body that is heightened in its exposure is a body that is modern, free, secure, conscious, human in contrast to the invisible body that is constrained and hidden in the shadows of vulnerability, and most saliently, *absent*. More than this, it is a commitment to a type of repetition, an attempt to secure this accessible, an unthinking "readiness to hand" freedoms that are marked on the very absent body of the Muslim woman. The veiled and unveiled are imbued in the belief that freedom and therefore, universal "truth" is only knowable and experienced when it is exteriorised and embodied.

The enjoyment of freedom as something to be visible, displayed, also raises the possibility that perhaps it is not the veil itself that signals unfreedom but the *unwillingness* to consume freedom in the mode of exercising available choices is what underlies the politicised terrain of veiled and unveiled bodies. The rise of hijab fashion throughout the Muslim world—particularly in Turkey, Lebanon, Egypt and Iran—is often understood as giving women more choices, more ways to enjoy and to express their individuality while adhering to the principle of modesty.[12] Though this trend is largely focused on the headscarf and not the veil, the role of consumption carries with it a humanising impulse that marks the veil as radically other. In the west, this desire to express individual freedoms for Muslims is at times coupled with the propensity to internalise deradicalisation discourses wherein consumerism becomes a form of therapy for radicalisation—"shop or the terrorists will win!"[13]—and to appear *more* human, more willing to participate in the logic of the same.

If the call to unveil denies Muslim women their own ontological truth—that is, identifying not her, but the liberal subject beneath the veil—the defence of the veil is similarly ensnared in this discursive logic of unveiling. With few exceptions such as Saba Mahmood, who looked at the embodied practices of the veil and the ways in which liberal traditions have made it intelligible through a language of agency as resistance,[14] the hermeneutic pattern of translating Muslim women as political subjects is an important area of research that has not been sufficiently undertaken. Looking beyond the epistemological focus, this book has offered other questions worth exploring: what *jouissance* is at work in the veiled subject invoked in counter-narratives? Who is the speaking subject of Islamic *jouissance*? What of the impossibility of articulating difference outside the discourse of liberalism, feminism, anti-racism and their acceptable forms of speech? Lila Abu-Lughod's inquiry into what Muslim women are being saved to[15] is re-cast so as to not only examine the west's saviour fantasy of saving Muslim women from the veil, but to ask: what is the Muslim woman *being decolonised to*? In other words, this book questions the possibility of decolonisation and the potential within emancipatory politics to escape the modern imaginary of bodies always in a "natural" state of casting out shadows through perpetual disclosure.

The limitations of this book are perhaps obvious for the reader as the investment in the veil is not entirely a western phenomenon. The book's focus was on the west's investment in the veiled woman, examining the power that this imagery of the veiled and unveiled enables and disables. Apart from the historical incidents and their political implications referenced, it did not delve into what degree this imagery has persuaded and shaped Muslim discourses. This book privileged the west's preoccupation with the veil because the veil in the west established and polices the political and epistemic parameters of relating to notions of freedom, modernity, democracy, nationhood, etc. The veiled and unveiled became an imperial tool of navigating the encounter with the Muslim and continues to influence and shape western and Muslim notions of self. Further research is required not to simply look at how the veiled and unveiled shape the responses of Muslim majority countries banning the veil such as Tunisia, Turkey and Egypt, but to look at how Muslim religiosity has developed within the discursive and psychic parameters of the veiled and unveiled. The west's investment in the veil is one of the nodal points to amplify the diffusion of European "modernity".

While the fantasy of unveiling is about securing a "natural" universal body as the location of unlimited *jouissance*, the veil appears as an attempt to secure the uncontaminated pre-colonial body of Islam. The veiled body is imagined as a site of discovering and recovering a historical loss, a return to an origin. It would mean building on Fanon's politicisation of the veil as an anti-colonial struggle,[16] and Leila Ahmed's historicisation of the veil's resonance in the colonial history of countries like Egypt, and how it has come to be adopted in Islamic revivalist movements.[17] Rather than basing the analysis on the history of the veil's politicisation, the postcolonial and psychoanalytic approach I have outlined in this book could unpack the relationship between the veil and the new ways of enjoyment that modernity has signalled for Muslims. If the body has been occupied by western universal truths, the important question remains: is there anything left of the body in the postcolonial Islamic imaginary? This book raises the possibility of investigating the fetishistic identification with the veil in Islamist discourses as a symptom of "putting back together" an Islam, which has been intimately entangled and invested in the image of the west.

NOTES

1. Jean Baudrillard, *The Conspiracy of Art: Manifestos, Interviews and Essays* (New York, CA: University of California, 2005), 187.
2. Houria Bouteldja, *Whites, Jews and Us: Towards a Politics of Revolutionary Love* (New York, CA: Semiotext(e), 2016), 75.
3. Lacan, *Ecrits: The First Complete Edition in English*, 693.
4. Berger, "The Newly Veiled Woman: Irigaray, Specularity, and the Islamic Veil," 107.
5. Abu-Lughod, *Do Muslim Women Need Saving?*, 68.
6. Rogers, *Law's Cut on the Body of Human Rights*, 51.
7. Laila Alawa, "I Am Not Oppressed," *Huffington Post*, April 10, 2013. https://www.huffpost.com/entry/i-am-not-oppressed_b_3052001.
8. Matviyekno, "The Veil and Capitalist Discourse: A Lacanian Reading of the Veil Beyond Islam," 8.
9. Abu-Lughod, *Do Muslim Women Need Saving?*, 55.
10. Macmaster and Lewis, "Orientalism: From Unveiling to Hyperveiling," 122–130.
11. Spivak, *A Critique of Postcolonial Reason: Toward a History of the Vanishing Present*, 9.
12. Filipa Ioannou, "Did Lady Gaga Do a 'Burqa Swag' Song?," *The Daily Beast*, August 9, 2013.

13. Jennifer Cotter, "Anti-Hijab and the Empire's New Morality," *The Red Critique* 7 (2002). http://redcritique.org/NovDec02/printversions/antihijabandtheempiresnewmoralityprint.htm.
14. See Mahmood, *Politics of Piety: The Islamic Revival and the Feminist Subject.*
15. Abu-Lughod, *Do Muslim Women Need Saving?*, 47.
16. See Fanon, "Algeria Unveiled."
17. See Ahmed, *Women and Gender in Islam: Historical Roots of a Modern Debate.*

REFERENCES

Abu-Lughod, Lila. *Do Muslim Women Need Saving?* Cambridge: Harvard University Press, 2013.

Ahmed, Leila. *Women and Gender in Islam: Historical Roots of a Modern Debate.* New Haven: Yale University Press, 1992.

Alawa, Laila. "I Am Not Oppressed," *Huffington Post*, April 10, 2013. https://www.huffpost.com/entry/i-am-not-oppressed_b_3052001.

Baudrillard, Jean. *The Conspiracy of Art: Manifestos, Interviews and Essays.* New York, CA: University of California, 2005.

Berger, Anne-Emmanuelle. "The Newly Veiled Woman: Irigaray, Specularity, and the Islamic Veil." *Diacritics* 28, no. 1 (1998): 93–119.

Bouteldja, Houria. *Whites, Jews and Us: Towards a Politics of Revolutionary Love.* New York, CA: Semiotext(e), 2016.

Fanon, Frantz. "Algeria Unveiled," In *Decolonisation: Perspectives from Now and Then: Rewriting Histories,* edited by Prasenjit Duara. London: Routledge, 2003.

Cotter, Jennifer, "Anti-Hijab and the Empire's New Morality." *The Red Critique* 7 (2002). http://redcritique.org/NovDec02/printversions/antihijabandtheempiresnewmoralityprint.htm.

Lacan, Jacques. *Ecrits: The First Complete Edition in English.* New York: W. W. Norton, 2006.

Macmaster, Neil, and Toni Lewis, "Orientalism: From Unveiling to Hyperveiling." *Journal of European Studies* 28, no. 1 (1998): 122–130.

Mahmood, Saba. *Politics of Piety: The Islamic Revival and the Feminist Subject.* Princeton, NJ: Princeton University Press, 2005.

Matviyekno, Svitlana. "The Veil and Capitalist Discourse: a Lacanian Reading of the Veil Beyond Islam." *(Re) Turn: Journal of Lacanian Studies* 6 (2011): 96–120.

Rogers, Juliet. *Law's Cut on the Body of Human Rights.* New York: Routledge, 2013.

Spivak, Gayatri Chakravorty. *A Critique of Postcolonial Reason: Toward a History of the Vanishing Present.* Cambridge: Harvard University Press, 1999.

INDEX